Hidden Truths

Magic, Alchemy, and the Occult

Religion, History, and Culture
Selections from The Encyclopedia of Religion

Mircea Eliade
EDITOR IN CHIEF

EDITORS

Charles J. Adams
Joseph M. Kitagawa
Martin E. Marty
Richard P. McBrien
Jacob Needleman
Annemarie Schimmel
Robert M. Seltzer
Victor Turner

ASSOCIATE EDITOR

Lawrence E. Sullivan

ASSISTANT EDITOR

William K. Mahony

Hidden Truths

Magic, Alchemy, and the Occult

EDITED BY
Lawrence E. Sullivan

Religion, History, and Culture
Selections from The Encyclopedia of Religion

Mircea Eliade
EDITOR IN CHIEF

MACMILLAN PUBLISHING COMPANY
New York
COLLIER MACMILLAN PUBLISHERS
London

Copyright © 1987, 1989 by Macmillan Publishing Company
A Division of Macmillan, Inc.

All rights reserved. No part of this book may be reproduced or transmitted in any form or by any means, electronic or mechanical, including photocopying, recording, or by any information storage and retrieval system, without permission in writing from the Publisher.

Macmillan Publishing Company
866 Third Avenue, New York, N.Y. 10022

Collier Macmillan Canada, Inc.

Library of Congress Catalog Card Number: 89–8286

Printed in the United States of America

printing number
1 2 3 4 5 6 7 8 9 10

Library of Congress Cataloging-in-Publication Data

Hidden truths: magic, alchemy, and the occult / edited by Lawrence E. Sullivan
    p.   cm. — (Religion, history, and culture)
  "Selections from the Encyclopedia of religion."
  Bibliography: p.
  ISBN 0-02-897404-2
  1. Magic. 2. Alchemy. 3. Occultism.   I. Sullivan, Lawrence Eugene, 1949– . II. Encyclopedia of religion. III. Series.
BF1611.H54   1989
133—dc20   89-8286
                                                                        CIP

CONTENTS

PUBLISHER'S NOTE   vii
INTRODUCTION   ix

PART 1: OCCULTISM

1. What is Occultism?
   Antoine Faivre   3
2. Wisdom
   Kurt Rudolph   10
3. Speculations about Nature
   Antoine Faivre   24
4. Esotericism
   Antoine Faivre   38
5. Hermetism
   Antoine Faivre   49
6. Gnosticism from the Middle Ages to the Present
   Ioan Petru Culianu   63
7. Witchcraft
   Jeffrey Burton Russell   69

PART 2: MAGIC

8. Theories of Magic
   John Middleton   85
9. Magic in East Asia
   Donald Harper   97
10. Magic in Greco-Roman Antiquity
    Hans Dieter Betz   102
11. Magic in Medieval and Renaissance Europe
    Ioan Petru Culianu   110
12. Magic in Eastern Europe
    Ioana Andreesco-Miereanu   116
13. Magic in Islam
    Toufic Fahd   122
14. Magic in South Asia
    Teun Goudriaan   131
15. Magic in Tribal Societies
    Donald R. Hill   136

PART 3: MAGICAL OBJECTS, TECHNIQUES, AND POWERS

16. Amulets and Talismans
    Theodor H. Gaster — 145
17. Astrology
    Ioan Petru Culianu — 151
18. Binding
    Giulia Piccaluga — 158
19. Cards
    Richard W. Thurn — 163
20. Divination
    Evan M. Zuesse — 165
21. Exorcism
    Geoffrey Parrinder — 177
22. Geomancy
    Erika Bourguignon — 191
23. Incantation
    Theodore M. Ludwig — 193
24. Necromancy
    Erika Bourguignon — 202
25. Oracles
    David E. Aune — 206
26. Spells
    Beatriz Barba de Piña Chán — 217
27. Magico-Religious Powers
    Robert A. F. Thurman — 224
28. Portents and Prodigies
    Raymond Bloch — 229
29. Fetishism
    Mesquitela Lima — 236

PART 4: ALCHEMY

30. What is Alchemy?
    Mircea Eliade — 243
31. Elixirs
    Allison Coudert — 248
32. Chinese Alchemy
    Nathan Sivin — 253
33. Indian Alchemy
    David White — 261
34. Islamic Alchemy
    Habibeh Rahim — 264
35. Hellenistic and Medieval Alchemy
    Henry and Renée Kahane — 269
36. Renaissance Alchemy
    Allison Coudert — 276

CONTRIBUTORS — 283
FINDING LIST OF ARTICLE TITLES — 284

PUBLISHER'S NOTE

Since publication of *The Encyclopedia of Religion* in 1987, we have been gratified by the overwhelming reception accorded it by the community of scholars. This reception has more than justified the hopes of the members of the work's editorial board, who, with their editor in chief, cherished the aim that it would contribute to the study of the varieties of religious expression worldwide. To all those who participated in the project we express again our deepest thanks.

Now, in response to the many requests of our contributors and other teachers, we take pride in making available this selection of articles from the encyclopedia for use in the classroom. It is our hope that by publishing these articles in an inexpensive, compact format, they will be read and reflected upon by an even broader audience. In our effort to select those articles most appropriate to undergraduate instruction, it has been necessary to omit entries of interest primarily to the more advanced student and/or to those who wish to pursue a particular topic in greater depth. To facilitate their research, and to encourage the reader to consult the encyclopedia itself, we have thus retained the system of cross-references that, in the original work, served to guide the reader to related articles in this and other fields. A comprehensive index may be found in volume sixteen of the encyclopedia.

Charles E. Smith
Publisher and President
Macmillan Reference Division

INTRODUCTION

MUST VALUABLE TRUTHS REMAIN HIDDEN TRUTHS?

The word *magic* calls to mind children's birthday parties or Las Vegas nightclubs, where entertainers dupe the gullible and "magic" is good for laughs. These images tempt us to conclude that magic is just a trick, an illusion. We forget that illusion lies at the foundation of human culture.

Magic is misunderstood and trivialized by the belief that only the naive take it seriously or that it is practiced only by charlatans or evildoers. These views fail to give us the full picture of the role of magic in culture and history. We might do better to hunt for a new term for the serious reality it is. Until someone offers us a better word, however, our best course is to learn something about the vital role magic plays in the history of ideas, art, science, literature, and religion. This volume recounts episodes of this fascinating story.

ILLUSION AND FAITH IN THE FOUNDATION OF CULTURE

Even parlor magic reminds us that culture is grounded in realities that cannot be seen at all times. Our way of seeing the world, our distinctively human stance toward reality, opens us to the constant possibility of illusion. The basic human outlook must always be one that remains vulnerable to deception, because realities are represented to us by signs, reports, or pictures that stand for something else. The digital codes on a compact disk, for instance, are not exactly the music of Sting or Winton Marsalis, no matter how high the fidelity may be, but only a faithful recording of signs that stand for the sounds these performers once made.

Art and culture flourish because humans face reality imaginatively—understanding reality and communicating about it through symbols. To speak, to listen, to understand is to enter a wonderland of signs, all pointing somewhere else. To venture through such a world requires a kind of faith that is not ordinarily equated with religious faith. The most ordinary actions are based on the extraordinary, and ultimately unprovable, belief that our signs represent something real and that we can correctly manipulate those signs and their meanings. Every word stands for something that is not fully present in that word itself, something that stands beyond or outside of that word. Each word serves as a sign of some "other" reality. Religious expressions that speak, for instance, of divine beings push this imaginative foundation to its ultimate height whenever these symbols come to represent realities that are "wholly other" than the ones seen in this world of signs.

But this situation is fraught with danger, misunderstanding, deceit, and obscurity. Like philosophy and science, magic reminds us how fragile and incomplete are our capacities to attend to the truths about reality, because truth is never fully grasped in its signs and reality is never exhaustively manifest in any of the quickly changing appearances of the world. Magic demonstrates right before our very eyes that our ingrained ways of acting, perceiving, and understanding can and do occasion our ultimate loss of control over meaning. Magic plays on the forms of chaos that lurk within the very symbolic orders we use to think and manage our lives. Throughout history magic has furnished specific and varying responses to hidden chaos and illusion: awe, confidence, fright, wonder, optimism, the promise of control, technology, hope in the future, transference of one's own blind forces upon another, love, and so on.

Magic reminds us that the world consists of signs, that every obvious reality is only a sign pointing to some more hidden one. But are all appearances merely signs? Is every statement of truth only a blaze on the trail to nowhere, to truths that can never be found? Where, precisely, are the truths to which all signs ultimately point? What realities are not just pointers but realities in themselves? It is easy to see why scientific, philosophical, and religious thinkers have perennially dedicated themselves to the study and practice of magic. One thinks, for example, of the occult practices of Roger Bacon, Marsilio Ficino, John Dee, Robert Fludd, Inigo Jones, Isaac Newton, and many others (Couliano, 1987: 179ff.)

ON THE BORDER OF LIFE AND WILL: WHERE TO DRAW THE LINE?

Magic questions where the line should be drawn between the mundane and the ultimate, the visible and invisible, the sacred and the profane. By highlighting the fragility of the relationship between a symbol and that to which it points, and by emphasizing the arbitrariness of the distance that appears to separate sign from reality, magic challenges the conventional or even willful nature of the "obscure void" that is deemed to separate appearance from reality. Are all valuable truths necessarily hidden behind or below their outward signs? By searching for order and clarity in the borderland that is supposed to exist between clear reason and murky irrationality, between the concrete experience of sense and the pure idea of the mind, magic dares to hope for more. By exposing the willful character of that border, magic aims to disclose and harness the power of the will that creates such borders.

Various magical theories have purported to discover powers of will at different depths: in human desire, affection, or intention; in the attractive or repulsive forces found in the elementary structures of all matter, such as gravity, magnetism, or absolute motion; in the creative love or jealous uniqueness of supernatural beings who affect all created reality, and so on. When magicians, alchemists, and occultists align themselves with the hidden forces that magic reveals (through divination, geomancy, necromancy, oracles, astrology, or identification with transmuted matter), magicians hope to explore, modify, or move the border between what we know and what we can only hint at with our knowledge, and between what we signal in our communication and what we are as forces in the world.

Magical diviners have organized the outward signs that disclose the inner structures of all existence into various systems of correspondences, much in the same way that chemists have mapped the variables that organize the relations among the elementary structures of matter into the periodic table of elements. Once the outward signs of inner structures are charted in this way, and once the controlling correspondences between the structure of the subject and objective reality are established, those signs can be manipulated at will to advance the frontier of knowledge. Matter conforms to the human will in the same measure in which the human being is empowered by making symbolic life conform to the fundamental structures of reality.

Magicians have viewed the imagination as covering both sides of the gulf between the seen and unseen, the known and the unknowable, because the image or symbolic gesture participates in both the inner realm of fantasy and in the outer realm of concrete expression. The imagination thus encompasses both poles of truth, both poles of reality. With this expansive faith in the imagination—the power of fantasy to conjure up images of the unimaginable and to craft concrete signs that embody the inner power of will—magic takes up residence in the space that otherwise separates what is evident from what is obscure, what is spoken from what is spoken about. A magical incantation, for example, often is the very power that it signifies.

From the point of view of many magicians, magic aims to close the gap between a sign and the real power to which it refers. Magical speech and acts bring into the light of day the power and truth that lie hidden behind the signs of ordinary discourse and gesture. Hidden realities are made visible in the fantastic images of the magician. The magical forces of fantasy can make present and subject to human control the powers hidden within the dynamic structures that create arbitrary order in culture and cosmos. As Sir Isaac Newton and Robert Boyle realized when carrying on their secret alchemical experiments, these willful orders include the structures inherent in the material world as well as in the epistemological structures of the mental universe. In *Coral Gardens and their Magic*, the anthropologist Bronislaw Malinowski emphasized that the magician's quest is at once both material and spiritual and that it has affinities with both science and religion insofar as it concretizes the hope that cultures can creatively explore the boundaries between scientific and religious modes of knowledge and experience.

Magic is the science of hope because it cultivates the human capacity to face the future—and all other forms of unknown, hidden reality. Magic allows hope to become a dominant, concrete force in structuring the world and restructuring time and space; through magic human hope allies itself with the forces that order the cosmos. Twentieth-century thinkers have examined this close tie that binds magic, hope, and the world. Jean-Paul Sartre's theory of emotions (in which the emotive changes in one's facial expression serve as magical signs that construct and deconstruct whole worlds of meaning and truth for the observer), Ernst Bloch's discussion of utopian magic (which shakes the known sociopolitical world), and Daniel O'Keefe's mention of recent Christian theologies of liberation (which aim to transform the current orders of the world by installing God as the all-defining future) all call attention to the fact that magic grounds truth and shapes strategies for change (Sartre, 1948; Bloch, 1970; O'Keefe, 1982: 74–75).

The religious optimism shared by magic and science predates the twentieth century. In the thirteenth-century book *Experimental Science,* the Franciscan philosopher and alchemist Roger Bacon longed to analyze the material conditions that would allow for the manipulation of unseen spirits and powers. Since in his view all visible objects of the material world, not just human beings, possess the inner force of fantasy, Bacon anticipated a time when science, based on the magical control of such empowering fantasy, would manipulate the inner essence of even inanimate objects. He predicted a day when physical objects would be driven by their own inner fantasy, essence, or energy vapors, projected outward (see Couliano, 1987). Were magic to allow science to penetrate the inner dynamism of material existence, Bacon speculated, boats would propel themselves over and under the sea, machines would launch themselves and fly through the air, and the inner force of mineral stones could be harnessed as they projected themselves outward in the form of exploding gunpowder. In proposing this, Bacon drew on earlier magical theories, especially the theory of universal rays put forward by the ninth-century Muslim philosopher al-Kindi, an author whose work was widely discussed through the sixteenth century (Couliano, 1987). In this view, because human fantasy has a material basis, the power of will and concentration cultivated in magical practice would allow humans to project their own inner forces outward by emitting rays that could manipulate physical reality in accordance with human hope and desire.

Human faith, belief, and understanding—in short, human culture—create the conditions for illusion. Illusion is a most important marker for human beings; it points to the opaque underpinnings of human possibilities as well as to the profound but not always fully visible realities that ground material existence. So far as we can tell, the ability to create illusions is a distinctive feature of our species. The history of magical ideas, systems, and techniques presented in this volume can be fruitfully set beside the study of the history of law, art, religion, science, ethics, politics, or other cultural forms of knowledge, which respond creatively to the tension that inevitably arises between what ought to be and what appears to be the case, between what we know to be true and what we will to have otherwise.

REFERENCES

Bloch, Ernst. "Man's Increasing Entry into Religious Experience," in *Man on His Own*. New York, 1970, pp. 147–240.

Couliano (Culianu), Ioan P. *Eros and Magic in the Renaissance*. Margaret Cook, trans. Chicago, 1987.

O'Keefe, Daniel. *Stolen Lightning: The Social Theory of Magic*. New York, 1982.

Sartre, Jean-Paul. *The Emotions: Outline of a Theory*. New York, 1948.

ONE

OCCULTISM

1 — WHAT IS OCCULTISM?

ANTOINE FAIVRE
Translated from French by Kristine Anderson

The term *occultism* is properly used to refer to a large number of practices, ranging from astrology and alchemy to occult medicine and magic, that are based in one way or another on the homo-analogical principle, or doctrine of correspondences. According to this principle, things that are similar exert an influence on one another by virtue of the correspondences that unite all visible things to one another and to invisible realities as well. The practices based upon this essentially esoteric principle express a living and dynamic reality, a web of cosmic and divine analogies and homologies that become manifest through the operation of the active imagination.

Occultism, as a group of practices, is to be distinguished from esotericism, which is, roughly speaking, the theory that makes these practices possible. [*See* Esotericism.] We may therefore accept the following distinction proposed by the sociologist Edward A. Tiryakian:

> By "occult," I understand intentional practices, techniques, or procedures which (a) draw upon hidden and concealed forces in nature or the cosmos that cannot be measured or recognized by the instruments of modern science, and (b) which have as their desired or intended consequences empirical results, such as obtaining knowledge of the empirical course of events or altering them from what they would have been without this intervention. . . . By "esoteric" I refer to those religiophilosophic belief systems which underlie occult techniques and practices; that is, it refers to the more comprehensive cognitive mappings of nature and the cosmos, the epistomological and ontological reflections of ultimate reality, which mappings constitute a stock of knowledge that provides the ground for occult procedures. By way of analogy, esoteric knowledge is to occult practices as the corpus of theoretical physics is to engineering applications.
>
> (Tiryakian, 1972, pp. 498–499)

To this must be added, however, that such a distinction has only become conceptually possible since the second half of the nineteenth century, an age of trivial esotericism during which the need for a word like *occultism* was strongly felt. Furthermore, it must be recognized that esotericism itself also has a practical dimension. It is not pure speculation, since the active knowledge, enlightenment, and imagination that constitute it correspond to a form of praxis. Similarly, occultism, in the most precise sense of the word, necessarily includes a form of theory. The problem of terminology is complicated by the fact that *occultism* is sometimes used in the sense of *esotericism,* as can be seen, for example, in the very title of an otherwise excellent work, Robert Amadou's *L'occultisme: Esquisse d'un monde vivant* (Paris, 1950), which mainly deals with esotericism and theosophy.

OCCULTISM BEFORE OCCULTISM

The first instances of something that can be called occultism appear in the early centuries of the Christian era, combined with esoteric and theosophical teachings. Theurgy can be found in the teachings of the fourth-century *Chaldean Oracles;* in the Alexandrine Hermetism of the *Corpus Hermeticum,* from the second and third centuries; and in the third-century Neoplatonism of Porphyry, that of Iamblichus in the fourth century, and that of Proclus in the fifth. [*See* Theurgy.] Alchemy flourished at Alexandria until the seventh century. [*See* Alchemy.] Even Stoicism had an occult aspect, insofar as it emphasized the necessity of knowing the concrete universe by harmoniously combining science and technique, and adopted an open attitude toward popular religion, especially toward all kinds of divination.

During the Middle Ages there was considerable interest in occultism. Sylvester II, who became pope in 1000, was among other things an astrologer and alchemist. The medieval interest in the occult was due in large part to the influence of Arabic thought, which combined a rational empiricism with a strongly mythologized vision of a world dominated by subtle, spiritual forces. During this period the Arabs themselves developed an interest in the esotericism and occultism that had been dormant since the sixth century, emphasizing the study of astrology and alchemy. They provided the Christian West with works such as the *Book of Images* by Pseudo-Ptolemy, *Picatrix,* the *Turba philosophorum,* the *Emerald Tablet,* the *Book of the Moon,* and the *Flower of Gold,* all of which discuss astrology, alchemy, or theurgy. These, along with the older Alexandrine writings already mentioned, became the historical foundation of occult philosophy in the West. The magical and Hermetic teachings of the Arabs also contributed to the spread of medical theories and practices.

Medieval interest in occult philosophy was stimulated by the symbolic orientation of Christian theology. The symbolic cosmos of the Middle Ages, a predecessor of the esoteric cosmological representations that multiplied rapidly in the Renaissance, was expressed through the Romanesque style, as in the works of Alain de Lille, Hildegard von Bingen, and Honorius. It promoted an interest in magic and the occult properties of natural things; hence the widespread taste for precious stones, their symbolism and their occult virtues, as in the *Liber lapidum seu gemmis* of Marbed. In astrology, the names of Roger of Hereford and John of Spain were prominent.

The year 1144 marked an important event: Robert of Chester's translation of the first important book of medieval alchemy, the *Liber de compositione alchemiae,* from Arabic into Latin. Other translations contributed to the spread of Proclus's influence, such as the *Liber de causis,* translated into Latin by Gerard of Cremona. There were also, in the twelfth century, numerous pseudo-Aristotelian writings, some of an alchemical, astrological, or pneumatological character, some concerning the occult virtues of stones and herbs, still others dealing with chiromancy and physiognomy. The most famous of these writings, the *Secreta secretorum,* a veritable handbook of occultism that placed a particular emphasis on astrology, was one of the most popular books of the Middle Ages.

Among twelfth-century works on magic, the Spanish and Latin translations of the *Picatrix,* compiled by the Arab Norbar, are important. Texts that attribute the origin of different occult traditions and treatises to Solomon also appear at this time; he is presented as a magician who received his occult knowledge through the revelation of an angel. These treatises were also believed to be dependent on the *ars notoria,* the art by which, it was thought, one could obtain knowledge of or communication with God through theurgical procedures such as the invocation of angels, the utilization of figures and designs, or the use of the appropriate prayers. To this category of writings belongs the *Liber secretus,* or *Liber juratus,* attributed to a certain Honorius, a book full of angels' names, theurgical prayers, and strange words derived from Hebrew and Chaldean.

In the thirteenth century, Albertus Magnus wrote a treatise on minerals and referred to both alchemy and magic. Thomas Aquinas himself believed in alchemy and attributed its efficacy to the occult forces of the heavenly bodies. Roger Bacon, too, took a close interest in the occult, since for him "experimental science" meant a secret and traditional science; that is, a concrete science, but one inseparable from holy scripture.

Astrology is best represented by the Scotsman Michael Scot, astrologer to Frederick II, a patron of seers and magi, and by Guido Bonatti, whose *Liber astronomicus* is undoubtedly the most important work of the period in this domain. Geomancy is represented by the great *Summa* of Bartholomew of Parma, published at Bologna. Iberian alchemy is best represented by the Catalan Arnau de Villanova, author of the *Rosarium philosophorum.* Indeed, the age's most beautiful work of literature, the *Roman de la rose,* begun by Guillaume de Lorris and continued by Jean de Meun, shows the influence of the science of Hermes.

The fourteenth century opens with the *Ars magna* of Ramón Lull, whose theosophical figures were intended for theological, medical, or astrological purposes. Lull's search for the absolute was carried out through these games played with number symbolism, which can be compared to the geometric schemes developed by Wronski at the beginning of the nineteenth century or to the famous "archaeometry" of Saint-Yves d'Alveydre. Alchemical literature progressed by leaps and bounds during the late Midde Ages and remained plentiful through the Enlightenment. Among its most powerful proponents were John Dastin, Petrus Bonus, Jean de Rupescissa, and Nicholas Flamel.

The occult philosophy of the Renaissance profited from this medieval legacy. It was also stimulated by the revival of Neoplatonism at the Florentine court that began in 1439 under the influence of George Gemistus Plethon and saw the translation of the *Corpus Hermeticum* by Marsilio Ficino (1463) and the christianization of the Qabbalah by Giovanni Pico della Mirandola. From then on there was a proliferation of magi and theosophists all over Italy, adhering to a truly philosophical esotericism and engaged in practices that prefigured the occultism of the nineteenth century.

Outside Italy, few people were as devoted to astrology and the occult arts as the monks. Astrology and medicine are directly connected in the work of the monk Jean Ganivet, whose *Amicus medicorum* (1431) went through many editions. Physiognomy was most notably represented by Michael Savonarola, the author of the *Speculum phisionomiae* and grandfather of the famous Florentine reformer. In this age, astrology and the Qabbalah held a larger place than alchemy. Trithemius (Johannes Heidenberg), for example, a father of Renaissance occult philosophy and the future teacher of Paracelsus, reserved only a modest place for alchemy. Nevertheless, alchemy could still be found in the new editions of older works written by George Ripley, Thomas Norton, and Bernhardus Trevisanus, and it was especially prominent in works of art.

In the Renaissance, we begin to hear of the "occult sciences," an expression that is common in the works of Blaise de Vigenère. Central to these sciences is the symbolic image of the two books: the "book of nature" and the "book of revelation," or, in other words, the universe and the Bible. The works of Paracelsus, who lived in the first half of the sixteenth century, best express the interest in the book of nature. Unlike the compilations of Heinrich Cornelius Agrippa or the abstract and laborious speculations of certain Christian qabbalists, Paracelsus showed a real interest in the concrete observation of nature. Like no one before him, he harmonized astrology and medicine in a philosophy of nature that is both typically Germanic and highly original, a philosophy that was to gain widespread acceptance. Plants, metals, minerals, relationships between the parts of the body and the planets—nothing escaped his observations. A powerful and genial wit, given to a rich and evocative use of language, Paracelsus transformed the medicine of his day by replacing the preconceived ideas of scholastic medicine with a genuine praxis. He was the great occultist of modern times, in the most elevated and noble sense of the word.

The concern for the book of nature found in magic, astrology, and alchemy was not as prominent in studies of the Qabbalah and Hermetism. Here again it can be helpful to distinguish between theosophy or esotericism proper and the occult sciences. In practice, however, things are often more complex. For example, Christian qabbalists like Pico della Mirandola and Franciscus Georgius Venetus made a rather forced effort to introduce astrology and alchemy into their qabbalistic works, in sharp contrast to the Jewish qabbalists, who paid little attention to alchemy. With the writings of Agrippa, however, an uninhibited syncretism appears, marking the beginning of modern occultism. In his influential work *De occulta philosophia libri tres* (1531), Agrippa combined magic, astrology, Qabbalah, theurgy, medicine, and the occult properties of plants, rocks, and metals. This work was an important factor in the spread of the idea of occult sciences. It should be noted, however, that Agrippa's work had been foreshadowed by a beautiful book by Ficino, his *De vita coelitus comparanda* (1489), and by the quite famous work of Giovanni della Porta, *Magia naturalis libri viginti* (1558).

It is only with some hesitation that one can classify the alchemy of this period as an occult science. In many ways it belongs more properly to esotericism. In spite of the inevitable presence of essentially practical alchemists, in the sixteenth and seventeenth centuries this "high science" increasingly became a technique of individual initiation, a spiritual activity involving a mystique of incarnation. Its rich iconography, particularly in the age of the German Baroque, was accompanied by texts laden with symbolism and philosophy. The metamorphoses of bodies and substances that these describe are given a metaphorical significance, and are intended to describe the procedure of the soul's transformation. For occultism in the strict sense, then, one must look not to alchemy but to astrology, which became dominant in Europe during the seventeenth and eighteenth centuries.

France in the seventeenth century in fact had an official astrologer, Morin de Villefranche, a professor of mathematics at the Collège de France, and the development of the printing press made possible the rapid diffusion of astrological literature. In 1666, however, astrology was banished from official teaching, when the Paris Academy of Science refused to recognize it. Nevertheless, this did not halt its popular expansion elsewhere. In 1791 the first monthly periodical devoted to astrology appeared in London. In its popular form, astrology was eventually reduced to a trivial occultism, devoid of a theology or even a consistent conception of the world. Originally, however, its foundations were esoteric.

The Illuminism of the eighteenth century, represented by thinkers such as Louis-Claude de Saint-Martin, Christoph Oetinger, and Jean-Philippe Dutoit-Membrini, was a spiritual current marked by a theosophy that often rose to a level worthy of its chief inspiration, Jakob Boehme. It too had its occultist side, which was sometimes exploited by entrepreneurs adept at profiting from human credulity. In addition to Illuminism, theurgy was also an object of sustained interest during this period, as can be seen from the works of Martínez Pasqualis.

OCCULTISM AND MODERNITY

The industrial revolution naturally gave rise to an increasingly marked interest in the "miracles" of science. It promoted the invasion of daily life by utilitarian and socioeconomic preoccupations of all kinds. Along with smoking factory chimneys came both the literature of the fantastic and the new phenomenon of spiritualism. These two possess a common characteristic: each takes the real world in its most concrete form as its point of departure, and then postulates the existence of another, supernatural world, separated from the first by a more or less impermeable partition. Fantasy literature then plays upon the effect of surprise that is provided by the irruption of the supernatural into the daily life, which it describes in a realistic fashion. Spiritualism, both as a belief and as a practice, follows the inverse procedure, teaching how to pass from this world of the living to the world of the dead, through séances of spirit rappings and table tippings, the table playing a role analogous to that of the traditional magic circle. It is interesting that occultism in its modern form—that of the nineteenth century—appeared at the same time as fantastic literature and spiritualism. The French term *occultisme* was perhaps first used by Eliphas Lévi (1810–1875), whose work is sometimes somewhat misleadingly identified with the beginnings of occultism itself. The English equivalent, *occultism,* was apparently first used by A. P. Sinnett in 1881. Like the fantastic and the quasi religion of spiritualism, nineteenth-century occultism showed a marked interest in supernatural phenomena, that is to say, in the diverse modes of passage from one world to the other.

Philosophically, occultism is founded on the theory of correspondences, and as such it of course comes under the heading of esotericism. In the nineteenth century, however, its representatives were generally more interested in various powers and phenomena than in salvational gnosis. Their works, which are often devoid of a sense of the sacred, generally lack theosophical range as well, or are characterized by a rather skeptical religious syncretism. The interest that they displayed in the science of their time, and their attempts to reconcile it with the supernatural, were often naive and awkward. It is regrettable that the result of such praiseworthy efforts was not a philosophy of nature worthy of the name, comparable to that of the German Romantics.

Although occultism was an important movement in many different countries, its leading exponents were, for the most part, French. Nearly all were affected by the anticlericalism that raged in France at the time, and it is not surprising that some of them adopted the anti-Christian attitudes of the militant atheists. Occultism in France also came to be associated with the *fin de siècle* period of Symbolist and "decadent" literature, as can be seen in the work of Joris-Karl Huysmans (*Là-bas*, 1891), or in the painting of Gustave Moreau. In fact, however, the literary influence of occultism was exerted somewhat later, on surrealism, which is not surprising, given the experimental nature of the latter.

Of the great number of magi, thaumaturges, and experimenters who proliferated at the turn of the century, those for whom occultism was not only a practice but also a form of esotericism are of particular interest. Four Frenchmen who fit this description exercised a profound influence. Besides Eliphas Lévi, already cited, there were Saint-Yves d'Alveydre (1842–1909), the thaumaturge Philippe Vachot (known as "Maître Philippe"), and, most famous of all, Papus (Dr. Gérard Encausse, 1865–1916), who was with good reason called the "Balzac of occultism," and whose influence, in France as well as abroad, is still powerful. He was one of those who best succeeded in harmonizing magic and spirituality, occultism and theosophy, in works that were rich, sometimes chaotic, but always imposing and, as a whole, relatively traditional. He founded the very active Martinist order and contributed to making Saint-Martin better known. After a brief period of association with the Theosophical Society, he distanced himself from what he judged to be its "orientalizing" tendency. He shared with it, however, the fault of an often confused erudition. Besides Papus, other names stand out, interesting in their own right, such as Stanislas de Guaïta (1861–1897), Joséphin Péladan (1890–1915), Paul Sédir (1871–1926), Grillot de Givry (1874–1929), Albert Jounet (Dr. Emmanuel Lalande, 1868–1929), Charles Barlet (Albert Faucheux, 1838–1921), the editor-bookseller Chamuel, and the librarian Augustin Chaboseau. Victor-Émile Michelet, who knew most of these people, drew a lively portrait of them in his book, *Les compagnons de la hiérophanie*.

The sociologist Edward A. Tiryakian has noted that in our age there is a connection between the modernization of Western society and the interest in present-day occultism. We have already seen how the appearance of occultism in the nineteenth century was linked chronologically with the industrial revolution. To this may be added the following comment by Tiryakian: "The occult revival, at least in terms of the receptivity of witchcraft among segments of the middle-class, could . . . be seen as another step in the modernization of Western society, in this context as a secularization of the demonic. Such a perspective would be consonant with the secularization hypothesis concerning the relation of religion to modern society" (Tiryakian, 1972, p. 492).

The French esotericist René Guénon professed to be a severe critic of these occultists. His objectivity as a critic was compromised, however, by his own dependence upon an esotericism suffused with Orientalism, hardly relevant to an impartial study or appreciation of Western occult traditions. His own personal commitments led him to ignore Paracelsism, for instance, as well as other true philosophies of nature. Nevertheless, his criticisms remain eminently valuable, for no one did a better job of denouncing the confusion of values and of levels in an age in which surrealism had laid claim to occultism, the confusion of the psychic and the spiritual reigned, and the most dubious syncretisms flourished.

This situation has hardly changed since then. The confusion has even been aggravated by the proliferation of cults and sects, especially in the United States. There, even more than elsewhere, the media—film and television in particular—help to popularize a polymorphous occultism that sometimes openly declares itself to be satanic but that is nevertheless rendered harmless precisely by such publicity. The taste for magic in all its forms finds a psychological outlet in fantasy films (Roman Polansky's *Rosemary's Baby* is one example among hundreds). Occultist sects have proliferated as rapidly as the films, offering themselves as a similar sort of spectacle for the world at large. Such cults are in a sense the manifestations of the desire to explore the unknown.

Occultism, like esotericism in general, has been the object of a great number of scholarly works, especially in the last generation or two. If Eliphas Lévi, Papus, and others of their era made poor use of their erudition, they at least had the merit of calling attention to the historical density of esotericism and occultism. Arthur E. Waite, himself an "initiate," and Paul Vulliaud drew upon them for inspiration. Today, historians such as Alain Mercier, Guy Michaud, and Jean Richer are throwing new light on the relationships between occultism, literature, and philosophy. Similarly, the works of Eugenio Garin, Paul O. Kristeller, Wayne Shuhmaker, and Frances A. Yates give us a more accurate picture of the *philosophia occulta* of the Renaissance and post-Renaissance. Thus, like the popularization of occultism by the media, current erudition too contributes a new facet to the subject: its sociocultural dimension.

BIBLIOGRAPHY

A comprehensive survey of the history of occultism from antiquity to the seventeenth century is provided by Lynn Thorndike in *A History of Magic and Experimental Science,* 8 vols. (New York, 1923–1958). For the Renaissance and later periods, see the bibliographical notes for "Esotericism" and "Hermetism." See also Will-Erich Peuckert's *Gabalia: Ein Versuch zur Geschichte der Magia naturalis im 16. bis 18. Jahrhundert* (Berlin, 1967). A full account of recent writing on the Renaissance and a valuable summary of the major tendencies is found in Wayne Shuhmaker's study *The Occult Sciences in the Renaissance* (Berkeley, 1972). On modern occultism and literature, see Alain Mercier's *Les sources ésotériques et occultes de la poésie symboliste, 1870–1914,* 2 vols. (Paris, 1969–1974). On esotericism and occultism in general, see Robert Amadou's *L'occultisme: Esquisse d'un monde vivant* (Paris, 1950). An illuminating sociological account is provided by Edward A. Tiryakian in his article "Toward the Sociology of Esoteric Culture," *American Journal of Sociology* 78 (November 1972): 491–512. Valuable, insightful approaches to the study of the occult can be found in *The Occult in America: New Historical Perspectives,* edited by Howard Kerr and Charles L. Crow (Chicago, 1983), and in Mircea Eliade's *Occultism, Witchcraft, and Cultural Fashions: Essays in Comparative Religions* (Chicago, 1976).

2 WISDOM

Kurt Rudolph
Translated from German by Matthew J. O'Connell

The term *wisdom* has been used with a great variety of meanings in the course of history. A survey quickly shows that every culture has or has had its ideal of wisdom and recorded it in oral or written sapiential literature. In particular, the relation, both historical and systematic, between wisdom on the one hand and religion and philosophy on the other, varies a great deal. This article can give only a limited selection from the broad range of sapiential traditions and ideas.

GENERAL TERMINOLOGY

As far as we can judge from the terms used and their history, wisdom was originally a practical matter, namely "insight" into certain connections existing in human life and in the world and modes of behavior derived from this insight and put into the service of instruction and education. The Indo-European root of the word *wisdom*, **ueid-*, connotes "perceiving, seeing" (compare Greek *idein*, "idea," and Latin *videre*, "to see"). The German language has preserved the ancient connection between *Weisheit* ("wisdom"), *Wissen* ("knowledge"), and *Wissenschaft* ("science"). A person's wisdom depends on what he or she has seen and thereby come to know. It is therefore a practical knowledge, the primordial shaper of human behavior toward the environing world (to the extent that this knowledge resists the pressures for immediate action). The same practical element is manifest in other cultures as well. Thus the Hebrew *hokhmah* has to do with "skill, ability" *(ḥkm);* the Akkadian *némequ* with "dexterity and skill"; Greek *sophia* with "cleverness" or "skill" in any of the arts or professions of life (carpentry, medicine, poetry, music, etc.). The Akkadian word for a teacher of wisdom or learned person, *ummanu,* was borrowed from Sumerian and originally meant "master craftsman." The cultivation and transmission of cumulative experience in coping intellectually with the world was done mainly in schools that were the seedbeds of literary culture and the forerunners of the later "schools of wisdom" or universities. Oral tradition was likewise controlled by specific groups that were responsible for the maintenance of tradition.

WISDOM, RELIGION, AND PHILOSOPHY

If religion can be broadly conceived as a way of coping, theoretically and practically, with the problems of the world, nature, and society, then wisdom is one part of this effort. In fact, wisdom and the various contents of the religions have historically been closely connected. Wisdom was regarded as an area of religious tradition and derived its authority from its relation to particular gods (especially the sun, as in Mesopotamia and Egypt) or religious principles (e.g., concepts of world order, such as the ancient Egyptian *maat*). In this form, wisdom contributed to the development of theological thought and is part of its history ("priestly wisdom"). Particular divinities were venerated in cult and magic (the two are difficult to distinguish) as protectors or representatives of religious knowledge (Ea and Marduk in Babylonia, Ptah in Egypt). The legitimation of wisdom by more or less religious figures, such as kings, teachers, and priests, belongs in the same context. We know instances of wisdom being personified as a divine hypostasis (e.g., in Buddhism, Judaism, gnosticism, Zoroastrianism). In many religions wisdom is an attribute of the divinities; in monotheistic religions it is an attribute of the supreme God. The wisdom of God transcends that of human beings and makes it pale into insignificance; in Christianity the wisdom of God even turns human wisdom into folly (see below). This Christian revaluation of the value set upon wisdom in antiquity did not, however, lead to an abandonment of wisdom but to its relativization and to a radical transformation of the whole concept.

This more or less positive relation between wisdom and religion is only one side of the coin. Just as often, wisdom went its own way alongside official religion; it was even, as in the ancient Middle East, in tension or conflict with it. To the extent that this was true, it was a profane, secular way of coping with the world that avoided or excluded any appeal to traditional religious entities (gods, cult, priests). It thus paved the way for philosophical and ultimately also for scientific thinking (see the etymological connection mentioned earlier between the German words for wisdom and science). This development is most easily seen among the Greeks, where the concept of philosophy, or "love of wisdom," took shape. According to tradition (Diogenes Laertius, 1.12; Cicero, *Tusculanae Disputationes* 5.3.8) the term went back to Pythagoras and was then taken over by Plato and Aristotle, who gave it its normative meaning. It is clear that the projection of the Platonic conception of philosophy and science back onto Pythagoras meant a reinterpretation of the latter's simple, prescientific notion of wisdom. Pythagoras was undoubtedly a teacher of wisdom, not a scientist or mathematician in the later sense of these words; his explanation of the cosmos had at its center a number symbolism that could not yet be called scientific, since in it number, ritual, and doctrine of the soul still formed a unity (Burkert, 1972). In any case, *philosophy* retained its practical meaning of "way of life" down through the centuries and has not lost it even today. Ancient Greek wisdom, documented in gnomic poetry (Hesiod, Mimnermos, Solon, Phocylides, Theognis), with its simple key idea of "moderation" *(mēden agan)* or "fitness of act to time and situation" *(kairon gnōthi),* found its extreme application in the so-called Sophists, who converted wisdom *(sophia)* into practical rationality and thereby brought its dangers to light for the first time. In contrast to the Sophists, Socrates avoided the concept of wisdom and reserved this quality for God alone (Plato, *Apology* 20–22). For Plato wisdom was the supreme virtue (*Republic* 441c–d). Aristotle distinguished between the practical wisdom of everyday life *(phronēsis)* and speculative wisdom *(sophia)*, which concerns itself with "first things" *(Nicomachean Ethics* 4.5.2, 15.1.5). The distinction marked the transition to systematic wisdom, or philosophy. Nonetheless, in the history of philosophy its ancient root—"wisdom for living"—has repeatedly surfaced; in particular it has found ever new expression in ethical systems and endeavors (e.g., those of Spinoza, Kant, Fichte, and Schopenhauer). In his *Wörterbuch der Philosophie* ([1910–1911] 1980, vol. 1, p. 446), Fritz Mauthner formulates the difference between wisdom and practical "prudence," and between wisdom and philosophy or science with their goal of theoretical knowledge, as follows:

> *In my opinion,* wisdom *seems to mean not only that those who have this quality, possession, or way of thinking are able on every occasion to act or think with rare prudence in pursuing their theoretical or practical goals; it means that in addition they are able to judge the value of the theoretical and practical goals in question. It also means perhaps that such persons act according to their judgments. Schopenhauer was certainly a philosopher but hardly a wise man. Montaigne was a wise man but not really a philosopher. We think of Socrates as being both wise man and philosopher.*

PROBLEMS OF A TYPOLOGY

Since it is not possible at present (or ever, in my opinion) to write a history of the various ideas of wisdom, scholars have quickly settled for providing at least a typology of the concepts of wisdom. Wisdom has taken these broad forms: an anthropological ability to cope with life (the oldest and most widespread form); a rational system (interpretation of the cosmos, philosophy, beginnings of science); and a personification, hypostasis, goddess, or attribute of God.

Any attempt at greater detail becomes mired in the problems of the given historical context. It is possible, for example, with Edward Conze to compare the Buddhist (Mahāyāna) Prajñāpāramitā ("perfect wisdom") with the figure of Sophia in early Judaism and to find surprising similarities (Conze, 1968, pp. 207–209). There are even chronological correspondences: the hypostatization of both ideas of wisdom began about 200 BCE and yielded similar conceptions. Yet differences of content are unmistakable: Prajñāpāramitā is a personification of Buddhist insight into the "emptiness" of the world and has no connection with an idea of God; the Jewish Sophia became a divine hypostasis that can also be mediator of creation and identifiable with the Law (Torah). The situation is the same with parallels between Egyptian, Mesopotamian, and Iranian ideas of wisdom, each of which retains its own special character and cannot be wholly assimilated to the others and made to coincide with them. By and large, the only common element is the shift in the thematization of wisdom from an anthropological skill to a central religious figure or person who mediates wisdom. In this shift wisdom changes from subject to object; an anthropological capacity for insight becomes a form of revelation about the cosmos or God. The content of wisdom as insight into the coherence of the world and life takes on a religious and, to some extent, esoteric character (as in the *Wisdom of Solomon,* gnosticism, and Mahāyāna Buddhism). This development did not occur wherever ideas of wisdom existed (thus except for Israel and Iran it did not occur in the Near East or in Greece). It looks as if a necessary condition of this development is the existence of a canonical literature that accepts the idea of wisdom. "Revelation" is identified with wisdom inasmuch as wisdom becomes the content of revelation and as a result either heightens the importance of canonicity or permits an extension of canonicity (as, for example, in the Prajñāpāramitā literature or the gnostic writings).

This literary documentation for the idea of wisdom makes possible some typological classifications that should not be overlooked. Thus the "typical" wisdom genre is the *gnōmē* (Lat., *sententia*), that is, the tersely formulated "sentence" or maxim, or, more generally, the proverb. The oldest collections of wisdom traditions are collections of proverbs that can be developed into literary works on the theme of wisdom or can at least supply material for such ("teachings," "disputations," dialogues). Omens, riddles, fables, parables, and metaphors are also frequently storehouses of wisdom. Wisdom is thus not limited to a particular literary form, although it is closely linked with the proverb and maxim. Its origin in the oral tradition of the preliterary period of history can be demonstrated only through inference from the presence of such traditions among contemporary nonliterate peoples. There is hardly a people that does not possess some stock of wisdom traditions; this stock is the source of wisdom in the original sense of the term. Its beginnings are lost in the darkness of prehistory. The question whether the often asserted "international" character of wisdom literature is to be explained by evolution (from an original common possession) or by diffusion (through spread and borrowing) cannot be further answered. There are many arguments for the second hypothesis, but the first theory can also be helpful in examining many cultures. In any case, both forms of development can be seen at work in the course of history (the ancient Near East is a classic example of the borrowing of wisdom traditions). The important thing, however, is what particular cultures, literatures, and religions did with the common treasury of wisdom; these results are attractively multifaceted and pluralistic.

THE MANY FORMS OF WISDOM

Space allows only a limited survey of some of the principal forms taken by ideas of wisdom. The emphasis will be on the ancient Near East, which decisively molded the image of wisdom (transmitted through the biblical heritage). Only a brief glance can be taken at India and East Asia, which developed an independent form of wisdom that has influenced the culture and life of these peoples down to our own day.

Mesopotamia (Sumer and Babylonia). The Near East possessed expressions of wisdom at a very early date, although these did not lead later on to a unitary concept of wisdom. The dominant element in this wisdom was skilled proficiency in insightful understanding of the world, human beings, and society. No one doubted the divine origin of wisdom, even if an increasing awareness of the difference between divine and human wisdom manifested itself in later literature and led to a crisis in the wisdom tradition. The basic idea of the wisdom tradition was what scholars have named the "act-consequence connection," that is, the early insight that specific actions have or can have specific consequences in the lives of human beings. People attempted to find rules of behavior by observing their human environment, but they did not advance as far as systematic reflection or even develop an ethic of behavior (this step was left for the Greeks and the Chinese). Their observations, handed down in the form of aphorisms, provided valuable counsel for kings, officials, and scribes.

The storehouse for this wisdom was the school, and its teachers were the scribes, who were therefore regarded as wise beyond others. Wisdom derived its authority from its being traced back to divinities (especially Utu, Shamash, Ninurta, Enki, Inanna) or prehistoric wise men (Shuruppak, Gilgamesh). Because of its origin and approach this wisdom had a eudaimonistic and at times even a mantic character, but in the late period it turned pessimistic and skeptical. The dogma of the act-consequence connection to a great extent prevented the raising of new questions; when these were finally asked they led to a helpless skepticism (the problem of Job, the suffering just man; the problem of a just world order). Modesty, uprightness, consideration for others (love of neighbor), and deliberation were the principal virtues; their cultivation brought life, happiness, children (sons), and God's providential care.

The decisive force in the development of ancient Mesopotamian wisdom was that of the Sumerians. The Akkadians for their part mainly translated, transmitted, and interpreted, while adding a few new forms of their own (*Wisdom of Ahikar,* omen literature). The beginnings of wisdom are to be found in the early "lists" or "inventories" in which language was used as a means of "inventorying" the world and thus to some extent ordering or systematizing it. This kind of wisdom has therefore been called "list wisdom" and understood as a first approach to scientific effort (Soden, 1936). More developed approaches led from a simple listing of objects to an appraisal of them; this has come down to us in the form of disputations (literature of disputes over relative values). This kind of wisdom has been described as "value wisdom" (Hans Heinrich Schmid, *Wesen und Geschichte der Weisheit,* Berlin, 1966). The rise of proverbs relating to occurrences in nature and society brought for the first time the formulation of simple factual situations (called therefore the "wisdom of events"). This stage paved the way for wisdom sayings in the narrower sense. The latter emerged from observation of human behavior (initially without thematizing the act-consequence connection), first in proverbs and then clearly in various "counsels," which unfortunately have come down to us only in fragmentary form *(Counsels of Shuruppak, Counsels of Wisdom).* Wisdom gradually made its way into various other genres; meanwhile links were also established between wisdom and ideas of a socio-ethical and legal kind from royal and legal texts (e.g., conceptions of protecting the weak, widows, and orphans; doing good and hating evil; practicing righteousness). Wisdom thus sought to formulate and thereby give insight into the basic rules governing the cosmos. The gods had established a just world order; it was for human beings to learn this order and act accordingly. The challenge to this outlook by, for example, historical events led to a crisis of wisdom, since the act-consequence connection came into question and the theme of the "suffering just man" became topical. This was the subject of the "Job poems," which followed the "complaint and response paradigm" *(ershahunga).* To this genre belong the following: *Sumerian Job,* the *Poem of the Righteous Sufferer* (also called *I Will Praise the Lord of Wisdom* [*Ludlul bel nemeqi*], from its opening words), the *Babylonian Theodicy,* and the satirical *Dialogue of a Master and Slave* (or *Dialogue of Pessimism*), which probably does not belong to the wisdom literature but is nonetheless very informative in regard to it. The conclusion reached in these works is that God's action is inscrutable and his wisdom different from that of human beings. The act-consequence connection is pushed into the background but not abandoned, since insight into the order governing the world is denied to human beings. In all this we can see wisdom in the process of leaving our earth and becoming a supratemporal system and part of the divine world (to which in fact it had always belonged).

Egypt. Unlike Mesopotamia, Egypt did not have a "list wisdom" as a preliminary stage of wisdom; instead the sapiential saying (maxim) served as the starting point of a wisdom literature (the various "counsels"). The sapiential saying either contained a simple statement about the world and social relationships or it already connected consequences with specific actions that were either recommended or disapproved. Unlike the Mesopotamians, the ancient Egyptians developed the concept of a cosmic order *(maat)* that became basic to the idea of wisdom. The goddess Maat was a daughter of Re, the sun god, and symbolized truth, justice, and order in cosmos and society. The pharaoh was her representative on earth. The wise had to act like Maat; agreement with her bestowed success, disagreement brought punishment (unhappiness). Subordination to Maat was therefore the mark of the wise. Wisdom supplied the needed rules, which were based on tradition and experience (which included successive reinterpretations). Examples of wisdom or, as Egyptologists prefer to say, of "counsels" or "instructions," go back to about 2800 BCE. Only the names of the earliest have come down to us *(Instructions of Imhotep, Instructions of Djedefhor)*. The *Instruction of Ptahhotep* is the oldest surviving document of this genre (fifth dynasty). It is filled with optimism about the order *(maat)* that exists and is known and with an unbroken confidence in the act-consequence connection. Modesty, uprightness, self-control, subordination, silence, are virtues of the wise. The idea of the silent sage influenced Egyptian biographical literature. Citations from the wisdom literature can be demonstrated in numerous inscriptions.

Most of the remaining "instructions" are from the Middle Kingdom (c. 2135–1660 BCE) and are "tendentious writings" that discuss problems of wisdom and are therefore also called "disputation literature." Among them are the *Instruction for Merikare* (tenth dynasty), in which the first mention is made of the judgment of the dead; the *Instruction of King Amenemhet to His Son Sesostris* (twelfth dynasty), which was probably a model for *Proverbs* 22:17–24:22, although the former is more pessimistic and materialistic; and the *Instruction of Cheti, Son of Duauf,* a piece of publicity for the civil service. The threat to the old order shows through in the *Admonitions of an Egyptian Sage* and the *Protest of the Eloquent Peasant*.

To the period of the New Kingdom (c. 1570–1085 BCE) belong the *Instruction of Ani* (eighteenth dynasty), which defends traditional authority against criticism, and the *Instruction of Amenemope* (twenty-second dynasty), which is strongly pietistic and calls for humility toward the hidden rule of the sun god. From the late period (first millennium CE) we have only the very homespun *Instruction of the Papyros Insinger* and the instruction of a certain Ankhsheshonk. Characteristic of later wisdom (from the eighteenth dynasty on) is the realization, in Egypt no less than in Babylonia, of the limitations of human knowledge and the freedom of the divinity; this meant that the act-consequence connection, though weakened, was not completely abandoned, but was considered to reside in the impenetrable recesses of the godhead. Authority, tradition, humility, circumspection, and silence continued to be themes of wisdom. In fact, in the late period wisdom and piety came to be more closely identified. Maat yielded to the godhead (Re). Devout individuals had as their partner no longer Maat but God; God became the guarantor of the act-consequence connection, which was hidden from the devout but which they nonetheless humbly accepted as existing. Wisdom now consisted in this knowledge of God and his free will, a knowledge that was familiar to the Bible and probably exerted an influence on it. For that matter, a monotheistic or henoheistic current runs through the entire wisdom literature.

Ancient Israel, Judaism. Israelite wisdom literature *(Proverbs, Job, Ecclesiastes)* underwent developments comparable to those in Babylonia and Egypt. [*See* Wisdom Literature.] In its earliest, preexilic form, wisdom is here, as in the ancient Near East generally, not specifically religious but focused on the act-consequence connection in the cosmos and in individual lives (see *Prv.* 22:13–23:11). It is not opposed to faith in Yahveh but on the other hand has only peripheral contacts with it (see *Prv.* 16:1–22, 16:28–29). Yahveh, like the ancient Near Eastern and Egyptian sun god, is guarantor of the cosmic order that governs the lives of human beings. Wisdom is primarily concerned with this-worldly questions affecting the order and security of human life; observation and insight into what goes on in the world and society play their part here. From a literary standpoint the proverb or maxim is the basic form of transmission *(Proverbs, Ecclesiastes;* later on, the *Book of Ben Sira* and the *Wisdom of Solomon).* Ascription to Solomon (c. 970 BCE) has a historical basis to the extent that international communication (especially with Egypt) flourished during that period (see the *First Book of Kings* 5:9–14). From that time on in Israel, as elsewhere, the "wise man" *(ish ḥakham)* had his place alongside the priest and the prophet, and the area of tradition with which he dealt soon became one of the most important in Israelite literature (see *Ben Sira* 24:3–7).

In its historical development this literature reflects shifting approaches to wisdom until the latter's crisis and disintegration *(Job, Ecclesiastes).* To begin with, ancient wisdom is increasingly theologized, that is, connected with the Yahvistic faith, but also systematized or dogmatized and reduced to a series of anthropological contrasts (see *Prv.* 10–15). The wise and the foolish are turned into contrasting types, as are the devout and the ungodly, the sensible and the ignorant, and so on. The act-consequence connection changes (in the postexilic period) to a connection between behavior and its results *(Prv.* 10:30, 11:3–4). Corresponding dualistic traits make their appearance as human beings are divided into the just and the wicked, and the cosmos into good and evil, just and unjust. Wisdom itself withdraws into heaven and is personified (see below). The ancient program of wisdom, which urged insight into human beings and the world through observation and its application, comes under the control of strict monotheism and the doctrine of creation, both of which leave little room for independent human thought. As a result, the crisis of dogmatized wisdom becomes radical and leads in the *Book of Job* to its rejection. As in the Babylonian world, an appeal is made at this point to the inscrutability of God (see *Jb.* 40), a solution that is accepted in later Judaism. At the same time, however, a return to the ancient, authentic concept of wisdom is urged *(Jb.* 38–39): understanding of the world consists in the acknowledgement of its given order, even though insight into it is limited. The most radical break with the wisdom tradition comes in the Hellenistic period in the person of Qohelet (the purported author of *Ecclesiastes),* who abandons the act-consequence connection as a means of insight, is skeptical about an order in the world, and demonstrates the meaninglessness of human existence. Wisdom is no longer available in this world (see also *Jb.* 28). Reverence is still shown toward creation and its distant creator, but the "historicality of human existence" and its transitory character are thematized for the first time. Qohelet offers no solution for the crisis; the world and human beings remain unintelligible.

This situation, which we meet only in the Bible, had consequences that probably led to the disintegration of the biblical worldview in gnosticism. But Jewish apocalypticism too had some of its roots in wisdom: the removal of wisdom from the world led to an eschatological hope; the introduction of dualism into the cosmos (see above) led to the apocalyptic doctrine of the two kingdoms; historical events had deprived the scribes, who were the transmitters of wisdom, of their ancient theater of operations, the royal court, and they dreamed of its future restoration. Gnosis and apocalyptic were connected.

Hellenistic influence probably played a part also in the complete transformation of the figure of wisdom (Hokhmah). It becomes a suprahuman, otherworldly personage, a divine hypostasis (*Prv.* 8:22–31; *Ben Sira* 4:11–19, 24:3–22; *Wis.* 6–9), a mediator of revelation and creation (*Prv.* 3:19, *Ben Sira* 24:3); it is even identified with the Torah, or Law, as the content of the word of God (*Ben Sira* 24:8, 24:23; *1 Bar.* 3:9–4:4). It takes on the traits of a goddess (perhaps Isis Panthea) and, as Lady Wisdom, becomes the antagonist of Lady Folly, another personification, modeled on Aphrodite or Astarte (*Prv.* 7:9–13, 9:1–18). [*See* Hokhmah.] "Kinship" with her, such as the just or the wise have, bestows immortality (*Wis.* 6:17) and even makes one like God (*Wis.* 6:18). This shift from a horizontal role, as an anthropological skill in understanding of the world, to a vertical role leads in the *Wisdom of Solomon* (first century BCE) and then especially in the work of Philo Judaeus (first century CE) to the idea of wisdom (Gr., *sophia*) as an otherworldly figure accessible only through esoteric "knowledge." Communication with this distant heavenly wisdom is accomplished in the philosophy of Philo through the Logos (the divine intelligible word), which represents "wisdom close to us." Sophia is thus accessible only through revelation and knowledge of the Logos. It is no longer available in this world, but has vanished from it (Ethiopic *Apocalypse of Enoch* 42:1–8, *4 Ezr.* 5:9–10, Syriac *Apocalypse of Baruch* 48:36). At this point the way is already being paved for the gnostic conception of wisdom.

Christianity and Gnosis. Early Christianity accepted the early Jewish conception of wisdom at various levels. On the one hand, the early Jesus tradition (the purported source of the sayings of Jesus, known as the Q source) took over the ancient Israelite proverbial wisdom (explicit reference is made to Solomon in *Mt.* 12:42, *Lk.* 11:31); on the other hand, Jesus himself is understood as the embodiment of wisdom (*Lk.* 7:35 and parallels; cf. *Mt.* 23:34–36 with *Lk.* 11:49). He is "filled with wisdom" from his childhood (*Lk.* 2:40, 2:52) and surpasses even Solomon in this respect (*Mt.* 12:42, *Lk.* 11:31). His deeds and teachings demonstrate his wisdom (*Mk.* 6:2, *Mt.* 13:54). Scholars therefore speak of a "wisdom-Christology" as one of the earliest forms of christological statement. In the letters of Paul wisdom plays an important role in his dispute with the community in Corinth *(1* and *2 Corinthians),* where a wisdom that was probably already interpreted in a gnostic manner was being preached and was finding expression in ecstatic utterances (revelations). In response, Paul conceives the momentous idea that Christian wisdom, represented by the Redeemer, is foolishness *(mōria)* to the world, this wisdom being the cross that as sign of the "weakness of God" *(1 Cor.* 1:25) is the very sign of his "strength."

God has destroyed "the wisdom of the wise" and turned it into "foolishness" (*1 Cor.* 1:18–22, 2:6–8). In the presence of the true wisdom of God, which has been revealed in Christ, the traditional wisdom of this world has been reduced to naught, but at the same time it has also been fulfilled. Those who believe in Christ possess "the power of God and the wisdom of God" (*1 Cor.* 1:24, 1:30, 2:10–12, 3:18). Old Testamental and Jewish wisdom literature of two centuries before the common era is here given a completely new interpretation and thereby rescued from the crisis into which it had fallen; on the other hand, limits are also set for any future Christian conception of wisdom. The critical acceptance of ancient wisdom traditions and the ambivalent response of Christian theology to philosophy both have their roots here (see Thomas Aquinas on the one side and Martin Luther on the other). Meanwhile, as the *Letter of James* in particular shows, the principle is still accepted that wisdom shows its truth in ethico-moral practice: Christian life is wisdom made manifest (*Jas.* 3:13–17; cf. *Jas.* 1:5). The ancient idea of wisdom is thus revived here; it becomes a Christian virtue for coping with life.

In my opinion, gnosticism has its roots in those parts of early Jewish sapiential teaching that, like *Ecclesiastes,* challenged the traditional picture of the world. Independently of this heritage from tradition and the history of ideas, gnostic literature too continues to present wisdom in the guise of transmitted sayings, for the most part in Christian form (from the Nag Hammadi corpus, the *Gospel of Thomas* and the *Gospel of Philip;* see also *Silvanus* and the *Sentences of Sextus*), but also in new forms of its own *(The Thunder, Perfect Mind).* Most notable, however, is the figure of Sophia, or Pistis Sophia ("faith wisdom"), an ambivalent embodiment of the gnostic Pleroma, especially in the Barbelo and Valentinian forms of gnosis. [*See* Sophia.] According to some heresiological accounts and original (Nag Hammadi) texts, Sophia is a companion of the most high God; more precisely, she is the feminine aspect of his first manifestation or emanation, whose masculine aspect or consort may be identified with the Primal Man, the Son of man, or Christ (Seth). A second, lesser Sophia must also be included in the series of "syzygies" (paired aeons) that derive from the first pair. Other passages— and these are in the majority—describe Sophia variously as one of the final aeons: the one that, as mother of the demiurge (Ialdabaoth), is indirectly involved in the fate of the created world. But she is simultaneously active in the work of redemption, repairing the harm done by the loss of the spark of light, inasmuch as Sophia herself, split into two parts—an upper and a lower, a greater and a lesser, a part of life and a part of death, of truth and of lie, or simply as Sophia and Achamoth (the Aramaic word for "wisdom")—suffers in an exemplary fashion the fate of the fall and redemption. This version is characteristic of the so-called Barbelo gnostics and of the Valentinians; it is also attributed to the Cainites and the Ophites, as well as to the Sethians. Several texts from Nag Hammadi also belong here (e.g., *Apocryphon of John, Hypostasis of the Archons, Gospel of the Egyptians, Trimorphic Protennoia*). Gnostic wisdom *(sophia)* serves to express many sides of gnostic thought. It serves as an image of the self-estrangement of God in emanation and reflection; thus it represents the feminine aspect in God, while leaving his perfect unity undiminished. But Wisdom is also (as aeon) the consort of the Savior and is intimately connected with both demiurgic (cosmological) and soteriological processes. This has nothing to do with feminist ideas; behind it, rather, stands the heritage of the Jewish wisdom tradition in its later form.

Iran and Zoroastrianism. It is often forgotten that Iran too has produced an extensive wisdom literature that goes by the Middle Persian name of *handarz* (early New Persian, *andarz*), meaning "advice, instruction." This too has been handed down in various forms of *gnomai*. It is preserved only in Middle Persian, but it doubtless had Avestan (Old Iranian) precursors (such as the now lost *Barish nask*). At the center of this literature is "wisdom" (MPers., *khrad,* or *xrat*), whose representatives or transmitters were kings of the prehistoric period (e.g., Jam, Ōshnar) and the Sasanid period (e.g., Chosrau I), viziers (e.g., Wazurgmihr ī Bokhtagān), and priests (e.g., Ādurbad ī Mahraspandān). Here again collection and transmission were the work of priestly schools or the (fire) temples. Since thought, along with speech and action, played a dominant role in Zoroastrianism, great attention was paid to the teaching of religious knowledge. This knowledge was identified with wisdom. But in fact the "knowledge" in question was not only religious, theological, and cultic. Iran had either taken over (via Hellenism) or had itself produced a great deal of secular knowledge.

Nonetheless, the religious framework within which the wisdom tradition was placed played a very important role. According to one of the principal works, *Mēnōg ī Khrad* (Spirit of Wisdom), all wisdom flows from a single wisdom that goes back to God. Two works in particular are important in this context. One is the sixth book of the encyclopedia *Dēnkard* (Acts of Religion); the other is *Dādistān ī Mēnōg ī Khrad* (Book of Judgments of the Spirit of Wisdom). Both originated in the Sasanid period but preserve older material as well. Book 6 of the *Dēnkard* goes back in part to the Avestan *Barish nask;* other material comes from oral tradition. Its content is largely religious and has to do with Zoroastrian teaching on cleanliness; it is therefore highly ritualistic in character. In this context wisdom is correct knowledge and correspondingly correct behavior in things religious. "This world was created by Ōhrmazd the Lord [Av., Ahura Mazdā] with knowledge *(dānāgīh)*. He maintains it with sagacity *(frazānagīh)* and manliness *(mardābagīh);* ultimately He will become joyful through it" (Shaked, 1979, sec. 311). This is interpreted as follows by the sages *(dānāgān):* "The thing of Wisdom *(khrad)* is this: sagacity *(frazānagīh),* manliness *(mardābagīh)* and the hope of the Renovation" (ibid., sec. 312). The same passage goes on to say: "The substance of wisdom *(khrad)* is similar to that of fire. For nothing in this world may become so perfect as that which is done by wisdom *(khrad)*" (ibid., sec. 313). In the *Dēnkard,* "character" *(khēm* or *xēm)* is superior even to wisdom, since "wisdom is in character; and religion is in both wisdom and character" (ibid., sec. 6; see also sec. 2). Ōhrmazd creates creatures through "character," "holds them with wisdom, and takes them back to himself by religion" (ibid., sec. 11).

In other, more secular *handarz* texts wisdom is at the head of the virtues and leads human beings to a knowledge of their duties. Ōhrmazd created the following spiritual realities that help human beings to that goal: "innate wisdom, acquired wisdom, character, hope, contentment, religion [*dēn*], and the consultation of the wise" (*Āyadgar ī Wazurgmihr* 43, cited in Shaked, 1979, p. xxvi). Acquired wisdom is gained through education; innate wisdom preserves human beings from fear and sin. Clearly, in Zoroastrianism wisdom is firmly embedded in a religious context (although secular wisdom is not completely absent). Wisdom is primarily a matter of Zoroastrian knowledge; the latter defines its essence. It is therefore the duty of the faithful to follow the "wise" (teachers, priests) and ask them questions; association with them brings God close to one. Parts of Iranian wisdom literature, however, are also marked by a fatalistic pessimism reminiscent of *Ecclesiastes* (Shaked, 1979, sec. D). "Destiny" *(bakht, brēh, zamān)* determines human beings; their action is geared to its accomplishment. We see here the influence of Iranian teaching on fate (i.e., Zurvanism), an influence also to be seen in modern Persian literature wherever this is in continuity with ancient Iranian wisdom traditions (proverbial literature, didactic poetry).

Wisdom clearly emerges as a heavenly person or hypostasis, the Spirit of Wisdom (Mēnōg ī Khrad), in the work of the same name. Wisdom is here viewed as one of the "holy immortals" (Amahraspandān; Av., Amesha Spentas); in fact, the author devotes more prayers to her than to the others (1.53). She is "original wisdom *(āsn khrad)* from the heavens and the worlds"; she dwells with Ōhrmazd and combines all wisdom in herself (57.3–32); she was created by Ōhrmazd (8.3, 8.8), and through her he created the world (1.11, 1.49, 57.5); through her Ōhrmazd keeps the world in existence (1.12). Her most important function is instruction or, as the case may be, revelation. Each of the sixty-two chapters following upon the introduction to the work begins with questions by an (anonymous) "wise man" *(dānāg)*, which Wisdom then answers at length. The book is thus a compendium or catechism of Zoroastrianism and derives its authority from the heavenly wisdom of God. The "wise man" who passes its contents on is evidently a representative of the Zoroastrian community or priesthood. He had wandered through the world, from land to land and city to city, looking for wisdom, until he realized that true wisdom was to be found in his religion; then this wisdom appeared to him in bodily form as Ōhrmazd's Spirit of Wisdom (Mēnōg ī Khrad) and instructed him (1.14–61). The most likely equivalent of this Wisdom in the Avesta is Vohu Manah (Vahuman, Vahman), the Good Mind; "primordial or inherent wisdom" *(āsn khrad)* is found in *Yasna* 22.25 and 25.18 *(āsnō khratush)* in connection with the Zoroastrian concept of faith ("the innate understanding Mazda-made").

India. Some of the earliest Indian wisdom literature is found in the collections of proverbial wisdom that were made for rulers or kings, as, for example, the well-known *Pañcatantra* or the *Hitopadeśa* (Instruction in What Is Beneficial). The *Mahābhārata*, the Indian national epic, contains in its didactic sections a good deal of ancient wisdom tradition; this includes the *Bhagavadgītā* in particular. The important part played by knowledge or insight *(jñāna)* in ancient Indian thought (especially in the Upaniṣads) has given wisdom a central position in India. [*See* Jñāna.] It is difficult to distinguish this wisdom from philosophy, and philosophy in turn from religion; each shares in the character of the others. The *Bhagavadgītā* praises "the way of knowledge or wisdom" in preference to the way of action *(karman)*: "A man of faith, intent on wisdom *(jñāna)*, his senses (all) restrained, wins wisdom; and, wisdom won, he will come right soon to perfect peace" (4.39; trans. Robert C. Zaehner, *The Bhagavad-Gita*, London, 1973). Brahmanic philosophy or religion did not, however, reach the point of personifying wisdom or knowledge. This step was taken only in Buddhism, in which the Indian ideal of knowledge, the way to deliverance from the cycle of births *(saṃsāra)* without reliance on the priestly tradition or extreme asceticism took new forms. But the objectification (hypostatization) of redemptive knowledge or transcendental wisdom *(prajñā;* Pali, *paññā)* came only in

Mahāyāna Buddhism, beginning in about 100 BCE in southern or northern India. A whole literature arose (originally in Sanskrit) consecrated to what it termed the "perfection of wisdom" (*prajñāpāramitā;* lit., "the wisdom that has gone beyond"). The earliest Prajñāpāramitā works were composed between 100 BCE and 150 CE; from the fourth to the seventh centuries CE compendia and short versions were redacted under the influence of the Mādhyamika school; from the sixth century on, Tantrism also gained control of these texts and gave them ritualistic interpretations (to the extent even of introducing antinomian practices). As mentioned above, there are a number of parallels between the Buddhist and the early Jewish conceptions of wisdom. The Buddhist "wisdom books" (Conze, 1975) introduce a specifically new type of knowledge about redemption: an insight into the "emptiness" (*śūnyatā*) of existence that promises deliverance. These teachings are presented in the form of dialogues between the Buddha and some of his disciples. The manner of presentation lends authority to the new teaching and gives it canonical status. Here the virtue (*pāramitā*) of "insight" (*prajñā, paññā*), perhaps under the influence of the South Indian mother goddess, is sometimes personified as a goddess of wisdom, Prajñāpāramitā. In this form she is regarded as "mother" of all the Buddhas (*buddhāmāti, jñāna mātā*) and *bodhisattva*s.

> If a mother with many sons had fallen ill,
> They all, sad in mind, would busy themselves about her:
> Just so also the Buddhas in the world-systems in the ten directions
> Bring to mind this *perfection of wisdom* as their mother.
> The Saviours of the world who were in the past, and
>   also those that are (just now) in the ten directions,
> Have issued from her, and so will the future ones be.
> She is the one who shows the world (for what it is), she
>   is the genetrix, the mother of the Jinas,
> And she reveals the thought and action of other beings.
>   (Conze, 1973, p. 31)

Prajñāpāramitā is depicted iconographically with two, four, six, ten, or twelve arms. Her color is gold or white; her symbols are the lotus and a book (colored blue or red). She often resembles depictions of Mañjuśrī (the male personification of wisdom) or Sarasvatī (the Hindu goddess of learning, eloquence, and intelligence) or Avalokiteśvara, Tārā, and Cunda. [*See* Mañjuśri; Avalokiteśvara; Sarasvatī; *and* Tārā.] To ordinary Buddhists she is a goddess who can be invoked and who bestows merit, well-being, and blessing. Buddhist theologians, however, see in her simply a "spiritual" manifestation of redemptive or enlightening ("*bodhi*-giving") wisdom, which contains and sustains all things and is called "mother of enlightenment." Here the very essence of Buddhist doctrine is manifested and personified. The various interpretations of this doctrine in the Mahāyāna schools (Mādhyamika, Yogācāra, Tantra) are also reflected in the figure of Prajñāpāramitā and the literature about her. One of the best-known hymns to her was composed by Rāhulabhadra (c. 150 CE):

> Homage to Thee, Perfect Wisdom,
> Boundless, and transcending thought!
> All Thy limbs are without blemish,

> Faultless those who Thee discern. . . .
> Teachers of the world, the Buddhas,
> Are Thine own compassionate sons;
> Then art Thou, O Blessed Lady,
> Grandam thus of beings all. . . .
> When as fearful Thou appearest
> Thou engender'st fear in fools;
> When benignly Thou appearest
> Comes assurance to the wise. . . .
> By all Buddhas, Single Buddhas,
> By Disciples courted, too,
> Thou the one path to salvation,
> There's no other verily. . . .
> By my praise of Perfect Wisdom
> All the merit I may rear,
> Let that make the world devoted
> To this wisdom without peer.
> (Conze, 1959, pp. 168–171)

The Tantric school produced magical incantations or formulas (*mantra*s) for Prajñāpāramitā, which were given by the goddess herself. The recitation of these sayings has liberating power; it is also meritorious on behalf of others. In this form of Buddhism the figure of Wisdom unites in itself all aspects of religion, both in theory and in practice. In fact, Prajñāpāramitā is probably its most notable expression. [*See also* Prajñā; Tathatā; Upāya; Buddhism, Schools of, *article on* Mahāyāna Buddhism; *and* Goddess Worship, *article on* The Hindu Goddess.]

China. Finally, I shall add a brief word on China, where, in contrast to India, wisdom has minimal connections with religion. In Confucianism it has an unambiguously ethico-moral character. [*See* Confucian Thought.] We are reminded of the Greeks when we find wisdom consisting in the avoidance of extremes and the following of the mean. *Chih* ("wisdom") is one of the five cardinal virtues that characterize the Confucian "wise man" *(chün-tzu)*. It includes knowledge of human nature and society, a command of language, and a practical behavior that obeys the Confucian rules *(li)*. [*See* Li.] "The sense of right and wrong is the beginning of wisdom *(chih)*" (Fung Yu-lan, 1952, vol. 1, p. 121). Every human being has the native ability to become wise and needs only instruction and practice, since in the prevailing Chinese view human nature is good (another point reminiscent of Greek thought). [*See the biography of Meng-tzu.*] Confucianism nonetheless also offers the ideal of the "noble man" or "holy man" *(sheng-jen)* who surpasses even the wise man, since he complies perfectly with all the principles *(li)*, lives in harmony with nature and society, and thus is the peerless teacher of an age. The ancient meaning of wisdom as the practical management of life through knowledge of the world and human beings has probably found its most impressive development in China and has for thousands of years profoundly shaped the character of the people. Wisdom is embodied in behavior and can be acquired by practice; it then becomes a habitual attitude.

[*See also* Knowledge and Ignorance.]

BIBLIOGRAPHY

There is no monograph that completely covers the concepts of wisdom that are found among various peoples and cultures. Only A. R. Gordon's "Wisdom," in the *Encyclopaedia of Religion and Ethics,* edited by James Hastings, vol. 12 (Edinburgh, 1921), attempts a survey; the areas most fully studied and described are the ancient Near East (including Israel), Greek thought, and early Christianity. The following bibliography lists other articles and books that I have found helpful and that can serve as an introduction to the subject.

Burkert, Walter. *Lore and Science in Ancient Pythagoreanism.* Translated by Edwin L. Minar, Jr. Cambridge, Mass., 1972.
Conze, Edward. *Buddhist Scriptures.* Harmondsworth, 1959.
Conze, Edward. *The Prajñāpāramitā Literature.* The Hague, 1960.
Conze, Edward. *Thirty Years of Buddhist Studies: Selected Essays.* Columbia, S.C., 1968.
Conze, Edward, trans. *The Perfection of Wisdom in Eight Thousand Lines and Its Verse Summary.* Bolinas, Calif., 1973.
Conze, Edward, trans. and ed. *Buddhist Wisdom Books, Containing the Diamond Sutra and the Heart Sutra.* London, 1975.
Conze, Edward, trans. *The Large Sūtra on Perfect Wisdom.* Berkeley, 1975.
Dijk, Jan van. *La sagesse suméro-accadienne.* Leiden, 1953.
Fohrer, Georg, and Ulrich Wilcken. "Sophia." In *Theological Dictionary of the New Testament,* vol. 7. Nashville, 1967.
Fung Yu-lan. *A History of Chinese Philosophy.* 2 vols. 2d ed. Translated by Derk Bodde. Princeton, 1952–1953.
Gese, Hartmut. "Weisheit." In *Die Religion in Geschichte und Gegenwart,* 3d ed., vol. 6. Tübingen, 1962.
Gladigow, Burkhard. *Sophia und Kosmos.* Hildesheim, 1965.
Kuchler, Max. *Frühjudische Weisheitstraditionen.* Freiburg, 1979.
Lambert, W. G. *Babylonian Wisdom Literature.* Oxford, 1960.
Langdon, Stephen H. "Babylonian Wisdom." *Babyloniaca* (1923): 129–194.
Mack, Burton L. *Logos und Sophia: Untersuchungen zur Weisheitstheologie in hellenistischen Judentum.* Göttingen, 1973.
Noth, Martin, and D. Winton Thomas, eds. *Wisdom in Israel and in the Ancient Near East.* Leiden, 1955.
Rad, Gerhard von. *Wisdom in Israel.* Nashville, 1972.
Ringgren, Helmer. *Word and Wisdom.* Lund, 1947.
Rudolph, Kurt. "Sophia und Gnosis." In *Altes Testament–Frühjudentum–Gnosis: Neue Studien zu "Gnosis und Bibel,"* edited by K.-W. Tröger, pp. 221–237. East Berlin, 1980.
Sasson, Jack M., ed. *Oriental Wisdom.* Special issue of the *Journal of the American Oriental Society* 101, no. 1 (1981).
Shaked, Shaul, trans. *The Wisdom of the Sasanian Sages: Denkard Book Six.* Boulder, 1979.
Soden, Wolfram von. "Leistung und Grenze sumerischer und babylonischer Wissenschaft." *Welt als Geschichte* 2 (1936): 411–464, 509–557.
West, Edward W., trans. and ed. *The Book of the Mainyô-i-khard* (1871). Amsterdam, 1979.
Wilcken, Ulrich. *Weisheit und Torheit.* Tübingen, 1959.

3
SPECULATIONS ABOUT NATURE

ANTOINE FAIVRE
Translated from French by Marilyn Gaddis Rose and William H. Snyder

In the West, "natural philosophy" and "philosophy of nature" have developed side by side and at times have been confused because of an ever-present ambiguity. They differ in principle, however: the first has been defined by Galileo, Comte, and Darwin as the pursuit of a total but essentially objective knowledge of phenomena, whereas the second has oriented such thinkers as Leibniz, Hegel, and Bergson toward an intuitive approach that nevertheless strives to be rigorous regarding the reality that underlies data derived from observation.

Among the thinkers of this second category, those who have come more and more to be labeled *Naturphilosophen,* or "philosophers of nature," since the time of German Romanticism occupy a special place. They are generally committed to grasping the concrete character of nonmechanical, nonphysical reality or, as Schelling put it, the "productivity" concealed behind sensible appearances, without, as a rule, neglecting the study of appearances themselves. That is, they are not satisfied with a natural philosophy based on empiricism alone. Their ideas indisputably bear the mark of the religious, indeed of gnosticism—not in the sense this word evokes when it is applied to the gnostics of the beginning of our own era, but in the sense of a frame of mind fixed on defining the nature of the relationships linking God, man, and the universe by means not relevant solely to the experimental method. The study and the discovery of these relationships define the activity of the theosophist, but whereas he most often takes God as the point of departure for his speculations, the *Naturphilosoph,* while conserving this tripartite schema as a basis of his program, mainly concentrates the efforts of his experimentation, speculations, and imagination on nature.

We must not, therefore, confuse them with the thinkers who are content to celebrate the beauty of nature and of mathematical formulas, or suggest that the natural order might well be found again in a spiritual order. Thinkers like Einstein certainly do propose the existence of a meaning beyond scientific analysis concealed behind the appearances of things; and this manifestation of respect is indeed quite different from materialist or positivist agnosticism. However, it must also be further distinguished from the approach appropriate to *Naturphilosophie.* The *Naturphilosophen* do not limit themselves to confirming that there is something other than the phenomenal world; they aspire to attain to the very secrets of the universe, that is, to know, as Goethe's Faust would, "Was die Welt an innersten zusammenhält" ("the inmost force that undergirds the very universe"). A kinship more important than their differences unites these thinkers in comparable forms of inspiration that, in Western civilization, are found among the pre-Socratics, in certain currents of medieval thought, in the Renaissance, and throughout German Romanticism.

ANTIQUITY: THE PRE-SOCRATICS, STOICISM, AND HERMETISM

Certain components of modern *Naturphilosophie* can be found in the writings of most of the pre-Socratics. In particular, they did not oppose matter to mind, soul to body, or subject to object, but had a tendency to approach nature with a nondualistic, noncategorical attitude. In such a view, all being is concrete. Yet their thinking contained dynamic and creative contradictions. Cosmologies and anthropologies rested on pairs of opposites. The pre-Socratics had a sense of analogy and homology insofar as they did not think in Aristotelian categories—and this for obvious reasons. Their imaginary world was grounded in concrete nature, interpreting and molding it into living structures. Hence the importance of the elements (whose inexhaustible symbolism would later be taken up again by the alchemists): water for Thales, air for Anaximenes, fire for Heraclitus. For these physicist-metaphysicians, especially Heraclitus, the logic of antagonism was primordial. "Night and day," he said, "they are one." Novalis, in eighteenth-century Germany, would not forget this lesson, as can be witnessed even in his poetry: nature expresses herself in her works; man works by expressing himself. We are, as the Stoics might say, nature's co-workers. Hence the pre-Socratics' labyrinthine style, which seems obscure because it is made of paradoxes and which later inspired Western alchemy. Parmenides was already moving away from such categories of nature with his linear thought, his *doxa,* which tended to annul these contradictions. Thus, too, Anaxagoras, who saw in nature a thinking principle that is co-present in the ordering of the world, but that also separates man from the cosmic ambience. Not until Empedocles do we once more find some of the elements belonging to *Naturphilosophie*. He affirmed six principles—reassemblage and dispersion, plus the four elements—and presented the history of the world as the reconstitution of a dislocated unity.

Stoicism, which continued throughout almost six centuries, prepared the way not only for Neoplatonism and certain gnostic and Hermetic currents but for *Naturphilosophie* as well. Indeed, it placed emphasis on the need to know the concrete universe, harmoniously blending wisdom and technique, and taught the necessity of a *savoir-faire* that rejects pure speculation and must lead to the knowledge of an organic whole, assuring the accord between things heavenly and terrestrial. This is a trait that appeared again and again in a more systematic manner as one of the important aspects of Alexandrine Hermetism, where several texts affirm that God is known through the contemplation of the world. Hence the preference of the Hermetica for the particular, the *mirabilia,* over the abstract and the general; science is not "disinterested" but aims to rediscover the general by means of an enriching detour through the concrete and through individual objects: nevertheless, the notion of "concrete" is not absolutely the same in Heraclitus, in the Stoa, in the *Naturphilosophie*.

This focus on the concrete did not occur in Neoplatonism, where the intelligible reality, the realm of the mind to which one strives to gain access, has no purpose at all in explaining the world of the senses. Instead, it aids us in quitting this world in order to enter more easily into the pure region where knowledge and happiness are possible. The sensual, of course, reflects the intelligible, but the *sens,* or meaning, of the sensual is of little importance. The essential thing is to go beyond the sensual to get to the world of ideas. Nevertheless, there is in Plotinus something like the outline of a *Naturphilosophie.* The diverse branches of early gnosticism, even more than Neoplatonism, were, by definition, hostile to all forms of *Naturphilosophie,* since according to most of them the world of the senses, which was the work of an evil demiurge, has nothing good to offer us and is not even capable of nurturing our knowledge. This hostility toward anything pertaining to nature is a dualist trait, one that reappeared later in Catharistic thought.

MEDIEVAL PERSPECTIVES

The ninth-century theologian John Scottus Eriugena was born in Ireland but later lived at the court of Charles the Bald. In his major work, *On the Division of Nature,* or *Periphyseon,* Eriugena proposed a philosophy of nature that was to nourish much of subsequent theosophic speculation up to the age of German idealism in the nineteenth century. The different kinds of nature that Eriugena distinguished and examined, particularly those of nature *naturans* and *naturata,* and of nature creating and created, were later, as it seems, to inspire qabbalistic literature. His philosophy of expansion and contraction appears much closer to the mechanics of Qabbalah than to classic Platonism.

Beginning in the ninth century, the Arabs translated many ancient texts and, inspired by Aristotle, wrote commentaries on them. But together with the rationalistic empiricism of Aristotle, and in the margins of a form of positivism, we see Arab thought also expressing a highly mythicized vision of a world ruled by spiritual forces that only intuition can aspire to grasp. The medieval West received this teaching by way of the Latin translations of Arabic texts that were often concerned with the theory and practice of medicine and magic.

The High Middle Ages. The twelfth century saw a return to the cosmological themes of Greco-Roman antiquity, in other words, to a universe conceived and represented as an organic whole, subject to laws that must be sought in the light of analogy. The "discovery" of these laws would entail twofold consequences: on the one hand, a powerful process of secularization was set in motion, so that the sense of the sacred was lost. On the other hand, a lasting renewal of what might be called the feeling of cosmic participation took place. This latter corresponded to the systematic and poetic elaboration of a network of relations between the visible and invisible realms of creation. The universe was approached by form of philosophical speculation that was committed to deciphering living, concrete meanings. According to Jean de Meun, nature became the "chamberlain," or vicar, of God—a God incarnated in stone in this age that saw the emergence of the only true sacred art of the West.

Nature, its unity and its laws, is what interested the Platonism of Chartres as it appeared in the works of William of Conches, who was much concerned with physics, propagated the teachings of Eriugena on the world soul, and undertook, like Bernard Silvestris of Tours, to integrate a Platonic philosophy of nature with Christianity. The Platonic doctrine of ideas, and the reflection on numbers, could certainly have incited the intellect to remove any form of reality judged to be absolute from the sensible world and to place it in the realm of the archetypes. The school of Chartres did not succumb, however, to this temptation inherent in true Platonism, from which Augustine had not escaped. They owed this integration of the intellect with the material world to the natural sciences, and their debt to Arabic science in this respect is quite evident—especially in medical science, which had only recently been made accessible to the West. The occult philosophy of the Renaissance, already a philosophy of nature in the sense of *Naturphilosophie,* was in many ways close to that of the school of Chartres.

Dominicans and Franciscans. In the thirteenth century two opposing tendencies divided philosophical and religious reflection. The Franciscan spirit, represented mainly by Bonaventure, showed renewed interest in all things in nature. This was followed by the Dominican spirit, derived from Aristotle and represented by Albertus Magnus and Thomas Aquinas, who elaborated a philosophy based on abstraction and practically devoid of the universal analogical correspondences in which the individual plays an integrating part. From another source came a third tendency, that of the school of Oxford, which shared with the spirit of Chartres a desire for universal intuition.

Aside from the mystic path, nature holds the largest place in the thought of Bonaventure. The "Seraphic Doctor" considered it equal to the Bible and considered it as a book whose signs must be deciphered. The spirit of Oxford blossomed further in the work of the early thirteenth-century bishop Robert Grosseteste. Neoplatonism and an interest in the sciences, two traits characteristic of both these English masters, appeared clearly in Grosseteste, a precursor of the modern *Naturphilosophen.* His preferred subject, speculations on the nature of light, made him interesting in the eyes of posterity. The nature of light as the "first corporeal form" *(lux)* accounts for the presence of all of the bodies of the universe and the constitution of the world by its expansion, its condensation, or its rarefaction. Grosseteste imagined that a point of light created by God was diffused in such a manner that a sphere of a finite radius was formed, which is the universe (a hypothesis that prefigured the "big bang" theory). The limit of its power of diffusion determined the firmament, which in turn sent back a light *(lumen),* which engendered the celestial spheres and the spheres of the elements. Adam Pulchrae Mulieris, a Parisian contemporary of William of Auvergne and another theologian of light, prefigured several of Grosseteste's intuitions with his *Liber de intelligentiis.* Five centuries later, in the age of German Romanticism, light examined from a similar perspective would once again be at the heart of the preoccupations of *Naturphilosophie.*

There has been a tendency in modern times to make Roger Bacon, a thirteenth-century Franciscan of Paris and Oxford, a rationalist precursor of the experimental method. This gives the false impression of a character bristling simultaneously with illuminism and experience. These two attitudes are here inseparable, for what Bacon called "experience" *(experimentum)* should be taken not in its current sense (related to "experiment") but in the sense of "the work of an expert." Thus, the practices of the alchemist and the astrologer fall under the heading of *experimenti.* Paracelsus would later reason in the same way when he dealt with "experience" in medicine. We must understand that this word means the study and knowledge of concealed natural forces. For Bacon, experimental science meant secret and traditional science, with the condition that concrete science not be separated from the scriptures but that the two be linked together for their mutual clarification. This is comparable to the science to which Friedrich Christoph Oetinger, following Paracelsus, would devote himself in the eighteenth century.

The Late Middle Ages. To these works must be added what was a relatively well-known genre in the thirteenth century, that of the *summae* ("sums") and *specula* ("mirrors"), of which Alexander Neckam's *De naturis rerum* is the first example. To this genre belong such works as the *Speculum majus* of Vincent of Beauvais, an exposé of natural history in the form of a commentary on the first chapters of *Genesis*. Aside from this, other works of the same sort worthy of note include *De natura rerum* by Thomas of Cantimpré and Bartholomew the Englishman's *De proprietatibus rerum*. Only occasionally do these works offer a philosophy of nature in the full sense of the term, but since they increase the number of histories and observations on the powers of plants, animals, and minerals, as well as on the heavenly signs, they prepare the way for the occult philosophy of the Renaissance.

The problem of nominalism versus realism, which was posed so sharply in the fourteenth century, entailed a debate with high stakes for the construction of a *Naturphilosophie* and, indeed, even for the survival of such lesser philosophies as prefigured it. Nominalism was loath to see in the laws and the realities of the sensible world a collection of analogous and homologous replicas of worlds hierarchically ordered in correspondences with one another. Nominalism emerged victorious from the debate, clearing the field for the development of modern science, beginning with physics. A heavenly mechanism assembled in the image of a terrestrial mechanism now filled the void left by the disappearance of the guiding intelligences. Thus the continuity between a spiritually structured universe and self-sufficient, purely physical laws, which had been sustained by traditional philosophies, was broken. At the same time, the influence of nominalism joined with that of Averroism and, in bringing about the downfall of the Avicennian concept of the universe, prepared the way for a sort of Cartesian *res extensa,* in itself incompatible with a *Naturphilosophie*. And yet realism itself was not a sufficient foundation for a *Naturphilosophie* because a good number of those who had defended it in the Middle Ages had generally done nothing more than distract attention from the reality of nature and of the individual for the aggrandizement of the universal.

For all that, however, *Naturphilosophie* did not die. It had not yet even seen its finest hour. The *Ars magna* of Ramón Lull, written in 1308 and inspired by Qabbalah, was an instrument of knowledge that claimed to be applicable at all possible and imaginable levels, from God himself down to the lowest orders of nature, by way of the angels, the stars, and the four elements. Lull's *Ars,* far removed from Scholasticism, was like a canal through which a part of the medieval Neoplatonism revived by Eriugena passed, in other words, a dynamic Platonism close to the Jewish mysticism then flourishing in Florence and Spain. Lullism enjoyed a broad dissemination, but only from the Renaissance onward. Nicholas of Cusa, Marsilio Ficino, and Pico della Mirandola drew a goodly part of their knowledge and their methods from it. A grandiose conception of nature is also found in the contemporary writings of Peter of Abano. Astrological Hermetism makes up half of his encyclopedic work, of which the *Conciliator* is the most important volume. Here nature is seen as controlled by the stars and objects are filled with spirits.

To all this the role of alchemy, which began to regain currency in the West in the twelfth century, was apparently added. It assumed three forms, which may have been complementary in the minds of certain alchemists, but which it is convenient to distinguish. These were simple research into procedures of metallic transmutation (for example, the production of gold); a "spiritual" alchemy, in which the chemical metaphors served as an aid to meditation, with a conscious or unconscious transformation of the experimenter himself as the goal; and third, an alchemy presented as a *Naturphilosophie,* as by Petrus Bonus in the *Pretiosa margarita novella* and by many other speculative adepts of the "high science" who were trying to harmonize Aristotle's philosophy with the ways of the "great work." In the middle of the fourteenth century, the Franciscan Jean De Rupescissa (or Jean de Roquetaillade) developed at length the idea that a "quintessence" is at work in each object, and he proposed theories on the four elements and the "principles"—in other words, on the nature of nature. All this heralds Paracelsus, but before him a great name emerged in the thought of the fifteenth century—Nicholas of Cusa, the apostle of a total science in which the *ars coincidentiarum* is clearly distinguished from the *ars conjecturarum* of common science. The first corresponds to the principle of the intellectual knowledge of objects, the second to the principle of a purely rational knowledge. Nicholas gives us a glimpse of the possibility of dynamic forms in science. What he called the *docta ignorantia* is a form of superior knowledge, a gnosis of the coincidence of opposites, or state of the unity of all things. [*See also* Alchemy, *article on* Renaissance Alchemy.]

THE RENAISSANCE, PARACELSIANISM, AND PANSOPHY

The Renaissance promoted the revival of a philosophy of nature, primarily in Germany. This country was thenceforth the preserver of a tradition characterized by a theosophy that embraces the fullness of the world. In the sixteenth century, when the Jewish tradition detached man from nature in order to place him once more in the hands of God, the idea that nature speaks to us of God was defined, whereas Jewish Qabbalah had not been exempt from such a tendency but was mainly concerned with a theosophy of the relationships between God and man. The idea of nature in the Middle Ages, even among the Franciscans of the schools of Chartres and Oxford, had not gone as far as the new theosophy, to which the name *pansophy* has sometimes been given, in order to emphasize its "universal" character, in the concrete sense of the term. This new theosophy stressed the possibility of knowing God by knowing nature. It was Paracelsus, the famous physician of Einsiedeln, Basel, and Salzburg, who here played the determining role, with his immense oeuvre and his abundant posterity. He made all of nature enter into Christian mysticism by joining the latter to the Neoplatonic tradition, at the same time transforming its contribution. For while Paracelsus preserved the Neoplatonic idea of intermediaries between man and heaven, he did so less as a spiritualist meditating on the nature of intermediary intellects than as a practitioner seeking to discover the analogical relationships between a concrete, living, dynamic heaven and the human being studied in all his constituent parts.

In opposition to Neoplatonism, nature for Paracelsus emerged directly from divine power. He distinguished two orders of suprasensible realities, or "lights." There was the "light of grace," of a uniquely spiritual order, a divine world to which man is related through his immortal spirit. This is the domain of pure mysticism and divine and human eternity. Paracelsus did not venture to occupy himself with it, except in order to be reminded by it of ontological preeminence and existence. His domain of research was the other "light," that of nature, or *philosophia sagax,* which was not the intellective approach of the Scholastics, and which he described as the autonomous power of revelation. Between these two lights he placed astronomy or astrology as a third area or term. Everything that concerns these three realms, as well as biology, human psychology, and even the arts, emerges from nature's light and obeys the laws of analogy, which it is increasingly important for us to decipher: correspondences among metals, the planets, the parts of the human body, and so forth. His is a complex universe and, despite all, heterogeneous; it is an expanding universe—one in which time itself, far from being considered a container, is nothing other than the growth of beings. In this construction, it is essential to continue to improve one's understanding, through observation and experiment, of the complexity of nature's divinely created unity. Chemistry and medicine are emphasized in the search for that comprehension. One must, as Paracelsus himself said, "acquire the wonders of God through the mediation of nature."

Paracelsianism spread through Germany and the rest of Europe at the end of the sixteenth century and the beginning of the seventeenth, at least two generations after the death of its initiator, whose work was not well known or widely published until then. Among his successors and disciples, Gerhard Dorn, Adam Bodenstein, Michael Toxites, Alexander von Suchten, and Oswald Croll occupy an important place. Their philosophy, like their master's, is not autonomous but is set within a theology; it has dynamic character that is found at all levels of their speculations, up to the level of God himself, who is by no means a *deus otiosus.* The manner in which they conceive the organic unity of the world with its multiple hypostases always results in a "sacred physics" far from the dryness that characterizes most of the cosmologies of the Middle Ages except those of the kind of Bonaventure or Hildegard von Bingen. The important thing is not so much the anatomy of the body of God and of the universe as it is God's physiology. Paracelsianism corresponds to the irruption of a "physiological" cosmology—or cosmosophy, rather—in the West.

This "pansophy," as it was called more and more often in the seventeenth century, subsequently led to three developments. First there was Paracelsianism proper, which seldom, because of the personal nature of Paracelsus's method (better characterized as "bubbling up" rather than systematic), appeared in the form that its initiator originally gave it. Next there was chemical philosophy, more or less influenced by alchemy, which practical science struggled to get rid of throughout the seventeenth and eighteenth centuries. This was a science that aimed to be objective and generally did not encumber itself excessively with theological considerations. Finally, there was pansophy, in other words, a theosophy that took into consideration the tissues of analogical relations between God, man, and the universe. It involved philosophers who sometimes had the tendency to go further than Dorn, Croll, or Paracelsus himself in the direction of theosophy.

This third current culminated in one of the major inspirational themes of the Rosicrucian movement—as the first manifestations of this movement, the *Fama* and *Confessio,* attest—and in the early seventeenth-century work of Robert Fludd and Jakob Boehme who, though more theosophist than pansophist, owed much to Paracelsus. For all of them, God is known through his works. Since he is immersed in nature, he participates in it in a thousand ways. To know nature is at the same time to know God—and conversely, as we discover the center of the whole by studying the whole, we discover the creator by studying his creatures. [*See* Rosicrucians *and the biography of Paracelsus.*]

THE DIRECT SOURCES OF ROMANTIC NATURPHILOSOPHIE

In the seventeenth century the influence of magnetism, and particularly the Boehmian type of theosophy, joined the influence of Paracelsianism. We must wait until the middle of the following century, however, before we see *Naturphilosophie* arise from the aggregate of these currents. The Swabian Friedrich Christoph Oetinger was the greatest German theosophist of his time, and, if we add to his name those of his satellites Johann Ludwig Fricker, Prokop Divisch, and Friedrich Rösler—known as the "theologians of electricity"—then he was quite possibly the first *Naturphilosoph* in the Romantic sense of the term. The current of Oetinger's thought is characterized by a continuing, simultaneous recourse to two sources of inspiration, which serve both as a heuristic and a verification: nature and the Bible. There develops from the seventeenth century onward a *"physica sacra,"* or "physicotheology," which might be considered the chronological link between the cosmosophical views of the Renaissance and the German *Naturphilosophie* of pre-Romanticism and Romanticism. Thomas Burnet, Joseph Addison, John Hutchinson, and George Berkeley (see his *Siris*) belong to this trend. The teaching of the one ought not contradict that of the other; on the contrary, they should clarify one another. Neither biblical literature nor biblical fundamentalism are at issue here, because if the revealed images are taken concretely—whether they have to do with the days of creation, the garden of Eden, or the vision of Ezekiel—they are understood in a perspective of spiritual realism that preserves and promotes interpretations at several levels. Almost immediately afterward, Mesmerism, that is, the works and teachings of Franz Anton Mesmer, popularized the taste of the age for magnetism by establishing a basis for it that appeared truly scientific. There was, at the turn of the eighteenth century, a great infatuation with anything touching on magnetism, galvanism, or electricity. Between Oetinger's Neo-Boehmian theosophy and the pragmatism of Mesmer, a physician little given to metaphysics, Romantic *Naturphilosophie* was born. It was not, however, a result of these two currents alone; at least three other factors now entered the picture.

The first of these is French naturalism. This might seem paradoxical, but with Buffon's *Histoire naturelle* and Diderot's *Rêve de d'Alembert,* a new physics appeared, presented more in the form of a literary exercise than as a scientific calculation. With Buffon we see emerging once again the old theme of the world soul. Buffon, and even Holbach, gave back to Germany what had originally come from there, that is, from Leibniz. But this was a Leibniz revised and corrected by French naturalism, which transferred the monad, an intelligible substance accessible to understanding alone, into phenomenal nature itself.

The second and more decisive factor was the philosophy of Kant. Schlegel, Novalis, and others were happy to find (particularly in Kant) a concept according to which the world is a product of the imagination, in other words, a synthetic, spontaneous activity of mind. Beginning with his *Anfangsgründe,* Kant had presented the two forces of Newtonian physics—attraction and repulsion—as the components of all nature. The Romantics further complicated this polarity in order to make it a key to the understanding of human nature, all the more so because to Kant's influence they added that of the contemporary Scottish physician John Brown, author of a theory also based on polarities, the *Elementa medicinae,* which was destined to enjoy considerable success in Germany. Then came Fichte, who tried to finish the work of Kant's critique by freeing the human mind from the only bonds that Kant had not removed, those of the "thing in itself." For Fichte, there is, in fact, no absolute existence outside of the subject, for it is the subject that creates the real. Schelling said that Fichte had restored fundamental confidence in the object, a natural confidence that is proper to the human being that had been shaken or destroyed first by Descartes and then by Kant. Fichte had reinstated it by positing the thing and our mental representation of it as identical.

The third factor involves religion and theology. The rediscovery of Spinoza at the end of the eighteenth century must be taken into account here for, having until then been considered an atheist, he was now fervently received as a man intoxicated with God. It was now recognized that his formula "Deus sive natura" ("God or nature") was not a profession of faith disguised by materialism, but rather an affirmation that nature is something divine. Thinkers came more and more to posit a God not identical with things—*Naturphilosophie* generally avoids pantheism—but conceived of as the source of energy, as a development of organic forces, from which the entire finite world proceeds. Guided more or less by the influence of Herder, the first German Romantics tended to replace the notion of cosmic organism—such as that found in Hamann and Jacobi—with that of a dynamic force, in order to erase the Spinozan concept of substance in favor of a more energetic concept. Moreover, at the moment when *Naturphilosophie* was emerging, religion was also undergoing a crisis. This was the age in which Chateaubriand, in his essay *Sur les révolutions,* was asking what kind of religion would succeed Christianity. In response to the *Génie du christianisme* by the same author, there appeared almost immediately a book that is perhaps the sole French work of *Naturphilosophie:* Louis-Claude de Saint-Martin's *De l'esprit des choses.*

ROMANTIC NATURPHILOSOPHIE

It was largely due to these factors that the study of nature in the last years of the eighteenth century, and for half a century thereafter, was approached in a very new way. In 1798 there appeared almost simultaneously the *Weltseele* (Soul of the World) of Schelling and the essay *Über das pythagoräische Quadrat in der Natur* (On the Pythagorean Square in Nature) by Franz von Baader. This twofold beginning was then furthered by A. K. A. Eschenmayer who, together with Baader and with the help of Schelling, contributed to some extent to the unification of the data of traditional pansophy with the new spirit of Kantian philosophy. Among the principal representatives of this school, which lasted almost until the death of Carl Gustav Carus in 1869, and in addition to those already cited, were Karl Friedrich Burdach, Wilhelm Butte, Joseph Ennemoser, Gustav Fechner, Justinus Kerner, Giovanni Malfatti, Adam Müller, Novalis, the Dane Jean-Christian Oersted, Lorenz Oken, Johann Nepomuk Ringseis, Johann Wilhelm Ritter, Gotthilf Heinrich von Schubert, Henrik Steffens, Gottfried Reinhold Treviranus, Ignaz Troxler, Johann Jakob Wagner, and Karl Joseph

Windischmann. These are primarily Germans or men attached to German culture. There is little to add from other countries except for two English philosophers somewhat influenced by this school: William Paley, who published *Natural Theology* in 1802, and Sir Humphrey Davy, author, in 1830, of *Consolations in Travel*.

For most of these philosophers, knowledge of the self and knowledge of the world go hand in hand. Together, knowledge of the self and knowledge of the world are passion, initiation voyage, and immersion in becoming. The consciousness of these Romantics was not solitary but, rather, interdependent with nature, with the entire cosmos; hence the interest of Baader, Schubert, Kerner, and others in metempsychosis, psychical and metaphysical research, somnambulism, and animal magnetism. Despite the impact of Newton and mechanism on the age, we see the idea of an intelligible interdependence of man and cosmos affirmed among these scholars and thinkers. It was expressed in a broad spectrum of speculations regarding light, electricity, and chemistry, and often used inspired, poetic tones. But this lyricism should never let us forget that German Romanticism was ultimately a philosophical and religious movement rather than a literary one. In this respect it was clearly a continuation of Paracelsianism and pansophy, but it benefited from the acquisition of the experimental sciences and placed emphasis on the figurative systems, the polarities, and architectonics in a spirit often recalling certain forms of Pythagoreanism. Nature is a text to be deciphered with the aid of correspondences and symbolic implications; as a consequence, rigorous experimental science is never more than an obligatory point of departure in the movement toward a gnostic apprehension of invisible processes. These, the real, are of a *natura naturans* that is always posited as a postulate or, more correctly, as an initial belief.

Thus physics and metaphysics are two sides of the same coin. Almost all of the representatives of Romantic *Naturphilosophie* were scholars working with the concrete: chemists, physicists, geologists, mining engineers, and physicians. It is not surprising, then, to see a Romantic image of the physician disseminated in the literature of the time. The picture is seductive because it is based on the analogy of the two activities medicine and poetry. The physicians Marcus and Roeschlaub embodied this twofold activity quite nicely. Marcus had, moreover, published—as had Schelling—in one of the scholarly journals serving as a forum for these ideas the *Jahrbücher der Medicin als Wissenschaft*. There we read, from the pen of Philipp Walther, a spokesman for the same idea: "How the cure of a malady takes place remains eternally hidden from understanding and is among those things that are quite simply incomprehensible. . . . Now, just as the idea blends in with the material in a work of art, so the physician who heals attempts a critical effort at healing the conflict. . . . And, likewise, in the work of art, beauty of form only proceeds from the marriage of the idea and the substance, just as health is produced by the artistic effort of the physician." We are not far from Paracelsianism, which should not surprise us greatly, since many of the *Naturphilosophen* of the time came to reinforce the position of Paracelsus, making themselves the heirs of a theosophy that supported the foundations of Paracelsian pansophy itself.

Certainly, not all *Naturphilosophen* were theosophists by any means, but theosophy—notably that of the Boehmian variety—colored the works of most of them. Baader was certainly the greatest theosophist of that school as well as the most appealing and profound. Conversely, the theosophists did not disdain to have recourse to science in the spirit of *Naturphilosophie,* as we can see in the works of Johann Friedrich von Meyer, the theosophizing qabbalistic theologian of Frankfurt. It was always essential to rediscover the constitutive principles of things by simultaneous experimentation and meditation. But, even as they are revealed to us in a symbolic manner and develop in clusters of meanings, everywhere there are intermediaries, mesocosmic elements (invisible structures, principles, angels, qualitative stages of light, etc.), and from these arises the polymorphic, richly peopled world. From this grows a veritable polytheism, which does not occur at the level of religious dogma and which remains compatible with Judeo-Christian monotheism. "Monotheism of the mind and of the heart," writes Schelling, "polytheism of the imagination and of art. This is what we need." This is because the creative imagination, a fundamental notion of this movement, lets the gods play in us in a harmonious world of the concrete where each occupies, alongside the others, a place of his own.

The most remarkable common denominator of all of these currents of thought is the affirmation of the identity of mind and nature. This is what posterity has always retained as most specific or most suggestive, doubtless because it poses the basic metaphysical question. This "philosophy of identity," to use Schelling's expression, is the belief in a relationship between man and nature in which each is bound partly to the other. This relationship refers neither to an abstract knowledge of nature nor to a practical or utilitarian exploitation of it, but to a level of comprehension and reality where the negative or destructive opposition of the two is surmounted. Mind—and not only the mind of man—becomes nature, spiritualized nature. "The more we advance this agreement," wrote Oersted in 1807, "between nature and mind, the more perfect you will find it, and the more easily you will agree with me in admitting that these two natures are the seeds of a common root." Understood in this dynamic way, this "agreement" is an animated and passionate dramaturgy, especially when attached to a mythic narrative.

These polarities, generally presented as a quaternary, constitute the basis of most of the vital and unifying schemas so characteristic of this philosophy. The fourfold structure underlying most of these polar representations is made of an undifferentiated pole (chaos, or primordial night); from it emerge two further terms that are opposite and complementary: fire and water, fire and light, masculine and feminine, or attraction and repulsion. Then appears the fourth term, which reflects the original one and which is the common product in which the two opposite terms combine. Such a quaternary makes a mythic narration possible, indeed, at times even necessary, and a thinker is theosophical to the extent that he emphasizes such a narrative. If we want to identify it by reducing it to its simplest elements, we can find it in what Schelling termed "the repressed mystery of Christianity," which is basically alchemy, but in the form of the Hermetic myth of the "redeemed redeemer." It is the story of a captive, or "captured," light that another light, having remained free, awakens. Here is the crux of this Romantic narrative, present in the form of an opposition between light and weight, the latter understood as a substance in which primitive energies have been swallowed up. Certain of these energies, which were once close to the Absolute, have become inaccessible since their capture by attraction, that is, by weight, but can reappear or be resuscitated. This progressive reappearance of light in the world, in life, establishes, implicitly or explicitly, the narrative of *Naturphilosophie.*

DECLINE AND EPIGONI: PERSPECTIVES

Consequent upon the decline of *Naturphilosophie,* even before the middle of the nineteenth century, a corresponding "estrangement" of nature occurred: the view developed that nature is savage, in the sense that it increasingly ceased to be felt by man as the place where he could recognize himself, where he lived, or where he felt at home. More and more, nature came to appear as "other." This process was prepared by Schopenhauer in 1819, with *The World as Will and Representation,* in that he considered nature, once and for all, as outside of the categories of understanding.

Goethe's case is rather special. His scientific works, especially those on the metamorphosis of plants and on color, place him close to the great choices of the *Naturphilosophen,* but he was most interested in grasping eternity in an instant, or infinity in an object. Finally, he was more interested in the differences among origins than in their commonality. Throughout his life and works he preserved the notion of a vital universe; but he did not ask what it is that things symbolize in the invisible.

Romantic *Naturphilosophie,* in no way a product of spontaneous generation, has never been completely extinguished and has always been more or less actualized as a "philosophy of nature," in the meaning given to that term here. Thus, from the beginning of the nineteenth century on, it became difficult to say precisely how much in the impulse of that movement—which was never fully interrupted in the West—could be attributed to German Romanticism, or whether it was, rather, a more general movement, to be understood as a form of *philosophia perennis.* Whatever the case may be, Romantic theories of the unconscious colored the ideas of nineteenth-century thinkers such as Eduard von Hartmann, and it is in Schubert, with his *Dream Symbolism,* and even more so in Carl Gustav Carus, that the sources of psychoanalysis should be sought. However, we need not see too much resemblance to *Naturphilosophie* in the various forms of vitalism and esotericism that followed for the next century. The philosophers Ludwig Klages, Hermann Keyserling, and Max Scheler have, to be sure, reclaimed some of this heritage, but in an essentially speculative manner; moreover, they are neither chemists nor geologists nor astrophysicists nor physicians.

We find the most obvious survival of Romantic *Naturphilosophie* in the concept of the unconscious, particularly in Schopenhauer's monolithic conception of it and in the slightly different but still monolithic unconscious as described by Freud, but also in that notion of the unconscious whose structure Jung has depicted—it is even a quaternary structure! Without a doubt, Jung is the last of this school. What is more, he has even given us the key to understanding it, for what he says of the alchemists—that what they saw in stone was, in fact, a constellation of their own personal unconscious—could undoubtedly be said of the German *Naturphilosophen.* Though they themselves did not make discoveries significant in the history of science (in this area Johann Wilhelm Ritter was a brilliant exception), they nevertheless expressed truths of a different order, which could well be that of the Absolute. They were the last representatives of an age when man—at least the scholar—felt at home on this earth, before the appearance of an entirely different, definitively alienated nature.

Judeo-Christian theosophy, or rather, the little of it that survives in the twentieth century, continues the tradition of a philosophy of nature, some of its branches pressing forward in a traditional direction. Thus, Rudolf Steiner, like Jung, teaches the restoration of human harmony at all levels, but in addition, like the disciple of Goethe that he has always been, he assigns that part that is beautiful to nature. Today it is not so much tradition that orients man to a return to a philosophy of nature, for there is scarcely anyone left who dares, as Oetinger did, to confront science and the Bible. Increasingly this orientation occurs in the scientific communities themselves. There are many members of these communities who, often unwittingly, take up anew or rediscover these elements of the past. In the so-called exact sciences alone, we may mention the idea of intelligent matter, which has been addressed more and more by the specialists (Arthur Stanley Eddington, V. A. Firsoff, Fritjof Capra, Jean Charon), and the corollary tendency to establish relationships between the concepts of modern physics and the ideas on which the philosophical and religious traditions of the Far East are based—it is true that our own traditions, even in these areas, are generally unknown. Thus, a sort of visionary physics is developing. Werner Heisenberg's physics approaches the microphysical structures of Platonic schemas; Jack Sarfatti argues that matter comes from light, which is gravitationally self-trapped. For Arthur Koestler, in *The Roots of Coincidence,* matter is modeled on the spirit. One can easily multiply the examples.

Let me conclude with a word about the Colloquium of Cordova in 1979. Although it did not deal directly with the question of Romantic *Naturphilosophie,* in the published proceedings emerges the idea of a universal interdependence in a science that, at its triumphant peak, had the power to eradicate this idea once and for all. Some observers are tempted to detect in this interdependence the polar, dialectic, and dynamic schemas, which are now organized according to arithmological laws, themselves containing symbolic schemas of which esotericism could not have been ignorant, or which pertain to *Naturphilosophie*. These are apparent in the work of the physician and biologist Stéphane Lupasco. The current tendency in the history of the sciences and in the work of science itself is often to place the emphasis on structural types, on models of hierarchization, and on other categories or formal research procedures. The theories of modern science could find new horizons in the texts of *Naturphilosophie*.

Of course, if *Naturphilosophie* in the full meaning of the term—that is, the Paracelsian or Baaderian—is to regain full citizenship, then it must once more incorporate a theology or true theosophy, a myth in the sense that Oetinger had of the word; and it must launch a scientific investigation that, in turn, will release new meanings from the scriptures, meanings that complement science. One must remember that even at the zenith of Romantic *Naturphilosophie,* men who were both true theosophists and *Naturphilosophen* were never numerous. What we may nonetheless imagine, for our own late twentieth-century age, is a form of speculative spirituality capable of encompassing the full richness of the world, as the Christian theology of the twelfth century tried to do, in order to develop a new vehicle for perceiving the ordering principles of the universe under the threefold and complementary sign of mind, anthropology, and the comprehension of the real. We speak here of a many-sided reality not limited to the projection of a single flat, truncated belief, but rather one that brings flesh and flame together.

[*See also* Hermetism; *for related discussion, see* Science and Religion.]

BIBLIOGRAPHY

Debus, Allen G. *The Chemical Philosophy: Paracelsian Science and Medicine in the Sixteenth and Seventeenth Centuries.* 2 vols. New York, 1977. This study and the work of Pagel listed below complement one another. Contains an extensive bibliography and many detailed surveys on various authors.

Epochen der Naturmystik: Hermetische Tradition im wissenschaftlichen Fortschritt. Edited by Rolf Christian Zimmermann and Antoine Faivre. Berlin, 1979. A collective work comprised of fifteen contributions in English, French, and German ranging from Ficino and Agrippa to Schelling.

Gode-von Aesch, Alexander. *Natural Science in German Romanticism.* New York, 1941. A highly readable account of many of the philosophical, religious, and literary theories of *Naturphilosophie* in the age of Romanticism.

Gusdorf, Georges. *Les sciences humaines et la pensée occidentale.* 13 vols. Paris, 1966–1985. See especially volumes 9, 10, and 11. Well-documented and extremely comprehensive.

Joël, Karl. *Der Ursprung der Naturphilosophie aus dem Geiste der Mystik.* Jena, 1906. An old, but still valuable conspectus of the problem in the history of philosophical and religious ideas.

Pagel, Walter. *Paracelsus: An Introduction to Philosophical Medicine in the Era of the Renaissance.* Basel, 1958. Extremely comprehensive and well documented. Treats not only Paracelsus but also Paracelsism in the Renaissance.

Sladek, Mirko. *Fragmente der hermetischen Philosophie in der Naturphilosophie der Neuzeit.* Frankfurt, 1984. A valuable synthetic survey of the relationship between hermeticism and the philosophies of nature.

4 ESOTERICISM

Antoine Faivre
Translated from French by Kristine Anderson

Prior to the mid-nineteenth century there was no single name for the body of ideas that we today refer to as esotericism, although one often spoke of "occult philosophy." We owe the word *esotericism* itself to a nineteenth-century "occultist," Eliphas Lévi. By whatever name it appears, however, esotericism has had a long history. It has been composed of a collection of ideas, each with its own character, but is, as a whole, remarkably coherent. Initially, the need to conceptualize the phenomenon as a single concept was barely felt; it was enough to name its constituents (theosophy, theurgy, astrology, alchemy) and each of its many traditions or schools as branches of the esoteric tree. Until around the fourteenth century this tree was integrated rather well into the surrounding cultural landscape and drew a heightened beauty and majesty from certain very widespread philosophical doctrines, such as Neoplatonism.

Considered in a very general way, the situation was changed by what may be called the secularization of the cosmos. This secularization began in the fourteenth century, when official thought began to adopt a kind of formal Aristotelianism and to reject the belief in a series of living relationships uniting God or the divine world, man, and the universe, relationships that had been fundamental to esotericism. The technical sciences profited greatly from this epistemological rupture, but the mind found itself impoverished by it, and philosophy was cut off from some of its most enriching sources. Modern esoteric currents—that is to say, those that have appeared since the Renaissance—have defined themselves as a reaction against this rupture and as the continuation of the earlier intellectual tradition, preserving or reestablishing a sense of the relationships that unite man, the world, and the divine. The definitions of esotericism that can be given vary according to broader or narrower conceptions of these relationships.

GENERAL CHARACTERISTICS

In its narrower sense, the word *esotericism* has a meaning that is apparent from its etymology (Gr., *esōteros,* "inner"), which refers to an "interiorism," an entry into the self through a special knowledge or gnosis, in order to attain a form of enlightenment and individual salvation. This special knowledge concerns the relationships that unite us to God or to the divine world and may also include a knowledge of the mysteries inherent to God himself (in which case it is, strictly speaking, theosophy). To learn these relationships, the individual must enter, or "descend," into himself by means of an initiatory process, progressing along a path that is hierarchically structured by a series of intermediaries.

According to the particular form an esoteric tradition takes, these intermediaries may be known as angels or spiritual entities, sometimes called Agent Intellects or *animae coelestes*. They may be more or less numerous, and more or less personalized. In all cases, however, they have something common in essence with the initiate, since otherwise the necessary relationships could not be established. Each of them must be known if the initiate is to progress successfully through the initiatory steps. The procedure requires total commitment, whether the initiate progresses alone, aided by the intentionally obscure texts that provide the keys to the mysteries, or whether with the aid of an initiator, who may be an isolated master or a member of an initiatory school. The function of the initiation is to regenerate consciousness through the reappropriation of primal knowledge that was lost to man after the Fall. Once attained, this knowledge makes possible a new experience in our relations with the sacred and the universe. Whether or not the initiate has a master, it is finally up to him to realize the knowledge of the bonds that unite him to superior entities (theosophy in the narrow sense) and to cosmic forces and living nature (theosophy in the broad sense).

Success on the initiatory path requires what is traditionally known as "active imagination," an essential key to esoteric knowledge. It is the active imagination that permits one to escape both the sterility of purely discursive logic and the disorder of fancy and sentimentality. In this way the initiate prevails against the dangers of the lower, less spiritual imagination, which, as Pascal says, is the mistress of errors and falseness. The active imagination, which is the real organ of the soul, puts us in contact with the *mundus imaginalis,* with what Henry Corbin has called the "imaginal" world, the place of intermediary beings, the mesocosm possessing a geography of its own and perceptible to each of us according to our respective cultural images. [*See* Images, *article on* The Imaginal.]

Understood in this way, esotericism corresponds to what is generally referred to as gnosis (knowledge), of which the gnosticism of the first centuries of our own era is but a particular case. It is, in fact, appropriate to distinguish the gnostic movement from gnosis in general, since the teachings of gnosticism can hardly be equated with those of the later esoteric traditions of the Middle Ages and of modern times. Gnosticism in most of its forms taught an absolute dualism, according an equal ontological footing to the powers of good and the powers of evil. The God of the Old Testament, for example, was presented as an evil demiurge. Gnosis, by contrast, should be understood more generally. [*See* Gnosticism, *article on* Gnosticism from the Middle Ages to the Present.] The Greek word *gnōsis,* is also the related Sanskrit *jñāna,* means both "learning" and "sapiential wisdom," a double meaning that it tended to lose in late Greek thought and in patristic Christianity. Its root, which also appears in the word *genesis,* in fact implies both learning and coming into being. Thus it was possible for the most important German theosophist of the nineteenth century, Franz Xaver von Baader, to devote part of his work to the ontological identity of knowing and begetting. By giving birth to us—or rather rebirth—gnosis unifies and liberates us. To know is to be liberated. It is not enough to know symbols and dogmas in a merely external fashion; one must be engendered by them.

Gnosis is thus not mere knowledge; between believing and knowing there is the knowledge of interior vision proper to the *mundus imaginalis,* or "imaginal" world, mentioned above. These various types of knowledge have been clearly distinguished within Islamic gnosis as intellectual knowledge *('aql),* knowledge of traditional facts that are the object of faith *(naql),* and knowledge through inner vision or intuitive revelation *(kashf).* It is this last that opens up the world of the imaginal. As Corbin says, gnosis is an inner vision, a recital, whose mode of exposition is narrative. Insofar as it believes, it knows, but inasmuch as what it believes does not give positive, empirical, or historical evidence, it believes. Gnosis is wisdom and faith; it is *Pistis Sophia.* According to Pierre Deghaye's elegant definition, the idea of gnosis is therefore the foundation of the idea of esotericism, if one understands gnosis in its primary sense of "superior knowledge which is added to the common truths of objective Revelation, or the deepening of that Revelation rendered possible by a particular Grace." It is what the eighteenth-century theosophist Friedrich Christoph Oetinger called the *philosophia sacra.* It is a sacred, saving philosophy, soteriological because it effects the inner transformation of man, not through discursive thought but, according to Corbin, through a narrative revelation of hidden things, a saving light that itself brings life and joy, a divine grace that operates and assures salvation. For the esotericist, to know what one is and where one comes from is already to be saved. It is not a theoretical but a practical knowledge which, for that reason, transforms the knowing subject.

MYSTICISM, GNOSIS, AND THEOSOPHY

Esotericism thus permits access to a higher level of understanding where dualities of all kinds are transcended in a unity that is not to be grasped in a purely conceptual fashion but is to be experienced by one's whole being. Various words have been used to refer to this higher level: "the inner man" (Saint Paul), "the supramental" (Aurobindo Ghose), "illuminative intuition" (René Guénon), "the transcendental ego" (Edmund Husserl), "enstasy" (Mircea Eliade). Raymond Abellio, who has drawn up a list of these terms, speaks of "infusion," and of a "concrete and permanent participation in universal interdependence," aimed at the fulfillment in man of the mystery of incarnation. Such infusion or enstasy aspires to express itself, to spread and communicate itself, not, however, merely in the form of emotional effusions, but in the form of oral or written traditions that speak through a veil of symbols.

Strickly speaking, gnosis should be distinguished from mysticism, even though they are usually found together. Mysticism, which is more "feminine," more nocturnal, voluntarily cultivates renunciation, although this does not exclude a taste for symbolism. Gnosis, more "masculine," more solar, cultivates detachment and is more attentive to structures. In his own journey, the mystic discovers the same intermediate entities as the gnostic. But while the gnostic views such entities as a source of enlightening and saving knowledge, the mystic limits their numbers as much as he can and aspires to pass beyond them and be united directly with his God.

The properly esoteric or gnostic attitude can thus be seen as a mystical experience in which intelligence and memory come to participate, expressing themselves in a symbolic form that reflects the different levels of reality. Or gnosis may be described, with the theosophist Valentin Tomberg, as the expression of a form of intelligence and memory that has effected a passage through mystical experience. In a sense, then, a gnostic is a mystic who is capable of communicating his own experiences to others in a manner that conveys the impact of the revelations he has received while passing through different levels of the imaginal world (the mirror of the spiritual world). Whereas the mystic proclaims his personal union with God, the gnostic formulates a doctrine. The mystic contemplates; the gnostic learns through revelation.

In addition to this gnostic side of esotericism, esotericism in the broad sense includes a theosophical dimension as well. Here gnosis is no longer restricted to the individual's relationship to the divine world, but pertains as well to the nature of God himself, or to the nature of divine personages and to the origin and hidden structure of the natural universe, its relation to man, and its ultimate ends. [*See* Theosophy.] It is in this general sense that one traditionally speaks of theosophy. Theosophy adds to esotericism in its restricted sense that cosmic or cosmosophic dimension that prevents the gnostic from falling into solipsism. It opens esotericism up to the whole universe, making possible a philosophy of nature. Occultism, in all its forms, draws or can draw its heuristic foundations from esotericism and from a philosophy of nature.

UNIVERSALITY AND SECRECY; ESOTERICISM AND EXOTERICISM

Esotericism thus is shown to be a way of life and an exercise of vision. The dangers of subjectivism are overcome by the presence of the world (when gnosis is combined with theosophy) and by the historical density of esotericism itself, which is dependent upon specific, revealed religious traditions. Every esotericist reinterprets his own tradition, adding his own personal commentary, and it can undoubtedly be said that active esotericism is the privileged form of hermeneutics. Esotericism presupposes that an esoteric tradition originally accompanies all revealed religions, even if this tradition becomes explicit only later, through commentaries such as the major texts of Jewish Qabbalah, for example, which are a theosophy of the Old Testament. These new interpretations do not exclude the preceding ones; rather, they extend and enrich them. Thus the Christian Qabbalah is a hermeneutic variation on the Jewish. In the same vein, Louis-Claude de Saint-Martin commented on the work of Jakob Boehme, who himself had commented on the book of *Genesis*. [*See* Qabbalah.]

Here we are far from the historicizing tendency that confuses historical truth with the truth of the sacred origins of each revelation, a tendency that is as well represented by the supporters of *Formgeschichte* as it is by the demythologizing orientation of Rudolf Bultmann and his followers. On the contrary, the esotericist begins with the assumption that these origins go beyond the human. He seeks to recapture both the structure and the living meaning of the language of symbols and myths, first in his own culture, but eventually in other cultures as well. Here we encounter what Seyyed Hossein Nasr has called the "relatively absolute." In reaching beyond his own tradition, the esotericist is not seeking to relativize his own faith. Rather he attempts to see, in the foundations of each religion, one of the many possible manifestations of the supreme Logos, and in each sacred book a manifestation of the supreme book—what Muslims call "the mother of the book" *(umm al-kitāb)*. He does this even if he believes that the whole truth was revealed in a privileged fashion in his own tradition. Consequently, esoteric activity is intent upon detecting the trace of the Absolute in all of its diverse manifestations. This makes esoteric literature as a whole a particularly rich resource for the spiritual needs of today's pluralistic world.

Esoteric traditions can be especially valuable in suggesting ways of thinking beyond the closed systems, abstract terms, and dehumanizing ideologies that characterize so much of modern life. They offer the immense depths of a traditional wisdom and hermeneutics, which are becoming progressively more accessible thanks to the progress of historical research and publication. Esotericism presents us with a form of nonreductive thought that reveals the richness of the correspondences uniting God, man, and the universe in the play of its reflecting mirrors. Its potential value for a renewal of the human sciences has yet to be realized.

The relation of esotericism to exotericism is a question often posed, along with its corollary: whether the idea of secrecy is the same as the idea of esotericism. Esotericism is, in fact, opposed to exotericism in the same way that what is reserved for an elite is opposed to what is addressed to all. The distinction remains valuable and fruitful as long as two mistakes are avoided. First, one must not believe them to be incompatible. In fact, exotericism and esotericism mutually qualify one another, as though they were two sides of the same coin.

Second, it is a mistake to believe that all esotericism is necessarily connected with the idea of secrecy and composed of elements that it is forbidden to divulge, whereas exotericism is a discourse intended for the public. Esotericism is not simply a *disciplina arcani,* a discipline of the arcane. Although the arcane sometimes plays a role, especially in certain initiation societies, to reduce esotericism to this single dimension can only be the result of bad faith, ignorance, or the desire to limit greatly the subject of one's research. In most cases, there is no conscious desire for secrecy. What the term *disciplina arcani* suggests (for example, in reference to a "secret" teaching that Jesus is said to have offered his apostles, or a certain ritual that an initiation society treasures and hides) is above all the fact that the mysteries of religion, the ultimate nature of reality, the hidden forces of cosmic order, and the hieroglyphs of the visible world do not lend themselves to immediate comprehension or to a didactic or univocal explanation, but must be the object of a progressive penetration at several levels by each seeker of knowledge.

In an essay published in 1906, Georg Simmel identified the essential elements of the sociology of secrecy and its function in constituting social structure and facilitating interaction. We may add that a "secret society" is not created with the intention to hide something, but, as Raymond Abellio has rightly reminded us, in order to make a small group of people "transparent" to one another; for the world at large, taken as a whole, is opaque. It is not doctrine that the initiate is supposed to keep secret, but, at the very most, the details of a ritual. Thus, for example, the fact that almost all the rituals of Freemasonry were published long ago is not at all a betrayal of the Masonic "secret." If a Freemason, or any member of an esoteric society, must keep the names of his affiliated brothers quiet, it is essentially a discretionary measure. A comparable situation existed in the religions of Hellenism; the "mystical" secret not to be revealed was not a piece of ineffable religious knowledge, but only the knowledge of a rite in its purely material aspect. The sacred, that which is set apart, requires a slender partition between itself and the secular world. One feels obliged to prevent the desecration of that which one values most highly and which was obtained only with difficulty through submitting to diverse trials. Finally, the apparent opposition between the hermeneutic activity (linked to speech, logos, endless "interpretation," etc., proper to esotericism) and the discipline of silence is more a dynamic and creative paradox—a hermeneutic tension—than a contradiction in the strict sense. It is best illustrated in a drawing printed in Achilles Bocchi's *Symbolicae questiones* (1555) that represents Hermes, the god of speech and of esoteric sciences, lifting a forefinger to his lips—a typical gesture of Harpocrates, interestingly transferred to Hermes by Bocchi. [*See also* Silence.]

HISTORICAL OVERVIEW

In the intellectual currents of the late Roman empire (Neo-Pythagoreanism and Stoicism, Alexandrian Hermetism, pagan Neoplatonism, and the work of Philo Judaeus), Western esotericism found the themes and elements that were to inspire it up to our own day. After Origen and Clement of Alexandria, theosophical speculation incorporated the angelic hierarchies and divine names established by Dionysius the Areopagite; it was further enriched by the work of Maximos the Confessor and reached a high point in the ninth century with the work of John Scottus Eriugena. Meanwhile, Greek Hermetism maintained a discreet presence. The Jewish Qabbalah of the period is known to us through the *Sefer Yetsirah*. At the dawn of the Middle Ages, the Arabs played the important role of preservers and translators, restoring to the Christian world some of the ancient traditions that had been forgotten.

Roman art and thought were dominated by images of the cosmos, the temple, and man. Alain of Lille, Hildegarde von Bingen, and Honorius were the bards of a symbolic universe in which both Hermetism and alchemy blossomed forth in new forms. The myth of Alexander, a movement known as the Fedeli d'Amore, ("devotees of love"), myths of chivalry, and, above all, the work of Joachim of Fiore also left their permanent mark on a Europe, which, during its thirteenth century, avid for new forms of spirituality, discovered the Franciscan spirit. The genius of this spirit was Bonaventure, whose work contained many theosophical themes; many spiritual alchemists were also to be found in the Franciscan milieu. The School of Oxford, with Robert Grosseteste and Roger Bacon, followed a similar path, while the great *summae* of Vincent of Beauvais, Bartholomew the Englishman, and William of Auvergne developed a foretaste of the *philosophia perennis* that would be so dear to the Renaissance. Theurgy, astrology, and medicine also headed in this direction, in an epoch that witnessed not only the works of Arnau de Villanova but also the *Roman de la rose*, the *Zohar,* and a form of Gothic sculpture connected with the "Great Work" and the earliest forms of Freemasonry.

Nevertheless, as early as the twelfth century a tendency best represented by the Salernitan School (School of Salerno) spread that was intent upon developing the *artes mechanicae* at the expense of the *artes liberales,* hence a secularization of space and time that entailed a "mechanization" of the image of the world. This tendency can be seen in the work and influence of the mathematician Jordanus Nemorarius, who flourished in the thirteenth century. Moreover, in the theology of the fourteenth century the influence of the Aristotelianism originally championed by Ibn Rushd (Averroës) led to the progressive disappearance of angelology, or the notion of intermediary worlds that had given the *mundus imaginalis* its specific character. Consequently, esotericism became marginal. At the same time there was a rapid development of Rhenish mysticism. This was also the age of Rulman Merswin, with his Fidèles de l'Île Verte ("devotees of the Green Isle"), who were spiritual cavaliers. The imagery of chivalry was more present than ever. Ramón Lull and Peter of Abano wrote their great works. Alchemy, well represented by John Dastin, Petrus Bonus, John of Rupescissa, and Nicolas Flamel, also influenced literature. Dante's *Commedia* became a source of inspiration for esoteric exegesis in the following centuries. So did the work of Nicholas of Cusa, which burst forth in the fourteenth century, the age of the initiatory romance as well as of a pervasive interest in astrology and alchemy, present even in book illumination and the plastic arts. The end of the century saw the conceptualization and systematization of esotericism and what would later be called "occultism." This was the work in large part of Marsilio Ficino of the Florentine Academy, whose "occult philosophy" was based on his studies of Plato and his translation of the texts of Alexandrian Hermetism into Latin. [*See* Occultism.] Indeed, thanks to Ficino's translations, nearly all of the Hermetic corpus became well known in Europe. At the same time, Pico della Mirandola introduced Christian Europe to the Jewish Qabbalah, maintaining that nothing proved the truth of Christianity more than the Qabbalah and magic.

In the sixteenth century esotericism appeared as a form of counterculture, even while appropriating a good number of the characteristic values and ideas of the Renaissance. It stood almost entirely under the triple sign of the Hermetism rediscovered by Ficino, the Christian Qabbalah, and Paracelsus. Ludovico Lazarelli, Giordano Bruno, and many others came under the influence of that renewed Hermetism, whose Alexandrian texts were considered a sort of new gospel coming to complete the gospel of Christianity. These were thought to be contemporary with Moses, when in fact they date from the second and third centuries of our own era.

If the presence of Hermetism was diffuse, the christianized Qabbalah was presented as a body of doctrine, and was elaborated little by little throughout the Renaissance and up to the middle of the seventeenth century. Especially after the expulsion of the Jews from Spain in 1492, people sought to "qabbalize" in a Christian context. The cardinal Egidio da Viterbo translated the principal texts of the Qabbalah into Latin, and the German humanist Johannes Reuchlin made them known by christianizing them. Heinrich Corneliius Agrippa, in his *De occulta philosophia,* a work characteristic of the literature on magic at the beginning of the Renaissance, studied the Qabbalah along with alchemy and astrology. Perhaps the most widespread work on the Qabbalah during the Renaissance was Galatin's *De arcanis catholicae veritatis.* The *De harmonia mundi* of Francesco Giorgi of Venice became, along with the works of Pico, Reuchlin, and Pietro Galatino, one of the principal sources for later Qabbalah. In France, the most celebrated name in this domain was Guillaume Postel.

Paracelsus initiated yet another movement. In his works, magic, medicine, an alchemical conception of the world, and a philosophy of nature are brought together on the unifying canvas of Christian Neoplatonism, in order to depict a universe throbbing with Germanic inspiration and poetry. In his wake, but in the margins and as if in contrast, we find the silhouette of the legendary Johann Faust, the black magician. The true disciples of Paracelsus, however, were Leonard Thurneysser, Leonard Fioravanti, and Gerard Dorn.

The seventeenth century was the recipient of this diverse heritage. It opened with the publication of the *Amphitheatrum sapientiae aeternae* by Heinrich Khunrath, a major book of Western esotericism that included alchemical and qabbalistic materials. The most outstanding qabbalistic work of the century, the famous *Cabala denudata* by Christian Knorr von Rosenroth, appeared somewhat later. Although there were other works on the Qabbalah produced at this time, such as the writings of Athanasius Kircher and Robert Fludd, who made the science known in England, the innovations of this period lie elsewhere: on the one hand, in the appearance of the myth of the "Rosy Cross" during the first half of the century; on the other, in the work of Jakob Boehme. Andreae Johann, with his manifestos *(Fama* and *Confessio)* and his initiatory and alchemical novel *(Chymische Hochzeit des Christian Rosenkreuz),* inaugurated the tradition called Rosicrucianism, which immediately inspired Robert Fludd and the "Great Hermeticizer," Michael Maier. [*See* Rosicrucians.]

Alchemy and Rosicrucianism were happily married in a golden age of esoteric iconography, when an alchemist could be sure of finding welcome at the court of the emperor Rudolf II. Jakob Boehme, the prince of Christian esotericists, inaugurated the rapid development of the great age of European theosophy, prefigured in the preceding century by the work of Valentin Weigel. In Boehme can be found all the theosophical themes that were to follow: the Fall of Lucifer and Adam, sophiology (prefigured in the work of Khunrath), androgyny, and so on. The poetry of the mystic Angelus Silesius, as well as of other Baroque authors, was inspired by Boehme. In the second half of the century, Johann Georg Gichtel became his great disciple. Pierre Poiret, Antoinette Bourignon, and Gottfried Arnold also left original work in Boehme's wake. In England, Boehme's works were translated and popularized by John Pordage and Jane Leade. Under the influence of Paracelsus and Boehme, faith and knowledge were increasingly unified, especially among the Neoplatonists of Cambridge, of whom Henry More is the most eloquent representative. But it was also during this period that esotericism became a marginal phenomenon. The scientific community's break with esotericism is symbolized by the exclusion of astrology in 1666 from the new Academy of Sciences founded in Paris.

At the beginning of the eighteenth century, Andreas Freher gave England one of the clearest and most faithful expositions of Boehme. At the dawn of the century of Enlightenment, the theosophy of Georg von Welling and Sincerus Renatus also revived esoteric thought in Germany, while Saint-Georges of Marsais and the authors of the Bible of Berlebourg in France mixed elements borrowed from the mysticism of Madame Guyon du Chesnoy with Boehmean teachings. New editions of alchemical and theosophical works multiplied, and little by little a form of esotericism that came to be called Illuminism emerged. Johann Kaspar Lavater, the pastor of Zurich, joined this trend, as did Heinrich Jung-Stilling and William Law. The most famous of the Illuminati was Emanuel Swedenborg, less a theosophist than a visionary and rather marginal to European Illuminism despite the considerable influence that his work continues to exercise. Friedrich Christoph Oetinger publicized him, but was himself more interested in Boehme and the Qabbalah.

If Oetinger was the greatest German theosophist of the eighteenth century, the most important in Europe generally was Louis-Claude de Saint-Martin, whose influence was the most profound and the most durable. Joseph de Maistre, whose work is colored by his teachings, saw him as "the most learned, the wisest, and the most elegant of theosophists."

The influence of Illuminism can be seen in early German Romanticism, in the writings of Novalis, Karl von Eckartshausen, and the first works of Franz Xaver von

Baader. Freemasonry was also touched by it, and initiatory obedience, rites, and systems proliferated. Thus emerged such traditions and movements as the Strict Templar Observance, the Illuminati of Avignon (Dom Pernéty's system), the "Egyptian" Freemasonry of Cagliostro (pseudonym of Giuseppe Balsamo), the Chevaliers Bienfaisants of the Holy City (the system of Jean-Baptiste Willermoz), the Rose-Croix d'Or, and many others. Willermoz owes the essence of his Masonic inspiration to Martínez Pasqualis, the founder of the theosophical and theurgical order called the Elus-Cohens, and secondarily to Saint-Martin. "Martinism," a rather vague esoteric current constructed out of elements borrowed from the ideas of Martínez, Saint-Martin, and Willermozian Masonry, spread through Russia, where the names of Nikolai Novikov, A. F. Labizine, and I. V. Lopuchin grew famous. Literature felt the effects of such esoteric societies, especially in Germany, where initiatory novels proliferated.

German Romanticism after 1800 gathered together a large part of this heritage and used it to develop a philosophy of nature. [*See* Nature, *article on* Religious and Philosophical Speculations.] Theosophizing philosophy appeared in the works of G. H. von Schubert, A. K. A. von Eschenmayer, Justinus Kerner, and later in Carl Gustav Carus. Theosophical philosophy appeared in the works of J. J. Wirz, Michael Hahn, and especially von Baader, the greatest of them all. In France, Antoine Fabre d'Olivet and Pierre-Simon Ballanche each developed a very personal work, while Swedenborgianism and Martinism became the subjects of commentaries and exegesis, and even influenced the writings of Honoré de Balzac. Also in the early nineteenth century, England experienced a renewal of interest in Boehme and, even more, in Swedenborg. German philosophy came increasingly under the influence of esotericism, an influence that extended beyond *Naturphilosophie.* Ernst Benz has shown the importance of esoteric sources and a secularized form of mysticism for Hegelian Marxism. In the ideology of modernism one can discern the influence of a distorted esotericism, which is translated into the expectation of a new universal order.

Occultism in its present-day sense appeared at this time, with Eliphas Lévi, the "New Agrippa" and a talented popularizer. As the offspring of the naturalistic magic of the Middle Ages and the occult philosophy of the Renaissance, occultism in general had no specifically Christian elements. Christianity, esotericism, and occultism nevertheless blended together well in the works of Papus (pseudonym of Gérard Encausse), the founder of the Martinist order and the most famous French magus of the *fin de siècle,* a time that also witnessed the flourishing of the works of Joséphin Péladan, Édouard Schuré, Saint-Yves d'Alveydre, Stanislas de Guaita, and Paul Sédir. Richard Wagner and the Symbolists also have roots in the esoteric tradition.

In the twentieth century esotericism scatters in different directions, mainly because of the decline of faith, the confusion with occultism, a growing infatuation with often badly assimilated Eastern doctrines, and the miracles achieved by science. On bookstore shelves labeled "esotericism" it is not unusual to see works dealing with unidentified flying objects, parapsychology, fakirs, and healers. The mysteries of religion are readily presented as problems to be solved scientifically, and scientific problems are presented as religious enigmas. People tend to confuse the psychic and the spiritual. Or they proceed to hasty syncretisms, mixing a poorly understood Western esotericism with a debased orientalism of the bazaar. The Theosophical Society, founded in 1875 by H. P. Blavatsky and still flourishing throughout the world, has not always been exempt from such doubtful syncretisms, despite much doctrine that is undeniably valuable. As René Guénon pointed out, even its title is a usurpation of the word *theosophy,* and *theosophism* would be a more accurate term. For the rest, traditional theosophical thought remains alive among certain Orthodox thinkers such as Vladimir Solov'ev and, closer to us, Sergi Bulgakov and Nikolai Berdiaev in Paris, and Leopold Ziegler in Germany. There is a little of it among most editors and commentators on Western esotericism of the past. Alchemy, both spiritual and practical, still has numerous followers, who readily quote Fulcanelli, a cryptologist inspired by the symbolism of cathedrals. Fulcanelli (a pseudonym) has found a disciple in Eugéne Canseliet.

Esotericism has colored the work of Czeslaw Milosz, Gustav Meyrink, William Butler Yeats, Thomas Mann, and many other writers. Its influence on literature is facilitated by the existence of numerous initiatory societies, many of which maintain the venerable title "Rosy Cross" (e.g., the Lectorium Rosicrucianum and especially AMORC, or the Ancient and Mystical Order of Rosae Crucis), but these do not always have a sufficiently specific body of doctrine and tradition. A small and very traditional element of present-day Freemasonry still continues the Illuminism of the eighteenth century. Also still alive, but divided into several branches, is the Martinism that continues the teachings of Papus. The Astrum Argentinum, an anti-Christian society emerging from the Golden Dawn, founded by Aleister Crowley, contains as much occultism as esotericism. The teaching of G. I. Gurdjieff rallies some of the better spirits, but without drawing much inspiration from the traditional currents of Western gnosticism. Nor has it exerted much influence on the most prominent esotericist of our time, René Guénon, who has been affected mainly by India and Islam. Guénon made himself the commanding and uncompromising defender of the idea of tradition; his merit in this domain is mainly in having recalled to intellectual rigor and a form of metaphysical precision many students of esotericism who had been content to leave things vague. Besides Guénon, two great names have marked the esotericism of our century: Rudolf Steiner, whose "anthroposophy" revived the tradition of Romantic *Naturphilosophie,* and C. G. Jung, the last representative of the latter school. Unlike Steiner, Jung never presented himself as a spiritual master, and he rarely made any kind of profession of religious faith. But his scientific work renewed psychoanalysis by exploring the visionary, or imaginal, dimensions of the psyche, which had previously been virtually ignored. He also contributed to a rediscovery of the treasures of alchemical thought by applying alchemical symbolism to the process of psychological integration, which he called "individuation."

Evidently less popular than Jung's work, but more and more numerous, are the scholarly works that have been appearing since the 1930s. Translations, new editions, critical apparatuses, monographs, and university dissertations have all improved our knowledge of the history of esotericism. Arthur E. Waite and Paul Vulliaud were pioneers; Gershom Scholem, Ernst Benz, Frances A. Yates, Henry Corbin, and many others are nearer to us. Mircea Eliade, Joseph Campbell, Gilbert Durand, and others reveal to specialists, as well as to a large cultivated public, anthropological dimensions of the subject whose existence had barely been considered. They restore esotericism to its rightful place in the study of myth, symbols, and the sacred. To be sure, we witness the most diverse tendencies in exegesis and interpretation, and interpretations that are often reductive. Nevertheless, thanks to the cross-disciplinary breadth of research in the human sciences, esotericism is currently being taken seriously, even if largely as a subject for historical research.

[*See also articles on specific esoteric traditions:* Astrology; Theurgy; Hermetism; *and* Alchemy.]

BIBLIOGRAPHY

There is no single book on the history of esotericism. An interesting general reflection on esotericism and tradition can be found in Seyyed Hossein Nasr's *Knowledge and the Sacred* (New York, 1981). On Islamic esotericism, see Henry Corbin's *En Islam iranien,* 4 vols. (Paris, 1971–1972). A philosophical approach is to be found in Raymond Abellio's *La fin de l'esotérisme* (Paris, 1973). On esotericism in the eighteenth century, see my *L'esotérisme au XVIIIe siècle* (Paris, 1973) and *Mystiques, théosophes et illuminés au siècle des lumières* (Hildesheim and New York, 1976); for a more general encompassing approach see my *Accès de l'esotérisme* (Paris, 1986). The classic work on the theosophy of Jacob Boehme is Alexandre Koyré's *La philosophie de Jacob Boehme* (1929; Paris, 1979). Well-documented studies on Christian theosophy include Will-Erich Peuckert's *Pansophie,* rev. ed. (Berlin, 1956); the commentaries on the works of Friedrich Christoph Oetinger published by Walter de Gruyter in Berlin from 1977 onward; the studies by Bernard Gorceix, *Flambée et agonie: Mystiques du XVIIe siècle allemand* (Sisteron, 1977) and *Johann Georg Gichtel, théosophe d'Amsterdam* (Lausanne, 1975); and articles by Pierre Deghaye and many others, some of them authors referred to above, that have appeared in *Cahiers de l'hermétisme* (Paris, 1977–) and *Cahiers de l'Université Saint-Jean de Jérusalem* (Paris, 1975–).

5 HERMETISM

ANTOINE FAIVRE
Translated from French by Kristine Anderson

It is appropriate, especially as a consequence of the distinctions in vocabulary suggested by Frances A. Yates, to restrict use of the word *hermetism* to designate in a precise manner the Alexandrian corpus—that is, the body of writings attributed to Hermes Trismegistos—and the various adaptations and commentaries that it has given rise to in modern times. The word *hermeticism* would then serve to designate a much broader ensemble of doctrine, beliefs, and practices, not necessarily dependent on the Alexandrian or neo-Alexandrian Hermetic tradition, but including Christian interpretations of Qabbalah and, in a general way, most of the forms that cloak modern esotericism. Unfortunately, this distinction in vocabulary, while perfectly legitimate and very useful, is not translatable into every language; it is in German (*Hermetismus, Hermetizimus*) but not in French. This is why I have suggested the use of the word *hermésisme* in the sense of *hermeticism,* with the corresponding adjective *hermésien* to describe this attitude of mind in French.

The Hermetic tradition owes its existence to a collection of Greek texts written in Alexandria between the first and third centuries of our era and attributed to the mysterious figure known as Hermes Trismegistos, "Thrice-Greatest Hermes." [*See* Hermes Trismegistos.] These writings, named after their supposed author and known collectively as the Hermetica, had a strange destiny. In the Middle Ages only a few rare extracts were known, and yet their author, clouded by an aura of mystery, was the subject of great interest. Not until the dawn of the Renaissance did the texts themselves come to light. Their discovery gave rise to a prodigious amount of interest, which was to last until the nineteenth century. In the twentieth century, they are mainly the object of erudite research.

The body of writings known as the Hermetica is not large. It consists primarily of the *Asclepius,* a text falsely attributed to Apuleius of Madaura and of which we have only a Latin version, and the *Corpus Hermeticum,* a collection of fifteen or seventeen Hermetic dialogues, the first of which, the *Poimandres,* is the most famous. *Poimandres* deals with the creation of the world, whereas other treatises of the series describe the soul's ascension through the celestial spheres and its divine sojourns, a process that brings about its regeneration.

Alexandrian Hermetism is one of the most important resources of modern esotericism. Both are characterized by an eclectic mentality, a philosophical attitude that favors the concrete and eschews ontological dualism, and by their common use of the scenario of fall and reintegration.

The eclectic state of mind accepts the possibility of quenching one's thirst in diverse streams—hence it tends sometimes to merge with the notion of a *philosophia perennis*—and consequently displays a great tolerance on the religious plane. Hermeticism promotes the most irenic tendencies among Roman Catholics and Protestants and embraces the ideal of universal concord, of a solidarity between man and the world. Hermetic optimism extends to the affirmation of the possibility of union with the divine, through the inscription of the universe within the human soul or intelligence. This optimism is tempered, however, by the recognition of the negative consequences of the Fall for the present state of both man and nature.

Philosophically, the Hermetica reject absolute ontological dualism and stress the positive, symbolic value of the universe. This can be seen in the treatise in which Nous ("mind") addresses Hermes. Here Nous teaches Hermes how to reflect the universe in his own spirit, seizing the divine essence of nature and impressing it on the interior of his soul. This process is made possible by the fact that man possesses a divine intellect. Here we meet the theme of the world as mirror of the divine and object of contemplation. The idea that the universe is a text to be read or deciphered is the great common denominator of esotericism. One knows God through the contemplation of the world. And since the universe is a forest of symbols, it is natural to become interested in all that it contains. Hence the taste of the Hermetica for the particular, the *mirabilia,* to the detriment of the abstract and the general. Hermetic science is anything but disinterested. It reaches the general only by means of an enriching detour through the concrete and the particular. Here we find Paracelsus and German Romantic *Naturphilosophie* in embryo: a taste for the concrete, a philosophy of incarnation, and hence an obvious affinity with Christianity. According to one Hermetic axiom, "nothing is invisible, even among the incorporeal," since the reproduction of bodies is an "eternal operation" and embodiment is "a force in action." Thus, in these passages of the *Corpus,* the *Geistleiblichkeit,* or "spiritual corporality," of Boehme's and Oetinger's theosophy is prefigured. [*See* Theosophy.]

A third point of convergence between esotericism and Hermetism is the reference to a myth of fall and reintegration. The theme of the fall of man through the attraction of the sensual, a theme so common in Western theosophy, is found already in *Poimandres,* where it is apparent that the imprisonment of Adam in the sensual realm was due to eros. This mythic theme should not be read as anticosmic. Rather it is an invitation to undertake the work of regeneration through reascent. This reascent is accomplished either by means of the intellect, which makes a connection with intermediary spiritual intelligences (such as angels), using them as a spiritual ladder, or by theurgical means, or by both at once. [*See* Theurgy.] The Hermetica thus permit us to better understand the theurgy of John Dee in the sixteenth century and Martínez Pasqualis in the eighteenth. The divine essence locked within man must be regenerated along specific paths, including initiations of various kinds. Thus, implicit in Alexandrian Hermetism is a belief in an astrological cosmos, which is the scene of an initiatory journey. By contrast, the astrology of modern times, especially since the seventeenth century, tends more and more to separate itself from initiatory processes and to become exclusively a form of divination.

Finally, in Alexandrian Hermetism we find the idea that, thanks to man, the earth itself is capable of improvement, of recovering its former glorious state and becoming truly "active." It is the idea of a prodigious fecundity that had already been promoted by a text of Paul (*Rom.* 8:19–22): man led nature to its fall; consequently man can help regenerate nature, if he will but regenerate himself. Here we have a possible basis for a metaphysically founded ecology!

EARLY ANTIQUITY AND THE MIDDLE AGES

The oldest references to the work of Hermes Trismegistos in the Christian tradition are found in the writings of two fathers of the church, Lactantius and Augustine. Lactantius (d. 340?) devoted several laudatory lines to him and considered him to be more ancient than Plato and Pythagoras. In two of the texts that he knew, the *Asclepius* and *Poimandres,* he detected a herald of Christ's coming. Augustine, in the *City of God* (8.13–26), condemned "Hermes the Egyptian, called Trismegistos" because of a passage in the *Asclepius*—which he cites at length— that discusses magical processes intended to animate the statues of gods by making spirits descend into them. In another passage (18.29), he confirms Lactantius's idea of the antiquity of Hermes Trismegistos, who, Augustine tells us, lived "a long time before the wise men and philosophers of Greece." Clement of Alexandria also mentions his name, attributing a great number of works to him (*Strōmateis* 6.4.35–38).

It seems that the *Asclepius* was the only one of the Hermetic texts known in the Middle Ages, though we do not have even a *testimonium* about it for the period from Augustine to the twelfth century. On the other hand, other alchemical and especially astrological texts in the same vein appeared, attributed to "the Thrice-Greatest" or simply to Hermes. One example is the *Liber Hermetis Trismegisti,* an anthology of astrological magic discovered and published by Gundel in 1936. It was not written before the fifth century, but the elements that compose it are drawn from earlier works. Several other pseudo-Hermetic texts in the genre of the *Liber Hermetis Trismegisti* existed during the Middle Ages. A good number of them are translations from the Arabic into Latin, for Hermetism returned to the West through the Arabs, who were strongly influenced by Hermetic and gnostic literature, especially at Harran. The famous *Picatrix* is one such text. Undoubtedly written in the twelfth century, it was cited during the Renaissance by authors interested in the Hermetica. It contains, in particular, a famous passage in which Hermes is said to have been the first to make use of magical images and is presented as the founder of Adocentyn, a marvelous city in Egypt. Hermes Mercurius Triplex is presented here in his triple role as Egyptian priest, philosopher-magician, and king or legislator.

Another famous text is the fragment entitled *Tabula smaragdina,* or *The Emerald Tablet,* attributed to Hermes but certainly later than the Alexandrian Hermetica. It too was translated into Latin from the Arabic, for the first time, it seems, by Hugo Sanctelliensis, bishop of Tarazona (Spain), along with the *Liber de secretis naturae et occultis rerum causis quem transtulit Apollonius ex libris Hermes Trismegisti.* The text of *The Emerald Tablet,* the most famous and most popular piece of Hermetic literature, is still known today. This is the text that begins with the well-known words "All that is above is like all that is below, all that is below is like all that is above, in order that the miracle of unity should be fulfilled." Soon after it was translated, a certain Hortulanus provided it with a commentary, which was to be frequently republished.

Among the Hermetic texts that appear in the twelfth century, we may also cite the *Liber de causis,* which contains a passage devoted to the "secrets of creation," attributed to Apollonius of Tyana. This passage, which deals with the creation of man, is presented as a revelation of Hermes. As the *Liber* describes it, the revelation comes "from the moon," where Apollonius appears as the spokesman of Hermes. Also noteworthy are the *Liber viginti quattuor philosophorum,* a short text in which the image of God as a circle whose center is everywhere and whose circumference is nowhere appears for the first time, and the *Liber compositione alchemiae quem edidit Morienus Romanus,* long considered to have been translated from Arabic into Latin by Robert of Chester in 1144, but probably of a later period. The latter book, which is the first text of medieval alchemy known to us, presents Hermes as the inventor of the arts and the sciences. From this time on, the name of Hermes will be associated with alchemy as well as with Hermetism proper. Finally, the twelfth-century pseudo-Hermetic *Liber Hermetis Mercurii Triplicis de VI rerum principiis* belongs in the same context. Hugh of Saint-Victor was influenced both by it and by the *Asclepius.*

The reputation of Trismegistos extends in fact beyond the limits of the esoteric tradition, which in the Middle Ages was still often difficult to distinguish from theological thought. During this period we find assorted references to Hermes and to Hermetic texts. Several authors refer to the *Asclepius.* Theodoric of Chartres and Albertus Magnus cite it, as does Bernardus Silvestris in his *De mundi universitate.* Alain de Lille gives extracts from it in his *Contra haereticos.* Vincent of Beauvais speaks of it on two occasions, and it is mentioned by William of Auvergne. In the fourteenth century, Thomas Bradwardine mentioned it in his *De causa Dei* and Roger Bacon referred to Hermes Mercurius as the "father of philosophers." On the eve of the Renaissance, it is still hard to distinguish between the Hermes of alchemy and the Hermes of the Hermetica, which is not surprising since they represent almost identical attitudes of mind. In the fifteenth century, the alchemist Bernard of Trévise identified Hermes as the restorer of alchemy in his *Liber de secretissimo philosophorum opere chemico.* These references must be understood against the background of a belief in a *prisca philosophia* or *prisca magia,* a primordial philosophy or magic that was already widespread during the Middle Ages. It was thought that Plato and his predecessors Orpheus and Pythagoras had visited Egypt in order to learn the oral and written philosophy of Moses and to study the secrets of an Egyptian wisdom that predated even Moses. Zarathushtra (Zoroaster) was believed to represent the Chaldean aspect of this primordial tradition, while Hermes represented the properly Egyptian aspect. Both were believed to precede Plato. Such a belief in a *prisca philosophia* or *prisca theologia* indicates a desire to avoid a hiatus in tradition and to preserve the continuity of history. At the beginning of the Renaissance, this belief in an ancient religion common to humanity seemed to be confirmed by Marsilio Ficino's translation of the *Corpus Hermeticum* into Latin. It was a belief favorable to the irenic tendencies typical of Renaissance thought, since it presupposed a fundamental divinity in man that went beyond exterior religious forms.

THE REDISCOVERY OF HERMES TRISMEGISTOS IN THE RENAISSANCE

Around 1460 an event occurred that assured the sudden, unprecedented influence of the Hermetica. A monk, Leonardo da Pistoria, brought to Florence a Greek manuscript containing the fifteen treatises that constituted what would later be called the *Corpus Hermeticum.* These treatises had undoubtedly already been brought together in the eleventh century, since it was in this form that Psellus knew them. Leonardo, who had found the document in Macedonia, thereupon presented it to Cosimo de' Medici, the ruler of Florence and a great patron of letters. At the end of 1462 or the beginning of 1463, Cosimo gave the manuscript to Marsilio Ficino to be translated into Latin. At this time Ficino was about thirty years old and had a successful career as a philosopher behind him. Although he had already agreed to translate the collected works of Plato, who was considered a religious author throughout the Renaissance, Cosimo asked him to begin with Trismegistos. By April 1463 the translation was complete. It appeared in 1471 and went through no fewer than sixteen editions before the end of the sixteenth century, not counting partial editions. That these texts were translated prior to those of Plato in the projected program of translations is a testimony to the interest they aroused and to the importance attributed to them even before they could be read. Their prestige was due, no doubt, to the veneration and admiration paid to their supposed author, Trismegistos, who was thought to have lived long before Plato.

Pico della Mirandola, younger than Ficino, more or less his disciple, and living in the same Florentine milieu, added to the *magia naturalis* of the Renaissance a "practical" or theurgical Qabbalah. Most important, having discovered Alexandrian Hermetism through Ficino, he was the first to join Hermetism to the Qabbalah, uniting both around the common theme of the knowledge of creation through the Word. This marriage of the Qabbalah and Hermetism had consequences that would be important for the evolution of Western esotericism. Pico thus initiated what Frances A. Yates has called the hermetico-qabbalistic tradition, a tradition that was to have a double character. On the one hand, it was theosophical, that is to say, speculative and Pythagorean; on the other hand, it included magical elements and was thus more theurgical than the works of Ficino. Pico presented his views in his famous nine hundred theses, or *Conclusiones,* defended at Rome in 1486, and in his *Defense* or *Apology* published in 1487, at the same time as his *Discourse on the Dignity of Man.* The *Discourse,* which expresses the spirit of the Renaissance, is the period's fundamental theoretical text on magic, a text of both a spiritual and practical gnosis introduced by Ficino and finished by Pico.

Pico's influence, to be sure, was not solely philosophical. Were not the true operative magi of the Renaissance the artists, as Yates suggests? Were they not Donatello and Michelangelo, who knew how to breathe divine life into their statues, after the manner of the *Asclepius,* by means of their art? Magic as Pico conceived it was, in the final analysis, that taught by the *Asclepius,* a text to which he explicitly refers. It was a knowledgeable or erudite magic, different from the often crude magic of the Middle Ages, as exemplified by the *Clavis Salomonis.* Pico's magic emphasized instead the philosophical aspects of a text like the *Picatrix* and indirectly prepared the way for the great Germanic theosophy that blossomed at the end of the Renaissance. In it, man is no longer merely the privileged spectator of the universe; he is not only a microcosm that reflects the entire macrocosm in himself; he is, as the *Asclepius* had already suggested, divine, or in any case he is in a position to exercise a demiurgic creative power. Man's dignity, his greatness, is now strongly emphasized. Did one not speak of the "divine" Raphael, the "divine" Leonardo, the "divine" Michelangelo? To this theme of the divinity in man, Pico, and with him all later Western esotericists, added the ancient injunction "Know thyself," which was now given a new, gnostic significance in the wake of the rediscovery of the *Corpus Hermeticum.*

The age of the Renaissance witnessed also the emergence of an explicitly Hermetic art. It can be seen in Botticelli's *Primavera,* which, painted in 1478, only seven years after the publication of the *Corpus Hermeticum* in Latin, is a veritable magical talisman, a "figure of the world." In 1488, an unknown artist inlaid a beautiful work in the floor tiles of the cathedral of Siena, a representation still visible today. It depicts Hermes Trismegistos as a bearded old man attired in a robe and cape and wearing a padded miter. He is surrounded by various other personages, and the whole is accompanied by a very typical inscription: "Hermes Mercurius Trismegistus Contemporeanus Moysii." A little later, Pope Alexander VI, Pico's patron, commissioned a large fresco abounding with Hermetic symbols and zodiacal signs to be painted by Pinturicchio in the Borgia apartment in the Vatican; there we see Hermes Trismegistos in the company of Isis and Moses.

Several other authors contemporary with Ficino and Pico referred to the newly rediscovered *Corpus Hermeticum,* and the *Asclepius* continued to draw the attention of some, such as Antonio Agli, the bishop of Fiesole, in his *De immortalitate animae* (1475). But soon new editions with enthusiastic and erudite commentaries appeared. The earliest was the work of Jacques Lefèvre d'Étaples, who, in 1494, published the first fifteen dialogues under the title of *Poimandres,* using Ficino's text and following it with a brief personal commentary. In 1505, he published the text again, this time commenting on it chapter by chapter and including the *Asclepius,* which, he claimed, had condemned operative magic. In addition, Lefèvre added a previously unpublished text entitled *Crater Hermetis* (The Basin of Hermes).

The author of the *Crater Hermetis* was a certain Ludovico Lazarelli, who exhibited an extreme fondness for Trismegistos. His book shows the influence of book 4 of the *Corpus,* which discusses the manner in which the master transmits regenerative experience to his disciple. In Lazarelli, as in Pico, variations on the maxim "Know thyself" appeared. Hermetism was to make a major contribution to the development of this theme of Christian Socratism, especially in the seventeenth century. In 1507, Lazarelli translated the newly discovered book 16 of the *Corpus,* which had been unknown to Ficino. Lazarelli also seems to have been the author of the *Epistola Enoch,* a text focused on the picturesque figure of Mercurio da Correggio, a sort of "Hermes' fool" who brought the Thrice-Greatest to the public eye. On Palm Sunday of 1484 he appeared in Rome in bizarre dress and in like company. On the banks of the Manara he put on winged shoes and a crown of thorns topped with a crescent moon bearing the inscription: "This is my son Poimandres, whom I have chosen." He mounted a white ass and made a speech in which he called himself the "angel of Wisdom, Poimandres, in the most sublime manifestation of the Lord Jesus Christ" and claimed to have descended from heaven. Then, making his way to the Vatican, he deposited diverse objects on the throne of Saint Peter. In 1496 he turned up again in Florence and then in Lyons, exhibiting himself always in the same way. Eventually he converted Lazarelli to Hermetism. Mercurio is of interest to the historian since, being illiterate, he provides evidence for the vogue of Hermetism among the common people. Interestingly, his exploits took place prior to the inscription on the tiles of the cathedral of Siena.

Also at this time, Symphorien Champier, an admirer of Ficino and disciple of Lefèvre d'Étaples, published his own collection of texts at Lyons (1507), reproducing most of the commentaries of his master and adding his own to them. He also added the Latin translation of book 16 just completed by Lazarelli and did not hesitate to derive all of Greek philosophy from Hermes. He considered the famous passage from the *Asclepius* on magic and animated statues to be an interpolation by Apuleius, and thus not to be attributed to Hermes. This tendency to downplay the magical aspects of the *Corpus Hermeticum,* and of the *Asclepius* in particular, in favor of a more noble, essentially philosophical interpretation, is typical of French Hermetism. It can be seen in Pontus de Tyard, bishop of Chalons (*Deux discours,* 1578), among others.

In England, the beginning of the sixteenth century witnessed the adaptation of Catholic theology and philosophy to Neoplatonism and the *prisca theologia,* notably in the work of John Colet, Thomas More, and their intellectual circle. Colet was a disciple of Ficino and had also been influenced by Dionysius the Areopagite. More's *Utopia* (1516) shows the influence of Hermetism, if only in the irenicism that is so central to it. Before the crises arising from confessional conflicts, More was able to propose religious Hermetism as a possible palliative for the century.

Let us follow the thread of chronology. The *De harmonia mundi* (1525) of Francisco Giorgi Venetus, one of the most beautiful books of Christian esotericism of the Renaissance, bears the stamp of Hermetism and strives to reconcile the *Corpus Hermeticum* with the teachings of Christianity. The most famous book of occult philosophy of the age, the *De occulta philosophia* (1533) of Heinrich Cornelius Agrippa, cites Hermes Trismegistos many times, and the same author, in his speech given at Pavia *(Oratio habita Papiae),* took for his subject "the dialogues on the wisdom and the divine power of Hermes." Like Lazarelli in his *Epistola Enoch,* Agrippa identified Hermes as a grandson of Abraham and attributed all kinds of inventions to him. Valentine Weigel, the father of Germanic theosophy, of which Jakob Boehme is the greatest exponent, cites the name of Hermes Trismegistos more than that of any other author before the sixteenth century, and thus more than that of Dionysius the Areopagite, Plato, or Augustine. Like Agrippa, however, Weigel invoked this prestigious name more often than he utilized the Hermetic texts themselves. Traces of Hermetic influence can also be seen in Copernicus, for he cites Hermes in reference to the sun considered as the visible God.

Between 1553 and 1556 the *Fragments of Stobaeus* appeared and were subsequently incorporated into the *Corpus Hermeticum.* They were partially edited by Trincavelli at Venice but were completed only in 1575, by Canter. Lazarelli's *Crater Hermetis* was published in French in 1549 and dedicated to the duke of Lorraine; this text reproduced the *argumentum* of Ficino and the commentaries of Lefèvre d'Étaples, though without mentioning their names. Finally, in 1553, Michael Servetus, a Catholic and disciple of Champier, who had undoubtedly introduced him to the works of Plato and the *prisca theologia,* wrote his *Christianismi restitutio.* Servetus claimed the ancients as his authorities, especially Hermes and the Platonic fathers. He believed that Plato owed his conception of the world of ideas and archetypes to Hermes. In Servetus there is a curious materialistic interpretation of the *Corpus Hermeticum,* a sort of inverse Platonic emanationism, since for him matter and the body are the source of all being.

THE GOLDEN AGE OF RELIGIOUS HERMETICISM

The succeeding years saw the publication of important new editions of the *Corpus,* with more or less plentiful commentaries. In 1554, through the efforts of Turnebus, the first edition of the Greek text of the *Corpus* appeared in Paris, based on the manuscript used by Ficino and accompanied by the latter's Latin translation, as well as by Lazarelli's translation of the additional treatise. A preface by Vergerius emphasized the resemblances of Hermetism to Christianity. Three years later, Lefèvre d'Étaples's collection was translated into French by Gabriel du Preau, accompanied by the *Crater Hermetis* of Lazarelli. Even more important than Turnebus's work was the new Greco-Latin edition of the *Corpus* (1574) by the bishop François de Foix de Candale, which was followed by a French edition in 1579, to which his own commentary had been added. Foix de Candale professed a kind of ecstatic religious Hermetism and seems to have put the *Corpus Hermeticum* on the same plane as the canonical writings of Christianity. His long commentary in French continues the apologetic tradition of Ficino, Lazarelli, and Lefèvre d'Étaples. This was also the age of the vague yet recognizable Hermetism that one finds in the *De aetatibus mundi imagines* (1545–1573) and *Da pintura antigua* (1548) of the Portuguese writer Francisco de Holanda. The intellectual context of these works is that of the Escorial, marked in the study of art and philosophy by a Hermetism nourished by speculations on the proportions and numbers thought to be hidden in the marvels of mythic and sacred architecture.

The end of the sixteenth century and the beginning of the seventeenth were the golden age of religious Hermetism (Dagens, 1961, pp. 5–15). In addition to the editors and commentators, many others came under the influence of Trismegistos. Jacques Gohory (d. 1576), also known as Leo Suavius, directed a kind of medico-magical academy at Paris. Between 1570 and 1580 the De la Boderie brothers published their translations of Ficino, Pico, and Giorgi. It was also at this time that Ficino's *Opera omnia* appeared (1576), followed six years later at Anvers by Philippe Duplessis-Mornay's famous book *De la vérité de la religion chrétienne,* written at a time when William of Orange was trying to establish religious tolerance at Anvers. Duplessis-Mornay, a Protestant, employed Hermetism in fashioning a religious position that stood above all religious conflicts, a position close to that of Erasmus but with an added esoteric dimension. He compared the *Corpus Hermeticum* with the *Zohar* and made mention of Orpheus, Zarathushtra, and the sibyls, but especially of Hermes, "the source of them all." As is common among the French, his Hermetism is mystical and theological. His book, translated into English by Sidney and Arthur Golding in 1587, is perhaps the most complete exposition of Hermetism in the tradition of Ficino. The work of another Frenchman, Du Bartas, is comparable to that of Duplessis-Mornay in this regard, although the Hermetism of the former is more sober.

The end of the sixteenth century also saw the appearance of the works of Hannibal Rossel and Francesco Patrizi, in addition to diverse writings by Giordano Bruno. *Pymander Mercurii Trismegisti,* written by the Italian Franciscan Rossel, appeared at Cracow in six volumes between 1585 and 1590 and was reissued in Cologne in 1630. It contained the text of Foix de Candale, as well as commentaries borrowed from Dionysius the Areopagite. Rossel's work consists of an enormous commentary on the *Poimandres* that makes an irenic use of Hermetism—hardly surprising in a time when active religious tolerance was being practiced in Poland. Patrizi's *Nova de universis philosophia* (1591) was dedicated to Gregory XIV. It consisted of the text of the *Corpus,* as established by Turnebus and Foix de Candale, and a new Latin translation. Patrizi portrayed the true magus as one who is devoted to God, and true *prisca magia* as the true religion. He claimed that a single treatise from the *Corpus* contained more philosophy than all of Aristotle and advocated the study of Plotinus, Proclus, and the early fathers, while discouraging the study of the Scholastics, whom he judged too Aristotelian. In the spirit of the Counter-Reformation, he took up the question of a new catechism and recommended the study of the *Corpus* to the Jesuits. He even went so far as to suggest to the pope that Hermetic Platonism be assigned in all Christian schools as an aid to converting the Lutherans. In 1592, Clement VIII, won over to some of his ideas, called him to Rome to teach Platonic philosophy at the university, but once there he incurred the displeasure of the Inquisition.

Giordano Bruno also recommended a "new" philosophy founded on Hermetism. Bruno's Hermetism, in contrast to that of Ficino and the French, represented a kind of aggressive return to Hermetic magic. It was scarcely Christian; he did not identify the *intellectus* and *Filius Dei* of the Hermetica with the second person of the Trinity. In 1591 he tried to win over Clement VIII in Rome, but as we know, his radical interpretations, unlike those of Patrizi, led him to the stake in 1600.

Religious Hermetism is above all gnostic and irenic. But in the 1590s, the Puritanism then flourishing in England brought about a weakening of the theological syncretism that had favored those tendencies. With Edward VI, the English Protestants had already begun to break with the past, going so far as to destroy books and libraries; under the reign of Mary a Hispano-Catholic intolerance further damaged the tradition. Puritan Anglicanism under Elizabeth had lost all trace of Erasmian tolerance, and Hermetism suffered accordingly, at least in the official milieux of the church and the university. It continued to develop within private circles, however, such as those that formed around Sir Philip Sidney and Queen Elizabeth's astrologer, John Dee. In addition to Sidney and Dee, who were primarily enthusiasts of esotericism, we may also mention Richard Hooker, who often cited the *Corpus* in his work *The Laws of Ecclesiastical Polity,* which began to appear in 1593. Despite these references, however, Hooker does not seem to have identified himself with the Hermetic tradition as such.

CASAUBON'S "REVELATION" AND SEVENTEENTH-CENTURY HERMETISM

At the beginning of the seventeenth century, Hermetism and the *prisca theologia* suffered a terrible blow, one that served to separate the Renaissance from the modern world. In 1614, the Genevan Isaac Casaubon, seeking to refute the arguments of a spokesman for the Counter-Reformation who had cited Lactantius's passages on Trismegistos, discovered and demonstrated in a definitive manner that the texts of the *Corpus Hermeticum* did not predate the first centuries of our era. That this discovery should have come so late is surprising, since in the sixteenth century there was no lack of good humanists capable of making it. The fact that it was so long in coming is an additional testimony to the vogue of the *Corpus* and of Hermes Trismegistos during that period. At first certain authors deliberately ignored the discovery; others, at least for a few years afterward, simply did not know about it. Nevertheless, Alexandrian Hermetism, now known to be much less ancient than previously believed, began to find ever fewer followers.

Sir Walter Raleigh devoted a whole section of his *History of the World* to Hermes, but he was writing while imprisoned in the Tower of London when Casaubon's book appeared. Tommaso Campanella's ignorance was also involuntary. On the other hand, it is surprising that Marin Mersenne, who, with Johannes Kepler, founded modern science and who was never slow to recognize a new argument against the followers of the *philosophia occulta,* still did not know Casaubon when he wrote his *Quaestiones in Genesim* in 1623—the more so since this was a huge work directed against the hermeticists and the qabbalists. Nevertheless, he made use of this argument a little later. Mersenne pointed his finger in particular at Robert Fludd, the most important theosophist of England, whose major work, *Utriusque cosmi historia,* had appeared six years earlier. Fludd responded with his *Sophiae cum Moria certamen* (1626) and *Summum bonum* (1629). Gaffarel supported him while Pierre Gassendi took Mersenne's part. Fludd was also involved in a controversy with Kepler, who nevertheless had cited the *Corpus* at length in his *De harmonice mundi* (1619).

Fludd himself did not seem to know about Casaubon's discovery, or at least pretended not to know about it. He gave as much weight to the *Corpus* as to *Genesis* or the *Gospel of John.* On almost every page of his works one can find a citation from Ficino's Latin translation. He evidently associated Hermetism with the Qabbala, in an original synthesis similar to Pico's, presented as an updated version of the occult philosophy of the Renaissance. If Bruno and Campanella spoke little about the Qabbala, if their Hermetic cult remained more or less naturalistic, Fludd himself returned to origins—in other words, to Ficino and Pico—and reinterpreted them. After all, he was more trinitarian than Bruno, and unlike the latter, his Christianity was genuine. On the other hand, his interest in Rosicrucianism, which appeared in Germany at the beginning of the seventeenth century, is well known. It is undoubtedly possible to see the latter as a prolongation of the Hermetic spirit of the Renaissance, to which a new tendency toward secrecy had been added, rendering it subterranean and restricting to minority groups what had still, in the preceding century, been the domain of the dominant philosophers. [*See* Rosicrucians.]

It is not surprising to find allusions to the *Corpus* and to its supposed author in the Neoplatonists of Cambridge. They generally accepted Ficino's idea of an uninterrupted transmission of ancient wisdom from Moses to Hermes, passing through Zarathushtra, Pythagoras, Plato, and Orpheus. Ralph Cudworth's position on this point is interesting, for it anticipates what an esotericist of today might think of that tradition; indeed, Cudworth believed that the Hermetica, no matter how weak in details, could well have preserved certain authentic Egyptian teachings. Other English authors contemporary with Cudworth readily cite Trismegistos, although they can hardly be thought of as his followers. One detects here the influence of Casaubon. Robert Burton, in his *Anatomy of Melancholy* (1621), mentioned Hermes no fewer than thirty times, along with Ficino, Pico, Paracelsus, and Campanella. One has the impression, however, that all these names are merely a show of erudition in the context of an enlarged humanism. The same reserved attitude is found in Sir Thomas Browne, a skeptical scholar as well as contemplator of the infinite. He often evoked the famous Hermetic image of the sphere whose center is everywhere and circumference nowhere, but he has obviously borrowed it from the *Liber viginti quattuor philosophorum* and not from the *Corpus Hermeticum.* Browne himself was not convinced that the ancient wisdom was superior to the modern. It was merely in his capacity as a collector of information and propagandist that he cited Trismegistos, as likely to find what he needed there as elsewhere: "The severe schools shall never laugh me out of the Philosophy of Hermes, that this visible world is but a

Picture of the invisible" (*Works*, ed. Keynes, 1928–1931, vol. 1, p. 17). Indeed, "where I cannot satisfy my reason, I love to humour my fancy." One finds similar references in the works of William Gilbert (*De magnete*, 1600), Henry Reynolds (*Mythomystes*, 1632), and Milton, who cites Hermes Trismegistos three times (in *Il Penseroso*, lines 87ff.; *Ad Joannem Rousum*, line 77; and *De idea Platonica*, lines 33ff.). An English version of the *Corpus* was provided by John Everard in 1650 and 1657, many times reedited afterward.

In France, Ficino's doctrines, still alive at the Palace Academy and in Queen Margot's circle, provided the occasion for several references to the Hermetic tradition, but these became less frequent after the scandal of Casaubon. "Hermes" and "Hermetism" developed into a notion that came more and more to refer to alchemy or theosophy—and eventually became hermeticism, or esotericism, in the modern sense of the term. This is the case in d'Espagnet's *La philosophie naturelle rétablie en sa pureté, avec le traité de l'ouvrage secret d'Hermès* (1651). But in 1659 Jean Desmarets de Saint-Sorlin could still devote four hundred pages of his lovely folio volume *Les délices de l'esprit* to the *Book of Revelation* and *Genesis* under the sign of Pico, through whom Hermes is evoked. Finally, Jacques-Bénigne Bossuet himself did not neglect the Hermetic themes that he found in the church fathers (in particular, Gregory of Nyssa and Lactantius). In his *Sermon on Death* (1662), for instance, he utilized Cicero's *De natura deorum*, a text of Stoic origins that had been incorporated into Hermetic literature and that had influenced the *Corpus Hermeticum*. Here again the references to Hermetism served to guarantee or reinforce confidence in human powers.

The Jesuit Athanasius Kircher gave Hermes Trismegistos and the *Corpus* almost as much importance as had Fludd in his own writings. Kircher's *Oedipus Aegyptiacus* (1652)—one of the works first to stir the Egyptomania that swept Europe over the next three centuries—is full of citations borrowed from Ficino's text of the *Corpus*, and particularly from the *Asclepius*. Kircher readily associated Qabbalah and Hermetism, and, like Ficino, saw Hermes as the inventor of the hieroglyphs; following the example of Renaissance Hermetism, he interpreted these as truths about God and the world, inscribed on stone monuments, and especially on obelisks. This is basically the inverse and complementary process to that of interpreting the Hermetica as a collection of *icones symbolicae*, since Hermes was also supposed originally to have written in hieroglyphs. Most of the hieroglyphs that Kircher referred to were demystified when Jacques-Joseph Champollion deciphered them in 1824. This was the second blow, after Casaubon, delivered to the "Egyptian" myth.

ASPECTS OF HERMETISM IN GERMANY

Translations of the *Corpus* into Dutch had been published in 1607 and 1643. The first translation into German seems to be the publication of extracts in *Occulta Philosophia* (1613). In Germany, the anonymous *Hermes Trismegisti Vere Aureus* (1610) carried a vibrant dedication to Trismegistos and was presented as a dialogue between Hermes and a disciple—a little like the *Corpus*, although the Alexandrian reference served more as a pretext than as a motif. In general, the Germans had little part in the golden age of European Hermetism, which lasted from Ficino to Kircher. Agrippa had written before the Reformation, and Kircher had composed his main works in Rome. During this period humanism made only slight progress in

Germanic lands, hampered by the barrier that Lutheranism had erected against it. Alexandrian Hermetism, by its very nature and as a legacy of ancient Greek literature and thought, remained a subject of study for the humanists, even after it had been translated into Latin by an Italian. As a consequence, the authors of almost all the great commentaries on the *Corpus* were also French and Italian: Ficino, Lefèvre d'Étaples, Foix de Candale, Patrizi, Rossel. The Christian Qabbala, which was almost contemporary with Hermetism and was sometimes confused with it, was also poorly represented in Germany, although better than the latter.

What is most remarkable is that Germanic esotericism of the sixteenth and seventeenth centuries was essentially "barbaric," in the sense that it did not owe much to the ancient legacy and developed in a more or less autonomous fashion. We have seen that Hermes Trismegistos was the object of a particular veneration in Weigel and Agrippa, although they made little use of the Hermetica. Paracelsus, Boehme, J. G. Gichtel, and most of the representatives of early *Naturphilosophie*—in other words, the whole theosophical current that had chosen Germany as its protector—owed practically nothing to Hermetism. This remained so, despite many similarities of thought, publications of Hermetica (such as the *Poimandres* of Rossel in Cologne), and the occasional references of theosophists like Abraham von Frankenberg and Josephus Stellatus (also known as Joseph Hirsch) to Hermetic materials. These references remained rather general and alchemical. One may well wonder if the disappearance of the *Corpus Hermeticum* and its author after the discovery of Casaubon did not result, either as a consequence, reaction, or compensation, in the reinforcement of the belief in a tradition, all the more secret or primordial because one could no longer date it. The Rosicrucian vogue, which appeared at exactly the same time as Casaubon's revelation, can perhaps be partially explained by such a reaction, as the historian R. C. Zimmermann has suggested.

In the Germanic countries, Hermetism at the end of the seventeenth century and at the beginning of the eighteenth appears to have been a manifestation of humanism, which appeared only with the beginning of the Enlightenment. One interesting presentation of Hermetism was a book by a certain Christian Kriegsmann, published in 1684 at Tübingen, *Conjectaneorum de germanicae gentis origine, ac Conditore, Herme Trismegiste, qui S. Moysi est Chanaan . . . Liber Unus*. In it the author endeavored to demonstrate by philosophical arguments that Hermes was the founder of the Germanic peoples. Ten years later, Johann Ludwig Hannemann cited Kriegsmann in his *Ovum hermetico-paracelsico-trismegistum*, a work devoted primarily to medical and occult chemical recipes, but which also contained a lively homage to Hermes, who is presented as having lived well before Christ—obviously Casaubon was not cited! A large place is also given to Hermes Trismegistos in the works of Johann Heinrich Ursinus (*De Zoroastre bactriano, Hermete Trismegisto* 1661) and Olaus Borrichius (*Hermetis Aegyptiorum*, 1674).

In 1706 the first complete German translation of the *Poimandres* appears in Hamburg, with commentaries by Aletophilus (W. von Metternich?), under the title *Erkenntnüsz der Natur und des sich darin offenbahrenden Gottes*. In the same period, the title of Ehregott Daniel Colberg's work *Das platonische hermetische Christentum* (1690–1692) was a vague reference to both spiritualists and theosophists, against whom the author took up arms, reserving only four pages of his book for Hermes himself. A little later, Gottfried Arnold made almost no mention of Hermetism in his voluminous history of sects and heresies, and Johann Heinrich Zedler's great dictionary, which appeared around 1730, gave only a very vague definition of it. Nevertheless, 1706 saw the publication of the first complete German translation of the *Corpus* at Hamburg, while Johann Albrecht Fabricius began to publish his monumental *Bibliotheca Graeca* (1705–1728), one of the first great surveys of Hellenism in Germany, in which Hermes was much discussed. Hermes also appeared in the *Theo-Philosophia theoretico-practica* (1711) by Samuel Richter (called Sincerus Renatus), one of the fundamental works of eighteenth-century German theosophy. Finally, Johann Jacob Brucker devoted an entire volume of his popular *Historia critica philosophiae* (vol. 14, 1743) to hermeticism, in both its broad and narrow senses.

NEW PERSPECTIVES

During the remainder of the eighteenth century and all of the nineteenth, the Hermetism of Hermes Trismegistos was confused with Egyptomania, Orphism, and Pythagoreanism. The rather muddled imagery that resulted nevertheless proved favorable to literary and artistic inspiration. Quintus Aucler and Pierre Jacques Devismes were a part of the neopagan current. Their work displays a taste for the cosmic harmonies that had so interested Giorgi Venetus and Fludd. In *Hermes Trismegisti Poemander* (Berlin, 1781), Dietrich Tiedemann had provided one of the very first scholarly editions, and under the same title, Gustav Parthey provided another version (Berlin, 1857), with commentary.

Nineteenth-century occultism made little use of Alexandrian Hermetism, but it helped to stimulate scholarly research into the subject of esotericism in the broad sense. As a result, the beginning of the twentieth century saw a proliferation of detailed works on Qabbalah, alchemy, and Freemasonry. On the other hand, neo-Rosicrucianism and the Theosophical Society of H. P. Blavatsky were concerned with Hermetism: in 1871, Beverly Randolph's *Hermes . . . The Divine Pymander* appeared in Boston; in 1882, John David Chamber's *The Theological and Philosophical Works of Hermes Trismegistos, Christian Neoplatonist*; and in 1885, Anna Kingsford and E. Maitland's *The Hermetic Works: The Virgin of the World,* as well as new editions of Everard's translation. Louis-Nicolas Ménard had presented the *Corpus* in 1867, trying to be simultaneously academic and esoteric. A similar endeavor can be found in G. R. S. Mead's *Thrice Great Hermes: Studies in Hellenistic Theosophy and Gnosis* (1906).

But the genuine academic work began only with the appearance of Richard Reitzenstein's *Poimandres* (1904). Most important on this academic level are the four volumes edited by Walter Scott and John Ferguson at Oxford (*Hermetica,* 1924–1936). Shortly after, a remarkable translation of the *Corpus*, with notes and commentaries, was published by Arthur Darby Nock and A.-J. Festugière, followed by Festugière's enormous and learned survey *La révélation d'Hermès Trismégiste*. Finally, numerous works have brought us up to date on the reception of Hermetism in the Renaissance and the seventeenth century, especially those of Brian P. Copenhaver, Eugenio Garin, Paul O. Kristeller, Wayne Shuhmaker, E. L. Tuveson, D. P. Walker, and Frances A. Yates, to cite only a few of the best.

Two streams thus go on running in parallel directions: the esoterically inspired and the objective, scholarly, and academic. Representative of the former in our century are the edition by the "Shrine of Wisdom" of *The Divine Pymander* (1923) as well as Duncan Greenless's *Gospel of Hermes* (1949) or Gerard Van Moorsel's *Mys-*

teries of Hermes Trismegistus (1955). But the academic works seem to be the most numerous. Thus having been an object of veneration, indeed, of particular devotion and then having been relegated to darkness, the Thrice-Greatest and his Hermetica have become, in our own day, the subject of studies for linguists as well as historians of literature and philosophy.

[*See also* Esotericism.]

BIBLIOGRAPHY

There is no single book on the reception of Hermetism from the fifth through the twentieth century. A summary, along with the best philosophical insights into this problem, is provided by a short but remarkable book, Françoise Bonardel's *L'Hermétisme* (Paris, 1985). Much useful material is found in Lynn Thorndike's *A History of Magic and Experimental Science*, 8 vols. (New York, 1923–1958). On Hermetism in the Middle Ages and its relationship to alchemy, see Julius Ruska's *Tabula smaragdina* (Heidelberg, 1926). The classic history of Hermetism in the Renaissance, Frances A. Yates's *Giordano Bruno and the Hermetic Tradition* (London, 1964), is a valuable conspectus of the major tendencies and is extremely well documented. See also Daniel P. Walker's *Spiritual and Demonic Magic from Ficino to Campanella* (London, 1958); Wayne Shuhmaker's *The Occult Sciences in the Renaissance* (Berkeley, 1972); and the collective work *Umanesimo e esoterismo*, edited by Enrico Castelli (Padua, 1960). An interesting account of later writings is found in Jean Dagens's article "Hermétisme et Cabale en France, de Lefèvre d'Étaples à Bossuet," *Revue de littérature comparée* 35 (1961): 5–16. See also Brian P. Copenhaver's *Symphorien Champier and the Reception of the Occultist Tradition in Renaissance France* (New York, 1978). New interesting insights concerning the direct and indirect influence of Hermetism upon Anglo-Saxon literature are provided by Ernest Lee Tuveson's *The Avatars of Thrice Great Hermes: An Approach to Romanticism* (Toronto, 1982). On the relationship between Hermetism and the philosophies of nature, a valuable synthetic survey is found in Mirko Sladek's *Fragmente der hermetischen Philosophie in der Naturphilosophie der Neuzeit* (Frankfurt, 1984).

6 — GNOSTICISM FROM THE MIDDLE AGES TO THE PRESENT

Ioan Petru Culianu

The existence of an underground gnostic tradition within Christianity, Judaism, and Islam, from the Middle Ages to the present, can be considered one of the near certainties of modern scholarship. Heretical Christian movements from Augustine to the eighteenth century fall into three different categories:

1. dualistic sects whose doctrines make use of gnostic and Manichaean mythological themes;
2. sects derived from Marcionism, which are not typically gnostic but which are dualistic, insofar as they make a distinction between a "just" divinity (that of the Old Testament) and a "good" divinity announced by Jesus Christ;
3. pauperistic movements (so called from Latin *pauper*, "poor"), which are fundamentally non-gnostic and nondualistic but which may be akin to the first two types of sects, insofar as they are strongly ascetic, encratic (i.e., rejecting marriage and sexual intercourse), antinomian (i.e., rejecting both worldly and religious institutions), anticlericalist, and sometimes vegetarian.

Furthermore, the doctrine of several medieval sects is a blending of a basic Marcionite lore with superimposed gnostic-Manichaean elements. The same situation faces us both in the two main trends of Islamic heresy *(zandaqa)*, the *ghulāt* and the Ismāʿīlīyah, and in the late Jewish qabbalistic school of Isaac Luria. The history of gnostic ideas and imagery is not easy to follow, since it is basically a history of interactions between gnostic and merely Marcionite movements.

As the cradle of late medieval heresy was eastern Europe, the cradle of early medieval heresy was Armenia, where Marcionites, gnostics, and Manichaeans had sought refuge from the prosecutions of the church in the fourth and fifth centuries. The Paulicians, a sect founded by Constantine of Mananalis at the end of the seventh century, might have been based on Marcionite lore. Prosecuted by both Christians and Muslims, the Paulicians were nearly destroyed in the eighth century, but managed to become important again under the reformer Sergius Tychikos (d. 835). Nearly one hundred thousand of them were killed under the empress Theodora. The officer Karbeas, who was a Paulician, crossed the border to Arab Armenia and founded there, with five thousand followers, the cities of Tephrike (modern-day

Divrigi) and Amara. Around 869, the Paulicians were about to send a mission to Thrace. One century later, the emperor John Tsimisces sent many of them to Philippopolis in Thrace, where they still were located in 1116.

The ideas of Priscillian of Ávila in Spain, condemned in 385 as a sorcerer and a "Manichaean," are hardly known. His sect was Marcionite during the fifth and sixth centuries. Late Priscillianism and Paulicianism shared the following distinctive features: cosmological and anthropological dualism, encratism, docetism (according to which Christ's passion was not real), antinomianism. All these were consequences of Marcion's distinction of two gods, of which the evil one (i.e., the god of the Old Testament) was also the creator of the visible world.

Gnostic, Manichaean, and Jewish messianic ideas are likely to have influenced the first representatives of Shī'ī gnosis. Just as Simon Magus was the archheretic of Christian gnosis, the archheretic of Islamic *ghulūw* ("exaggeration") was a certain 'Abdallāh ibn Saba', a Jew belonging to the adepts of the imam 'Alī in the town Kufa in Iraq. Ibn Saba' fostered, after 'Alī's death, messianic expectations likely to be explained in the light of his Falasha background. Different sects of *ghulāt* ("extremists, exaggerators"), in which one or another descendant of 'Alī was divinized and/or expected to come back as the Messiah long after he was dead, have been important among the Shī'ah from the early eighth century to the present. Their last remnants are, today, the Syrian Nuṣayrīyah, or 'Alawīyūn. To the Kufic *ghulāt* belongs the book *Umm al-kitāb* (Mother of All Books; late eighth century), an apocalypse containing unequivocal gnostic motifs. Another apocalypse, in use among the Nuṣayrīyah, the *Kitāb al-azillah* (Book of Shadows), is equally based on gnostic mythology.

Ismā'īlī gnosis, a distinct trend of *zandaqah,* was founded in the ninth century by a certain 'Abdallāh of Hūzistān, perhaps a son of that Maimūn who was known to be a disciple of the Bardayṣan heresy. 'Abdallāh, together with his acolyte al-Ahwāzī, fled to Syria, where an offshoot of the sect developed in the village of Salamīya. Al-Husayn, the fourth descendant of 'Abdallāh, went to North Africa and became the founder of the Fatimid dynasty. Al-Ahwāzī founded in Kufa, Iraq, a second branch of the sect known as the Qarāmiṭah after the name of a certain al-Asch'at, surnamed Qarmaṭ, a disciple of al-Ahwāzī. The Qarāmiṭah of Iraq sent missions to Yemen, to countries bordering Yemen, and to Persia. The twelfth-century sect of the Assassins was a branch of the Qarāmiṭah. Today, different Ismā'īlī sects are to be found in Syria, Lebanon, Yemen, and northwestern India. Among the most important are the Druze, a group dating from the early eleventh century that today lives in Syria, Lebanon, and Israel. The oldest writing of the Ismā'īlīyah is *Kitāb al-kashf* (Book of Revelation). Its most ancient passages seem to have been composed at Salamīyah. The cosmogony of *Kitāb al-kashf* is based on the gnostic myth of the pride and ignorance of the demiurge, a theme resumed in the Druze treatise *Kashf al-ḥaqā'iq* (Revelation of All Truths). The most important Ismā'īlī thinker is the eleventh-century Iraqi Neoplatonist al-Kirmānī.

How might gnostic myths have reached the Ghulāt and the Ismā'īlīyah? They were probably transmitted by the so-called *mawāli,* or "clients," from Kufa. The *mawāli* were foreigners converted to Islam after the conquest of Persia's capital, Seleucia-Ctesiphon (Arabic, al-Madā'īn), and its transfer to Kufa under the Umayyads (637–638 CE). Among the *mawāli,* Jewish, Christian, Zoroastrian, gnostic, and Manichaean ideas were represented.

In the Christian world, a dualistic movement containing unequivocally gnostic elements burst forth in Bulgaria in the tenth century under the influence of the Paulician mission. This heresy was named after its founder, the priest Bogomil, active at the time of the emperor Peter (927–969). Cosmological and anthropological dualism, antinomianism, docetism, anticlericalism, encratism, asceticism, and vegetarianism characterized Bogomilism.

The basic creation myth of the Bogomils has an authentic gnostic flavor, but it derives in all probability from Inner Asian folklore. Similar myths occur elsewhere in dualistic religious contexts, such as in Persian Zurvanism. Bogomilism spread to Thrace and Asia Minor and reached the capital of the Byzantine empire in the eleventh century as an underground movement. At the beginning of the twelfth century, its leader in Constantinople was a doctor named Basilius. Some basic myths of the Byzantine strain of Bogomilism (the creation of Adam, the seduction of Eve) are unequivocally gnostic.

If twelfth-century Catharism was directly influenced by Bogomilism, earlier Western movements might have appeared either as a result of intermittent Bogomil influences or as a spontaneous revival of dualistic ideas.Religious groups sharing such beliefs as dualism, docetism, encratism, antinomianism, vegetarianism and anticlericalism were found and prosecuted during the eleventh century in towns throughout Europe: Orléans (1017–1022); Liège, Arras, Toulouse (1028); Monforte (northern Italy, 1028); Goslar (Saxony, 1052); Chalons-sur-Marne (1043–1062); Agen (1090). Of these sectarians, only those of Orléans, Liège, Arras, and Agen were certainly dualists. The European interviewers, who were not yet properly "inquisitors" (the Inquisition was established in 1227–1235), did not show the same forbearance as Alexius, emperor of Byzantium, who, in 1111, spent many days listening to the Bogomil Basilius before sending him to the hippodrome to be burned alive. If the heretics were not convinced within one morning to abjure their faith, they faced certain condemnation. Therefore, one should not expect from Western ecclesiastical historians such accurate descriptions of heretic doctrines as Eastern historians gave concerning the Byzantine Bogomils. Western sectarians of the eleventh century were, in most cases, so-called crypto-heretics who continued to go to church and to take sacraments. In some cases, they gladly accepted martyrdom after having been found guilty. Since vegetarianism was widespread among them, their refusal, for instance, to kill a chicken was considered sufficient cause for execution (as in Goslar in 1052), just as later the refusal of a young woman to have intercourse with the inquisitor was held to be sufficient evidence for condemning her as a Cathar.

Bogomilism spread westward as a mass movement in the middle of the twelfth century. Catharist churches were established in northern Italy and southern France. The churches grew, and a crusade was organized against them in 1208. A second crusade in 1227 resulted in the fall of Montségur (1244), the last stronghold of the Cathari. The movement declined, although it continued to face its prosecutors for about another century.

French and Italian Cathari were dependent on two mother churches in eastern Europe, a fact emphasized during the Council of Saint-Félix-de-Caraman (near Toulouse) when the priest Niketas, bishop of the Byzantine Bogomils, converted Italian and French Cathari from the Ordo Bulgariae to the Ordo Drugunthiae, to which he belonged. The Ecclesia Bulgariae, or Ordo Bulgariae, held a mitigated form of dualism, while the Ecclesia Drugunthiae (probably refering to Dragovitsa in Thrace, near Philippopoli) held a radical dualism. Italian Cathari were divided between the Ordo Bulgariae and the Ordo Drugunthiae. A third church existed in Italy, at Bagnolo San Vito, near Mantua, belonging to the Sclavini, or Sclavi ("Slavs"), a sect deriving from the Bogomil church of Bosnia.

Like the Bogomils, the Cathari professed cosmological and anthropological dualism, encratism, asceticism, antinomianism, anticlericalism, docetism, and vegetarianism. Their myths bore the incontestable imprint of Manichaeism, a fact that has not so far met with a convincing historical explanation.

Neither has the revival of gnostic myth in the qabbalistic school of Safad (Palestine) been explained historically. The founder of this school was Isaac Luria (1534–1572). Lurianic Qabbalah had two influential schools: the Palestinian one, represented by Hayyim Vital (1543–1620), and the Italian one, represented by Yisra'el Sarug (fl. 1590–1610). The fundamental doctrine of Lurianic Qabbalah was that of *tsimtsum,* or "contraction" of God within himself in order to free a zone outside himself, which is accordingly deprived of God and filled up with creation. Later in the process of creation, the spiritual "vessels" broke *(shevirat ha-kelim)* and were filled up with matter, while the "shells" *(qelippot)* fell in the void of creation. The mythologem of the broken vessels, found in the Valentinian treatise *The Gospel of Truth,* is an ancient gnostic tradition.

Lurianic Qabbalah was influential in Western thinking. The Lutheran qabbalist Friedrich Christoph Oetinger (1702–1782) was acquainted with the works of the Lurian adepts Hayyim Vital and 'Immanu'el H'ai Ricci ben Avraham (1688–1743). Oetinger took over, in his own works, the theory of *tsimtsum* and the Marcionite distinction between God's justice and bounty, a distinction that also played a role in Lurianic Qabbalah. According to Ernst Topitsch ("Marxismus und Gnosis," in *Sozialphilosophie zwischen Ideologie und Wissenschaft,* Neuwied-Berlin, 1966), Hegel's early writings were very much influenced by Oetinger's philosophy, and thus both Hegel and his materialist disciple Marx might be considered direct descendants of gnosticism. Yet the idea of a gnostic "devolution" is alien to Marx, who is a typical evolutionist. It is true that the proletarians are viewed as redeemers of the world and communist lore as a gnosis, but this analogy is not sufficient to make a gnostic of Marx.

Gnosis has left an indelible imprint on other products of Western culture, for instance on Goethe's *Faust.* During the nineteenth century, several Romantic poets seemed to reinvent gnostic myth, to describe a position that was no longer gnostic but was essentially nihilistic. These poets were P. B. Shelley (*Prometheus Unbound,* 1818–1819), Lord Byron (*Cain,* 1821), Giacomo Leopardi (*Ad Arimane,* 1833), Alphonse de Lamartine (*La chute d'un ange,* 1837), Victor Hugo (*La fin de Satan,* 1854–1857), and Mihail Eminescu (*Muresanu* and *Demonism,* 1872). Apart from Leopardi, who was acquainted with ancient gnosticism, the other writers were compelled to invent mythologies that corresponded, sometimes in detail, with gnostic mythologies (this is especially true of Byron and Eminescu). Their desire to foster human liberation from the bonds of Christianity, especially as far as its Old Testament inheritance was concerned, stimulated these inventions. One way or another, each of these Romantics arrived at the Marcionite idea that the god of the Old Testament, who is also creator of this world, is an evil god who must be opposed. Only Shelley set against this evil god a sort of transcendent pleroma and a supreme and bounteous Father. Byron and the other poets eliminated this distinctive gnostic feature from their literary myths. For them, the world and man had become worthy of salvation from the clutches of the religious tyrant, and a sort of active nihilism was the way to reach that goal. This position of the Romantics was precisely the reverse of the gnostic position, insofar as the latter expressed a metaphysical denial of the world on behalf of transcendence, while the former expressed a nihilistic denial of transcendence on behalf of this world. Thus, while the mythological products of Romanticism were surprisingly akin to those of gnosticism, they were expressive of a completely different ideology.

In recent scholarship, the confusion between gnosticism and modern nihilism has grown. All sorts of philosophical and literary works were labeled as "gnostic" because of their nihilistic implications. Only in a few cases are analogies with gnosticism meaningful, for instance in the case of the philosopher Theodor W. Adorno, who reinvented several gnostic myths (e.g., the myth of the descent of the Great Ignorance upon the modern world in his *Minima Moralia* of 1944–1947; this myth was expressed in another form by the secondcentury gnostic Basilides).

Gnosticism has been a source of inspiration for a few modern writers, such as Anatole France (1844–1924), Aleksandr Blok (1880–1921), Albert Verwey (1865–1937), and Hermann Hesse (1877–1962). Social criticism took on gnostic accents in the novel *The Master and Margaretha* (1966) of the Russian writer Mikhail Bulgakov (1891–1940). The psychologist C. G. Jung (1875–1961) was very impressed by gnostic imagery and even produced in 1915–1916 a "gnostic" work, *Septem Sermones ad Mortuos,* inspired by Basilides' speculations.

In modern philosophy and literary criticism, the words *gnosis* and *gnostic* tend to be indiscriminately used to indicate the nihilistic character of a specific school of thought, the presence of a transcendental capacity in man, the emanationistic character of a system, or simply some "knowledge," esoteric or not. Such use of the word *gnosis* has little to do with gnosticism, which is characterized by dualism and extreme metaphysical nihilism. Even modern religious scholarship has not thus far come to agreement on the meaning of *gnosis* in its stricter sense. Louis Massignon and Henry Corbin, for instance, have enlarged the concept of "Islamic gnosis" to include many authors and trends of Islam that have nothing to do either with the *ghulāt* or with the Ismāʿīlīyah. Eric Voegelin, in *Science, Politics, and Gnosticism* (Chicago, 1960), defined gnosis broadly, both as a Christian heresy and as a perennial antinomian tendency worthy of condemnation. If gnosis was a *Weltreligion,* as Gilles Quispel asserts in *Gnosis als Weltreligion* (Zurich, 1951), this was due entirely to the historical continuity between gnosticism, Marcionism (sometimes considered a form of gnosticism), Manichaeism, Priscillianism, Paulicianism, the *ghulāt,* the Ismāʿīlīyah, Bogomilism, Catharism, and Lurianic Qabbalah.

Romantic mythology is nihilistic, not gnostic, and the history of modern nihilism has to be kept apart from the history of gnosticism. The same confusion between gnosis and nihilism occurs in the works of those authors who have tried to show, for instance, that existential philosophy or modern biology is "gnostic." The too liberal use of the words *gnosis* and *gnostic* can only bring these terms to semantic impoverishment, without any real profit for modern scholarship.

[*For discussion of Christian interpretations of some movements referred to in the foregoing article, see* Heresy, *article on* Christian Heresies; Marcionism; Manichaeism, *article on* Manichaeism and Christianity; Cathari; *and* Waldensians. *For Islamic interpretations, see* Shiism; Ismāʿīlīyah; Qarāmiṭah; ʿAlawīyūn; *and* Druze. *For Jewish interpretations, see* Qabbalah.]

BIBLIOGRAPHY

A somewhat dated but not unreliable survey of the history of heresy from Priscillianism and Paulicianism to Catharism is Ignaz von Döllinger's *Beiträge zur Sektengeschichte des Mittelalters,* vol. 1, *Geschichte der gnostisch-manichäischen Sekten im frühen Mittelalter* (1890; reprint, New York, 1960). Döllinger emphasizes the historical continuity between ancient gnosticism and medieval heresy but makes no distinctions between gnostic, Marcionite, and pauperistic trends. An up-to-date bibliography on this problem can be found in Giulia Sfameni Gasparro's "Sur l'histoire des influences du gnosticisme," in *Gnosis: Festschrift für Hans Jonas,* edited by Barbara Aland (Göttingen, 1978).

The most reliable monographs on Shīʿī gnosis are Heinz Halm's *Kosmologie und Heilslehre der frühen Ismāʿīlīya* (Wiesbaden, 1978) and *Die islamische Gnosis* (Munich, 1982).

On the history of medieval heresy, there is a succinct but useful general presentation by Malcolm Lambert, also containing the best bibliographical survey to date, *Medieval Heresy: Popular Movements from Bogomil to Hus* (London, 1976).

On Lurianic Qabbalah and its influence on the Shabbatean messianic movement of the seventeenth century, the best survey to date is Gershom Scholem's *Sabbatai Sevi: The Mystical Messiah, 1626–1676* (Princeton, 1973).

Gnosis und Politik, the proceedings of a symposium edited by Jacob Taubes (Paderborn, West Germany, 1984), is a well-documented collection of essays on several theories concerning gnosis and the history of modern ideas, from the beginning of the nineteenth century to date.

7 WITCHCRAFT

JEFFREY BURTON RUSSELL

The term *witchcraft* embraces a wide variety of phenomena. The word *witch* derives from the Old English noun *wicca,* "sorcerer," and the verb *wiccian,* "to cast a spell." The original concept of witchcraft is sorcery, a web of beliefs and practices whose purpose is to manipulate nature for the benefit of the witch or the witch's client. Three quite different phenomena have been called witchcraft. The first is simple sorcery, which is found worldwide in almost every period and every culture. The second is the alleged diabolical witchcraft of late medieval and early modern Europe. The third is the pagan revival of the twentieth century. This article will distinguish sharply among these three phenomena, because the connections between them are tenuous and few.

SIMPLE SORCERY

The simplest sorcery is the mechanical performance of one physical action in order to produce another, such as performing sexual intercourse in a sown field to assure a good harvest or thrusting pins into an image to cause an injury. However, sorcery often goes beyond the merely mechanical to invoke the aid of spirits. Thrusting pins into the image of a god is usually intended to release latent divine power rather than to cause harm, but such power may also be sought by direct appeal. For example, if a member of the Lugbara tribe of Uganda was injured, he went to the shrines of his dead ancestors and invoked their aid. The distinction between the magical invocation of a god and religious prayer to a god is not clear, but the tendency of magic is to attempt to compel, or at least assure, the god's assistance, whereas the tendency of religion is to implore or beseech his cooperation.

Simple sorcery, which can also be called low magic, is usually practiced by the uneducated and unsophisticated. It assumes a magical worldview, implicitly and preconsciously, in distinction to the sophisticated magical worldview of high magicians such as astrologers and alchemists, whose philosophy is often highly structured. High magic is quite different from low magic, or simple sorcery, and has never been called witchcraft. The magical worldview professed explicitly by the high magicians and held implicitly by many sorcerers is a belief in a coherent universe in which all the parts are interrelated and affect one another. In such a universe a relationship exists between individual human beings and stars, plants, minerals, and other natural phenomena. Both science and magic make this assumption, but where science looks for empirically demonstrable connections, magic assumes a nexus of occult, hidden connections. High magic resembles natural science; simple sorcery resembles technology. A sorcerer fertilizes his field by slitting a rooster's throat over it at midnight, a technologist by spreading steer excrement on it at dawn.

The thought processes of sorcery are intuitive rather than analytical. They often spring from an emotionally charged experience that becomes a critical incident in one's life. In a rage you curse someone who has offended you; shortly afterward the person dies; you are filled with sensations of power and guilt; henceforth you are convinced that certain powers are available to you. Empirical methodology ignores such critical events because they cannot be verified by repetition, but societies whose worldviews are not empirical regard such events as direct and convincing evidence.

The Azande of the southern Sudan distinguished three types of sorcery. One was a benevolent magic involving oracles, diviners, and amulets; it was aimed at promoting fertility and good health and at averting evil spells. This benevolent magic was an accepted means of achieving justice in Zande society. The second kind of sorcery was aimed at harming those whom one hated or resented, perhaps for no just cause. A means of distorting or unbalancing justice, it was condemned as antisocial. The third kind was peculiar to the Azande: possession of *mangu,* an internal spiritual power that a male Azande could inherit from his father and a female from her mother. Those possessing *mangu* held meetings at night at which they feasted and practiced magic; they used a special ointment to make themselves invisible; they sent out their spirits to seize and eat the souls of their victims; they had sexual relations with demons in the form of animals. They represented essential evil and were a source of terror to the other Azande. Yet the Azande used them as helpful scapegoats; every misfortune befalling the Zande community or an individual Azande could be blamed upon the dreaded *mangu.*

Sorcery ordinarily fills certain societal functions. In some societies it merges with public religion, and a priest or priestess may perform ritual acts to make rain, ripen the harvest, procure peace, or ensure victory in war. When such acts are performed publicly and for the public good, they are as close to religion as they are to magic and are generally considered to have a positive social function. But when they are performed privately and for private purposes, they are often regarded with suspicion. The Voodoo cults of Haiti and the Macumba cults of Brazil both make formal distinctions between public religious sorcery and private sorcery; the latter is condemned. The distinction between public and private magic often becomes the most usual distinction between "good" and "bad" magic.

Sorcery may have a variety of social functions: to relieve social tensions; to define and sustain social values; to explain or control terrifying phenomena; to give a sense of power over death; to enhance the solidarity of a community against outsiders; to provide scapegoats for community disasters; even to supply a kind of rough justice. Private sorcery has the additional functions of providing the weak, powerless, and poor with a putative way of obtaining revenge. In periods of great social tension, such as plague or defeat in war, recourse to sorcery tends to grow more common and more intense. In such situations the witches themselves may become the scapegoats for a community whose magic has failed. Under such circumstances of tension, anthropologists have observed, sorcery can often be dysfunctional, exacerbating and prolonging social tensions rather than relieving them.

Witch doctors, medicine men, or *curanderos* are sorcerers who by definition have a positive function in society, for their business is to cure victims of the effects of malevolent magic. Individuals consult witch doctors to obtain relief from disease or other misfortunes attributed to witchcraft; tribal and village authorities summon them to combat drought or other public calamities. Dances or other rituals, such as those performed by the *ndakó-gboyá* dancers of the Nupe tribe, serve to detect and repel witches and evil spirits. The *ndakó-gboyá* dancers wore tall, cylindrical disguises and identified sorcerers by nodding these weird shapes at them. Such protective sorcery assumes special social importance in times of famine, war, or other severe stress in the community.

Sorcery is less a well-defined body of beliefs and actions than a general term covering marked differences in perceptions among societies and within a given society over time. Among the Nyakyusa of Tanzania it was believed that malevolent sorcerers might be of either sex. They were often accused of eating the internal organs of their neighbors or drying up the milk of cattle. The Pondo of South Africa usually thought witches to be women whose chief crime was having sexual intercourse with malevolent spirits. One reason for the difference is that the Nyakyusa were sexually secure but nutritionally insecure and so expressed their insecurities in terms of food, whereas the Pondo were more insecure sexually and so expressed their fears in sexual terms. The function of witchcraft has changed over time among the Bakweri of Cameroon. Before the 1950s the Bakweri were threatened by poverty and a low fertility rate, and they translated these threats into widespread fear of sorcery. In the 1950s their economic status improved radically owing to a boom in the banana crop. The new prosperity occasioned first a cathartic purging of suspected sorcerers and then a decline in accusations and a relative period of calm. In the 1960s bad economic conditions returned, and fear of sorcery revived.

Patterns of sorcery exist in virtually all present societies and have existed in virtually all past societies. The classical Greco-Roman and Hebrew societies from which Western civilization sprang entertained a great variety of sorcery, from public rituals that melded with religion to the activities of the hideous hags described by the classical poet Horace. Clothed in rotting shrouds, with pale and hideous faces, bare feet, and disheveled hair, they met at night in lonely places to claw the soil with their taloned fingers and invoke the gods of the underworld. The Greeks made theoretical distinctions among three varieties of magic. The highest was *theourgia*, a kind of public liturgy "working things pertaining to the gods [*theoi*]," in which magic and religion blended. [*See* Theurgy.] *Mageia* was the next variety; its practitioners worked technical magic privately to help themselves or their clients. *Goēteia* was the lowest form; "howlers" of incantations and mixers of potions, its practitioners were crude, ignorant, and widely feared.

The sorcery of most cultures involved incantations supposed to summon spirits to aid the sorcerer. In many societies the connection between sorcery and the spirits was not explicitly formulated. But in both Greco-Roman and Hebrew thought the connection was defined or elaborated. The Greeks believed that all sorcerers drew upon the aid of spirits called *daimones* or *daimonia*. A Greek "demon" could be either malevolent or benevolent. It could be almost a god *(theos)*, or it could be a petty spirit. In the thought of Plotinus (205–270 CE) and other Neoplatonists, the demons occupied an ontological rank between the gods and humanity. The Hebrews gradually developed the idea of the *mal'akh,* originally a manifestation of God's power, later an independent spirit sent down as a messenger by God. In Greek translations of Hebrew, *mal'akh* became *angelos,* "messenger." Christians eventually identified "angels" with the Greek "demons" and defined them as beings ontologically between God and humanity. But a different element gained influence through the apocalyptic writings of the Hellenistic period (200 BCE–150 CE): the belief in evil spirits led by Satan, lord of all evil. The idea had limited precedents in earlier Jewish thought but gained prominence in the Hellenistic period under the influence of Iranian Mazdaism, or Zoroastrianism. Under such influence the Christians came to divide the Greek *daimones* into two groups, the good angels and the evil demons. The demons were supposed to be angels who, under Satan's leadership, had turned against God and thereby become evil spirits. Sorcerers sought to compel spirits to carry out their will, but angels under God's command could not be compelled; thus it was supposed that one practicing sorcery might well be drawing upon the aid of evil demons. This was the central idea of the second main variety of witchcraft, the alleged diabolism of the late medieval and Renaissance periods in Europe.

EUROPEAN WITCHCRAFT

Although simple sorcery had always existed, a new kind of diabolical witchcraft evolved in medieval and early modern Europe. The Christian concept of the devil transformed the idea of the sorcerer into that of the witch, consorter with demons and subject of Satan. Since 1880 this kind of diabolical witchcraft has been subject to four major schools of interpretation. The first, rooted in classical nineteenth-century liberalism, perceived witchcraft as an invention of superstitious and greedy ecclesiastics eager to prosecute witches in order to augment their own power and wealth. The second school, that of Margaret Murray, argued that witchcraft represented the survival of the old pagan religion of pre-Christian Europe. This religion (which never existed in the coherent form she believed) she supposed to be the religion of the majority of the people down into the seventeenth century, although subject to constant persecution by the Christian authorities. Murray's theory had great influence from the 1920s through the 1950s; unsupported by any credible evidence, it is now rejected by all scholars. The third school emphasizes the social history of witchcraft, seeking to analyze the patterns of witch accusations in Europe much as anthropologists have done for other societies. The fourth school emphasizes the evolution of the idea of witchcraft from elements gradually assembled over the centuries. Most scholars currently belong to one or the other of the last two schools.

Historical Development. The first element in diabolical witchcraft was simple sorcery, which existed in Europe as it did elsewhere. It persisted through the period of the witch craze and indeed has persisted to the present. Without this fundamental element, witchcraft would not have existed. The second, related aspect was the survival of pagan religion and folklore in Christian Europe, or rather the demonstrable survival and transmutation of certain elements *from* paganism. The Canon Episcopi, a legal document of the Frankish kingdom issued about AD 900, condemns "wicked women . . . who believe that they ride out at night on beasts with Diana, the pagan goddess. . . . Such fantasies are thrust into the minds of faithless people not by God but by the Devil." The wild ride with Diana (the classical name applied to the Teutonic fertility goddess Hilda, Holda, or Bertha) was a form of the "wild hunt," a troop of spirits following a male or female Teutonic deity. Such spirits were believed to ride out at night blowing their horns and striking down any human that had the temerity or ill fortune to encounter them.

Another element in the development of diabolical witchcraft in Europe was Christian heresy. The classical formulation of witchcraft had been established by the fifteenth century. Its chief elements were (1) pact with the Devil, (2) formal repudiation of Christ, (3) the secret, nocturnal meeting, (4) the ride by night, (5) the desecration of the Eucharist and the crucifix, (6) orgy, (7) sacrificial infanticide, and (8) cannibalism. Each of these elements derived from one or another charge made against medieval heretics. Heresy became the medium through which sorcery was linked with the Devil. At the first formal trial of heretics in the Middle Ages, at Orléans in 1022, the accused were said to hold orgies underground at night, to call up evil spirits, to kill and cremate children conceived at previous orgies and use their ashes in blasphemous parody of the Eucharist, to renounce Christ and desecrate the crucifix, and to pay homage to the Devil. The history of such charges goes at least as far back as the court of Antiochus IV Epiphanes of Syria (176–165 BCE), who made similar accusations against the Jews; the pagan Romans used them against the Christians, and the early Christians used them against the gnostics. An early eleventh-century pedant must have resurrected the charges from patristic accounts of gnostic heresy and applied them to the Orleans group, applying the archetypal thinking common in the Middle Ages: a heretic is a heretic, and whatever one heretic does another must also do. Thus the *idea* of heresy, more than any actual heresy itself, became the basis for the connection of heresy with witchcraft. Some later heretical groups, such as the sect of the Free Spirit, also were accused of similar diabolical crimes. Not all heretics were so charged, however. On the whole the accusations were limited to those who had some connection with dualism, the doctrine that not one but two eternal principles existed. One evil and one good, the two principles struggled for control of the cosmos. Dualist influence on most medieval heresies was indirect, but upon Catharism it was both direct and pronounced.

Catharism was a dualist heresy imported into western Europe from the Balkans in the 1140s. [*See* Cathari.] Strong in southern France and northern Italy for well over a century, it dominated the culture of Languedoc and the Midi in the years around 1200; it was suppressed by the Albigensian crusade and eradicated by the Inquisition. The Cathari believed that matter, and the human body in particular, were creations of the evil god, whose intent was to hold the spirit imprisoned in the "filthy tomb of the flesh." The evil god is Satan, lord of this world, ruler of all material things and manipulator of human desires for them. Money, sex, and worldly success were the domain of the Devil. These doctrines brought the Devil closer to the center of attention than he had been since the time of the Desert Fathers a thousand years earlier. If only to refute Catharist theories, scholastic theologians had to give the devil his due. The Catharist designation of Satan as the lord of the things of this world may also have led some who desired those things in the direction of Satan worship.

Scholastic theology was the next major element in the formation of the witch concept. Tradition going back to the early church fathers had suggested that the Christian community, which formed the mystical body of Christ, was opposed by an opposite group forming the mystical body of Satan and consisting of pagans, heretics, Jews, and other unbelievers. It was not only the right but the duty of the Christian to struggle against this evil host. Saints' lives and legends of the intense struggles of the desert fathers against demonic forces kept this tradition alive, and it was reinforced by Catharist dualism. In the twelfth through fourteenth centuries the Scholastics developed the tradition of the body of Satan, refined its details, and supplied it with a rational substructure. They extended the Devil's kingdom explicitly to include sorcerers, whom they considered a variety of heretic. Simple sorcerers had become, in the dominant scholastic thought of the later Middle Ages, servants of Satan.

The link between sorcerers, heretics, and Satan was the idea of pact. The notion of pact had been popularized in the eighth century by translations of the sixth-century legend of Theophilus. In this story, Theophilus was a clergyman who sold his soul to the Devil in exchange for ecclesiastical preferment. He met the Devil through a Jewish magician and signed a formal pact with "the evil one" in order to fulfill his desires. The Scholastics derived a number of sinister ideas from the legend of Theophilus. Their theory transformed the person making the pact from a relatively equal contracting party to an abject slave of Satan who abjured Christ, did feudal homage to "the dark lord," and kissed his master's genitals or backside in token of his submission. The Scholastics also broadened the idea of pact to include implicit as well as explicit consent. One did not actually have to sign a contract to be a member of Satan's army; anyone—heretic, sorcerer, Jew, Muslim—who knowingly opposed the Christian community, that is, the body of Christ, was deemed to have made an implicit pact with the Devil and to number among his servants.

The shift from Platonic to Aristotelian philosophy in the thirteenth and fourteenth centuries encouraged the process of demonizing the witches. Platonic thought allowed for the existence of a natural, morally neutral magic between divine miracle and demonic delusion; but Aristotelianism dismissed natural magic and denied the existence of occult natural forces. If no natural magic existed, it followed that wonders were worked either through divine miracle or demonic imposture. Magicians compel or exploit supernatural powers, and since God and the angels cannot be compelled or exploited, the powers with which sorcerers deal must be demonic, whether they know this explicitly or not. Thus scholastic logic dismissed simple sorcery as demonic witchcraft.

Theology, then, made a logical connection between witchcraft and heresy. Heresy is any persistently held belief counter to orthodox doctrine. One who used demons serves the Devil rather than God, and if one serves the devil, one acknowledges that correct theology involves serving the Devil rather than God: this was the worst imaginable heresy.

The final element in the transformation of sorcery into diabolical witchcraft was the Inquisition. The connection of sorcery with heresy meant that sorcery could be prosecuted with much greater severity than before. Late Roman laws against sorcery were extremely severe, but during the early Middle Ages simple sorcery, or natural magic, was treated with relative leniency. Often it was ignored; when detected, it might bring no more than a fairly stiff penance. Elements of simple sorcery were incorporated into Christian practice, as seen in the combination of Christian prayer and pagan spells commonly said by parish priests in England during the tenth and eleventh centuries. Penalties for heresy, on the other hand, were severe. Suppression of heresy in the earlier Middle Ages was inconsistent, but in 1198 Innocent III ordered the execution of those who persisted in heresy after having been convicted and excommunicated. Between 1227 and 1235 a series of decrees established the papal Inquisition. In 1233 Gregory IX accused the Waldensian heretics, who were in fact evangelical moralists, of Satan worship. In 1252 Innocent IV authorized the use of torture by the Inquisition, and Alexander IV (1254–1261) gave it jurisdiction over all cases of sorcery involving heresy. Gradually almost all sorcery came to be included under the rubric of heresy.

The Inquisition was never well organized or particularly effective; in fact, most cases of witchcraft were tried before the secular courts. Nonetheless the Inquisition provided one essential ingredient of the witch craze: the inquisitors' manuals. These manuals told inquisitors what signs of Satanism to look for, what questions to ask, and what answers to expect. Having obtained the answers they expected by using torture or the threat of torture, the inquisitors duly entered the answers in formal reports, which then added to the body of "evidence" that witches flew through the air, worshiped the Devil, or sacrificed babies. It is unlikely that no one in the period ever practiced Satanism, but it is even more unlikely that any widespread Satanism existed. The great majority of the accused were innocent, at least of diabolism.

The Witch Craze. The number of executions for witchcraft was measured in the hundreds until the end of the mid-fifteenth century, but from 1450 to 1700—the period of the Renaissance and the origins of modern science—a hundred thousand may have perished in what has been called the great witch craze. The witch craze can be explained by the dissemination, during a period of intense social unrest, of the intellectual elements summarized above by the Inquisition, the secular courts, and above all the medium of the sermon. The popularity of the sermon in the later Middle Ages and in the Reformation explains how beliefs about witches spread in a period when the leading intellectual movements, such as nominalism and humanism, downplayed or even ignored witchcraft. For example, the mystic Johannes Tauler, who was capable of great theological sophistication, was also capable of exploiting lurid demonology in his sermons in order to impress his didactic message upon his congregations. The invention of the printing press did its part in spreading the evil. In 1484 Pope Innocent VIII issued a bull confirming papal support for inquisitorial proceedings against the witches, and this bull was included as a preface to the *Malleus maleficarum* (The Hammer of Witches), a book by two Dominican inquisitors. Published in 1486, the *Malleus* went into many editions in many languages, selling more copies in Protestant and Catholic regions combined than any other book except the Bible. The *Malleus* colorfully detailed the diabolical, orgiastic activities of the witches and helped persuade public opinion that a cosmic plot directed by Satan threatened all Christian society.

Fears of cosmic plots increase in periods of high social tension. The fifteenth and sixteenth centuries witnessed a growth of eschatological anxiety, a widespread belief that the Antichrist, the return of the Savior, and the transformation of the world were at hand. As the religious split between Catholicism and Protestantism widened during the sixteenth century and flared up into religious warfare, eschatological fears deepened. Catholics saw the Protestants as soldiers of Satan sent to destroy the Christian community; Protestants viewed the pope as the Antichrist. Terror of witchcraft and prosecution of witches grew in both Catholic and Protestant regions, reaching heights between 1560 and 1660, when religious wars were at their worst. No significant differences distinguished Catholic from Protestant views of witchcraft. The Protestants, who rejected so many of the accretions of doctrine in the Middle Ages, accepted beliefs about witches almost without modification. Luther declared that all witches should be burned as heretics in league with Satan; persecutions in the regions ruled by the Calvinists were comparable to those in Catholic and Lutheran areas. Millions were persecuted and tens of millions terrified and intimidated during one of the longest and strangest delusions in history. The craze was restricted almost exclusively to western Europe and its colonies. Since diabolism is virtually meaningless outside a Christian conceptual framework, it could not spread to non-Christian areas. Although the Eastern Christian church shared the same beliefs in the powers of Satan as the Western church, it experienced no witch craze. The absence of the witch craze in the Eastern church illustrates the hypothesis that for a craze to break out, three elements are required: (1) the appropriate intellectual structure; (2) the mediation of that structure from the elite to the people at large; (3) marked social tension and fear.

Skeptics such as Johann Weyer (fl. 1563) and Reginald Scot (fl. 1584), who wrote against belief in witchcraft, were rare and were often rewarded for their efforts by persecution; Weyer, for example, was accused of witchcraft himself. More typical of the period were the works of the learned King James I of England and VI of Scotland (d. 1625). Personally terrified of witches, James encouraged their prosecution, wrote a book against them, encouraged the statute of 1604 against pact and devil-worship, and commissioned a translation of scripture (the Authorized Version or King James Bible) that deliberately rendered certain Hebrew words (such as *kashshaf*) as "witch" in order to produce texts such as "Thou shalt not suffer a witch to live," which supported the king's design of suppressing witchcraft legally. In 1681 Joseph Glanvill was still able to publish a popular second edition of a work supporting belief in diabolical witchcraft. But by that time the craze was beginning to fade. Cartesian and scientific thought had no room for witchcraft; ecclesiastical and civil authorities agreed that witch prosecutions had got out of hand; and European society was settling down to two centuries (1700–1900) of relative peace and prosperity. The greatest outburst in those centuries was the French Revolution; it occurred in an intellectual context (the Enlightenment) in which revival of witch beliefs was impossible. European society found other rationales by which to demonize aristocrats, Jews, communists, capitalists, imperialists, or whoever was selected as an object of hatred. The date of the last execution for witchcraft in England was 1684, in America 1692, in Scotland 1727, in France 1745, and in Germany 1775.

Witchcraft and Society. The most important social function of the belief in diabolical witchcraft was scapegoating. Sometimes this process was conscious and cynical, as when Henry VIII added witchcraft to the list of charges trumped up against Anne Boleyn. Much more often it was unconscious. If one is impotent, or one's crops fail, or one becomes ill, it helps to blame a witch, not only because it relieves one of guilt but also because the belief that a witch has caused one's problems gives one the illusion of being able to solve them. If God or fate has caused your illness, you may have no remedy; if a witch caused it, then you may recover once the witch has been found and punished.

Another function of the belief in the existence of witchcraft was to promote the cohesion of Christian communities by the postulation of a powerful external foe. Witches thus served a purpose similar to that of external enemies in modern warfare, for they united the people against a common threat.

Historians have noted correlations between witch accusations and social position. Persons between the ages of forty and sixty were most commonly accused; the accused had fewer children than normal; children were seldom accused of witchcraft but were often believed to be its victims; people accused of witchcraft had been previously accused of other crimes more frequently than normal, especially offensive language, lying, theft, and sex offenses. Chronic grumbling, abrasive personality, quarreling, and cursing also increased one's chances of being accused. The social status of accused witches was usually low or lower middle, though sometimes magistrates, merchants, and other wealthy persons were involved. Anyone connected with medicine, especially midwives, was prone to suspicion, because illness and death could so easily be blamed upon witchcraft.

The most striking social correlation is between witchcraft and women. Although in certain areas and for brief periods of time more men were accused than women, the opposite has almost always been true, and over the entire history of the witch craze women outnumbered men by at least three to one. In New England, for example, 80 percent of the accused were women. In the sixteenth century many more women were living alone than men. Given the patriarchal structure of European society at the time, a woman living alone without the support of father or husband had little influence and little legal or social redress for wrongs. Such women sometimes struck back at society with clandestine crimes such as arson or sorcery, which were difficult to detect. They also naturally tended to grumble or curse more than persons having effective influence in society. A physically weak, socially isolated, financially destitute, and legally powerless old woman could hope to deter only with her spells. But the explanation lies only partly in specific social conditions. The misogyny underlying the association of women with witchcraft sprang from deep and ancient psychological roots. C. G. Jung, Mircea Eliade, Wolfgang Lederer, and others have commented on the powerful ambivalence of the feminine in religions, mythologies, and literatures dominated by males. The male view of the archetypal feminine is tripartite: she is the sweet, pure virgin; she is the kindly mother; she is the vicious, carnal hag. From the twelfth century, Christian society developed a compelling symbol incarnating the first two types in the Blessed Virgin Mother of God. As the power of the symbol of the Virgin Mother grew, the shadow side, the hag symbol, had to find outlet for its corresponding power. In ancient polytheistic religions the dark side of the female archetype had been integrated with the light side in the images of morally ambivalent goddesses such as Artemis. Split off from the positive side of the archetype, the Christian image of the hag became totally evil. In the period of the witch craze, this one-sided image was projected upon human beings, and the witch, no longer simply a sorceress, became the incarnation of the hag. Other androcentric assumptions in maledominated religions encouraged the connection. God, the chief power of good, was imagined in masculine terms, and so the devil, the chief power of evil, was supposed to be masculine also. Since it was believed that the Devil's followers submitted to him sexually, it was naturally supposed that they should be women, some of whom described their intercourse with the Devil in lurid detail.

The outbreak of witch trials in Salem, Massachusetts, during 1692 has been the subject of careful social analysis. Although the first hanging of a witch in New England occurred in 1647, it was at Salem in 1692, when the craze was already fading in Europe, that the colonies produced their most spectacular series of witch trials, in which nineteen persons were executed. After a group of little girls became hysterical while playing at magic, their elders suggested that they might be the victims of a spell, and the witch hunt began. At the time, Salem village was in the throes of a long dispute concerning the church. An unpopular minister, John Bayley, was succeeded by a controversial one, Samuel Parris, in 1689, just at the time when England was undergoing a revolution and the lines of authority were blurred. The villagers split into factions supporting and opposing Parris, and, since no structured means of expressing dissent existed, its release took the form of vituperation and slander.

The outbreak was the violent expression of deeply felt moral divisions; the moral divisions were generated by the quarrel over the governance of the church, and the quarrel over governance was exacerbated by strongly felt neighborhood and family problems. Salem was a small, premodern village in which everyone knew everyone else, a situation that encouraged people to correlate unfortunate events with unpopular individuals and to blame them for their misfortunes. Intensely religious to a degree seldom paralleled in Europe at the time, the New England Puritans could not view the strife in their village in purely natural, personal, political terms. They interpreted it in religious terms, as a manifestation of the cosmic struggle between Christ and Satan, good and evil. The tradition of belief in the existence of witchcraft was a vehicle perfectly adapted to the expression of such assumptions. Many towns and villages had political controversies without becoming centers of the witch craze; clearly such controversies do not automatically produce witch accusations and cannot be considered their cause. Most sophisticated scholars give full weight to the history of religious concepts and avoid simplistic correlations between external phenomena and witch beliefs. Disasters and controversies can produce witch accusations only in the presence of certain value systems. But such social tensions, once those value systems are there, can provoke the outbreak of a witch persecution.

MODERN WITCHCRAFT

The eighteenth and nineteenth centuries in Europe, with their secularism, scientism, and progressivism, were not conducive to witch beliefs of any kind. Yet already in the nineteenth century the basis had been laid for a new permutation, which became the third main variety of witchcraft: neopaganism. Franz-Josef Mone, Jules Michelet, and other writers of the mid-nineteenth century suggested that European witchcraft was really a widespread fertility cult surviving from pre-Christian paganism. Such arguments influenced anthropologists and folklorists at the turn of the century, such as James Frazer, Jessie Weston, and Margaret Murray. A fraudulent document entitled *Aradia: The Gospel of the Witches* was published by Charles Leland in 1899. Allegedly evidence that witchcraft was the survival of a fertility cult, *Aradia* influenced Murray and other twentieth-century anthropologists. Meanwhile, interest in the occult gained fashion among intellectuals and poets such as Algernon Blackwood and Charles Baudelaire. By the early part of the twentieth century, occultism enjoyed a certain popularity, especially among dandies and bohemians, and magicians such as Aleister Crowley, who styled himself "the Great Beast," attracted a following. Their doctrines were a mixture of high magic, low sorcery, affected Satanism, hedonism, dubious historical and philosophical arguments, and mere irony.

The occult tradition of Crowley merged with the spurious fertility-cult anthropology of the followers of Margaret Murray during the 1940s and 1950s to produce a new phenomenon. Around the time that the famous litterateur Robert Graves was writing his imaginative and wholly unreliable *White Goddess* (1948) about an alleged worldwide cult of the earth and moon goddess, modern witchcraft was being created in the mind of an Englishman named Gerald Gardner. According to his followers, Gardner, who was born in 1884, was initiated into the ancient religion in 1939 by a witch of the New Forest named Old Dorothy Clutterbuck. In fact, Gardner had invented the religion on the basis of his reading of the Murrayites and Aleister Crowley, and his experiences in occult organizations such as the Hermetic Order of the Golden Dawn and Crowley's Order of the Temple of the Orient. Gardner's claim to be the mediator of an ancient religion was spurious, but he launched a growing religious movement that has gained many adherents, especially in Anglo-Saxon countries. Whatever its origins, it has become a small religious movement in its own right.

The overall world numbers of the witches must be fewer than a hundred thousand. There are numerous schismatic groups. The tenets of witchcraft as it has evolved include a reverence for nature expressed in the worship of a fertility goddess and (sometimes) a god; a restrained hedonism that advocates indulgence in sensual pleasures so long as such indulgence hurts no one; the practice of group magic aimed (usually) at healing or other positive ends; colorful rituals; and release from guilt and sexual inhibitions. It rejects diabolism and even belief in the Devil on the grounds that the existence of the Devil is a Christian, not a pagan, doctrine. It offers a sense of the feminine principle in the godhead, a principle almost entirely forgotten in the masculine symbolism of the great monotheistic religions. And its eclectic paganism promotes a sense of the variety and diversity of the godhead.

This modern neopaganism has few connections with simple sorcery, and virtually none with diabolism. Diabolism has in fact almost ceased to exist in the late twentieth century, though a few self-styled and self-conscious Satanists can be found here and there. Among other problems, Satanism suffers from a glaring contradiction: in order to worship Satan, the Satanists redefine him as good according to their own ritualistic and hedonistic views. Simple sorcery, on the other hand, continues to flourish worldwide. *Curanderos* in Mexico and the American Southwest still practice healing with herbs and charms. Fear of sorcerers persists as widely as sorcery itself. In Germany those who suspect that they are the victims of malevolent sorcery still call upon the *Hexenbanner,* professional witch doctors who sell remedies, spells, and countermagic to protect their clients from witchcraft.

Sometimes sorcery has been transmuted by conceptions taken from Christianity or other more sophisticated religions. Voodoo, for example, is a syncretistic religion pieced together from West African religions, sorcery, Christian religion, and folklore. [*See* Voodoo.] It has become the real religion of many of the people of Haiti, including those who are nominally Catholic. Voodooists worship *lwa* ("spirits") whom the Catholics claim are demons; the Voodooists claim that the *lwa* are morally ambiguous and can be summoned for good or ill. Voodoo practices are in the shadowy area between religion and magic: it is difficult to define the Voodooists' address to their spirits as either prayer or magical incantation. Yet Voodooists themselves distinguish between religion, which is good, and sorcery, which is always evil whether worked mechanically or with the help of the *lwa*. Voodoo sorcery, a mixture of European and African elements, includes incantations, spells, the use of images, rain making, and a cult of the dead.

In syncretistic cults such as Haitian Voodoo and the Macumba cult of Brazil, it is difficult to distinguish native from Christian elements, particularly because a similarity of themes worldwide seems to precede any cultural diffusion. One of the most surprising aspects of the study of witchcraft is that African, Asian, and European witchcraft all postulate the following: witches are usually female and often elderly; they meet at night, leaving their bodies or changing their shapes; they suck the blood or devour the internal organs of their victims; they kill children, eat them, and sometimes bring their flesh to the secret assemblies. Witches ride through the air naked on broomsticks or other objects; they have familiar spirits; they dance in circles; they hold indiscriminate orgies; they seduce sleeping people. The similarities go beyond the possibility of coincidence or cultural diffusion; the most likely explanation is that such ideas have an archetypal ground in the psychic inheritance shared by all humanity.

CONCLUSIONS

Witchcraft will continue to be examined theologically, historically, mythologically, psychologically, anthropologically, and sociologically. No single approach can completely explain the phenomenon; even together they do not seem to provide full understanding of such a diverse subject. Witchcraft dwells in the shadowy land where the conscious and unconscious merge, where religion, magic, and technology touch dimly in darkness. Its forms are so varied that it cannot be said to represent any one kind of quasi-religious expression. Modern, neopagan witchcraft is a naive, genial, nature religion. Simple sorcery is usually located across the border into magic yet is frequently combined with religion in two important ways: it is often incorporated into the liturgy of public religion; its charms and spells are often amalgamated into prayers. The Anglo-Saxon clergy of the tenth and eleventh centuries, for example, christianized charms by taking over from wizards the right to say them and then introducing Christian elements into them. By incorporating the sign of the cross or an invocation of the Trinity into a pagan charm, the clergy legitimized the magic. They argued that everything that occurred resulted from God's power and will, and that the use of herbs and charms simply drew upon benevolent forces that God had appointed in nature. It was essential to use them reverently, with the understanding that they were God's and that whatever one accomplished through them was achieved only by appeal to him.

Simple sorcery could be malevolent as well as benevolent. Malevolent sorcery, practiced for private, unjust purposes, was universally condemned. But in late medieval and early modern Europe, evil sorcery merged with diabolism, the result being a different dimension in the religious meaning of witchcraft. This dimension is that of transcendent, transpersonal, or at least transconscious evil.

The sense of the witch as a manifestation of an uncontrollable, superhuman force of evil is not peculiar to Christianity. The Azande, for example, considered the witch a superhuman force of evil. The witch is often on the border between mortal and spirit; she expresses the same characteristics as the Lilitu of the Sumerians, the Lilith of the Hebrews, and the *ranggda* of Malaysia, evil spirits that roam the world at night sucking blood, killing babies, and seducing sleeping men. In many societies the witch is supposed to be a wholly evil being. In Christianity, with its belief in a supernatural power of evil, the witch became a human associate of the devil, closely associated with demons and occasionally indistinguishable from them. The witch came to be seen as a pawn of Satan, a tool used in his efforts to destroy humanity and block God's plan of salvation. Thus the witch in Christianity was a minor symbol of that transpersonal evil of which Satan was the major symbol.

Many people feel that evil exists in the world to a degree far beyond what one would expect in nature, and many are not satisfied by the traditional theodicy argument that evil arises from free will (which God creates for the greater good). We observe people performing monstrous acts of destruction and cruelty against their own self-interest as well as against that of the community; and we sense in ourselves monstrous urges transcending anything that we might consciously desire. Thus a power of evil seems to exist that exceeds our own personal limitations, ignorance, and sin. This brooding, pervasive power, whose purpose is to corrupt and destroy the cosmos, may be perceived as coming from an external being, or it may be felt to operate from within the soul. In either case it transcends the conscious, and, as Jung observed, one might as well call it the devil. The witch, melding the two archetypes of human hag and evil demon, is a powerful metaphor whose power may be diminished from time to time but is unlikely to disappear.

BIBLIOGRAPHY

One bibliography of recent books on European witchcraft is Carl T. Berkhout and Jeffrey B. Russell's *Medieval Heresies: A Bibliography, 1960–1979* (Toronto, 1981), part 16, "Witchcraft," items 1809 to 1868. Anthropological and sociological works on witchcraft that are particularly significant include Maurice Bouisson's *Magic: Its History and Principal Rites* (New York, 1960); E. E. Evans-Pritchard's *Witchcraft, Oracles, and Magic among the Azande*, 2d ed. (Oxford, 1950); and Lucy Mair's *Witchcraft* (London, 1969), a good survey. The sociology and psychology of Salem witchcraft are best explored in Paul Boyer and Stephen Nissenbaum's *Salem Possessed: The Social Origins of Witchcraft* (Cambridge, Mass., 1974), and John Putnam Demos's *Entertaining Satan: Witchcraft and the Culture of Early New England* (New York, 1982). Similar treatments of European witchcraft include Alan Macfarlane's *Witchcraft in Tudor and Stuart England: A Regional and Comparative Study* (London, 1970); E. William Monter's *Witchcraft in France and Switzerland: The Borderlands during the Reformation* (Ithaca, N.Y., 1976); and Keith Thomas's *Religion and the Decline of Magic* (New York, 1971). Other works approach witchcraft from the point of view of the history of ideas: K. M. Briggs's *Pale Hecate's Team: An Examination of the Beliefs on Witchcraft and Magic among Shakespeare's Contemporaries and His Immediate Successors* (London, 1962); Julio Caro Baroja's *The World of the Witches*, translated by O. N. V. Glendinning (Chicago, 1964); Norman Cohn's *Europe's Inner Demons: An Enquiry Inspired by the Great Witch-Hunt* (New York, 1975); Mircea Eliade's *Occultism, Witchcraft, and Cultural Fashions: Essays in Comparative Religions* (Chicago, 1976); Richard Kieckhefer's *European Witch Trials: Their Foundations in Popular and Learned Culture, 1300–1500* (London, 1976); Edward Peters's *The Magician, the Witch, and the Law* (Philadelphia, 1978); Hugh R. Trevor-Roper's *The European Witch-craze of the Sixteenth and Seventeenth Centuries and Other Essays* (New York, 1969); and my own studies, *Witchcraft in the Middle Ages* (Ithaca, N.Y., 1972) and *A History of Witchcraft: Sorcerers, Heretics, and Pagans* (London, 1980).

TWO
MAGIC

8

THEORIES OF MAGIC

JOHN MIDDLETON

Magic is a word with as many definitions as there have been studies of it. In most societies it is an integral part of the sphere of religious thought and behavior; in others, especially in the industrialized West, it is more generally accepted as superstition and even as a form of sleight of hand used for entertainment. [*See* Superstition.] In addition it has almost always been thought to mark a distinction between Western and so-called primitive cultures, or between Christian and non-Christian religions. It is not really feasible to consider "magic" apart from "religion," with which it often has been contrasted, as many of the definitions of magic derive from their opposition to the nonmagical elements of religion.

Magic is usually defined subjectively rather than by any agreed-upon content. But there is a wide consensus as to what this content is. Most peoples in the world perform acts by which they intend to bring about certain events or conditions, whether in nature or among people, that they hold to be the consequences of these acts. If we use Western terms and assumptions, the cause and effect relationship between the act and the consequence is mystical, not scientifically validated. The acts typically comprise behavior such as manipulation of objects and recitation of verbal formulas or spells. In a given society magic may be performed by a specialist.

For example, a man may plant a yam, fertilize it, weed it, and, when the tuber is ripe, harvest it: this is a straightforward technical activity. He may also perform rites, cast spells, or perform other acts that are thought to help the yam grow and ripen. To a Western farmer these are magical acts and any link between them and their intended consequences is a mystical one, existing in the mind of the performer and not in any scientifically verifiable actuality. We therefore distinguish two kinds of performance. Whereas we make this distinction, however, the performers may not do so, regarding both performances as efficacious. In fact, it appears from the available ethnographic evidence that performers of magic may distinguish the two forms of activity but consider both as techniques effective each in their own way in ensuring that the yam ripens.

We must consider the kind of evidence available for the performance and efficacy of magic. Much of it is inaccurate, sensational, and inadmissible, the kind of material found in the many travelers' tales of mysterious powers possessed by exotic practitioners whose behavior they have never actually seen, or the conjuring of devils by accused witches in late medieval Europe. There are, however, other kinds of evidence. One example is the accounts of trained anthropological observers, who can speak the local languages and ask questions of the actual practitioners; another is the writings of scholars of historical societies where there is reliable documentation from original sources. An example of the first kind is the work of Bronislaw Malinowski (1935, 1948), who witnessed and described yam planting and other magical acts in Melanesia. Accounts of this kind have the immense advantage of being placed in the contexts in which the rites are carried out. Examples of the second kind are those of G. E. R. Lloyd (1979) on the ancient Greeks and Keith V. Thomas (1971) on post-seventeenth-century England.

Scholars of many kinds have been writing about magic, its aims, its origins, its methods, and its believed efficacy since before the days of the ancient Greeks. But it seems sensible here not to attempt a historical survey about magic using as sources those who have accepted its validity for themselves but rather to deal with the writers who have tried to understand the practice of magic among other societies whose systems of thought they have not shared at the outset but that they have come to understand during their researches. Little can be gained from the writings of those who could not remain objective observers: for example, the writings of the late medieval inquisitors or of King James I of England are important as data for analysis but in themselves they throw no more light on theories of magic than would the verbal statements of a Melanesian yam magician.

Certain basic questions that have been asked by writers on magic include those of the relationship of magic to science and to religion, its instrumental and technical efficacy, its social and psychological functions, its symbolism, and the nature of its thought. If we omit the once popular concern with magic's evolutionist implications—that it marks an archaic stage of cultural evolution—these questions essentially concern either the functions and efficacy of magic or the nature and processes of the system of thought that lies behind it. It has generally been accepted by those studying magic that magical performances do not "work" in an immediately technical or instrumental sense: Trobriand yams are not affected by magical spells, other than in the indirect sense that a yam farmer might take greater care of magically protected yams and that neighbors might be wary of damaging them. Clearly many cases lie on the borderline: alchemy, which contained much that is generally accepted as magic, did at times stumble onto scientifically correct relations between phenomena and events.

Questions of systems of thought deal with these same problems, but at another level, at which arise questions of symbolism, interpretation, and translation between cultures. Perhaps the most long-standing problem is anthropology (and to a lesser extent in psychology, history, and philosophy) involves the distinction between the notions of "primitive" and "civilized," a distinction that can gather such pejorative implications that the terms are now rarely used, although there are scholars who use the word *primitive* in the sense of "primal." Theories of magic have essentially been concerned with the problem of the relationship between what are usually referred to as "traditional" and "scientific" modes of thought. Other terms that have been used in this context include "prelogical/logical," "prescientific/scientific," "irrational/rational," "preliterate/literate," and "closed/open" beliefs in magic, the performance of magical rites being identified with the first term in each of the above pairs. The discussion of whether these are meaningful distinctions that actually exist between societies begins in the work of Lucien Lévy-Bruhl, discussed below. Much later work has been devoted to refining, refuting, and assessing the worth of his findings, especially once it became clear that if there are indeed two contrasting modes of thought they are normally found together in any particular society, so that references to a dichotomy between "primitive" and "civilized" are misleading.

At the risk of oversimplification it may be said that in the history of theories of magic the battle has been between what have been called the "literalists" and the "symbolists." Briefly, the literalists suggest that performance of magical actions is instrumental, so that the thought behind them (depending on the views of the writer) is either similar or dissimilar to that behind scientific experiments. Therefore the world may be divided into those societies whose magicians try to achieve a cause-and-effect relationship in events, whether technical or psychological, and those where the magician's place is taken by the scientist. The symbolists argue that this distinction misses the point. What is important for them is that magicians and scientists may or may not be trying to achieve the same results but are using different conceptual systems: they speak different "languages," the one symbolic and the other concrete, and translation or interpretation between them is meaningless until this fact is taken into account. The main questions, therefore, are those of the nature of the different modes of thought and how they may be translated into one another.

MAGIC IN SOCIAL AND CULTURAL EVOLUTION

The first important writers on magic whose views retain currency are those nineteenth-century evolutionists generally known as the Intellectualists because they based much of their work on their opinions of what prehistoric and archaic peoples would have thought about the world, as imagined from Victorian academic armchairs.

The most influential of these writers were E. B. Tylor (1832–1917) and James G. Frazer (1854–1941). Both distinguish magic from religion as distinct modes of thought and ritual performance. Both claim to base their definitions and analyses on voluminous ethnographic material, although much of it is in fact erroneous and faulty. The method, which they referred to as "comparative," suffers because the data are not placed in their social and cultural contexts; their approaches are essentially psychological in the sense that they depended upon their own assumptions about the behavior of other peoples rather than on categories formulated by those peoples themselves.

Tylor defined magical knowledge and performance as "pseudo-science": the magician and his public (Tylor's "savages") postulated a direct cause and effect link between the magical act and the intended result, whereas the link was not a scientifically valid one but one based on the association of ideas only. Tylor considered magic to be "one of the most pernicious delusions that ever vexed mankind" but nevertheless regarded it as based on a rational process of analogy that he called the "symbolic principle of magic." His predecessors had taken a belief in magic as a sign of the infantile and ignorant thinking of early mankind. To argue that "savages" were capable of rational thought, even in a scientifically unfounded context, was a significant advance. He was also concerned to demonstrate why "savages," capable of rationality, accepted magic even though it was clearly ineffective. His views, which have been accepted by all later anthropologists, were that magical and empirical behavior are often coterminous, in that natural processes often achieve what the magician claims to do; that failure can be attributed to hostile magical forces on the part of rival magicians or to the breaking of taboos; that there is great plasticity of definitions of success and failure; and that the weight of cultural tradition and authority validates the practice of magic. Finally Tylor maintained that "magic" and "religion" are complementary parts of a single cultural institution and are thus not merely stages in the evolutionary development of mankind, although he believed that magical belief and practice decrease in the later stages of human history.

The other great evolutionist of the period, Frazer, held rather different views, which have long persisted in popular thought on the subject. He built up an evolutionary scheme with three main stages of thought, each paramount in turn: magical thought he placed as the most primitive, then religious thought, and finally scientific thought. He contrasted magic with religion and with science, although he discerned certain resemblances between magical and scientific thought. He placed magic at an earlier stage in human development for three reasons: (1) because in his view it is logically simpler; (2) because it persists as superstition even in industrial societies and so forms an underlying and persistent substratum; and (3) because the Australian Aborigines (at that time taken as the extreme case of an archaic remnant people) believe in magic rather than in religion (in this, Frazer's ethnographic facts were simply incorrect). So in his schema magic was the earliest form of thought and behavior involving the supernatural; as people came to realize that magical techniques were ineffective, they postulated the existence of omnipotent gods that controlled nature and needed to be supplicated and propitiated; finally, men began to recognize the existence of empirical natural laws, first by alchemy and later by true science, and religion came to join magic as a superstition. The "evidence" for this development was virtually nonexistent outside Frazer's mind, but he fit a vast amount of data into "proving" his deductive hypothesis.

Frazer defined the magical according to his belief that magical performances are sympathetic rites based upon his Law of Similarity ("like produces like . . . an effect resembles its cause") and the Law of Contact (by which things that have been in physical contact then act upon one another even at a distance). He defined magic based on similarity as Homeopathic Magic and that based on contact as Contagious Magic, and he added taboo as negative magic acting according to the same "laws." Since much of science seemed to him also to be based on the same premises, he linked it with magic by accepting Tylor's earlier view of the existence of a rational link between cause and effect in the magician's mind, magic thus being a "spurious system of natural law." It is easy today to point to the flaws in these "Intellectualist" arguments, citing their authors' projection of their own modes of thought onto other cultures. But at the time these theories were highly influential.

Tylor and Frazer were followed by many less original scholars who refined their predecessors' somewhat crude schemata of evolution. In England were R. R. Marett (1866–1943), Andrew Lang (1844–1912), A. E. Crawley (1869–1924), and others. Marett maintained that in the earliest stages of human evolution religion could not be differentiated from magic, because at that prior preanimistic stage of development religion did not condemn magic as mere superstition. He coined the term *magico-religious,* a blanket term that has muddled the issue of the natures of magic and religion for over half a century. Marett held that magic arises from the recourse to make-believe acts that the magician considers symbolic and different from their realization and as a means of resolving emotional tensions. Magic is a substitute activity that gives courage and confidence, a view later reflected in the work of Malinowski. Crawley, writing less specifically, held that "primitive" peoples' mentalities are totally religious or superstitious, so that magic cannot be differentiated from religion, because both are based on fear in the face of an omnipotent unknown. In the United States, Alexander A. Goldenweiser (1880–1940) made the point against Frazer that magic and science are in fact not similar, in that only the scientist sees order and the working of regularities in nature, whereas the magician is unaware of them; he suggested that in early societies magic was closely linked with religion but that later they grew apart, religion becoming more centrally associated with the formal structure of society and magic assuming a place on the fringes of legality and organized religion.

These were not the only psychologically minded scholars to discuss the nature of magic. An important figure was Wilhelm Wundt (1832–1920), who held that magical thinking, as the earliest phase in the development of religious thought, was based on emotional processes, the principal one being the fear of nature, which appears hostile to human well-being and which is conceptualized as an evil force that can be controlled by magic. In the same line of development came Gerardus van der Leeuw (1890–1950), who maintained that the magician believes that he can control the external world by the use of words and spells, and Sigmund Freud (1856–1939), whose notion of the omnipotence of thought was basic to his argument. Primitive magical rites and words correspond to the obsessional actions and spell-like speech of neurotics, who believe that they can affect reality by their own thoughts and wishes. Freud accepted the gross evolutionist schema of Frazer as a parallel to the psychological development of the individual. It is tension in the face of the sense of impotence that gives rise to magical thought both in the child and in early man: magic is wish fulfillment. Unfortunately this analogy has no basis in the ethnographic data supplied by anthropologists and must be considered a "just-so story" that puts a pattern of coherence into Freud's psychological work but tells us little of the nature of magic and magical thought.

THE SOCIOLOGY OF MAGIC

In the years around 1900 the works of other kinds of thinkers became influential and have continued to be more so than that of the Evolutionists and Intellectualists. The principal theorists among these more sociologically minded scholars were Émile Durkheim (1858–1917), Marcel Mauss (1872–1950), and Lucien Lévy-Bruhl (1857–1939) in France and Max Weber (1864–1920) in Germany.

The three French writers followed Auguste Comte in substituting sociological explanations of social processes for psychological ones. For them religion, including magic, is a social fact, brought into existence by collective action and then possessing an autonomy of its own; it is not merely an illusion (Durkheim realized that the religious and the magical persist in "scientifically" based societies). The "religious" is defined as sacred, a realm set apart by the religion's adherents, whose beliefs and rites unite them into a single moral community or church. Religion is a collective practice, there being no religion without a church in the sense used above. Magic, however, is an individual affair in the sense that although magical rites are also collectively defined as being sacred, the magician has a clientele and not a church. In magic, therefore, the function of ritual to fortify the faith of the group is lacking, and instead the magician attempts to bring about certain consequences by the use of magical or sacred objects and words. Durkheim's study of magic formed an unimportant part of his main study of Australian Aboriginal religion (Durkheim, 1912) and seems to be included there mainly for completeness of his treatment of what had conventionally been included under the "religious." However, in a sense the gap had already been filled by Marcel Mauss's essay of eight years earlier, wherein he set out his general theory of magic (Hubert and Mauss, 1904). Here he preceded Durkheim in defining a magical rite as "any rite which does not play a part in organized cults—it is private, secret, mysterious and approaches the limit of a prohibited rite." Both Mauss and Durkheim thus defined magic not by the structure of its rites but by the circumstances in which these rites occur. Much of Mauss's book is taken up with the relationship of magic to religion and science, the latter being similar to magic by analogy, the former being similar to magic in that both are based on beliefs in *mana* and the sacred.

Lévy-Bruhl (1910) did not present any theories of magic as such, but he was centrally concerned with the mode of thought, which he called prelogical or prescientific, that most later writers have associated with belief in magic. He argued that modern Western societies are scientifically oriented in their thought whereas "primitive" societies are mystically oriented toward using the supernatural to explain unexpected and anomalous events. Prescientific "collective representations" inhibit cognitive activities that would contradict them, so that events attributed to causes that are prescientific are not put to objective verification. "Prescientific" or "prelogical" thought (Lévy-Bruhl was later to withdraw the latter term) contravenes the rules of science and Western logic, but otherwise it is rational and builds up into a single coherent system. Examples are beliefs in the effects of witchcraft or of magical rainmaking. It is important to realize that Lévy-Bruhl stresses the content of thought, which is determined by a society's culture, and not the process of thinking, which is not a social phenomenon but a psychological and physical one (a point on which he has often been misunderstood). A person's perceptions are determined by his culture's notions of the social and ritual value of those elements of experience that are perceived rather than merely being seen: that is to say, "primitives" do not perceive "mystically" because they are some way mentally inferior but perceive phenomena as significant on account of the mystical properties given to them by the culture. Lévy-Bruhl called such thought "mystical" because "primitive" thought, unlike Western scientific thought, does not distinguish between the "natural" and the "supernatural" but considers them to be a single system of experience. There is therefore a "mystical participation" between the "primitive" and what Western science would call the natural, the social, and the supernatural, a participation that composes the "primitive's" total social personality.

In Germany the scholar Max Weber was working on somewhat different yet related problems. He was particularly interested in the problem of rationality and its relationship to economic and political growth and development and based his work mainly on comparisons between precapitalist religions in Europe and in China and India. His main argument was that magic has been the most widespread form of popular religion in pre- and proto-industrial societies and that in many parts of the world (especially in Asia, where capitalism might have been expected to develop early but did not) the recourse to magic prevented the rationalization of economic life. Before this rationalization "the whole world is full of magical powers working in an irrational fashion," a generalization that Weber held particularly true of peasant societies. The power of magic might be broken by the appearance of prophets (of whom magicians were the precursors) who introduced new and rational schemes of reward and salvation. As will be mentioned below, much of the significance of Weber's work lies precisely in his views as to the relationship between the decline of magic and advances in technology: for him the former was a necessary forerunner of the latter, a view that has since met with considerable and sustained opposition from more "literalist" writers.

MAGIC IN ITS SOCIAL AND CULTURAL SETTING

The writers just mentioned were the last of the classic anthropologists and sociologists to have written about magic. Their successors based their findings and hypotheses on their own field research, where the importance of what people who believe in magic actually do and say about it and of the social contexts of their actions and statements become evident. The era of armchair scholars, however brilliant, was over. On the other hand, most recent work may be seen at one level to be based largely on proving, disproving, and refining the theories of the classic scholars. The later researches and reports may be usefully divided into the "literalists" and the large and more diverse group of "symbolists," although it must be stressed that these labels are only rough and ready ways of identifying them.

The leading literalist was the Polish-born Bronislaw Malinowski (1884–1942), the first important anthropologist to present a coherent theory of magic based upon his own field research in the Trobriand Islands of Melanesia during the first world war. He recognized that among the Trobriand Islanders what is generally defined as magic is quite different from religion: religion refers to the fundamental issues of human existence while magic always turns round specific, concrete, and detailed problems. For the Trobriand Islanders magic was of several kinds and had several functions. First, its use lessens chance and risk and induces confidence in activities where risk is high and/or linked to techniques that may therefore easily be ineffective. His famous example is that of the use of magic when fishing in the open sea but not when fishing in the shallow lagoon. Besides acting as an extension to the technical, magic extends men's abilities into the realm of the miraculous, as with love magic, by which an ugly man attracts beautiful women, old men become rejuvenated, or a clumsy dancer becomes an agile one. And magic can also extend into the super-material or super-moral, as with the use of black or evil magic, or sorcery, that is thought to kill at a distance: magic is to be expected and generally to be found whenever man comes to an unbridgeable gap, a hiatus in his knowledge or in his powers of practical control, and yet has to continue in his pursuit.

However, he goes further, in an important way: he stresses that the islanders' land is well watered and fertile and their sea rich in fish, so that the use of magic is not merely an extension of technical competence. The production of food provides, in addition to physical nourishment, a means of gift-giving and exchange whereby interpersonal bonds are recognized and prestige made and kept. Magic protects people from failure and enables them to achieve success in which emotional and social involvement are high. Magic raises the psychological self-confidence of its believers, may help them achieve higher stages of technological and moral development, and may enable them better to organize their labor and to control the cooperative work on which the well-being of society's members depends: magic "ritualizes man's optimism." Malinowski stressed also that among the Trobriand Islanders the basis of magic lies in the immaculate saying and transmission of words and spells, which are validated by myth that creates an inviolable tradition as to the magic's efficacy.

Malinowski projected his findings among the Trobriand Islanders onto all mankind, making their particular cultural beliefs, thoughts, motives, and actions into universals, and he has rightly been criticized for so doing. But at the same time he did witness and participate in the magical practices of a "primitive" people: he was not adducing the functions of magic from his own thoughts as to what they might do and think but started from the ethnographic experience itself. It is true that, although he came to know the Trobrianders well, he may be suspected of projecting his own thoughts, emotions, and motives onto them when discussing the psychological functions of magic that he considered so central. Nonetheless, Malinowski revolutionized the study of magic.

Malinowski was essentially a successor to Frazer (who wrote the introduction to his first book on the Trobriand Islanders, [1922]. The first important immediate successor to the writers of the sociological school of Durkheim and Mauss was A. R. Radcliffe-Brown (1881–1955), who carried out research among the Andaman Islanders of the Bay of Bengal ten years before Malinowski's Trobriand work and published *The Andaman Islanders* in 1922, a book that was a landmark in the development of anthropological studies of religion and magic. In his work he does not rigidly differentiate between religion and magic. The Andamanese recognize certain objects and substances as possessing magical qualities in the sense that a magician may use them to cure sickness, control the weather, and the like. The magician acquires magical power and knowledge by coming into contact with spirits that possess a mystical power that is both dangerous and beneficial, for which Radcliffe-Brown uses the Polynesian word *mana*.

He argues that the power of spirits and the substances and objects in which *mana* is manifest, or can be made manifest by a magician, is used to mark the importance of social position when the latter is being changed (e.g., at birth, death, in sickness). When undergoing these transitions people become vulnerable to the dangers inherent in *mana,* and so they must observe taboos and fears of pollution, which are removed by the use of this power in a magical performance. By this means the community is kept aware of the importance of cooperative ties between its members and, thus, of their sense of interdependence. The rites both give confidence to the individual and (more importantly, in Radcliffe-Brown's view) demonstrate the importance of the activities magic marks off in this way—fishing for large animals, for example. These are important precisely because they represent communal activities and dangers and so emphasize the importance of dependence of members on one another. In brief, Radcliffe-Brown introduced to theories of magic the new dimension of ritual and social value and played down its relationship to technical knowledge and science.

THE LATER "SYMBOLISTS"

Behind the work of both Malinowski and Radcliffe-Brown lay the problem of Lévy-Bruhl, that of the nature of the "prelogical" or magical mode of thought and worldview, for which the terms "mythopoeic" and "prescientific" have also been used. Since his work there has been continual discussion on the points that he raised. The most important figure in this context has been E. E. Evans-Pritchard (1902–1973), whose *Witchcraft, Oracles, and Magic among the Azande* (1937) has been the most influential of all writings on these topics. Like Radcliffe-Brown and Malinowski, Evans-Pritchard carried out extensive field research, in his case among the Azande people of the southwestern Sudan, largely with the intention of testing Lévy-Bruhl's hypotheses. His book deals with Zande views on mystical causation in the contexts of accusations of witchcraft, of the use and working of oracles and divination to determine the identity of witches, and of the recourse to magic and the performances of magicians. He presents a detailed firsthand account of Zande magical beliefs and practices, setting them in their social contexts and stressing especially the modes of thought and the "collective representations" that lie behind them. Zande magic is based on the use of "medicines," mainly plants and vegetable substances, in which lie magical powers, that are inert until activated by the verbal spells of the "owner," the magician, and which may be used for protection, production, and punishment of evildoers.

Most magical performances are private, carried out by individuals, but there are also public magicians who perform magic that has consequences such as war, rain, and vengeance for death. Magic is in the hands of men, who consider themselves more responsible to use these powers than are women.

In an earlier paper, published in 1929, Evans-Pritchard contrasted Zande magic with that of the Trobriand Islanders described by Malinowski. Among the former there is no concept akin to that of *mana* that provides the power of magical objects for the Trobrianders, and the spell is of less importance and used essentially as a directive to the mystical power of the "medicines." Whereas among the Trobrianders magic is "owned" by clans, as are the myths that validate it, among the Azande it is spread out among the entire community, the distinction being due to differences in social organization, ownership of land and crops, and political authority. Evans-Pritchard emphasized the social context far more than did Malinowski and also stressed that magic cannot be understood as an isolated phenomenon but only as part of a "ritual complex" composed of magic, witchcraft, divination, and oracles; indeed, without belief in witchcraft Zande magic would have little meaning. Making an important point that went back to that made far earlier by Radcliffe-Brown, he concluded that the main objective of the use of magic is not to change nature but rather to combat mystical powers and events caused by other people. It followed that the long-argued link between magic and science falls away: it is the network of social links, tensions, and conflicts that is central.

Evans-Pritchard also discussed the reasons that magic persisted despite what would appear to be its frequent failure: believers in magic have a "closed" system of thought that inhibits verification in a scientific sense. His argument goes back to Lévy-Bruhl and has been taken up by later writers who have contrasted closed and open systems of thought, a dichotomy that has perpetuated the long-standing contrast between magic and science. Lévy-Bruhl had remarked that ignorance is culturally determined, and Evans-Pritchard stressed that what appeared to be failures in magical performances were attributed by the Azande not to their inefficacy in a technical sense but to failure of the magician to perform the magical rites correctly and to the counter-activities of hostile magicians or witches: the system answers its own problems in its own terms.

Later writers, in particular Robin Horton, have enlarged on the contrast between open systems of thought, where efforts are made objectively to prove or disprove hypothesized causal relations between scientific acts and natural consequences, and closed systems of thought, where this kind of verification is not attempted and success and failure are seen in the light of the already culturally accepted worldview. Other writers, especially those in *Modes of Thought,* a collection of essays edited by Horton and Ruth Finnegan in 1973, enlarged on the social and cultural factors, like literacy or division of labor, associated with this basic distinction between closed and open systems.

The discussion was taken further by suggesting that although the causal links in both magic and science are based on analogy, as had been said by Frazer and all later writers on magic (although using such terms as metaphor, metonymy, homeopathy, and the like), the analogies were of different kinds. Stanley J. Tambiah, for example, distinguishes "scientific" analogy from "persuasive," "rationalizing," or "evocative" analogy. He points out that the Azande themselves recognize the analogical or metaphorical basis of magical performances that have as their aim the transferral of a particular property or quality to a recipient person or object: because of the similarity and/or difference between two objects, the magical rite transfers the desirable quality of the one to the other. The performance of the magical rites achieves and marks changes of quality or state through the "activation" of the analogy by the "performative" rite of magic.

The implication of these remarks is that the discussion of magic has widened in recent years from its relationships to religion and science to the mode of culturally determined thought behind it and to the social contexts of magical performances. The discussion has relied largely on the pioneering work of Lévy-Bruhl and Evans-Pritchard, but it has not all taken place among their anthropological followers. Important work has been done by philosophers such as Peter Winch and Martin Hollis, classicists such as G. E. R. Lloyd and E. R. Dodds, and others. A historian whose work merits mention here is Keith V. Thomas; his *Religion and the Decline of Magic* is concerned with the factors that led to the decline of magic in England from the seventeenth century onward. He stresses that, historically, magic cannot be separated from astrology and witchcraft, the relationship between them being both intellectual and practical.

Before the seventeenth century, religion and magic could not easily be distinguished, but with the rise in England of forms of Protestantism there came a separation between the two and the importance of magic declined. Thomas follows Weber in seeing this decline as permitting the "rationalization" of economic life, but he analyzes the historical situation with greater subtlety. He suggests that factors that led to the decline of magic included the growth of popular literacy and education, greater individual mobility, the development of forms of banking and insurance, and the rise of the new disciplines of economics, sociology, and statistics that were to remove much chance and uncertainty from everyday life. He also stresses the importance of optimism and aspirations in science and in medicine: even though available technology had not yet greatly advanced, people considered that it could and would. For the history of English magic, at least, he considers the views of Weber as of more relevance than those of Malinowski: even if the latter are correct for the Trobriand Islanders they are not so for what have become industrial societies. Malinowski's view, put neatly by Godfrey and Monica Wilson as "magic is dominant when control of the environment is weak," can be shown not to hold for "historical" and industrial societies.

Another influential scholar in this context is Claude Lévi-Strauss, who has been concerned for many years with the nature of the magical worldview. He made the point that by his performance the magician is making "additions to the objective order of the universe," filling in links in a chain of causation between events that are distant from each other in space or in time. Magic may therefore be seen as a "naturalization of human actions—the treatment of certain human actions as if they were an integral part of physical determination," whereas in contrast religious rites bring about a "humanization of natural laws." Religion and magic there imply each other and are in that sense complementary and inseparable, neither having priority of any kind over the other.

Lévi-Strauss has suggested that the notion is similar to that of *mana*. Both are subjective notions, used by Westerners to mark off "outside" thought as different from our own "scientific" thought and by the Azande (for example) to distinguish surrounding peoples as more involved with magic and thus inferior to themselves (much as Westerners might call other peoples "superstitious" rather than "religious"). If magic is a subjective notion in that sense then it can have little or no meaning in cross-cultural analysis and understanding. The concept of magic is in itself empty of meaning and thus susceptible to the recognition of any meaning that we care to give to it; following this, Lévi-Strauss has implied that the category of magic must be "dissolved."

Lévi-Strauss's observations notwithstanding, magic remains a category that has been and is used in accounts of systems of belief and ritual and so does merit continued discussion. Rather like the notion of totemism, which has also been "dissolved" by Lévi-Strauss, its shadow remains, and to understand most writings on comparative religion, its history as a concept must be analyzed. This cannot yet be the final word, and arguments about magic indeed continue, but essentially in the wider contexts of differentiation between culturally determined modes of thought and forms of society rather than in the earlier terms of its relationship to religion and science.

[*See also* Witchcraft; Miracle; *and* Spells. *For further discussion of the history of theory, see the biographies of the scholars mentioned herein.*]

BIBLIOGRAPHY

Three important studies of theories of religion in general warrant mention here. E. E. Evans-Pritchard's *Theories of Primitive Religion* (Oxford, 1965) is an excellent summary of anthropological theories of religion and magic, with emphasis on the work of Tylor, Frazer, Durkheim, and Lévy-Bruhl. *Modes of Thought,* edited by Robin Horton and Ruth Finnegan (London, 1973), is a collection of essays on the differences between magical and scientific worldviews, and Claude Lévi-Strauss's *La pensée sauvage* (Paris, 1962), translated as *The Savage Mind* (London, 1966), is a brilliant discussion of the same problem.

Of the numerous works on magic, five are classic. James G. Frazer's *The Golden Bough,* abr. ed. (London, 1922), is a summary of his twelve-volume third edition, a mass of ill-comprehended data that has had enormous influence far beyond its real importance. Henri Hubert and Marcel Mauss's "Esquisse d'une théorie générale de la magie," *Année sociologique* 7 (1904), translated as *A General Theory of Magic* (London, 1972)—the first sociologically oriented discussion of magic—is based on acute analysis of the data then available. Émile Durkheim's *Les formes élémentaires de la vie religieuse* (Paris, 1912), translated as *The Elementary Forms of the Religious Life* (1915; reprint, New York, 1965), is a highly influential study of Australian totemic religion. Lucien Lévy-Bruhl's *Les fonctions mentales dans les societés inferieures* (Paris, 1910), translated as *How Natives Think* (London, 1926), is a seminal work that, although outdated, has led to much fruitful work on the magical worldview. Max Weber's *The Sociology of Religion,* edited and translated by Talcott Parsons (Boston, 1963), contains passages on the problems of rationality from several of Weber's original German works.

Later basic anthropological accounts of magic include Bronislaw Malinowski's *Coral Gardens and Their Magic,* 2 vols. (London, 1935), a detailed ethnographic account of Trobriand magic, and *Magic, Science and Religion* (New York, 1948), a collection of earlier papers on Trobriand religion and magic. A. R. Radcliffe-Brown's *The Andaman Islanders* (1922; 3d ed., Glencoe, Ill., 1948) is an ethnographic account that has had great influence. E. E. Evans-Pritchard's *Witchcraft, Oracles, and Magic among the Azande* (1937; 2d ed., Oxford, 1950), the most important anthropological account yet published on the working of magic, has influenced all later work on the subject. Also noteworthy is his brilliant comparative essay "The Morphology and Function of Magic: A Comparative Study of Trobriand and Zande Ritual and Spell," *American Anthropologist* 31, (1929): 619–641, reprinted in *Myth and Cosmos,* edited by John Middleton (Garden City, N.Y., 1967).

Finally, there are two important historical works that deserve mention: Keith V. Thomas's *Religion and the Decline of Magic* (London, 1971), a historical account of the decline of magic in England since the seventeenth century, and G. E. R. Lloyd's *Magic, Reason, and Experience: Studies in the Origins and Development of Greek Science* (Cambridge, 1979), an innovative study of the relationships between magic and science.

9 MAGIC IN EAST ASIA

Donald Harper

Magic and mantic arts are endemic in Chinese life and prominent in the religions of China, both in popular religion and in Buddhism and Taoism. The same is true of Korea and Japan, where indigenous beliefs have been overlaid by the cultural influence of China. The magical practices of China found ready acceptance in Korea and Japan. Although many of the practices traveled on their own, religion—chiefly Buddhism, which had already absorbed elements of Chinese popular beliefs and of Taoism—was an important vehicle for the transfer of Chinese magic. The result was an amalgam of magical lore in East Asia, with Chinese knowledge often providing a frame to which specifically Korean or Japanese practices and permutations were affixed.

CHINA

In general, we should distinguish between magic, which provides a means to accomplish specific ends (through spells, gestures, amulets, talismans, and the like), and various occult sciences (such as yarrow-stalk divination with the *Book of Changes*, astrology, hemerology, geomancy, and alchemy), even though this distinction was not strongly maintained in the traditional Chinese schema of magic and the occult. There was in fact a fluid boundary between magic (where there was no cause for rationalization) and occult sciences, which were elaborated in terms of a theory of symbolic correspondence based on the concepts of *yin-yang* dualism and of Five Actions (*wu-hsing*: water, fire, wood, metal, and earth). Not only was this theory the product of prior conceptions of the magical power of fire, water, and other primary forces in nature (e.g., wind), but even after its full elaboration the symbolic correspondences did not negate the validity of magical practices. Not infrequently, occult theory supplied a *modus operandi* for magic and religious worship. For example, an astrological instrument designed to calculate the position of the Big Dipper (Chinese archaeology has recently brought to light a second century BCE specimen of the device) was used by the usurper Wang Mang to direct the power of the Dipper against his enemies in 23 CE. From the beginning, this astrological instrument served as one means for conjuring the god of the Dipper and polestar (talismanic replicas of the constellation cast in metal were also used). The same instrument was influential in Taoist star magic, and it was the model for an astrological *mandala* in the esoteric Buddhism of the T'ang period (618–907 CE). Similarly, the hemerological symbols of the calendrical cycle were not simply neutral signs marking the passage of time; they constituted a succession of spirits whose magical powers could be summoned through spells and talismans.

The Warring States (403–221 BCE), Ch'in (221–207 BCE), and Han (206 BCE–220 CE) periods were the formative age for Chinese magic. Earlier, magic was employed in dealings with the spirits and was important in the royal ancestral religion of the Shang and early Chou (c. sixteenth–eighth centuries BCE). But the proliferation of magical arts, and an increasing differentiation between magic as employed in archaic religion and magic for its own sake, began during the Warring States and continued to develop in Ch'in-Han times. The history of Chinese magic in later centuries followed from the developments of this period. It was during the same period that the theory of symbolic correspondence was formulated, and developments in occult sciences paralleled significantly those in magic.

Before the Warring States the principal practitioners of magic were the *wu,* a class of female (and in lesser numbers, male) shamans who mediated between the human and spirit worlds. Their methods included trances in which spirits might descend into their bodies or in which the shaman might journey into the spirit world, invocations and maledictions, and the utilization of magical materials to either attract or repel the spirits. Their functions overlapped those of incantators *(chu)* and other ritual officiants; however, the latter did not engage in ecstatic trances. The Warring States and Ch'in-Han periods witnessed the decline in prestige of these shamans, who came to be increasingly associated with witchcraft; the rise of occult specialists *(fang-shih,* literally "masters of recipes"), whose skills extended to magical operations; and the formation of a Taoist clergy, who adapted magic to fill the needs of the newly emergent religion (organized Taoist religious communities made their first appearance in the second century CE). The general populace also practiced forms of superstitious magic in the course of daily life.

Historical records of Han rulers who favored shamans and masters of recipes provide an important source of information about ancient Chinese magic. Liu Ch'e (posthumously titled Wu Ti; r. 140–87 BCE), for example, established cults for shamans and made his court a gathering place for masters of recipes who claimed to possess magical powers and the secrets of immortality. One master of recipes, Li Shao-weng, was a psychopomp who gained Liu Ch'e's favor by conjuring the ghost of the ruler's recently deceased concubine; he was executed after he was exposed for fabricating portents. Near the end of Liu Ch'e's reign the court was paralyzed by an outbreak of a type of shamanic witchcraft known as *ku.* The word *ku* referred to a demonic affliction that attacked its victim as the result of witchcraft. According to some accounts, *ku* was a poison produced by sealing certain creatures in a vessel until only one remained, which became the *ku.* The tradition that the *ku* is a magical potion cultivated by women and passed down through generations is still alive today. Men who ingested the *ku* were believed to die and become the demon-slaves of the *ku* and its keeper. In two of the witchcraft incidents at Liu Ch'e's court the *ku* agent was discovered to be a wooden effigy buried in the ground, where it was intended to bring harm to the ruler. There were other cases of witchcraft during the Han period in which shamans were hired to work black magic.

Accusations of charlatanism against masters of recipes and fear of shamanic witchcraft were widespread during the Han period. A negative perception of magical practices crystallized around the government's concern for its own political and spiritual authority. All magic and occultism were potentially subversive. They incited social unrest and infringed upon the holiness of the monarch, whose position as the Son of Heaven made him the only legitimate authority to oversee dealings with the spirit world. Popular religious cults not under the direct control of the government were branded "abusive worship" *(yin-ssu)*, and ordinary citizens could be executed if caught illicitly performing magic or uttering imprecations. Such practices were identified as the "way of the left" *(tso-tao)*. The word *left* did not connote the sinister aspects Western cultures associate with the left. Rather, in cosmo-ritual symbolism the left was the ruler's position of honor, and those who practiced the way of the left were abusing powers belonging properly to the ruler.

The Taoist sects that arose in the second century CE inveighed against those who placed their faith in shamans, worshiped demons, and believed the occultists' shams. These practices were an offense to the true deities of the Tao. Taoist liturgy incorporated many elements of popular worship, however, and the clergy engaged in many of the magical practices that they condemned in others. Indeed, in the eyes of the Han government the Taoist sects were rebel organizations whose religion represented simply another outbreak of "abusive worship." For the Taoist sects the fundamental issue was heterodoxy—the use of magic not sanctioned by religious authority. But in the continual process of syncretization that occurred over the centuries as Taoism interacted with popular religion and with Buddhism, the standard of orthodoxy fluctuated.

The Buddhist attitude toward magic was similar. Illicit magical practices fell under the category of the "arts of Māra" *(mo-shu)*, Māra being the tempter and chief of malevolent demons. *Mo-shu* parallels other Chinese terms such as "shamanic arts" *(wu-shu)* and "way of the left" in referring to the forms of magic prohibited by the orthodox church (and the government). However, as early as the fifth century CE there was a tradition of Buddhist spell-casting in China rivaling the Taoist practices. Buddhist magic was most prominent in the esoteric practices of Tantrism. The Tantric literature contained magical formulas to be used to gain prosperity or harm adversaries; Tantric *mantras*, *mudrās*, and *maṇḍalas* were utilized as instruments for working magic. Tantric magic incorporated elements of native Chinese magic and occultism, while at the same time enriching Taoist and popular practices.

Most of our knowledge of actual magical procedures in premodern times comes from Taoist and Buddhist writing, which naturally reflect the practices of Taoism and Buddhism. Recently, Chinese archaeologists have discovered manuscripts from the third and second centuries BCE that describe magic as it was practiced in the ancient popular religion and occult tradition. Two of the manuscripts are almanacs that are strikingly similar to Chinese almanacs in use today and attest to a continuity in magic and occult practice. The Chinese almanacs combine information on portents to watch for during the year with material on spells, talismans, and other magical devices.

Many of the common forms of magic described in premodern sources are still practiced. There are spells to summon deities and to drive off demons (versions of popular, Taoist, and Buddhist spells are preserved). Spitting and spouting water over which a spell has first been uttered is another common device (sometimes Taoist or Buddhist priests will spout ignited alcohol). Substances believed to have magical properties are often identified in traditional materia medica. Amber, for example, wards off nightmare demons and is used in making headrests. Amulets to be hung in the open or worn on the body exist in many forms. Peachwood amulets are perhaps the most ancient. Talismans *(fu)* made from strips of silk and inscribed with undecipherable writing have been discovered in a second century BCE tomb. A medical manuscript discovered in the same tomb includes a recipe for curing *ku* witchcraft by burning a talisman, scattering its ashes over sheep broth, and bathing the victim with the brew. Water over which the ashes of talismans have been scattered has been used in Taoism to cure sickness since the time of the earliest Taoist sects. Taoism talismans inscribed with symbols and magic writing have many uses. The deities are summoned with talismans, which may be used in conjunction with spells. And, in addition to using the ashes, Taoists may wear talismans as phylacteries or swallow them in order for them to take effect. Love magic is represented in a second century BCE manuscript that provides recipes for two philters with which a person can "obtain the object of desire." Another example in the same manuscript is a recipe that instructs a person engaged in a lawsuit to write the opponent's name on a slip and insert it in a shoe, magically trampling the opponent.

KOREA AND JAPAN

In Korea, cults formed around female shamans were a source of native Korean magic. This popular religion is known as Mu-sok ("shamanic customs"). Contacts between Korea and China began well before the T'ang, but increased markedly during that period. Knowledge of Chinese magic and occultism was part of the general flow of Chinese culture into Korea. And the initial impact of Chinese religion—before, for example, there was a more sophisticated understanding of Buddhist theology—was an admiration for its great magical power as compared with native practices. Chinese political institutions and ethics were also influential in the formation of the early Korean kingdoms. In general, the antagonism between government and practitioners of magic, and between Buddhism and popular religion, followed along lines similar to the situation in China.

In the native religion of Japan, which came to be known as Shintō ("way of the spirits") after Buddhism took hold, there were two categories of religious personnel. The *miko* (female shaman) was a medium into whose body a spirit might descend, sharing essential characteristics with shamans throughout East Asia. The *kannushi* (spirit controller) was more in the nature of a priest who oversaw the worship of the spirits. As with the shamans in China, the *miko* were increasingly associated with witchcraft, whereas the *kannushi* came to function as officiants in the state cult. Esoteric tantric Buddhism had a strong influence in Japan, leading to a syncretism of Shintō and Chinese-Buddhist magic. Buddhist ascetics called *hijiri* (sage) and *yamabushi* (mountain recluse) traced their origins to the eighth century CE and were renowned for their magical powers. As in Korea, in Japan other forms of Chinese magic and occultism were absorbed into the culture.

BIBLIOGRAPHY

Blacker, Carmen. *The Catalpa Bow*. London, 1975. A well-documented and groundbreaking study of shamanistic traditions in Japan, both from a historical and contemporary perspective.

Chang Chu-keun. "Mu-sok: The Shaman Culture of Korea." In *Folk Culture in Korea,* edited by Chun Shin-yong, pp. 59–88. Seoul, 1982. A more popular account of Korean shamanism.

Groot, J. J. M. de. *The Religious System of China* (1892–1910). 6 vols. Reprint, Taipei, 1967. A comprehensive description of religion in China, valuable for its copious translations of primary sources.

Haguenauer, Charles M. "Sorciers et sorcières de Corée." *Bulletin de la Maison Franco-Japonaise* (Tokyo) 2 (1929): 47–65. A scholarly examination of shamanism and magic in Korea.

Ngo Van Xuyet. *Divination, magie et politique dans la Chine ancienne*. Paris, 1976. An excellent study of magic and occultism in the formative Ch'in-Han period, including a translation of the chapter of biographies of occult specialists in the *Hou Han shu* (Documents of the Later Han).

Sieffert, René. "Le monde du sorcier au Japon." In *Le monde du sorcier,* "Sources orientales," vol. 7, pp. 355–389. Paris, 1966. An excellent survey of the practice of magic in Japan, with a detailed discussion of magic in Buddhism and Shintō.

10 MAGIC IN GRECO-ROMAN ANTIQUITY

Hans Dieter Betz

From the beginning, magic was an essential part of Greco-Roman culture and religion. Over the course of history, however, it changed in appearance, scope, and importance from being an element of simple rituals to becoming highly complex systems claiming the status of science and philosophy. To the extent that magical ideas were presupposed in early agrarian and sacrificial rites, purifications, and burial customs, magic even preceded the culture of the Greeks. Later, magical beliefs and practices steadily grew in significance and diversity. In the Hellenistic period that followed Alexander the Great (d. 323 BCE), magical material increased considerably. In Classical Greece of the sixth to fifth centuries BCE, Thessaly and Egypt had already been known as the prime sources of magical knowledge; but only Hellenistic syncretism produced the abundance of material now available. Within the Greco-Roman world magic formed to some extent a common tradition, yet at the same time each cultural region put its own stamp on it. The main traditions were those of Greek, Greco-Egyptian, Roman, Jewish, and Christian magic. While clearly distinguishable, these cultural contexts also overlapped to a considerable degree and produced a variety of syncretic forms.

SOURCES

The material to be considered falls into two categories. First, there is an abundance of primary sources: amulets, magical gems (often with pictorial and verbal inscriptions), curse tablets, spells on papyrus and on strips or sheets of metal, inscriptions, symbols, drawings, paintings, small figurines and larger sculptures, tools, and finally handbooks of magicians that collect the materials they used (especially the Greek Magical Papyri). Second, there is also a vast amount of secondary source material. Almost every ancient author presents literary and artistic descriptions of magical beliefs and practices. There are also many short references to such beliefs and practices as they existed at the time. Philosophers discussed the matter from early on. Scholarly investigations from the Hellenistic and Roman periods are extant (Plutarch's *On Superstition*; Pliny's *Natural History* 30). At that time the distinction between acceptable and unacceptable forms of magic became common, making it possible for even the educated to use magic in some positive way. Legal provisions had to be developed to deal with magic, especially with forms of it that were reputedly used to harm others.

Despite its reputation as illicit, fraudulent, and superstitious, magic was an essential part of daily life at all levels of society. The uses of magic seem to have been unlimited. In any case, they were also connected with legitimate forms of ritual, myth, symbol, and even language in general. Magic was presupposed in all forms of the miraculous, and in medicine, alchemy, astrology, and divination. Even so, magic retained its dubious reputation, and there were always those few who viewed it with total skepticism.

TERMINOLOGY

The phenomenon of magic is designated by several Greek terms, especially *mageia, pharmakeia,* and *goēteia.* The term *mageia* is derived from *magos* (pl., *magoi*), originally a Persian word *(magush).* Herodotus describes the Magoi (Magians) as a Median tribe. Later they were assumed to be priests and scholars of astrology, divination, and related subjects. Whereas Plato (*Alcibiades* 1.122) still speaks of *mageia* in a positive sense as referring to "the magian lore of Zarathushtra," Aristotle uses the term also in a negative sense as we do today (frag. 36; also Theophrastus, *History of Plants* 9.15.7). This negative meaning, which has little to do with the original meaning, becomes predominant in the Hellenistic period, when new words develop besides *magos* and *mageia,* as for instance *mageuein* and *magikos.* The positive meaning, however, is found in the writings of the magicians themselves, especially in the Greek Magical Papyri.

The negative meaning was taken over by the Romans; in Latin the terms are *magia, magicus,* and *magus,* as well as *maleficium* and *maleficus.* Modern English has inherited this negative meaning, with the exception of the Magi of *Matthew* 2:1.

DESCRIPTIONS OF MAGIC

What constitutes magic was already disputed in antiquity. Roman officials and intellectuals reflect the negative reputation that magic had acquired. Pliny (*Natural History* 30.1–2) points out its fraudulent and dangerous character and has a theory about its origins as a decadent mixture of elements from medicine, astronomy, and religion. Apuleius (*Apology* 26) sums up the view of it as being vulgar and making preposterous claims. By contrast, practitioners of magic provide favorable descriptions of the art (Apuleius, *Apology* 26; Greek Magical Papyri, passim), or they distinguish between lower and higher forms; *goēteia* became the lower, *mageia* the general, and *theourgia* the higher magic. This distinction allowed Neoplatonic philosophers, especially Iamblichus and Proclus, to accept theurgy as a form of philosophical magic. [*See* Theurgy.]

GREEK AND ROMAN MAGIC

For reasons of methodology it is important to distinguish between primary (performative) and secondary (descriptive) material.

Primary Sources. Primary sources for ancient magic consist of various kinds of artifacts, images, symbols, and written texts. Collections of such sources are today housed by public museums and libraries or with private collectors. The cataloging and publishing of these widely dispersed materials are still in progress.

Amulets. Greco-Roman antiquity has left us a large number of amulets of different kinds and purposes. The word *amuletum* occurs in Pliny and corresponds to the Greek *phulaktērion*. Amulets were magically potent objects that averted evil or increased a person's or a deity's divine power. [*See* Amulets and Talismans.] They were worn around the neck or on the head, or arm, or were posted in various places in the house (on doors, at thresholds, etc.). Amulets come in many shapes and forms. Best known are the Egyptian scarab, the hand showing the *fica* (the obscene gesture called "the fig"), the phallus, the eye. Other forms are divine symbols and figurines, replicas of other parts of the human body, animals, and plants. Precious and semiprecious gems engraved with images of deities, inscriptions, and magical symbols were very popular. Often amulets were placed in capsules *(bullae)*. While Egypt was the classical land of amulets, they were known in all parts of the ancient world. Among Jews the *tefillin* and the *mezuzah* should be mentioned, and among Christians the cross and the fish.

Curse Tablets. Curse tablets, or *defixiones* (from Lat. *defixio,* "binding spell"; Gr., *katadesmos*), are known from Greece since the time of Homer. [*See also* Cursing.] A large number of lead lamellae are extant from fifth-century Greece, but curse tablets exist also in the form of ostraca, seashells, and papyri, upon which the curse formulas were inscribed, often with the names of the cursed and the curser. The tablets were deposited in the ground near places where the spirits of the dead were believed to be or in such places as houses, baths, and sports arenas, so as to be communicated to avenging underworld deities (especially Hermes, Hekate, Persephone, and Typhon). Curse tablets were used for a variety of purposes, especially in erotic magic, court trials, political intrigues, and sports (gladiators, horse races). From the earlier and simpler curse developed the later, more elaborate, syncretistic forms of the Hellenistic and Roman eras; besides the magical formulas, inscriptions often included so-called *voces magicae,* characters, or drawings. A special form was the magical letter to the underworld deities.

Curse Figurines. Curse figurines, of which several examples and descriptions have survived, were also widely used. To curse someone, one made a wax or clay figurine of the person and then stuck needles or nails into the figurine or mutilated it, while curse formulas were spoken over it. Like curse tablets, the figurines were deposited in the ground. This form of curse was apparently popular in erotic magic.

Drawings. Drawings have magical power in themselves, as extant magical papyri show. The subjects of the drawings can be deities, persons, or animals.

Tools. Magical tools are known to have existed and have in fact been found (nails, disks, etc.). The most important discovery was a set of tools found in Pergamum.

Symbols. A large number of magical signs and symbols appear on amulets, gems, and tablets. Although seemingly in use since Pythagoras (see Lucian, *Pro lapsu* 5), most of them are still unexplained today. The magicians called them *charactēres.* In gnosticism they were also taken over by Christian magic *(Book of Jeu, Pistis Sophia).*

Incantations. Incantations belong to the magic of the word. [*See* Incantations.] They consist of magical formulas, prayers, and chants. The term comes from the Latin *incantamentum,* "incantation, spell" (Gr., *epōidē*). Many examples of *incantamenta* are found in inscriptions, papyri, and literature, where they are quoted or described. They were widely used in medicine (healings, exorcisms), weather magic, cultic invocations of gods and demons, and erotic magic. Their significance for philosophy and rhetoric was recognized by the Sophists and Plato. They also appear as literary motifs in sagas, novels, myths, aretalogies, mystery cults, and collections of oracles.

Hymns. Hymns to the gods are closely related to incantations. In terms of poetry and religion, hymns are more and even highly developed forms. They were composed metrically and sung, with accompanying cithara and dance. Their basic form included the invocation of the gods, the gods' names and epithets (expressed in relative clauses, participles, adjectives, etc.), and the petition. Hymns existed from Archaic times on. Major extant collections include the Homeric Hymns (mainly from the eighth to the sixth centuries BCE), the Orphic Hymns (probably from the second century CE), and the hymn fragments inserted in the Greek Magical Papyri, some of which may be ancient.

Magical Handbooks. Magicians collected the material they needed in handbooks, some of which are extant, as for example the great magical papyri of Berlin, Leiden, London, and Paris. Such handbooks include a wide variety of spells to be used by the magicians themselves or to be sold to customers. There are also rituals for acquiring assistant demons *(paredroi daimones),* initiation rituals, deification rituals, invocations for oracular séances with deities, and procedural matters (preparation of ingredients, instructions about when various procedures can be undertaken, etc.). Among the spells, those designed to attract a lover, harm an enemy, or restrain anger are most numerous. Other spells have to do with various illnesses, bedbugs, business problems, catching thieves, and horse races. To find out what the future holds, a host of mantic spells and longer rituals are provided. Outstanding among all these collections are the so-called Mithraic Liturgy, which exhibits yet unexplained relationships to the Mithraic cult, and the "Eighth Book of Moses," which contains three different versions of an initiation ritual. In addition to collecting magical material, the handbooks told magicians how to make and use amulets, curse tablets, figurines, and drawings, and how to use tools.

Secondary Sources. Whereas primary sources present magical practices and beliefs directly, secondary sources presuppose, describe, or discuss them. The literature of Greek and Roman antiquity contains innumerable examples of such secondary sources, but careful distinctions must be made: while many authors have real knowledge of popular magic or even access to primary sources of magical literature, there is at the same time a purely literary tradition in which the same themes, motifs, and terms show up again and again. Therefore some authors simply imitate the descriptions of magical acts found in earlier authors or attempt to supersede them. While both kinds of authors may flourish simultaneously, some authors may have received their information from secondary sources exclusively.

Literary Texts. Magic is a common literary motif in both Greek and Latin literature. Homer's *Iliad* and *Odyssey* contain many allusions to and descriptions of magical acts. Pliny (*Natural History* 30.1) states that the *Odyssey* in particular was recognized simply as a book of magic. In fact, Homeric verses were used later as magical formulas. Magic plays a role in Odysseus's encounter with the witch Circe (*Odyssey*

10.274ff.) and his descent into Hades and consultation with the seer Teiresias (*Odyssey* 11.14ff.). The Homeric Hymns have numerous references to magic, some of which (depending on whether the hymns actually were used in the cult) may be primary rather than merely secondary sources. The *Hymn to Demeter* 228–230 is especially important because of its reference in the Demophon episode to a ritual baptism of fire. From the beginning, literary interests were focused not only on erotic magic but also on death and the underworld with its deities, especially Hekate and Persephone (e.g., Hesiod's Hekate episode in *Theogony* 411–452). There is also, of course, a close relationship between the literary and the pictorial art. Greek drama took to the subject as well, expressing it either in episodes (e.g., the calling up of the ghost of Darius in Aeschylus's *Persae* 619–842) or in whole tragedies (e.g., Euripides' *Medea,* treating one of the great witches of antiquity). Ancient comedy used magic for its own purposes, as in the description of a *goēs* ("quack") in Aristophanes' *Plutus* (649–747) or Menander's *Deisidaimon* and *Theophoroumene*. Theocritus's second idyll, entitled *Pharmakeutria* (The Witch), became a literary prototype for many later poets.

The superstitious man as a literary and ethical type was described by Theophrastus (*Characters* 16). The hymnic tradition was continued by the third-century BCE poet Callimachus (*Hymn to Demeter* 3–6; *On the Bath of Pallas* 9) and his pupil Apollonius of Rhodes, whose *Argonautica* included several magical sections (3.7ff., invocation to Erato; 744–911, Medea's preparation of magical drugs; 1163–1224, Jason's nocturnal sacrifice to Hekate; 1225–1407, Jason's magical defeat of the giants). Especially popular were descriptions of scenes of necromancy. In the Roman period the second-century Greek satirist Lucian of Samosata provides an almost complete inventory of magical beliefs and practices, as did the Greek novels.

In Roman literature the tradition continues with an increasing interest in the dramatic and the bizarre. Vergil's eighth eclogue (64–110) describes a magical ritual performed by a deserted lover that shows exact knowledge of magical details, although it is based upon Theocritus's second idyll. In the *Aeneid,* dramatic magical scenes are connected with the death of Dido (4.504–676). Horace's fifth epode has a macabre scene of the abduction and murder of a child.

Philosophical and Scientific Investigations. According to ancient tradition, philosophers have been preoccupied with magic since pre-Socratic times. The names of Heraclitus, Pythagoras, Empedocles, and Democritus appear several times in connection with magic, and spells under the names of Pythagoras and Democritus are found in the Greek Magical Papyri. Although the historical value of these references is doubtful, philosophers seem to have investigated magical phenomena since Pythagoras, who also may have been the first to make a positive use of it.

Greek philosophy in general rejected magic. The Skeptics, Epicureans, and Cynics produced an entire literature combating magic. But the attitude gradually changed with the development of demonology, mantic, and astrology. The Hermetic writings and the Neoplatonic philosophers Iamblichus and Proclus (and probably even Plotinus) accepted forms of magic and integrated them into their systems.

Scientific compendia of magical beliefs and practices are extant from the Roman period. Pliny's *Natural History* contains a history and theory of what he calls the *magicae vanitates* (30.1–18) and a large collection of remedies (see also book 28). Although written as an apology, Apuleius's *Apologia (De magia)* is in fact a compendium of magic. Apuleius's other works are also valuable sources for the magical beliefs of his time (see especially the *Metamorphoses*).

Legal Provisions. Ancient law had no provisions for prosecuting magicians for the practice of magic. However, there are numerous accounts of trials in which magic played a role. These were trials not only of magicians and witches but also of philosophers (e.g., Anaxagoras, Socrates, Apollonius of Tyana, and Apuleius of Madaura). According to ancient writers, these persons were accused of murder by poisoning *(pharmakōn)* or of failure to honor the gods properly *(asebeia)*, accusations broad enough to add emotional furor to a wide range of charges. If magic as such was not a reason for prosecution, harming a person by means of magic was. Plato included legal provisions against such injury in his *Laws* (11.933.D). The Romans went further and included property damages caused by weather or agricultural magic in the *Tabulae XII*.

JEWISH MAGIC

Magic played a somewhat different role in Judaism as compared with neighboring religions. The Old Testament shows that Israelite religion was well aware of the importance of magic in the religions of Egypt and Babylon, but on the whole it viewed magic negatively. For the Old Testament, magic is either foreign or marginal. Magicians are called in by Pharaoh (*Ex.* 7–10) or Nebuchadrezzar (*Dn.* 2:2); they serve Jezebel (*2 Kgs.* 9:22) and Manasseh (*2 Chr.* 33:6). The prophets warn against magic (*Is.* 47:9–15, *Jer.* 27:9, *Ez.* 13:17–19, *Na.* 3:4, *Mal.* 3:5, *Mi.* 5:11–12). The religion of Israel is believed to be more powerful than all magic, which is excluded by law (*Ex.* 22:18; *Lv.* 19:26, 19:31, 20:6, 20:27; *Dt.* 18:9–22). Especially important is the necromancy in the story of the witch of Endor (*1 Sm.* 28).

This picture, however, is deceptive. Pre-Israelite religions, most of them saturated with magic, have left numerous traces in Israelite religion; furthermore, popular Israelite religion must not be confused with what the Old Testament conveys. In this popular religion, magic has a firm place that was often approved of even by "official" religion (e.g., Moses' and Elijah's magical wands in *Ex.* 4:20, 17:8–13; *2 Kgs.* 4:29, 4:31; Urim and Tummim, ephod and terafim in *1 Sm.* 2:18, 14:3, 14:18; *Jgs.* 17–18; *Dt.* 33:8). More important than amulets and rituals was the magic of the word, especially curses and blessings and above all the name of Yahveh (see especially *Jgs.* 13:6, 13:17–18; *Ex.* 3:14). The name of Yahveh became the most important magical element in Judaism and, beyond it, in Hellenistic syncretism. Therefore the God Iao plays an enormous role in the Greek Magical Papyri, and on the magical gems and amulets of the Hellenistic and Roman period.

These various developments persist on a far broader scale in rabbinic Judaism. The official rejection of magic in rabbinic literature must be seen against the background of popular religion and the whole mystical tradition (Merkavah, Qabbalah), both of which were very open to magical beliefs and practices.

CHRISTIAN MAGIC

For early Christianity, magic presented difficulties. On the one hand, Christians had inherited Judaism's negative attitude toward magic (see *Gal.* 5:20, and the typical attitudes expressed in *Acts* 8:9–24, 13:6–12, 19:13–19). On the other hand, the emphasis on miracles and sacraments implied approval of some forms of magic. Jesus' activities as a miracle worker were soon attacked as being the work of a magician possessed by Beelzebub (*Mk.* 3:22–27 and parallels). Beginning with the presynoptic sources of the Gospels, New Testament apologetics was increasingly preoccupied with defending Jesus against classification with the magicians. Since his exorcisms and miracle work could not be ignored, distinctions were introduced to separate miracles from magic. Similarly, miracles worked by Christian healers had to be separated from those of non-Christians. This was accomplished by treating the latter as acts done by magicians.

Problems arose also because of the close affinities between the epiphanies of the crucified and resurrected Christ and the magical concept of the return as demons of persons who had died of violence *(biaiothanatoi)* (see especially *Lk.* 24:36–43, *Jn.* 20:19–23). Moreover, magical presuppositions in the rituals of baptism and the Eucharist led to practices approved by some and disapproved by others (see especially Paul, who tried to correct misuse in *1 Cor.* 1:10–16, 8:1–11:1, 11:17–34, and in *Rom.* 6:3–10). Paul first distinguished between abuse (magical misconceptions) and proper use (sacraments) of these rituals. The fundamental theological problems stated or implied in these early texts continued to assert themselves throughout the history of Christianity and have led to ever new conceptualizations.

From the second century on, popular Christian religion showed greater interest in amulets, relics, symbols, and signs (see the apocryphal gospels and *Acts*). The gnostics also made positive use of magic (see especially the *Book of Jeu,* the *Pistis Sophia,* and the writings found at Nag Hammadi, Egypt). The official church, through its bishops, synods, and the writings of the church fathers, was forced to combat and suppress new Christian forms of magic and superstition. The extant wealth of amulets, spells, relics, holy places, symbols, and images indicates that complete suppression was impossible. Still, Christian theology was able to contain and restrain the lower forms of magic by accepting some forms of christianized magic while eliminating other, unwanted forms. Liturgy and sacramental theology developed special kinds of magic thought to be compatible with the doctrines of the church. By the end of antiquity, the church had become the home of many forms of magic that coexisted in an uneasy and tenuous symbiosis. Some magic was banned, some was tolerated, some was approved, but none achieved domination.

BIBLIOGRAPHY

No complete collection of the vast remains of ancient magic exists, but there are useful editions and translations, indices, and surveys of literature. For new publications, see the annual bibliography in Marouzeau, *L'annee philologique,* section on "Magica."

Texts and Translations

Betz, Hans Dieter, ed. *The Greek Magical Papyri in Translation, Including the Demotic Spells.* 2 vols. Chicago, 1986. Volume 1 contains English translations of the papyri in Preisendanz's work and those published thereafter (until 1983), with introductions, notes, and a glossary. Volume 2 will have an index of Greek words by Edward N. O'Neil and a subject-matter index by Marjorie A. Menaul.

Kropp, Angelicus M. *Ausgewählte koptische Zaubertexte.* 3 vols. Brussels, 1930–1932. Volume 1 has the edition of Coptic texts; volume 2 has their German translation; volume 3 is introductory.

Preisendanz, Karl. *Papyri Graecae Magicae: Die griechischen Zauberpapyri.* 2 vols. Edited by Albert Henrichs. 2d ed. Stuttgart, 1973–1974. Edition of Greek texts, with German translation, notes, and bibliography.

Studies

Abt, Adam. *Die Apologie des Apuleius von Madaura und die antike Zauberei.* Giessen, 1908.

Aune, David E. "Magic in Early Christianity." In *Aufstieg und Niedergang der römischen Welt,* vol. 2.23.2 (Berlin and New York, 1969), pp. 1507–1557. A comprehensive bibliographical report.

Bonner, Campbell. *Studies in Magical Amulets, Chiefly Graeco-Egyptian.* Ann Arbor, 1950.

Burkert, Walter. *Griechische Religion der archaischen und klassischen Epoche.* Stuttgart, 1977. Translated as *Greek Religion* (Cambridge, Mass., 1985). Important and up-to-date comments on various aspects of magic in the archaic and classical periods of Greek religion.

Grant, Robert M. *Miracle and Natural Law in Graeco-Roman and Early Christian Thought.* Amsterdam, 1952.

Herzig, Otto. *Lukian als Quelle für die antike Zauberei.* Würzburg, 1940.

Hopfner, Theodor. *Griechisch-ägyptischer Offenbarungszauber.* 2 vols. Leipzig, 1921–1924. Still the best survey of the entire range of material.

Hopfner, Theodor. "Mageia." In *Real-Encyclopädie der classischen Altertumswissenschaft,* vol. 14 (Stuttgart, 1928), pp. 301–393. Mostly a summary of the former work.

Luck, Georg. *Arcana Mundi. Magic and the Occult in the Greek and Roman Worlds.* Baltimore and London, 1985. A useful collection of sources in translation, with brief introductions and notes.

Nilsson, Martin P. *Geschichte der griechischen Religion.* 3d ed. 2 vols. Munich, 1967–1974. Has important sections on magic at the various stages of development in Greek religion.

Scholem, Gershom. "Der Name Gottes und die Sprachtheorie der Kabbala." *Eranos-Jahrbuch* 39 (1970): 243–297.

Thee, Francis C. R. *Julius Africanus and the Early Christian View of Magic.* Tübingen, 1984. The volume contains the *Kestoi* of Julius Africanus (c. 160–240 CE) in translation, together with commentary, extensive introduction, and a survey of the early Christian views on magic.

Thorndike, Lynn. *A History of Magic and Experimental Science,* vols. 1–2, *The First Thirteen Centuries of Our Era.* New York, 1923. Written from the perspective of the history of science; incomplete series of studies.

Trachtenberg, Joshua. *Jewish Magic and Superstition* (1939). Reprint, New York, 1982.

Trumpf, Jürgen. "Fluchtafel und Rachepuppe." *Mitteilungen des Deutschen Archäologischen Instituts,* Athenische Abteilung, 73 (1958): 94–102.

Widengren, Geo. *Religionsphänomenologie.* Berlin, 1969. References on various aspects of magic can be found in the index, s.v.v. *Magie, Magier.*

11

MAGIC IN MEDIEVAL AND RENAISSANCE EUROPE

Ioan Petru Culianu

A history of magic during the Middle Ages and the Renaissance has yet to be written. New discoveries and, above all, new interpretative viewpoints, have made obsolete the few existing syntheses, like those of Lynn Thorndike, Kurt Seligmann, or Émile Grillot de Givry. Any scholar who still relies on these works—and especially on the first—is by no means better off than would be an anthropologist who relied exclusively on James G. Frazer.

EARLY MIDDLE AGES

The magic of late antiquity survived into the early Middle Ages along several different lines. The archbishop Synesius of Cyrene (c. 370—413), who before becoming a Christian had been a pupil of the Neoplatonist Hypatia of Alexandria (martyred in 415), laid in his treatise *On Dreams (Peri enhupniōn)* the foundations of a new theory of magic that was to be particularly influential during the Renaissance. Synesius took over the notion of "spirit" *(pneuma)* from the medical and philosophical traditions of antiquity, from Empedocles to Galen and from Zeno of Citium and Aristotle to Proclus.

The *pneuma* was a vapor of blood, which was supposed not only to give life to all animal organisms but also to form the material substratum upon which the activity of both the five senses and the intellect was based. According to this "subtile physiology," which remained unquestioned down to the eighteenth century, the spirit also forms a sixth or "inner" sense, whose function is to grasp the messages of the five external senses and to codify them so that they become intelligible to reason. The language of the spirit, whose seat as an inner sense, or phantasy, is either the heart or the head, is formed by phantasms *(phantasmata)*, or inner images. According to Aristotle, later recalled by Thomas Aquinas, the human reason is unable to understand anything without the aid of phantasies *(aneu phantasmatos—sine conversione ad phantasmata)*.

For Synesius, the phantasy of man is the very place where the upper and the lower world come together. According to a principle that all of the greatest philosophical schools of antiquity—Platonism, Aristotelianism, and Stoicism—had affirmed on different grounds and stressed with various intensities, man is a compendium of the universe. Synesius's "magic," which is no more than a blending of Platonism, Aristotelianism, and Stoicism, stems from the postulate that there is interaction between man and universe and that this interaction can be practically realized and controlled by means of the *sensus interior,* or phantasy. This represents a continuation of the popular magic of late antiquity, insofar as the latter was equally based on the conceptions of *pneuma* ("spirit") and *pneumata* ("spirits, ghosts"). It also represents a conspicuous improvement over that tradition, insofar as the concept of *pneuma* now becomes a part of a general theory that was labeled as scientific and, accordingly, was endowed with immense prestige.

Synesius's theory, which became known through Marsilio Ficino's 1489 translation of the treatise *On Dreams,* as very influential during the whole of the Renaissance. It also stood in the background of the most outstanding early medieval system of "intellectual" magic, that of the Arab al-Kindī (d. c. 873), whose treatise *On Rays* has been preserved in a twelfth-century Latin translation *(De radiis).* The work was much appreicated by Roger Bacon and Ficino. In the sixteenth century, Al-Kindī's ideas became the center of a debate between defenders and opponents of magic and astrology. According to al-Kindī, all terrestial and superterrestrial beings send forth rays that are never identical, since there are no identical things in nature. Rays are susceptible to manipulation, and the power to manipulate them can be acquired through will and concentration of the human phantasy *(spiritus ymaginarius).* This phantasy emits rays that have an impact upon the universal system of rays everywhere. In other words, human desires expressed in phantasies are, under special conditions, transitive; that is, they can have an influence on someone else's phantasy and even on inanimate objects. Magic is actually the knowledge of these special conditions that make possible manipulation by means of the spirit. Such special conditions, and, consequently, special results, can be reached through appropriate sounds, figures, images, and sacrifices.

As far as popular magic is concerned, one could argue that the Jewish *Sefer ha-razim* (Book of Mysteries), compiled in the sixth or seventh century CE and published in 1969, gives room to the hypothesis that early medieval Jewish magic forms the background of such anonymous treatise of practical magic as the *Clavicula Salomonis* (Small Key of Salomo), which circulated from the late Middle Ages to the nineteenth century. This is not actually the case. Whereas the *Clavicula* describes a system of planetary angelology, and, consequently, of astrological magic, the *Sefer ha-razim* is a treatise of *merkavah* mysticism transformed to include the magical conjuration of angels, and it is based on a more rudimentary cosmology. The *Clavicula Salomonis,* otherwise a farraginous text, is a more sophisticated example of magic than the *Sefer haprazim.*

During the late Middle Ages, a book of practical magic translated from Arabic into Latin that enjoyed much popularity was the *Picatrix,* in Arabic *Ghāyat al-ḥakīm fi-al-siḥr* (The Goal Pursued by the Sages through Magic), ascribed to the philosopher al-Majrītī (d. 1004—1007). The influence of the *Picatrix* on Renaissance magic, which was of a quantitative kind, has been certainly overrated.

LATE MIDDLE AGES

Two late medieval personalities connected with magic deserve special mention: Albertus Magnus (c. 1200—1280) and Roger Bacon (C.1220—1292). Accounts of other magicians, like Michael Scot (c. 1175—1235), are so affected by the traditional and atemporal typology of the "magus" that is is impossible to separate truth from legend. Others still, like Guido Bonatti of Forlì, Peter of Abano, Ramón Lull, or Arnaldus of Villanova were skilled in astrology, alchemy, the art of memory, or, occasionally, geomancy (a form of divination imported from the Moors), but they do not properly belong to the category of actual authors or performers of magic.

The Dominican monk Albertus Magnus was truly well versed in popular magic; a universal man, he could discourse with equal enthusiasm and skill on tin mining or the faculties of the human soul. He was famous through the ages for having discussed at length the properties of stones and plants. His *Book of Minerals* contains the traditional lapidary, with ninety-nine descriptions of precious stones that, among other qualities, are supposed to confer happiness, riches, strength, success in war, and skill in business. They can also stop breathing, protect against theft, prevent storms and hail, provoke or prevent miscarriage, and further cure all sorts of ailments and diseases. The sixth book of Albertus's treatise *On Plants* contains references to the magic and apotropaic properties of plants. Albertus's lapidary and herbary were frequently reprinted during the Renaissance; together with the *Picatrix* they formed one of the principal sources of practical Renaissance magic.

The mere fact of Roger Bacon being a Franciscan may account for the contempt he repeatedly showed toward Albertus. Surprisingly enough, Bacon, like Albertus, was a supporter of natural magic. In his *Experimental Science* he drew a wonderful vision of the new world that was to come about with the application of his "science": he described self-propulsive boats and engines, flying machines, and submarines. Bacon cultivated a form of astrological magic and was also a practitioner of alchemy.

THE RENAISSANCE

The father of Renaissance magic was undoubtedly Marsilio Ficino (1433—1449), author of the 1489 *De vita coelitus comparanda,* widely copied or paraphrased by representatives of "spiritual" magic like Heinrich Cornelius Agrippa (1486—1535) and Giordano Bruno (1548—1600). Another kind of magic, of which Ficino himself gives an extensive account, was magic by means of demons; it was a sort of astrologic magic akin to that described in popular books like the *Clavicula Salomonis.* Its greatest representative was the abbot Trithemius of Würzburg (1462—1516). This "demonic" magic left indelible traces in the compilation *Occult Philosophy* of Agrippa and in the magical works of Bruno, who followed both Agrippa and Trithemius.

Another kind of magic, which is neither "spiritual" nor "demonic," is the "natural" magic of the Neapolitan Giambattista della Porta (c. 1535—1615), author of the treatise *Natural Magic,* which grew from four books in its first printing of 1558 to twenty books in the second of 1589 and which has had innumerable reprintings. Like Trithemius in the third book of his *Steganographia,* unlike Ficino, Bruno, or even the mere compiler Agrippa, della Porta is not much of a theoretician. Although it contains several interesting details, his treatise is a catalogue of curiosities rather than a book of magic in the Renaissance tradition.

Spiritual Magic. Like al-Kindī, Marsilio Ficino recognized a universal force radiating into the remotest corners of the universe; but he called this force "love," whereas the Arab philosopher called it "rays." In his treatise *On Love (De amore),* loosely a commentary on Plato's *Symposium,* Ficino resumes the medieval tradition of love as a serious illness of the spirit. Love is a natural form of magic, in which the spell is unconsciously cast by the beauty of the beloved. It is important to recognize that there is no essential difference between the mechanism of love and that of magic. In fact, the latter represents a conscious (as opposed to an unconscious) manipulation of someone (or something) else's spirit by means of one's own spirit. Magic works only under certain conditions, which are governed by the positions of the stars in heaven. Ficino's magic is a more or less complicated astrological magic, consisting of the knowledge and exploitation of the astral influences stored in earthly matter such as those of minerals, plants, and animals. If magic in general is intersubjective, that is, if it works from the spirit of a person (the manipulator) to the spirit of another person (the object of the operation), Ficino's magic, which is also frequently termed "theurgy," represents a particular case of intersubjectivity: it is actually intrasubjective in that it is meant to direct spiritual influence upon the subject himself. By following a diet that is astrologically beneficial and by surrounding himself with objects and persons in which the qualities of the three beneficient planets (the sun, Jupiter, and Venus) inhere, the Ficinian magus could obtain a clean, elastic, and firm spirit, which would open to him the gates of superior contemplation.

This is pure spiritual magic, but it is not free from demonic interferences, since demons, it might be said, are but bodiless spirits. (In fact, demons are also other things, planetary spirits, for instance, of which Ficino speaks at some length in his *De vita coelitus comparanda*.) We may safely state that there is no contradiction between spiritual and demonic magic, since spiritual magic comprehends demonic operations, and demonic magic does not exclude operations by the human or extra-human spirit. Of course, there are also cases of pure demonic magic.

Demonic Magic. Paradoxically enough, the greatest wizard of the sixteenth century, Trithemius of Würzburg, was also a fierce opponent of witchcraft, against which he recommended the most drastic measures, according to the doctrine of the *Malleus maleficarum* (1486). Until he was fifteen, Trithemius was an analphabet, but his desire of learning was so intense that, after an angelic vision, the boy was given the possibility of realizing his dream, which he did with astonishing quickness. He claimed from that time to have constant communication with angels. As a result, he became a Benedictine monk at the age of twenty, and, at twenty-three, he was elected abbot of Sponheim, the poorest convent of the Palatinate. In twenty years, Trithemius transformed the convent into the most famous place of pilgrimage in all humanistic Europe. Its library contained the rarest manuscripts of the time. In 1505, the library possessed almost two thousand volumes, an exceptional number. The Sponheim library probably contained a great many works on practical magic; several are possibly listed in Trithemius's *Antipalus maleficiorum* (1508), which, ironically enough, was a refutation of witchcraft dedicated to the abbot's highest protector, the emperor Maximilian.

Trithemius is the author of two treatises on cryptography: *Steganographia* (posthumously printed) and *Polygraphia* (1508). The former, which was to become one of the most intriguing books of the sixteenth century, was not preserved in its entirety: the extant parts contain the first two books and a fragment of the third. Whereas the first two books really constitute a cryptographic manual, the fragment of the third book presents a bold method of magic that would permit the magus to communicate at great distances by means of planetary demons, properly summoned for this purpose. It is probable that Trithemius thought that through similar methods a magus would be able to know at every moment all things happening in the world. It is likely that the abbot himself destroyed the rest of his *Steganographia,* which logically would have dealt with divination. In the ecclesiastical jurisprudence of the time, demonic invocations were considered to be sacrilegious, whereas divination was heretical. Trithemius would not admit to such a sin.

Heinrich Cornelius Agrippa was Trithemius's disciple. As a matter of fact, his compilation *On the Occult Philosophy,* written from 1509 to 1510 and printed in 1533, is a blending of Ficinian spiritual magic and Trithemian demonic magic; he was also acquainted with treatises in practical magic, and the compilation is a systematic exposition of all these matters.

Erotic Magic. Ficino and Trithemius could hardly claim absolute originality in their magic methods, and Agrippa was merely a compiler, but there was one genuinely creative work of Renaissance magic, the two manuscripts by Giordano Bruno entitled *De vinculis in genere* (On Bonds in General). Educated in a Dominican cloister at Naples, Bruno early came into conflict with church authority. Exiled to Protestant countries, he never obtained there the friendly reception he might have expected. For all Christian denominations at that time, Giordano Bruno, a specialist in the mysteries of the art of memory and a magus in the Renaissance tradition, incarnated precisely the archenemy of faith. He was eventually burned at the stake as a witch.

Bruno's work on magic includes a number of compilations *(De magia, Theses de magia,* and *De magia mathematica)* and the two manuscripts entitled *De vinculis in genere.* These manuscripts carry to an extreme end the Ficinian theory of love as a form of natural magic. Thus, if any affection conceived by the spirit of the operator is transitive, then it is enough to produce erotic phantasms loaded with the emotion of passion, in order to be able to influence another person. This person would receive the phantasms through his own spirit and would thus become the prey of the magus. The magus is, however, supposed to be perfectly continent, lest he become himself a prey of his own phantasms. Bruno conceives a world in which everything is manipulable through the same mechanism of phantasmic production. The operator may have three distinct hypostases: he may be a physician, a prophet, or a magus. As a physician, he is responsible for the spiritual healing of his patients; as a prophet, he is able to bind *(vincire)* masses of people and to make new religions; as a magus, he is able to find the appropriate bonds *(vincula)* in order to bind anyone's will through phantasms. As a poet, Bruno described several times the psychic condition of such an operator, who is supposed to be at once burning with desire and completely cold and indifferent toward his own passion.

Phantasms at Work. Giordano Bruno's magic is based not only upon the Ficinian tradition but also on techniques relating to the art of memory. This art consisted of a manipulation of phantasms or inner images, whose purpose varied from the mere learning by heart of a text to mystical contemplation. At any rate, the art of memory as a discipline pertained to rhetoric. The first to envisage explicitly the art of memory as a magico-mystical enterprise was the Friulian Giulio Camillo Delminio (c. 1480–1544). Giulio Camillo tried all his life to build up a "theater" of memory organized in seven planetary fields embracing practically all objects and persons. He was followed by the Friulian rhetorician Fabio Paolini, who published his *Hebdomades* at Venice in 1589. Paolini replaced Giulio Camillo's "theater" with a mental scheme of seven series of planetary influences, to be simply filled in with the phantasms of things supposed to reflect the respective planetary characters (for instance, a lion under the sun, etc.). Paolini was convinced that a rhetorician-magus, at any moment during his speech, could call up such a phantasm before his internal sense. The phantasm would not fail subsequently to influence the spirit of the auditors, their emotions, and their decisions.

Giulio Camillo's ideas had an important impact on the aesthetician Giovanni Paolo Lomazzo (1538–1600). Lomazzo is a representative of the magical theory of the subjective value of colors. In his *Idea del tempio della pittura* (1590) he made a sevenfold classification of painting and painters in conformity with the sevenfold classification of Giulio Camillo.

THE MODERN DEBATE ON RENAISSANCE MAGIC

The spiritual principle of Renaissance magic and the inner coherence of this discipline have been, for the first time, carefully investigated by Daniel P. Walker (1958). Walker's approach made obsolete the traditional historical approach in search of "origins" and influences. According to the traditional approach, Renaissance magic was a blending of Hermetism and Qabbalah. Further investigations into the figure of the Renaissance magus—John Dee (1527–1608), for instance—have shown that, at a later time, "the Renaissance magus turned into Faust" (Yates). Frances A. Yates seems also to consider—in her last work (1979)—the possibility that the Renaissance magus was turned into a grim and deluded follower of Satan by the ideology of the Reformation. This idea is given particular emphasis in my book *Éros et magie à la Renaissance* (1984).

BIBLIOGRAPHY

The principles of spiritual magic are the foci of Daniel P. Walker's excellent *Spiritual and Demonic Magic: From Ficino to Campanella* (London, 1958). The evolution of erotic magic from Ficino to Bruno has been followed by my *Éros et magie à la Renaissance* (Paris, 1984). Another general work on Renaissance magic, handy but unreliable, is Wayne Shuhmaker's *The Occult Sciences in the Renaissance* (Berkeley, 1972). Magic in the Elizabethan age is the subject of Frances A. Yates's *The Occult Philosophy in the Elizabethan Age* (Boston, 1979). Several works on individual authors are recommended. Excellent articles on the herbary and lapidary of Albertus Magnus by J. Stannard, J. M. Riddle, and J. A. Mulholland are found in *Albertus Magnus and the Sciences,* edited by James A. Weisheipl (Toronto, 1980). The best book to date on Trithemius of Würzburg is Klaus Arnold's *Johannes Trithemius, 1462–1516* (Würzburg, 1971). Two reliable books on Heinrich Cornelius Agrippa are Auguste Prost's excellent biography *Les sciences et les arts occultes au seizième siècle: Corneille Agrippa, sa vie et ses œuvres,* 2 vols. (1881–1882; reprint, Nieuwkoop, Netherlands, 1965), and Charles G. Nauert, Jr.'s reliable *Agrippa and the Crisis of Renaissance Thought* (Urbana, Ill., 1965). Peter J. French has devoted his attention to John Dee in *John Dee: The World of an Elizabethan Magus* (London, 1972). There are a multitude of studies concerning Marsilio Ficino and Giordano Bruno, but none of them is dedicated to their magic. For both these remarkable personalities, the reader should refer to my books, to the books of Daniel P. Walker, and to my article "La Magie de Giordano Bruno," *Studi e materiali di storia delle religioni* 49 (1983): 279–301.

12 MAGIC IN EASTERN EUROPE

IOANA ANDREESCO-MIEREANU
Translated from French by Brunhild Biebuyck

Demonology, introduced by Christian religious thought in the fifteenth and sixteenth centuries, profoundly affected western European thought with respect to its conception of magic. The transformation of the witch into an expression of the demon who seeks to ensure his power on earth and prepare for his own advent obscured popular thinking, which possessed its own type of representations and its own system of values inherited from a rather deep-rooted paganism. In eastern Europe, where this intervention did not occur in the same way, the phenomenon of magic continued to evolve in its primary form, as a unified practice anchored in a popular culture of which it represented only one facet.

For so long isolated from the historical and sociological upheavals that affected western Europe, the peoples of eastern Europe still hold to a different worldview and use different means to account for the human condition. As Mircea Eliade states in his *De Zalmoxis à Gengis-Khan* (1970): "As in all other provinces of the Roman Empire, autochthonous religious realities outlived, more or less transformed, both the romanizing and the christianizing processes. There is enough proof of a pagan heritage" (p. 73). The common inherited substratum preserved by the Romanian and Balkan populations is considered by Eliade as "the principal unifying element in the entire Balkan peninsula" (ibid., p. 183). As early as the 1930s, Pierre Bogatyrev, in the introduction to his *Actes magiques, rites et croyances en Russie subcarpatique* (1929), noted a renaissance of paganism among ethnic groups practicing orthodox religions, even though he insists that this renaissance evidently took place "under the aegis of the Revolution and Soviet government." He adds: "Orthodox religion and witchcraft, the rival sisters, . . . form an unexpected ensemble. All of village Russia is divided into witchcraft parishes that do not yield to ecclesiastical parishes."

Given the importance of the pagan heritage (not to mention the circulation of motifs, sociocultural exchanges, and so on), it is not surprising that a rather large body of magical practices is shared by the majority of the traditional societies of southeastern Europe. In fact, there is no domain in which magic is not practiced; magic crosscuts all spheres in which human beings move. But recourse to magic becomes especially obligatory for the different phases of the life cycle; in this way it ensures its principal function, that of integrating individuals into their own collectivity and their own development. Throughout this region, for example, the Fates, those fabulous beings whom the Bulgars call "women or fairies of fate" and whom the Greeks name simply Morai ("fates"), participate in the "programming" of an entire life, from birth to death, including marriage. They are the ones to whom a woman addresses herself (even today, in a hospital setting) on the third day after childbirth:

> You, the Saints,
> You the Good Ones,
> You the Fates
> Predestine this child,
> This newborn.
> Come as sweet as honey,
> Come as smooth as water,
> And as good as bread,
> As gay as wine,
> As limpid as water,
> And give him intelligence and wisdom.
> To this child newborn,
> Give him health and good fortune in life.
> May he be protected by God.

In Romania, especially in the region known as Little Walachia, the Fates intervene in the principal magical rites dealing with marriage and love through the intermediary of their plant, the mandrake. When, for example, a mandrake is unearthed during rites designed to determine a young woman's mate, the Fates are addressed in the same terms as those used to ask about a child's destiny: "You, the Saints, / You the Good Ones, / You the Pure, / I give you honey, wine, bread, and salt. / Let me know the destiny of [so-and-so]." The Fates are also invoked through their plant in incantations that accompany magical rites aiming to reunite separated couples:

> You mandrake,
> You the Benefactress,
> Herb of the Saints,
> Know her lot.
> And if her husband had been destined to marry,
> If this union be his fate,
> Bring him back
> And reunite them,
> Keep them bound forever. . . .
> Give them a second chance. . . .
> If God had wanted them to separate,
> May they separate.
> But if not,
> Bring them together, you, Benefactress,
> Herb of the saints.
> Unite them a second time.
> Enliven her home. . . .

At times of death, the Fates through their plant are once again asked to intervene in a sort of ritual magic that is experienced and felt as a form of euthanasia. After the mandrake is unearthed "in order to summon death," an act performed in complete silence and sadness; it is boiled and the ill person is bathed with the decoction; at this time the Fates are invoked and asked to declare the lot they have selected for the sufferer: death or life. If it is death (as is usually the case), they are asked to palliate the victim's suffering: "May his fate be decided. / If it be death may it come quickly. / May he not suffer any longer." This type of magic ritual also appears in the Balkans, at least among the Bulgars, as Christo Vakarelski (1969) demonstrates.

Many other magical practices are shared by these traditional societies. Among them, the most important are the rites aiming to vitiate the contamination associated with childbirth and those aiming to avoid the contamination of death—all intended to ensure the separation of worlds that should not intersect. An extended comparative study, for example, could be undertaken on the magical precautions taken so that the dead remain dead and do not transform themselves into vampires, who are today still dreaded, feared, and fought. Represented as wild or monstrous carnivorous animals, these eternally unsatisfied beings are doomed to seek out earthly pleasures. They refuse to be relegated to the beyond and, instead, assume human form in order to finish on earth what they could not realize in life. In order to make sure the dead do not become vampires, certain preventive measures can be undertaken. One can, for example, deposit nine stones, nine marble chips, and nine millet grains under the person's head and utter the following incantation:

> Your mouth, I petrify.
> Your lips, I marbleize.
> Your teeth, to millet I transform.
> So that harm shall you never wreak.

Numerous magical practices (echoing religious rites) are also associated with the cyclical succession of the seasons and with the household. Incantations surrounding the home usually seek to expel malevolent forces and bring good luck:

> Just as the waters melt in March,
> Just as they are transported by the torrent
> And just as they clean and carry
> All the rust,
> All the trash,
> May my home and all those who live in it also be
> Cleansed
> Of all malfeasance, all bad luck,
> All illness, all ill will
> That may be in its walls.

These incantations and the rites they accompany are essential, for they situate man in a context of rituals that integrate him with nature and the order of the cosmos. In fact, it is in this domain that, from Romania to Bulgaria to Russia to Greece and Albania, the magical rites most resemble each other in both form and content.

Magical practices are also directed at administrative and legal authorities. For villagers the power of persuasion is the best weapon against these authorities with whom they are usually involved in a "battle of words." Silencing the authorities is seen as the ultimate form of persuasion, and many incantations thus request that they be silenced just like the dead:

> Just as the dead have now grown cold,
> May all members of the tribunal grow as cold.
> May no one be able to proclaim my guilt.
> May they stop speaking,
> May they lose their voice
> Just as the dead have lost theirs.
> The arms of the dead are crossed over their chest.
> May the case made against me grow as cold as they.
> May it go away.

In many regions of eastern Europe one could say that folk culture was not profoundly modified by the more or less important changes that occurred in modes of production. It is, however, not easy to speak of magic and witchcraft as it is currently practiced and experienced in these countries, because both official discourse and research data relegate these practices to an obscure past or consider them forms of charlatanism. A series of field trips conducted in Romania in recent years, however, confirms that folk beliefs remain very much alive and that recourse to magical practices in frequent, especially when it concerns the health of children, the prosperity of the home, the productivity of animals, and so on. In fact, one does not have recourse to magic merely on an occasional basis; it is the imaginary fabric into which all individuals are enveloped. There are few mothers, for example, who do not know one or another incantation to neutralize the effects of the evil eye (belief in the evil eye is found throughout the Mediterranean Basin and elsewhere). The following Romanian example is expressed in extremely violent terms:

> May he burst, the envious one.
> Evil eye he cast.
> May he explode.
> If a virgin spellbinds him,
> May her braids fall off.
> If his wife spellbinds him,
> May her milk dry up,
> May her breasts wither,
> May her child die of hunger.
> If a youth spellbinds him,
> May he burst completely.

Many practices and incantations form part of any individual's basic knowledge, but one seeks recourse to magic only if one has the gift, the power, the desire, and the daring to do so. The specialists commonly known as witches possess the gift and the daring to practice a distinct form of magic. A witch is frequently described as someone who uses supernatural forces to do evil (although most witches will say they do what they do for the good of mankind). Witches were and still are enormously feared because they are said to "give life or death." Consulting them always means incurring some form of danger, especially since they are thought to collaborate with the Devil (who appears in his diverse forms during the séance). Access to witches is also difficult and troublesome: they live often in faraway places (necessitating a tiresome journey, waiting one's turn among the others who have come for consultations, sleeping in a strange place); one can only see them on specific days and at specific times (at night, for example); one must be recommended to them by someone in whom the witch has confidence. Thus access to specialized magic could be said to presuppose a kind of punitive expiatory path.

People have recourse to witchcraft especially in cases of serious disequilibrium or when a significant disturbance has disrupted the natural order of things. Witches are especially sought out, for example, in cases in which a marriage is endangered by the intervention of a third party (usually the husband's mistress, a rival who wishes to substitute herself for his legitimate wife). Indeed, marital relations and extramarital ties are a source of great conflict and violence, and the greater part of specialized forms of magic is played out in this arena.

To control her husband, who should not waste his energies elsewhere, a woman has recourse to two forms of specialized magic, both of which aim to reunite the legitimate couple. In the first form the wife attempts to kill the intruder (the "rival," the "stranger") or to eliminate her from the protected sphere. In the process, the two women enter into a kind of magical battle using a number of possible weapons: a charmed knife that must symbolically reach the other; dolls made from scraps of the man's or the mistress's clothing: a yellow plant *(dosnica)*, described as "terrifying," which causes the rival to wander to the ends of the earth; the mandrake, which can make people go mad; and an insect or a frog (seen as the mistress's substitute) captured under special conditions and made to suffer the worst treatments.

Specific procedures accompany the use of any of these means. For example, while piercing a symbol representing her rival with the charmed knife, the woman will utter the following incantation:

> You, charmed knife,
> Go into her body.
> Beat her,
> Crush her,
> So that her blood spouts forth.
> If she is alive, pierce her heart.
> If she is dead, seek her out in the Beyond.

While thinking of her rival a woman may prick an insect with a needle or a knife and utter:

> May the one who is breaking my home,
> The one who does not let me live with my man,
> The one who gives me no peace,
> May that one die and disappear.

In the second form—identified as the "magic of filth"—the wife will simply attempt to dissolve the soiled relationship in which her husband is involved in order to reestablish her original tie with him. She will use decoctions made from urine, semen, menstrual blood, fecal matter, sweat, or other secretions of intimate life (which serve as substitutes for the people concerned). These decoctions may be clandestinely fed to the husband. If he eats his own secretions (an act of autocannibalism), he is said to devour himself, thus reintegrating the forces and energies he seeks to dispense elsewhere. If he eats the substitutes of his wife, he is said to become impregnated by her, filled with her person.

Incantations accompany the administration of these decoctions; if, for example, the wife uses menstrual blood, she utters the following words (similar to those used in practices on certain Greek islands today):

> Just as the menses are cyclical,
> Have their hour and time,
> So, to each of my words
> May he likewise return.
> May he return to my body,
> May he return to my desire. . . .
> May my husband cling to me,
> May he explode, may he burst,
> May he not do without me.

The wife may also manipulate these secretions in other ways. She may, for example, take the earth on which her rival has trod and place it on her husband's feces, uttering an incantation all the while.

One could speak at length about these and other forms of magic still practiced in Romania and other east European countries. Indeed, despite all the sociocultural modifications and modernizing trends that have taken place in this part of the world, magic has adapted itself to its new environment. It is not a survival of a bygone era but an integral aspect of popular culture; it provides people with the power and know-how to understand their world and their position within it. Magic is still the arena through which different communities find a common language, a discourse through which they recognize themselves.

[*See also* Incantations.]

BIBLIOGRAPHY

Argenti, Philip P., and H J. Rose. *The Folk-Lore of Chios*. Cambridge, 1949.
Bîrlea, Ovidiu. "Descîntecul." In his *Folclorul românesc*, vol. 2. Bucharest, 1983.
Bîrlea, Ovidiu, and Ion Muslea. *Tipologia folclorului: Din raspunsurile la chestionarele lui B. P. Hasdeu*. Bucharest, 1970.
Bogatyrev, Pierre. *Actes magiques, rites et croyances en Russie subcarpathique*. Paris, 1929.
Eliade, Mircea. *De Zalmoxis à Gengis-Khan*. Paris, 1970. Translated as *Zalmoxis, the Vanishing God: Comparative Studies in the Religions and Folklore of Dacia and Eastern Europe* (Chicago, 1972).
Eliade, Mircea. *Occultism, Witchcraft, and Cultural Fashions: Essays in Comparative Religions*. Chicago, 1976.
Gorovei, Arthur. *Descîntecele românilor*. Bucharest, 1931.
Kabbadias, Georgios B. *Pasteurs-Nomades méditéranéens: Les Saracatsans de Grèce*. Paris, 1965.
Krauss, Friedrich S. *Slavische Volksforschungen*. Leipzig, 1908.
Lorint, F. E., and Jean Bernabé. *La sorcellerie paysanne*. Brussels, 1977.
Megas, George A. *Greek Calendar Customs*. 2d ed. Athens, 1963.
Stahl, Paul-Henri. "L'organisation magique du territoire villageois roumain." *L'homme* 13 (1973): 150–162.
Vakarelski, Christo. *Bulgarische Volkskunde*. Berlin, 1969.

13 MAGIC IN ISLAM

TOUFIC FAHD
Translated from French by David M. Weeks

Magic in Islam forms part of what are called *'ulūm al-ghayb*, "the occult sciences," which include divination, astrology, oneiromancy, and all fields of learning relating to prophecy. Magic (Arab., *siḥr*) is an important branch, like divination and astrology, with which some forms of magic overlap.

Following the very rich literature of magic in Islam, I shall here treat the various categories of *siḥr* in three sections: black magic (*'ilm al-siḥr*), theurgy (*'ilm al-khawāṣṣ wa-al-ṭalāsim*), and white or natural magic (*'ilm al-ḥiyal wa-al-shaʿwadhah*). The first section will deal with divinatory magic, exorcism of demons, spells and the summoning of spirits into bodily forms. The second section will examine the properties of divine names, numbers and certain spells, sympathetic magic or sorcery, amulets, talismans and potions, charms, and the properties of medicinal plants. The third section will consider the mutual connections between effective and efficient forces, the ability to vanish instantly from sight, and prestidigitation.

BLACK MAGIC

From the many Qur'anic verses relating to magic (sixty-six, of which only three were revealed in Medina), one might conclude that the phenomenon of *siḥr* occurs in the revelation only in the form of a condemnation of pagan practices. In certain verses, however, magic appears as a fragment of a celestial knowledge that was given to humans by fallen angels such as Hārūt and Mārūt (surah 2:102). These angels revealed to humans secrets "that they ought not to have known" (*Apocalypse of Enoch* 64:10). Thus, "God decided, in his justice, that all the inhabitants of the world would die [by flood], for they knew all the secrets of the angels, and possessed the hateful power of the demons, the power of magic" (ibid., 64:6). Another group of verses, condemning this almost instinctive quest by humans to penetrate the will of God, connects magic with divination.

Divinatory Magic. The boundaries between magic and divination remain blurred. In their classification of the sciences, the Muslim encyclopedists, such as al-Afkānī, Tāshköprüzade, and Ḥājjī Khalīfah, call divination a branch of magic. According to Edmond Doutté, the transition from magic to mantic takes place via a phenomenon of "objectivization of the desire" (Doutté, 1909, p. 352). Whether inductive or intuitive, divination partakes of magic in certain of its techniques. One of the sources of knowledge common to the magician and the seer is demonic inspiration. Furthermore, the Arab seer *(kāhin)*, and especially the female seer, practiced magic and divination concurrently (see my book *La divination arabe*, Leiden, 1966, pp. 92ff.), so that in Islamic magical literature, the two run parallel without mingling. Both make use of supernatural means to predict natural elements; both share a practical and nontheoretical character. One searches in vain for a theoretical definition of magic in the Qur'ān or the *ḥadīth* (prophetic traditions).

Exorcism and Spells. If divinatory magic has recourse to secrets revealed by fallen angels, the magic of incantations and spells is meant to compel the *jinn* and the demons to accomplish a desired end, by pronouncing the formula "'Azamtu 'alaykum" ("I command you"). The Qur'ān and the *ḥadīth* say nothing of this, but theological consideration led to the following conclusion, formulated by Ḥājjī Khalīfah:

> *This thing is possible and lawful, according to reason and the law; whoever denies it is not highly regarded, because he winds up failing to acknowledge the omnipotence of God: to subjugate the spirits, to humble them before him, and to make them subordinate to men, is one of the miracles of* [God's] *creation.*
> (Ḥājjī Khalīfah, ed. Flügel, 1955–1958, vol. 4, pp. 205–207)

Two kinds of conjuring, however, may be distin-guished. One variety consists in directing the mind toward an object other than God, and thus being unfaithful to him. When this unfaithfulness appears as one of the elements making up the magical act through one of the means used to realize it, it becomes forbidden magic. In this case, the magician acts in a manner that is wicked and harmful to others, and, indeed, a controversy arose among medieval jurists concerning the question of knowing "whether they must be killed because of the unbelief which is antecedent to the practice [of sorcery], or because of their corrupting activity and the resulting corruption of created beings" (Ibn Khaldūn, trans. Rosenthal, 1967, vol. 3, p. 159.).

On the other hand, the conjuring of spirits is permissible when it is performed "with perfect piety and the complete absence of all unlawfulness, in solitude and isolation from the world and in surrender to God" (Ḥājjī Khalīfah, op. cit., pp. 205–207). This interpretation is basically consistent with the demonological conception of Islam, which considers the *jinn* servants of God, somewhat in the manner of humans and angels.

The writers differ on how this power derived from God is applied. Fakhr al-Dīn al-Rāzī sums up the opinion of the theologians thus:

> *When the conditions are brought together and the incantations pronounced, God makes the latter like a mighty devastating fire, encircling the demons and the* jinn, *until the [four] corners of the world close in around them, and there is no place left for them to hide, nor any other choice than to come out and resign themselves to do as they are commanded. What is more, if the performer is skillful, being of good conduct and praiseworthy morals, God will dispatch powerful, rough, and strong angels to the demons to inspire them and lead them to obey and serve him.*
> (quoted in Ḥājjī Khalīfah, loc. cit.)

Summarizing the views of the Muslim theologians, Ḥājjī Khalīfah adds: "The obedience of demons and *jinn* to humans is not something unimaginable, either from the standpoint of reason or from the standpoint of accepted practice." The best illustration of this conception of magical incantation is given by certain exalted mystics, the North African marabouts, or *ṭālibs*, who transform the old pagan magic and subordinate it to the omnipotence of the one God. How, in this case, can obtaining a miracle by divine favor be distinguished from the effects of magic?

For the philosophers, whose views are summed up by Ibn Khaldūn,

The difference between miracles and magic is this: a miracle is a divine power that arouses in the soul [the ability] to exercise influence. The [worker of miracles] is supported in his activity by the spirit of God. The sorcerer, on the other hand, does his work by himself and with the help of his own psychic power, and, under certain conditions, with the support of devils. The difference between the two concerns the idea, reality, and essence of the matter.

(Ibn Khaldūn, op. cit.)

Ibn Khaldūn himself locates the distinction in external criteria, which he defines as follows:

Miracles are found [to be wrought] by good persons for good purposes and by souls that are entirely devoted to good deeds. Moreover, [they include] the 'advance challenge' [taḥaddī] of the claim to prophecy. Sorcery, on the other hand, is found [practiced] only by evil persons and as a rule is used for evil actions, such as causing discord between husband and wife, doing harm to enemies, and similar things. And it is found [practiced] by souls that are entirely devoted to evil deeds.

(ibid.)

He adds that "this is also the view of the metaphysicians," and he concludes that "among the Ṣūfīs some who are favored by acts of divine grace are also able to exercise an influence upon worldly conditions. This, however, is not counted as a kind of sorcery. It is effected with divine support" (ibid.).

One should point out, finally, that wishing does not make a magician; indeed, to be a magician presupposes a disposition and a preparation not required of the worker of miracles. "This art," the Pseudo-Majrīṭī tells us, "can be practiced and applied only by one who has [the power of] it in his nature" (al-Majrīṭī, ed. Ritter, 1933, p. 187), and Ibn Khaldūn says that the philosophers "think that a sorcerer does not acquire his magical ability but has, by nature, the particular disposition needed for exercising that type of influence" (op cit., p. 167). This disposition is called *al-ṭibā' al-tāmm*, "the perfect nature"; the person who possesses it attains "knowledge of the secrets of creation, of natural causes, and of the mode of being of things" (al-Majrīṭī, op. cit., p. 187; cf. Fahd, 1966, p. 192, n. 29). Pseudo-Majrīṭī's quotation from the so-called *Book of Hermes the Sage* defines this perfect nature in these terms:

The microcosm that is man, if he possesses the perfect nature, has a soul like the solar disc, unmoving in the heavens and illuminating every horizon with its rays. It is the same with the perfect nature whose ray is found in the soul; it flashes out, touches the translucent forces of wisdom, and draws them to the soul that is its point [of origin], just as the sun's radiance attracts the forces of the universe and lifts them up into the atmosphere.

(al-Majrīṭī, op. cit., pp. 193–194)

The progressive assimilation of the magician to the forces that he conjures, evokes, or invokes contributes to the effectiveness of his work and the success of his endeavor. The spiritual beings *(rūḥanīyah)* then appear to him as if in person, speaking to him and teaching him all things.

Evocation of Spirits. In conjuring and incantation, the magician relies on the service of *jinn* and demons to accomplish his ends; in evocation, he compels the spirits of the dead, the demons, and the planets to carry out his wishes.

Necromancy, which really belongs with divination, is steeped in black magic. Like the summoning of demons, it generally involves two phases: a material phase, consisting of the preparation of a mixture of various products belonging to a special pharmacopoeia and fumigations of every kind, plus an intellectual phase, consisting of the formulation of a prayer naming all the qualities and attributes of the spirit invoked and stating the wishes to be realized.

The evocation of the spirits of the planets is based on the knowledge of the qualities and properties of each of them: its color (red-gray for Saturn, white-gray for Jupiter, the yellow-green-red of red-gold for Mars, redgold for Venus, a mixture of all colors for Mercury, and green-white for the Moon), its odor, and its flavor (for details, see al-Majrīṭī, op. cit., pp. 140, 150–156). To evoke the spirit of a planet, one must be dressed in its color and perfumed with its scent; further, by means of ingestion, one must assume its essence and flavor. Having done so, one must watch for the moment when the planet reaches the point corresponding to it in the zodiac, on a direct line that does not cross the line of another planet of a different nature. When this is so, the line from the planet to earth will be straight and uninterrupted.

Next, from metals attributed to the planet, one must fashion a cross, hollow from top to bottom and with a hole at the top, resting on two feet. This cross is to be mounted on the image of whatever it is one plans to ask of the spirit invoked: that of a lion, for example, or a serpent, in case one desires to go to war or to overcome an enemy, of a bird if one wishes to escape danger, of a man seated on a throne if one aspires to fame, power, or respect, and so on. Likewise, to gain control of someone, one carves that person's likeness from a stone characteristic of the planet that presided over his birth, at the proper time and in the position described above. This image then serves as a base for the cross. The choice of a cross has to do with the fact that every body takes this shape; thus it serves to establish a connection between the higher spiritual entity and an image that resembles it. An incense burner made of the same metals as the cross is also used; it must have only one opening at the top of the cover, for the smoke to escape.

To summon a celestial spirit, a proper location must be selected, completely open to the sky. The ground should be strewn with plants of the same properties as the planet whose strength is to be attracted, on the principle that like attracts like; there must be nothing else on the ground or in the area. Incense of the same essence as the planet being evoked must be burned so that the fumes, escaping from the single opening in the burner, will pass through the hollow cross from bottom to top. All this must be done at a propitious time. If all these conditions are met, the upper world will be in harmony with the lower and thus the request will be received favorably. (See al-Majrīṭī, op. cit., pp. 182–186; for a French translation, see Fahd, 1966, pp. 170–171.)

THEURGY

Other techniques aimed at tapping the planetary and stellar virtues lie on the borders between magic and theurgy. The distinction between the two, according to Ibn Khaldūn, lies in the fact that

> *the sorcerer does not need any aid, while those who work with talismans seek the aid of the spiritualities of the stars, the secrets of numbers, the particular qualities of existing things, and the positions of the sphere that exercise an influence upon the world of the elements, as the astrologers maintain. The philosophers, therefore, say that sorcery is a union of spirit with spirit, while the talisman is a union of spirit with body.* (Ibn Khaldūn, op. cit., p. 166)

"As they understand it," Ibn Khaldūn continues, "that means that the high celestial natures are tied together with the low [terrestrial] natures, the high natures being the spiritualities of the stars. Those who work with [talismans], therefore, as a rule, seek the aid of astrology" (ibid., p. 167).

Such is the theory, but in practice it is rare to find mention in the texts of a magical act carried out without recourse to a material support. While the talismanic art assumes a perfect technique, grounded in astronomical, astrological, and other data, this is not required for the practice of magic, which is performed with the help of prayers, evocations, and attempts to unite spirits, demons, and stars by magical means.

The Talisman. According to Ḥājjī Khalīfah, the art of talismanry is intended

> *to combine the active celestial forces with the passive earthly forces at moments favorable to the desired action and influence, with the help of vapors [able] to strengthen and attract the spirit of the talisman, with the intent of producing unusual manifestations in the world of generation and decay. In comparison with magic, this science is more accessible, for both its principles and its causes are known. Its usefulness is obvious, but mastery comes only after a great deal of effort.* (Ḥājjī Khalīfah, op. cit., pp. 165ff.)

In fact, skill in talismanry can be acquired only by one who understands its principles, which spring from the branches of knowledge making up natural philosophy, in particular mathematics, physics, and metaphysics.

A great many elements come into play in the creation of a talisman. In addition to ease and efficiency, sympathy and antipathy, time and place, there is relativity, a basic principle of the talismanic art, the relationship between the planet and the object of the talisman as well as the similarities and parallels among its various components. To be effective, these connections should be located on the straight line crossing the talisman's field of influence.

Time plays a fundamental role in talismanry. Indeed, the proper moment is a condition *sine qua non* for the success of the undertaking. In order to seize it, one must observe the planet until it arrives at its operative position, the most favorable point in its influence, its conjunction with the other planets and its position with respect to them, the exact instant when the talisman must be set in place, and so forth. Position plays an equally important part, in particular the observer's vantage point, the spot where the talisman is made and set up, and the place of origin of the materials used to fabricate it. Numbers, as the measure of time and moment, are, like speech, necessary for the expression of quantity.

Quality, meanwhile, is equivalent in talismanry to causality. The object on which the talisman acts must bear a perfect resemblance to the quality transferred to it, so that its sphere of activity can spread. This is the basis of the connection between the higher and lower natures. Quality here is none other than inherent nature, the source of causality. Its role is therefore essential, not only in the discovery of the limited properties and influences of the planets but also in the diffusion of these same properties and influences. This leads to an increase in the quality of the material of which the talisman is made, by causing equivalent qualities to act upon it (al-Majrīṭī, op. cit., pp. 99–100).

The Properties. In the words of Paul Kraus, the properties of beings are

the virtues proper to minerals, plants, and animals, their sympathies and antipathies, as well as the use of these virtues in the various arts and in medicine. The miraculous occupies an important place here, and affinities with magic are undeniable. Men, animals, and plants are no longer considered objects of reasoned inquiry, but are endowed with occult powers, able to heal any malady and to procure happiness and miraculous power of man.

(Kraus, 1942–1943, vol. 2, p. 61)

Among the physical properties, those of stones hold pride of place in talismanic practice, and knowledge of them is one of the essential conditions for a talisman's success, likewise for the properties of animal bodies, where magic comes to the aid of medicine; the latter are considered healthful even for incurable diseases. Plants possess many properties used in the rich magical repertoire of fumigations. A large number of these are found in the geographical compilation known as *Nabatean Agriculture*, and Pseudo-Majrīṭī also collected many of them. Among the plants used in magical operations are laurel, marshmallow, mandrake, elm, pennyroyal, myrtle, olive, horseradish, darnel, rice, beans, chickpeas, watermelon, and chicory.

The magical powers of plants are commonly connected with the natures of the planets. These natures impart their virtues to whatever responds to them. The fact that a plant sprouts in one soil and not in another comes not from the particular nature of the soil but from the marriage of a fixed disposition with given conditions of air and water. "The prime cause of this lies on the line crossing the horizon of this piece of ground and marking the zone of influence of certain planets on certain countries; thus the existence of plants and specific features in a given country to the exlusion of others" (al-Majrīṭī, op. cit., pp. 385ff.).

This learned theurgy, which systematically and "rationally" exploits the virtues of animal, vegetable, and mineral kingdoms, is marked by its Hellenistic origins and by the rich syncretism from which it emanates. [*See* Theurgy.] Popular magic in Islam has preserved this spirit, while opening it to new influences in the various islamized countries, hence the existence of magical practices peculiar to each of the major Muslim regions.

128 Hidden Truths: Magic, Alchemy, and the Occult

There are innumerable survivals of ancient theurgy in Muslim tradition, where many instances are ascribed to the Prophet himself, and in the abundant magical literature that spread out throughout the Muslim world. A saying attributed to the Prophet reflects an important principle of ancient magic, namely the magical power of the spoken word: "There is," he is supposed to have said, "a kind of utterance that is none other than magic" (quoted in al-Majrīṭī, op. cit., p. 9). By virtue of this principle, onomatomancy became widespread in Muslim lands, and the ninety-nine "most beautiful names" of God, like the most ancient surahs of the Qur'ān, played a very great role in spells, amulets, and potions. Muslim magic was based in large part on the knowledge of the letters that made up the supreme name of God. At the base of these speculations, we find the theory asserting that the letters of the alphabet, being at the root of creation, represent the "materialization" of the divine word.

However, according to Ibn Khaldūn, there is

> *a real difference between persons who practice talismanry and those who work with the secret virtues of names, regarding the manner in which the soul is made to act on living beings). . . . This soul has inherently the ability to encompass nature and control it, but its effect, among those who operate by means of talismans, is limited to drawing down from above the spirits of the spheres and tying them to certain figures or numerical supports. . . . It is otherwise with those who, to give their souls the ability to act, make use of the secret properties of names; they must be illuminated by the celestial light and sustained by divine help.*
>
> (Ibn Khaldūn, op. cit., pp. 175ff.)

These latter avoid giving the name of magic to practices consisting of the use of secret properties of letters, numbers, and names. Nonetheless, in practice, "they fall under the idea of sorcery" (ibid., p. 181), although they tend to locate their activities in the legitimate realm of natural magic.

WHITE OR NATURAL MAGIC

The branch of magic known in English as white magic, or natural magic, is denoted in Arabic by two terms: one, *sīmiyā'*, of Greek origin *(sēmeia)*, and the other, *nīrinjāt*, Persian *(neyrang)*. Both are applied generally to illusionism, prestidigitation, fakery, and legerdemain.

According to Ḥājjī Khalīfah (op. cit., pp. 646–647), natural magic involves imaginary phenomena, occurring in space and having no correspondence to anything palpable. Their production and causes remain a secret known only to the practitioners. Often it includes mixtures concocted by the magician out of natural essences, ointments, liquified materials, or even special words with suggestive powers. The range of such practices is very large: aerial illusions, atmospheric vapors, playing with fire, tricks with bottles, cups, and glasses, illusions with eggs, fruits produced out of season, wax figures, animal taming, discovery of hidden objects, preparation of magic ink, and so on.

In the *Ghāyat al-ḥakīm* of Pseudo-Majrīṭī, the term *nīrinjāt* is applied to charms that have an extraordinary power over human beings and natural phenomena alike, such as a magic ring that transfixes anyone who looks at it, amulets that ward off bad weather or neutralize weapons held by enemies, and so on (al-Majrīṭī, op. cit., pp. 242ff.). The making of these *nīrinjāt* requires extreme precision and careful handling of the poisonous materials used in their composition. These are potions that act by mans of absorption or fumigations of various powders and oils. The anticipated effects of these potions vary, and their application depends upon astrological conditions, as in all magical activity, and on the simultaneous utterance of a formulaic spell containing incomprehensible names.

In the same class of magical activity belongs the rainmaker, who commands the stars and who alternates between a demanding, coercive, and occasionally even insulting tone toward the heavens and flattery toward God. The imprecations he pronounces have a clearly magical character: often they include the use of the divine names with the aim of bending the will of heaven. The author of the *Theology of Aristotle*, followed by Ibn Sīnā (Avicenna), affirms that "prayer influences the sun and the stars, by imparting a certain motion to them, because the parts of the world form a single whole, like a 'single animal'" (quoted in A. Goichon, *Directives et remarques*, Paris, 1951, p. 250). For greater effectiveness, the rainmaker stood inside a circle *(mandil)* or a magic square.

In this same category is also included the evil eye. Ibn Sīnā explains it as "an admiring tendency of the soul that exercises, by this property, a weakening influence on the object of its admiration" (ibid., p. 523). For Ibn Khaldūn, the effect is

> *natural and innate. It cannot be left alone. It does not depend on the free choice of its possessor. It is not acquired by him. [It is] an influence exercised by the soul of the person who has the evil eye. A thing or situation appears pleasing to the eye of a person, and he likes it very much. This [circumstance] creates in him envy and the desire to take it away from its owner. Therefore he prefers to destroy him.*
> (Ibn Khaldūn, op. cit., pp. 170–171)

It may be concluded from the foregoing that Islam, the heir of ancient civilizations, has preserved for us, in its rich cultural and folkloric patrimony, remnants of Semitic and Hellenistic notions that were developed and intermingled in the wide expanse of the ancient and medieval Near East.

BIBLIOGRAPHY
Primary Sources

Būnī, Aḥmad ibn ʿAlī al-. *Shams al-maʿārif wa-laṭāʾif al-ʿawārif.* 4 vols. Cairo, 1905. A most important source for practical and theoretical understanding of Islamic magic. There are three versions of this work: short, medium and long. It exists in several lithographs and numerous manuscripts.

Ḥājjī Khalīfah. *Kashf al-ẓunūn.* 8 vols. Edited by O. Flügel. London, 1955-1958. A large encyclopedia with material arranged in alphabetical order. See especially the articles on *siḥr, sīmiyāʾ, ṭalāsim,* and the keywords given therein.

Ibn Khaldūn. *Al-muqaddimah.* Edited by M. Quatremère. Paris, 1858–. Translated by Franz Rosenthal as *The Muqaddimah: An Introduction to History,* 2d ed., 3 vols. (Princeton, 1967). The emphasis in this work is on the theoretical aspect of magic.

Majrīṭī, Maslamah ibn Aḥmad al-. *Ghāyat al-ḥakim.* Edited by H. Ritter. Leipzig, 1933. Translated by H. Ritter and M. Plessner as *"Picatrix": Das Ziel des Weisen Pseudo-Majrīṭī* (London, 1962). A study of magic and theurgy from the double perspective of theory (*ʿilmī*) and practice (*ʿmalī*). Completed in AH 395/1004 CE, it is the most important work in this field.

On the question of its attribution to Maslamah al-Majrītī ("of Madrid"), see H. Ritter's article in *Vorträge der Bibliothek Warburg* 1 (1921–1922): 95–124.

Secondary Sources

Fahd, Toufic. "Le monde du sorcier en Islam." In *Le monde du sorcier*, pp. 157–204. Paris, 1966. Includes an extensive bibliography. The present article owes much to this study.

Doutté, Edmond. *Magie et religion dans l'Afrique du Nord*. Algiers, 1909. An important study on magical practices in North Africa.

Kovalenko, Anatoly. *Magie et Islam*. Geneva, 1981. A 721-page volume containing a detailed description of magical procedures, with an exhaustive bibliography. This is an invaluable reference work.

Kraus, Paul. *Jābir Ibn Ḥayyān*. 2 vols. Cairo, 1942–1943. A valuable tool for the study of the occult sciences in Islam and their relationship to Hellenism.

Mauchamps, Émile. *La sorcellerie au Maroc*. Paris, n.d. A posthumous work preceded by a study on the author and the work by Jules Bris. Mauchamps's investigation into magical practices in Morocco is an exemplary model; every Muslim region needs such an inquiry.

14 MAGIC IN SOUTH ASIA

Teun Goudriaan

South Asian religious history offers a unique documentation textually recorded over three thousand years of the manipulation of the powers of the universe in a great variety of methods, aims, and social conditions.

IDEOLOGICAL POSITION
The oldest preserved corpus of Indian religious tradition, the Veda, is a rich source of magical ideas and devices. In the world view of the Vedic ritualists, all phenomena in the world are interrelated. No fundamental distinction is made between substances or beings and their qualities; powers and processes; symbols and the symbolized, and so forth. Reality is built up from various networks of affinities or connections *(nidāna)*, which can be detected, evoked and activated by man. Many of these similarities are also known from elsewhere. Thus, clear water not only purifies the body but also serves to wash off the impurity caused by untruth *(Śatapatha Brāhmaṇa* 1.1.1.1). In the ritual, the effect-directed interrelations *(bandhu)* between the material and the spiritual, the human and the cosmic levels are employed systematically. Very important as a key to the hidden reality is the realm of sound, which can be manipulated by the power of the sacred, ceremonially uttered word *(mantra)*. [*See* Language, *article on* Sacred Language.]

In Vedic religion, a demarcation between "magical" and "religious" ritual ideologies is difficult to maintain and partly depends on the definition of "magic." One might better, with Hermann Oldenberg, distinguish between unspecified, nonsacerdotal or private magic *(māyā, yātu)* and magical powers manipulated in the cultic sphere *(brahman, tapas)*. The aim of the ritual procedure is to keep the life process of the universe moving, to maintain good relations with the powers of the Unseen, to secure cosmic order on which human welfare depends. Within this decidedly religious context, magical thought patterns and actions find their natural place. If it is true that religion focuses on encounter and magic on manipulation, one can say that both aspects are often present in the intricate religious ceremonies such as the Rājasūya or Aśvamedha described in Vedic texts. Magic predominates, however, when important *mantra*s are applied outside their original context for specified, immediately mundane objectives (e.g., the Ṛgvedic hymns discussed in the Ṛgvidhāna).

In post-Vedic Hindu tradition, supernatural powers are ultimately derived from the Supreme Power, in this connection most commonly Śiva, who in several of his aspects functions as the magician's chosen deity; in popular Buddhism, such powers are subject to Lord Buddha. The spheres of religion and magic continue to overlap, though on a much more restricted scale than in the Vedic period. Although deities are invoked during ceremonies of what we would call magic and magical elements sometimes feature in otherwise purely religious contexts, the distinction between magic and religion is ever present in the popular mind. A distinction is also made between socially approved and disapproved kinds of magic.

TERMINOLOGY

Of the four branches of Vedic literature, especially the *Atharvaveda* (of sometimes disputed authority) contains a rich collection of spells and magical rites. Later generations distinguished two kinds of Atharvavedic lore: the *ātharvaṇaḥ*, aiming at positive welfare *(puṣṭi)* or pacification *(śānti)* of evil influences, and the *āṅgirasaḥ*, directed against inimical powers or individuals. Vedic and later Sanskrit literature mention different kinds of supernatural power; there is no exact counterpart to our term *magic*. In nontechnical literature, *māyā* perhaps comes closest. The term denotes a creative faculty originally in the possession of superhuman beings and applicable to good as well as evil purposes. [*See* Māyā.]

A prominent feature of *māyā* is the creation by its possessor *(māyāvin)* of deceptive phenomena (e.g., a wild animal or one's own double, or even the phenomena of existence) by which the victim is beguiled or subjugated. In younger texts (especially the *Mahābhārata*), divine *māyā* is associated with the subjugation of creatures by the tricks of fate or supernatural agency. This divine faculty can be appropriated by human performers who emulate or associate themselves with divine prototypes renowned for their powers of *māyā* (Indra, Viṣṇu). *Māyā* has also epistemological and metaphysical connotations that dominate its semantic field; in recent Sanskrit literature, the term is seldom used in a purely magical context.

Other Sanskrit terms cover related meanings, partly overlapping each other but never entirely synonymous. To mention a few: *brahman* is wielded by the specialist of the sacred word for the weal of the Aryan community. *Tapas* (internal heat) is a special possession of yogins and ascetics. *Yātu* is the dreaded power of the inimical sorcerer *(yātudhāna)* or sorceress; the term survives in the Hindi *jādū*. The most encompassing term for rites of magic in Sanskrit is simply *karman* ("deed, act"); indeed, all human activity is felt automatically to create its consequence. From the same root is derived *kṛtyā* ("creation"), known since the *Atharvaveda* as a female evil spirit dispatched by a sorcerer. Also yoga ("method, practice") is used in a magical sense; among the people, a yogin often functioned as a miracle worker.

Specialists developed a voluminous literature in Sanskrit and vernaculars on magically applied ritualism, most often called *mantravāda* ("doctrine of *mantra*"). They continued to distinguish rites of protection *(śānti)* and aggression *(abhicāra)*, while realizing the relative value of this criterion: the protection of A might imply the downfall of B. Widely known is a series of "six acts" *(ṣaṭ karmāṇi)*: subjugation *(vaśīkaraṇa)*, immobilization *(stambhana)*, eradication *(uccāṭana)*, causing dissension *(vidveṣaṇa)*, liquidation *(māraṇa)*, and pacification *(śānti)*. There are varieties to this standard list. This theoretical framework was devised to cover a multitude of sophisticated and popular devices actually practiced by unscrupulous brahmans and others. The subject is treated in Tantras, religious books of the non-Vedic esoteric tradition (Hindu and Buddhist) or in monographs derived from these. Influence of this sanskritized tradition of magic is also traceable in Jainism, in Buddhist countries, in tribal cultures of South Asia, and in Indonesia (especially Bali).

PRACTICES AND CONDITIONS

The Veda-oriented theorists distinguished three contexts for ritual action: regular, motivated (i.e., performed on special occasions such as festivals), and desire-oriented *(kāmya;* e.g., curing of disease, prolongation of life, elimination of rivals, softening of a beloved's heart, exorcism). A performer's ritual activity is again held to comprise three spheres: thought, word, and action, the latter subdivided into the rites proper, the preparation and handling of paraphernalia, and corporeal particulars such as symbolic gestures or a powerful glance. The *mantra,* although changing its outward form after the Vedic period, maintains its predominant position. [*See* Mantra.] Very often, elements from Sanskrit *mantras* persist in the spells uttered by tribal or low-caste magicians. Usually, such spells contain invocations of deities who are ordered to execute the performer's command. In *mantravāda,* initiation into a *mantra,* which is phonic manifestation of the world-sustaining power, can only be obtained under the guidance of a guru and implies several preparatory procedures such as astrological computation, protracted recitation, and regulation of breath. The *mantrin* should always carefully concentrate his thoughts and will upon the desired effect.

Descriptions of the rites proper tend to contain gaps while the social context is often altogether omitted. Actual practice includes prognostication, divination, witchfinding, manipulation of spirits or deities, exorcism (e.g., by striking with a broom over the patient's body while muttering spells) application of herbs or potions, innumerable small protective rites and customs (e.g., burying the placenta of a newborn child within the house's precincts) and aggressive rites of many kinds, such as piercing a small image representing the enemy. Besides, we find ample reference in literature to the art of *indrajāla,* which enabled clever performers to make a living by fascinating the public with hypnotism or juggling. Many magical practices have entered folklore as convention or customs that may persist for a considerable period along with alternatives such as medical aid; charms or amulets continue to be worn as "ornaments."

Magic is of course most prominent in exceptional circumstances when human life or welfare are at stake and psychic stress is intensified: sickness of children or other members of the family, or of cattle; attacks by poisonous snakes or other dangerous animals; pollution ("poisoning") of food or water; barrenness; tensions between families. The community needs protection in case of epidemics or plagues, drought, and so forth. In the past, magic was a necessary complement to military operations.

Those who cherish private desires or grudges (envy, fear) may also have recourse to magic. Antisocial rites of sorcery are proscribed by common opinion; countermagic, however, is desirable against malevolent ghosts such as *churel*s (women who died in childbirth) or deceased first wives who appear envious of their husband's second partner. Aggressive rites of countermagic are also well known from Sri Lanka *(kodivina)* and elsewhere. Witchcraft is still widely believed in and women in certain positions (e.g., daughters-in-law) are often suspected of it. Persecution of witches is occasionally reported.

MAGICIANS AND THEIR POSITION

In South Asian religious tradition (Buddhist as well as Hindu) the common opinion has always been that the endeavor to manipulate superhuman powers, even if possible, is inferior (because motivated by immediate worldly ends) and therefore detracts man from his ultimate purpose: release from mundane existence. But practice and theory are widely divergent. Ironically, creative and influential religious leaders who were guides on the road to release have often been credited by the popular imagination with powers of miracle working. Thus, for instance, the Buddha is said to have miraculously crossed the Ganges only a moment before his death *(Mahāparinibbāna Sutta)*. Of his disciples, especially Moggallāna (Skt., Maudgalyāyana) is known to have possessed an enormous store of supernatural power (Pali, *iddhi, Aṅguttara Nikāya* 1.23, etc.), which he used for such ends as the humiliation of conceited supernatural beings. In later Indian Buddhist as well as Hindu tradition, Siddha Nāgārjuna (eighth century CE?, often confused with the philosopher Nāgārjuna) has earned fame as an alchemist, inventor of elixirs, and author of magical books. [*See also* Alchemy, *article on* Indian Alchemy.]

In practice, magic is most often entrusted to a recognized specialist. As religious functionaries, the brahman, the village priest, and the diviner or exorcist can act on complementary levels. The latter might be characterized by his knowledge of *mantra*s (probably corruptions from some Tantric written source), his familiarity with and supremacy over relevant lesser deities and spirits, his ability for the diagnosis and cure of disease, and his strength of character, which inspires confidence in his clients. After thorough training, he settles as an independent practitioner who is remunerated by his clientele; his status depends on his personal qualities, not on ascription or heredity. In different regions, he bears different titles, for instance *ojha, gunia, baiga,* or *bhagat*. These titles can also overlap and be in vogue in the same place for different functions; thus, the *bhagat* may work through possession by his favorite deity, while the *ojha* claims mastery over the spirit world by means of his mantric expertise. In hinduized regions, the *ojha* can be a degraded brahman; in Buddhist countries, magic is sometimes practiced by monks. Also in tribal communities, the functions of village priest and healer-magician tend to be separated, although the village priest can help people through possession by or invocation of his deity. The functionary who sincerely and successfully works for the common weal is highly respected; but unscrupulous people who lend themselves to antisocial activities are disliked and feared.

Magic in South Asia is rooted in both high-status religion (where it has been relegated to a marginal position) and popular (or tribal) tradition. Although it is usually associated with the latter, there has been constant interaction between the two spheres. But respectable people, even if not denying the possibility that "things are done," have a definite conviction that they are done in circles of low repute.

BIBLIOGRAPHY

A comprehensive historical or phenomenological study of Indian magic has not yet been written. Data must be gathered from extremely dispersed sources. Vedic magic is covered in Hermann Oldenberg's *Die Religion des Veda,* 2d ed. (Stuttgart, 1917), pp. 465–522, and in Jan Gonda's *Vedic Literature (Saṃhitās and Brāhmaṇas),* vol. 1, fasc. 1, or *A History of Indian Literature* (Wiesbaden, 1975). Studies on Vedic magic most often concentrate on the *Atharvaveda;* see Maurice Bloomfield's*The Atharvaveda and the Gopathabrāhmaṇa* (Strassburg, 1899), N.J. Shende's *The Religion and Philosophy of the Atharvaveda* (Poona, 1952), and Margaret Stutley's *Ancient Indian Magic and Folklore: An Introduction* (Boulder, 1980). Many particulars on "sanskritized" magic can be found in my book *Māyā Divine and Human* (Delhi, 1978). Two of the many books and articles concerning the role of magic in tribal communities of South Asia by dedicated workers in the field are *Tribal Religion* (Delhi, 1978), by Joseph Troisi (see especially pages 199–237), and *Maria Murder and Suicide,* 2d ed. (Oxford, 1950), by Verrier Elwin (see pages 61–81). Although much of the data in William Crooke's *The Popular Religion and Folk-lore of Northern India* (1894), 2 vols., 2d ed., rev. (Delhi, 1968), is antiquated, there is much of interest to recommend it. Beni Gupta's *Magical Beliefs and Superstitions* (Delhi, 1979), although substandard, is also recommended for its interesting data on popular Hinduism. Gupta concentrates on Rajasthan. A recent historical study of witchcraft and sorcery is Rajaram N. Saletore's *Indian Witchcraft: A Study in Indian Occultism* (New Delhi, 1981). For an interesting article on witchcraft, see Scarlett Epstein's "A Sociological Analysis of Witch Beliefs in a Mysore Village," in *Magic, Witchcraft and Curing,* edited by John Middleton (Garden City, N.Y., 1967), pp. 135–154. Data from Sri Lanka can be found in Paul Wirz's *Exorcism and the Art of Healing in Ceylon* (Leiden, 1954) and in a more recent study by Gananath Obeyesekere, "Sorcery, Premeditated Murder and the Canalization of Aggression in Sri Lanka," *Ethnology* 14 (1975): 1–23.

15 MAGIC IN TRIBAL SOCIETIES

Donald R. Hill

Magic, in the view of many anthropologists and other scholars of small-scale societies—those in which effective political control is restricted to a village or group of villages—is the manipulation of enigmatic forces for practical ends. Magical means are said to be extranatural or supernatural, and the objectives of magical intervention, natural. The magician prepares a variety of special objects or "bundles," "spells," "incantations," or "potions," which are thought to bring about, in some mysterious way, real changes in a person, object, or event.

In the simplest foraging societies everyone knows some magic, and a shaman is usually a part-time specialist in healing and divination who may be called on for public religious ritual. In agrarian and other, more complex societies magicians tend to work for private clients in curing illnesses, in ensuring a positive outcome of an intended act, or in modifying the behavior of a third party. Magic in these societies, where there is greater specialization, tends to be practiced in private and, at times, against the public interest.

Some anthropologists of the late nineteenth and early twentieth centuries believed that so-called primitive peoples confused magical causality and natural causality. Today most anthropologists hold that magicians can distinguish the one from the other. Magic is used to coax nature to do its job, not to replace it; that is, the magician tries to engender a desired natural process as opposed to some other natural process, and this he accomplishes principally through the use of metaphor—the "power of words"—or other magical formulas. The magician may also deceive the client into imagining that some noxious natural substance "removed" from the client's body is the source of his sickness or whatever supernatural harm has befallen him (when, in fact, the magician comes upon the substance through a trick and does not remove it from the client's body). Magic may be used to supplement natural causality so that no chances are taken. When natural causality is not known, use of magic may still be rational: that is, given that many actual or perceived dangers are beyond human control, one must at least try something.

Typically, magic is contrasted with science and religion. It differs from both in that its purposes are practical, not theoretical or cosmic. It shares with science the desire to obtain a utilitarian understanding of everyday events, and with religion the use of extranatural processes. Thus magic is neither primitive science nor the religion of primitive people, contrary to views prevalent among nineteenth-century theorists; rather it supplements each. In small-scale societies magic may be entwined with science and religion to such a degree that their disengagement is arbitrary. Observers of these societies tend to label communal rituals and beliefs "religion" and private uses of mysterious forces for personal gain "magic." In such societies, applied science is craft—the ability to make utilitarian tools and other objects—or the practical knowledge of planting, hunting, or curing. Here again magic is inexorably tied to science in a supplementary way, in that magical procedures give the craftsperson, gardener, or herbalist a measure of confidence in a risky endeavor: magic can protect a newly built canoe against sinking, keep insects out of gardens, and heal the sick. Magic is never an alternative to practical science or technology; rather it is an attempt to tip the odds in the favor of the practitioner in the likely event that scientific knowledge is limited.

In small-scale societies magic may represent the instrumental aspect of religious belief: the same myths—the stories that explain a people's origins or an ultimate cause—validate religion and magic. However, in religion the myths are believed to be universally applicable and are used to support the public good or the established order, whereas in magic the myths are fragmented and used for individual purposes. Thus the conflict between the social good and individual need sometimes finds expression as a conflict between religion and magic. As manifested in Europe, that conflict involved the church and the practice of witchcraft. Anthropologists have applied the term *witchcraft* to practices outside Europe, but the conflict with well-established religion that the use of this term suggests is not necessarily present in simple societies.

The terms *sorcery* and *divination* have also been applied to magical traditions outside Europe. Although there is substantial variation from society to society and among scholars who use these terms to describe indigenous beliefs, witchcraft usually refers to the involuntary practice of magic, and sorcery to the deliberate practice of magic. Witchcraft is thought to be involuntary, since at times the witch may be unaware of the condition. Furthermore, a witch may be possessed against his or her own will. Witchcraft receives greater attention in the literature than does sorcery, possibly because witchcraft appears to be more common and because anthropologists are interested in the social implications of accusations of witchcraft. Witchcraft activities may have good intentions ("white" magic), or they may have evil intentions ("black" magic), although here again field data suggest that such a distinction is not always clear. Divination is not identical to magic, as no manipulation of natural events is sought. Yet it is not entirely separate from magic. Divination is the attempt to reveal hidden information by "reading" the mystical symbolism found in otherwise ordinary objects or action. The oracle exposes the probable result of an intended action. The person who consults the oracle may then choose the action if that result is desired, or he may select some other course of action if it is not. Divination may not necessarily involve foretelling the future. An oracle may reveal the cause of some community problem: someone is a witch and so is the source of harm. Identifying the problem suggests its solution: exorcise the witch. Thus the diviner taps the same mystical forces that the magician employs. But, unlike the magician, the diviner does not attempt to change events; rather he seeks to know what has happened or what will happen.

An early interpretation of magic was set forth by James G. Frazer (1854–1941) in *The Golden Bough,* a massive study of supernatural practices around the world. In common with many social philosophers of the late nineteenth century, Frazer held that use of magic was typical of early societies. Human thought progressed from magic to religion and thence to science. Magic is like science in that both explain the causality of ordinary events by suggesting that cause A has effect B. However, magic is pseudoscience in that it confuses supernatural efficacy with natural results. Today most anthropologists disagree with Frazer on this point and follow the interpretation of Bronislaw Malinowski (1884–1942), who held that the magician is well aware of the distinction between the supernatural and natural realms.

Scholars look more kindly upon Frazer's classification of types of magic, if only for the sake of convenience. According to Frazer, magic follows the "law of sympathy": magical causes may have distinct effects through one or the other of two procedures. The first is homeopathic magic: the magician acts out a procedure on models of the intended victim, and what he does is mysteriously transmitted to the victim himself. "Like produces like" is the principle here. A pin stuck in a doll that represents the victim causes harm to the victim himself. The second type of sympathetic magic is contagious magic: items that have been in contact with the victim, such as his hair or nail clippings, may be magically manipulated to produce harm in the victim.

Malinowski best explicated what is today a commonly held view among scholars: that magic and science supplement each other and are not to be confused. In extensive fieldwork among inhabitants of the Trobriand Islands off northeast New Guinea (1914–1920), Malinowski found that these gardening and seafaring people were highly empirical in their approach to horticulture, canoe building, and sailing. Yet they consistently tempered their pragmatism with magic. In sailing, they ordinarily relied on their craft skills and seamanship, but they understood, too, that native craftsmanship and seamanship were at times insufficient aids in withstanding the unexpected foreboding condition, like a capricious storm on open water. For these possibilities the Trobrianders used magic: it seemed to make the unknown amenable to human action and therefore provided psychological reassurance for a potentially perilous voyage. For Malinowski, then, there is no evolution from magic to religion and ultimately to science; rather these three facets of human behavior must be understood together, as aspects of a cultural system.

In his classic study of a people of Zaire, *Witchcraft, Oracles, and Magic among the Azande* (1937), E. E. Evans-Pritchard (1902–1974) took up Malinowski's argument that magic has its own logic. If one accepts the Zande worldview, then belief in magic follows. "Witchcraft, oracles, and magic are like three sides to a triangle," wrote Evans-Pritchard. "Oracles and magic are two different ways of combatting witchcraft" (p. 387). Consultation of oracles in divination can locate the source of witchcraft, and use of magic can combat it. For example, the Zande hold that all human death is caused by witchcraft. True, if a man walks under a cliff, is struck by a rock, and subsequently dies, the Zande would not deny empirical causality: surely the rock caused the death. Yet they would also claim an attendant causality: what, it could be asked, caused that person to walk under the cliff in the first place? Why did the rock fall just as the person was under the cliff? Surely some witch was responsible. To discover the identity of the witch, the Zande would consult the oracles.

The pioneering work of Malinowski and Evans-Pritchard contributed much to the development of the modern anthropological view of magic: specifically, that it has social, cultural, and psychological functions; that it is a rational activity akin to but separate from science; and that its use is not restricted to the so-called primitive peoples but may also be found in complex societies. These scholars emphasized the practical use of magic, as a private act in a social matrix. But there is a related stream of anthropological thought that concerns magic as an individual's ritual or cognitive act.

In his *Elementary Forms of the Religious Life,* Émile Durkheim (1858–1917) saw magic and religion as embedded in each other. Both contain beliefs and rites, but whereas religious rites are concerned with the sacred, magical rites are directed toward the utilitarian. Religion works toward communal goals while magic deals with private ends. It is this that explains the abhorrence with which organized religions reject magical practices. Religion involves a church operating in public, while magic involves an individual operating in private.

Marcel Mauss (1872–1950), Durkheim's son-in-law and intellectual heir, saw magic as "private, secret, mysterious and tending at the margin towards the forbidden rite" (Lukes, in Sills, 1968, p. 80). Like Durkheim, Mauss emphasized the similarity between magic and religion. In Mauss's view, both involve mystical power. Magic is a "social fact," a fundamental unit of society. Every rite that is not communal involves magic. For peoples of Oceania, the supernatural or mystical force in magic is *mana,* a nonsentient supernatural power. Similar notions are found in many other parts of the world, and anthropologists have labeled them *mana* as well. *Mana* may be located in objects or people. It is the power transmitted through the laying on of hands when one is cured of illness. *Mana* resides in the "ghost shirt," a special garment worn by some nineteenth-century Plains Indians to protect against bullets. And *mana* is to be found in all lucky charms. The transfer of *mana,* or the aura given off by an object or person with *mana,* is at the heart of many magical practices: the transfer is said to ensure supernatural protection.

Central to any discussion of magic are a number of puzzling questions. How can people actually believe that a special garment will protect them against bullets? Why do people let themselves be duped by the hocus-pocus of the magician? Are people so credulous as to believe that placing a photograph of an intended victim in a coffin will actually harm that person?

Lucien Lévi-Bruhl (1857–1939) provided one answer to these questions. Like Frazer, Lévi-Bruhl developed an evolutionary scheme to account for cultural differences. He focused on human thought, however, not social institutions. For most of his career he held to what was essentially an elaboration of the racist notion that socalled primitive peoples are less fully evolved than "civilized" peoples, and that their thinking, which Lévi-Bruhl labeled "prelogical," is fundamentally childlike. Civilized peoples, in his view, think rationally, logically. Prelogical thinking involves a different order of perception: mystic properties are attached to inanimate objects or to living things. Magic is thus part of prelogical thinking, as are many other aspects of so-called primitive culture: language, enumeration, memory. Toward the end of his career, Lévi-Bruhl modified his position on the inherent difference of certain groups of human beings. Humans taken as a whole, he came to believe, have capacities for the various styles of thought: prelogical mentality is to be found everywhere, but it is emphasized more in primitive societies.

This brings us close to Claude Lévi-Strauss's view of the "savage mind." Magical action is, in his view, a subset of analogical thought, the mental activity emphasized in simple societies. Magic involves an assumption that metaphors work according to physical or natural laws. The case of the Zande peripatetic hit by a falling rock might be solved in this fashion: human intent of harm to that individual was paralleled by the natural event of the falling stone.

Lévi-Strauss formulated his own contrast between magic and religion: religion is "a humanization of natural laws," while magic is "a naturalization of human actions—the treatment of certain human actions as if they were an integral part of physical determinism" (1962, p. 221). Lévi-Strauss envisages no evolutionary sequence beginning with magic: magic, religion, and science all shade into one another, and each one has a place in human society.

The contemporary scholar S. J. Tambiah also sees analogy at work in science. Science, however, begins with known causal relationships between phenomena and then, through analogy, discovers the identical causal relations between unknown phenomena. Meaning imbued in the magical act is analogously transferred to the natural activity. This is not, Tambiah argues, faulty science but a normal activity of human thought: magic is a specialized use of analogy and the imputation of meaning from the magical procedure to a natural referent. Thus magic does what science cannot: it helps create a world of meaning. Seemingly bizarre magical behavior is to be understood as an exercise in the exploration of meaning in practical activity, not as a refutation of natural law.

Many anthropologists would argue that magic is part of the normal daily routines of people in modern, complex societies. Clearly magic is involved when a baseball player, in order to get a hit, crosses himself or picks up a bit of dirt before batting. *Mana* is the "charisma" of the persuasive individual; it is also the "prestige" of the person of high social station. Magical protection is afforded the automobile driver who places the statue of a saint on the dashboard. And magic is involved in the daily ritual of personal ablutions and grooming: "I must always wear this tie with that suit," "If my hair is not styled just so, I won't feel right." The doctor says, "Take two pills and call me if you don't feel better in twenty-four hours," and we take his advice, since, like most laymen, we tend to see the science of the expert as a form of magic. And this is necessarily so, as we cannot all be experts in everything, yet we still need to reduce our anxiety and gain a sense of order and meaning in our lives.

BIBLIOGRAPHY

With the publication of *The Golden Bough: A Study in Magic and Religion,* 2 vols. (London, 1890), James Frazer put the study of magic forever on the agenda of anthropologists, folklorists, and all scholars of small-scale societies. Frazer's library study eventually grew to twelve volumes (3d ed., rev. & enl.; London, 1911–1915) plus an *Aftermath* (London, 1936). An abridged, single-volume version, entitled *The New Golden Bough,* edited by Theodor H. Gaster, was published in 1959 (New York).

In a theoretical essay entitled *Magic, Science, and Religion* (New York, 1948) Bronislaw Malinowski criticized Frazer's armchair scholarship, and it is with Malinowski's *Coral Gardens and Their Magic,* 2 vols. (Bloomington, Ind., 1935), that the modern anthropological field study of magic really begins. E. E. Evans-Pritchard's *Witchcraft, Oracles, and Magic among the*

Azande, 2d ed. (1937; Oxford, 1950), is a classic field study of magic among a traditional African group. Religion in small-scale societies, especially among the indigenous peoples of Australia, is the subject of Émile Durkheim's *The Elementary Forms of the Religious Life* (1915; New York, 1965). Greater depth is given to the Durkheimian approach to magic in Henri Hubert and Marcel Mauss's "Esquisse d'une théorie générale de la magie," *L'année sociologique* 7 (1904). Subsequently translated as *A General Theory of Magic* (London, 1972), this important essay is quoted by Steven Lukes in his article on Mauss in the *International Encyclopedia of the Social Sciences,* edited by David L. Sills (New York, 1968), vol. 9, pp. 78–82. The racist position that the use of magic is an outcome of "primitive" thought is set forth by Lucien Lévy-Bruhl, especially in his *Primitive Mentality* (New York, 1923).

The nature of magical thought, as a species of normal human thought, is spelled out by Claude Lévi-Strauss in his classic essay *The Savage Mind* (Paris, 1962). Summations of anthropological ideas concerning magic and religion in simple societies can be found in Ruth Benedict's "Magic," in the *Encyclopaedia of the Social Sciences* (New York, 1933), vol. 10, pp. 39–44; Nur Yalman's "Magic," in the *International Encyclopedia of the Social Sciences* (New York, 1968), vol. 9, pp. 521–527; E. E. Evans-Pritchard's *Theories of Primitive Religion* (Oxford, 1965); and the various editions of *The Reader in Comparative Religion: An Anthropological Approach,* edited by William A. Lessa and Evon Z. Vogt. Stanley J. Tambiah's article entitled "The Form and Meaning of Magical Acts: A Point of View" appears in the fourth edition (New York, 1979) of the reader.

THREE

MAGICAL OBJECTS, TECHNIQUES, AND POWERS

16 AMULETS AND TALISMANS

Theodor H. Gaster

An amulet is an object, supposedly charged with magical power, that is carried on the person or displayed in a house, barn, or place of business in order to ward off misadventure, disease, or the assaults of malign beings, demonic or human. A talisman is an object similarly used to enhance a person's potentialities and fortunes. Amulets and talismans are two sides of the same coin. The former are designed to repel what is baneful; the latter, to impel what is beneficial. The employment of both (which is universal) rests on the belief that the inherent quality of a thing can be transmitted to human beings by contact.

The choice of objects used as amulets and talismans is determined by several different criteria. They may be (1) of unusual form, such as perforated stones; (2) rare, such as four-leaved clovers; (3) medicinal herbs or flowers, such as mugwort (thought to ease childbirth) or various kinds of febrifuges; (4) parts of animals exemplifying certain characteristics (for example, of a hare for swiftness or a bull for strength), or deemed potent in protecting from attacks by those animals; (5) relics of holy or heroic persons, or even dust from their graves, regarded as imbued with those persons' "numinous" charisma; (6) figurines of gods and goddesses; (7) models of common objects to which a symbolic significance is attributed, such as miniature ladders exemplifying the means of the soul's ascent to heaven; (8) exotic objects of foreign provenience, which are held to contain powers not normally available in a given society. The color of an object may also be decisive, on the basis of "like affects like"; a red stone, for instance, may be thought to relieve bloody flux or menstrual disorders and a yellow stone, to ward off jaundice. Ubiquitous also are models of the male and female genitalia, to increase procreation and sexual pleasure, and threads, to bind evil spirits.

Nor is it only in material things that magical power is thought to reside. Since, in primitive thought, the name of a person is not a mere verbal appellation but an essential component of his being (like his shadow or voice), that of a god or demon written on a slip or engraved on a gem or a medallion can serve as an effective amulet or talisman. Similarly, a text relating some feat or special benefit, especially the discomfiture of a demon, dragon, or monster, associated in traditional myth and folklore with a god or hero, may be regarded as charged with the power that accomplished that deed, so that to carry such a text on one's person transmits that power and perpetuates it. Scrolls or scripts containing excerpts from scriptures accepted as divinely inspired and therefore instinct with the divine essence, or (in medieval Christian usage) copies of letters said to have fallen from heaven are likewise favored.

Sometimes, however—especially when an amulet is directed against human rather than demonic enemies—the procedure adopted is not to enlist the influence and charisma of gods or "numinous" objects but to scare potential attackers by exhibiting in houses statuettes or figurines of monstrous, terrifying creatures. The Babylonians, for instance, fashioned models of the head and body of the grim demon Pazuzu, and one form of Greek amulet was the head of a gorgon whose eye could petrify would-be assailants.

Of salient importance is the material out of which an amulet or talisman is made, since the magic power is inherent in, not merely associated with, the object itself. Gems have to be of substances and colors believed to convey qualities efficacious for particular needs and written texts have to be inscribed on specified skins and in special inks or pigments.

Amulets and talismans borne on the person take the form of ornaments— brooches, lockets, pendants, seals, and sachets. Indeed, it is maintained by several authorities that what came eventually to be mere decorations were originally designed for protection. [*See* Jewelry.]

A cardinal feature of amulets in many cultures is that they are esoteric and although, to be sure, they are often exhibited in full view on the walls of rooms and buildings, when they are carried on the person it is often a requirement that they must not be revealed to anyone except to the one who uses them on a specific occasion, to the magicians who make and dispense them, and to the hostile beings against whom they are directed. For this reason they are commonly concealed in the clothing or tucked away in bags or small cases. Moreover, in the case of written texts, they frequently employ cryptic alphabets or are couched in gibberish (known as *ephesia grammata*—perhaps a distortion of *aphasia grammata,* i.e., "unutterable letters"), supposed to be the scripts and languages of gods and demons. (These can sometimes be identified as genuine ancient scripts and tongues garbled in the course of the ages.) Signs of the zodiac and conventional symbols of constellations and metals also appear, because such signs are, like names, part and parcel of what they represent and because the inherent properties of constellations and metals are believed to control human fate and fortune. Common too are permutations of letters spelling out in esoteric fashion the words of the text. Thus (to use English equivalents) z will substitute for a, y for b, and so forth. In much the same way, the initial or final letters of words in a scriptural verse will be used instead of writing it out in full, and in alphabetical systems (like Hebrew) where each letter also possesses a numerical value (i.e., $a = 1$, $b = 2$, etc.), a combination of letters that add up to the same total as those of the word intended—a device known as gematria (probably a distortion of the Greek *grammateia*)—is employed. (The Library of Congress possesses the manuscript of a complete Hebrew Bible so written as a manual for the preparation of amulets!) A further device is the use of magical squares, each vertical column and each horizonal line of which adds up to the same sum, and all of them together spelling by gematria the name of God or of a protective angel.

The esoteric character of amuletic texts, it may be added, is matched in oral spells by having them recited in a whisper or crooned in a low voice. Indeed, this is the primary meaning of the term *incantation*.

Written amulets frequently express their numinous character by beginning with the words "In the name of [this or that god]" (e.g., the Arabic Bismillah, "In the name of God, the Merciful, the Compassionate") and by being interspersed with religious signs (e.g., the cross, swastika, or shield of David), and their efficacy is increased by marks or letters (*ss* or *kh*) indicating that their recitation is to be accompanied by hissing and spitting to ward off demons. They also feature strings of vowel letters standing cryptically for the powers of angels or planets. Sometimes too the power of a written amulet is conveyed not simply by wearing it but by immersing it in water that is then drunk.

Amulets and talismans seem to have been in use even in prehistoric times, for cowrie shells, celts, arrowheads, and stones buried with the dead (a practice surviving throughout the ages) were evidently intended to protect them in the afterworld. Amuletic too were the pictures of eyes painted on prehistoric walls and monuments; these represented the providential vigilance of benevolent gods or spirits, countering the evil eye of the malevolent demons.

It is obviously impossible in the space of this article to describe in detail the whole host of amulets and talismans current all over the world. We shall therefore confine ourselves to representative examples of the principal types drawn from various cultures ancient and modern.

Historically, the oldest amulets came from Egypt. Dating as far back as the fourth millennium BCE, these take the form of images and figurines made of faience, feldspar, carnelian, obsidian, jasper, and the like wrapped in the bandages that swathed mummies. Each limb of the corpse had its appropriate amulet, usually placed over it. In addition to figurines of gods and goddesses there are miniature hearts, eyes of Horus, frogs, ladders, and steps. The eyes of Horus (usually a pair), made of gold, silver, lapis lazuli, hematite, or porcelain, represented the all-powerful might and watchfulness of that god and were worn also by the living to bring health and protection. The frog, emblematic of teeming abundance, symbolized life in the broadest sense, including resurrection of the body. The miniature ladder stood for the means of ascent to heaven. Miniature ladders are still set up beside graves by the Mangors of Nepal, and a ladder made of dough was traditionally placed next to coffins in some parts of Russia. One recalls also Jacob's ladder in the Bible (*Gn.* 28:12) and the reference to the same notion in Dante's *Paradiso* (21.25ff.)

Ubiquitous also was the familiar *ankh*. What it actually portrays is uncertain; some say it represents a combination of the male and female genitalia and hence (eternal) life. It was carried also in the right hand of deities, where, of course, it was not amuletic but a symbol of immortality. Scarabs (a species of beetle) were also interred with the dead. This particular type of beetle, one that continually rolls pellets of dung until they become larger and larger, symbolizes the process of continuous creation.

Mention should be made also of the so-called Horus *cippi*, stelae or plaques inscribed with legends of that god and portraying him standing on, or beside, serpents he had vanquished. A Canaanite version of this myth has recently been recognized in a Canaanite magical text from Ras Shamra (Ugarit) in northern Syria. The *cippi* were displayed to ward off malign spirits.

Other ancient Near Eastern amulets, common among the Babylonians, Assyrians, Canaanites, and Hittites, take the form of cylinder seals, usually made of diorite or hematite, engraved with mythological scenes depicting the discomfiture of demonic monsters by gods or the vanquishing of the formidable Huwawa, guardian of the sacred forest of cedars, by the heroes Gilgamesh and Enkidu. Sometimes, too, pictures of men supplicating gods, the beneficent sun rising between mountains, or a goddess bountifully pouring water from two jugs are featured. In interpreting these "mythological" amulets it is important to bear in mind that the scenes depicted may be simply mythologizations of general principles. Thus the goddess who pours water may be simply an illustration of bountiful profusion. Often, indeed, the basic meaning may be elicited by matching the glyptic portrayal with a corresponding verbal metaphor.

Another popular Mesopotamian and Canaanite amulet was a plaque portraying the ravages and eventual dispatch of a demonic hag or wolf who stole newborn babes. This has analogues in many parts of the world, for example, in Armenia, Ethiopia, and the Balkans, and especially in a Jewish charm, the so-called *Kimpezettl* (a Yiddish distortion of the German *Kindbettzettel,* "childbirth note"), in which the beldam is identified with Lilith.

Despite the monotheistic orientation of the writers of the Old Testament, amulets seem to have been used by the masses in ancient Israel. The prophet Isaiah castigates women who wore charms (3:20), and a silver amulet inscribed with the words of the Priestly Blessing (*Nm.* 6:24-27) and purportedly dating to the sixth century BCE has been found in Palestine. On the other hand, a figurative reference to amulets in *Deuteronomy* 6:8 was later taken literally and led to the modern Jewish practise of affixing to doorposts a small cylinder *(mezuzah)* containing excerpts from the Pentateuch and of wearing phylacteries *(tefillin)* on the brow and arm at morning prayer.

More modern Jewish amulets are the hexagram, fancifully termed the shield, not star, of David. This, however, is simply a judaized version of a magical symbol of disputed meaning that is widely used elsewhere. Its counterpart is the equally universal pentagram, known to Jews as the seal of Solomon. Common too are metal amulets in the shape of the divine hand (likewise fairly universal), often engraved with the letter *h,* an abbreviation of Je*H*ovah. A favorite written amulet is a strip of paper on which is inscribed the legend "Abracadabra" (variously interpreted) in a series of lines, each of which has one more letter cut off at the end, so that the whole forms an inverted triangle ending with the single letter *a.* In recent times a further popular amulet is a golden pendant or brooch shaped in the form of the letters of the Hebrew word *ḥai* ("life, living").

Of special interest is a class of gems or semiprecious stones (sard, beryl, chalcedony, onyx, etc.) found mainly in Egypt of the Greco-Roman period (but later also in other lands), featuring fantastic images—often part human and part animal—of Egyptian and other gods accompanied by magical inscriptions such as the mysterious "Ablalhanalba," which is said to be a distorted palindrome of the Hebrew phrase "Av lanu [Aram., *lan*] attah," "Thou art a father to us." Prominent among the deities depicted is a certain Abraxas (or Abrasax), who is an important figure in the teachings of the gnostics. These have therefore been termed gnostic amulets, but the attribution is increasingly questioned by modern scholars. When these amulets came to be current in Christian circles the mysterious name *Ablalhanalba* was explained as equivalent by gematria to *Jesus.*

In many countries, written amulets are more common than any other. Among Muslims, for instance, the most popular type is a small case containing excerpts from the Qu'rān or a list of the ninety-nine epithets of God. The Copts use pictures illustrating the defeat of a monster by Saint George of Lydda, and the Ethiopians, scrolls relating the praises of the Virgin Mary, or grotesque representations of the divine eye or face. This, however, by no means precludes the use of ornamental amulets. Christians most often carry miniature crosses or crucifixes, but equally common is the written legend "Sator Arepo," which is really "Paternoster" spelled cryptically.

The Japanese use, besides relics, two forms of amulet that deserve mention. One of these is an image, painted on pillows, of an animal who swallows bad dreams. The other amulet is a pair of dead sardines affixed to a stick of holly at the entrance to a house to keep away noxious spirits at the annual festival of Setsubun. (This finds a parallel in the use of garlic elsewhere.)

The use of colors in amulets is influenced also in medieval magic by the belief that they carry the charisma of the sun, moon, and the seven planets. Thus, yellow stones (amber, topaz) bear the "influence" of the sun; whitish stones (diamond, mother-of-pearl), of the moon; red stones (ruby), of Mars; green stones (emerald), of Venus; black stones (jet, onyx, obsidian), of Saturn; and so forth. Moreover, each stone "controlled" a specific condition. Agate, in Italy, is deemed efficacious against the evil eye, and in Syria against intestinal disorders. Crystal cures dropsy and toothache; diamond neutralizes poisons and also averts thunderstorms. Furthermore, gems promote human passions and affections. Beryl gives hope; carbuncle, energy and assurance; ruby, love; and of coral it is said that it fades when a friend dies. There is also a stone for every month, and these are often featured in brooches inscribed with zodiacal signs portraying a person's horoscope.

Lastly, with regard to the use of exotic objects as amulets and talismans, a curious fact is worth mentioning. Many years ago the present writer had occasion to examine a number of ceremonial costumes worn by African shamans and found that several of them included a pouch worn on the breast. Opening these, he discovered that their contents consisted mainly of European hairpins, scissors, cigarette butts, London omnibus tickets, and similar foreign paraphernalia deemed magical.

Like myths and popular tales, the actual forms of amulets migrate from one culture to another as the result of trade relations, conquests, importation of captives, intermarriage, voyages, and the like, but new meanings are then read into them in order to accommodate them to the beliefs and traditional lore of those who adopt them. Thus (as we have said) the hexagram became to Jews the shield of David, the cross to Christians a symbol of Christ, and the dung-rolling beetle (heper) to the Egyptians the emblem of the creator god Hepera and the pellet as the orb of the sun that he rolled across the sky. It is necessary, therefore, in interpreting these vehicles of magic, to get behind such particular local explanations of them and to attempt to recover their underlying, subliminal significance. This approach, however, is inevitably fraught with the perils of subjectivism and has led, indeed, to any number of psychological fantasies and absurdities. But *abusus non tollit usum;* a spurious coin does not invalidate currency, and the basic nature of amulets will never be understood unless the attempt is made to do so.

[*See also* Stones; Relics; *and* Images.]

BIBLIOGRAPHY

For English readers the most serviceable survey and discussion is E. A. W. Budge's *Amulets and Talismans* (reprint, New Hyde Park, N.Y., 1961), originally entitled *Amulets and Superstitions*. Useful also is Frederick Thomas Elworthy's *The Evil Eye* (New York, 1970), although this work tends at times to go too far afield and to indulge in untenable theories. C. W. King's *The Gnostics and Their Remains, Ancient and Mediaeval,* 2d ed. (London, 1881), gives a good survey of the "Abrascas" and kindred amulets, but it is a bit antiquated in its interpretations. Arabic amulets are treated fully in Edward W. Lane's classic *An Account of the Manners and Customs of the Modern Egyptians*, 5th ed. (New York, 1973), and in Edmond Doutté's *Magie et religion dans l'Afrique du Nord* (Algiers, 1909). Jewish amulets are discussed in Joshua Trachtenberg's *Jewish Magic and Superstition* (1939; New York, 1982).

17 ASTROLOGY

Ioan Petru Culianu

When astrology, a product of Hellenistic civilization, appeared at the end of the third century BCE, its origins were ascribed to the revelations of the Egyptian god Hermes (Thoth). However, its practitioners were usually called "Chaldeans," a formula devoid of any actual historical reference to Mesopotamia. Hellenistic astrology was actually a combination of Chaldean and Egyptian astral religion and Greek astronomy and methods of computation. [*See* Sky, *article on* The Heavens as Hierophany.] Even though Hellenistic astrology and the astrology of late antiquity took on the features of different local traditions when exported to India, China, or Islamic countries, their basic ingredients are, in all places, Greek science and Chaldean and Egyptian astral lore.

The actual contribution of the latter to Greek astrology is debatable, for the Chaldean and Egyptian traditions were widely divergent on some points. However, the idea of two malefic planets—Mars and Saturn—is genuinely Chaldean; genuinely Egyptian, but no older than the third century BCE (although based on a more ancient doctrine of the *chronokratores,* the "rulers of time") is the invention of the thirty-six decans of the zodiac. The latter was called *zōidiakos* (from *zōidion,* "carved figure") by the fifth-century Greeks, after the shapes of figures that they imagined were in the heavenly constellations. One of the oldest astrological treatises, a Hellenistic compilation dating from the second century BCE, is also said to be Egyptian in origin. It is attributed to the mythical Egyptian pharoah Nechepsos as well as to the priest Petosiris, who may be the same as the Petosiris whose mummy was found in a fourth-century BCE tomb discovered at Eshumēn in Upper Egypt.

Eudoxus of Cnidus (408–355 BCE), the father of Greek astronomy, was also versed in the principles of universal and meteorological astrology. The great astronomer Hipparchus (fl. 146–127 BCE) studied the correspondences of planetary signs with the people and the geographic features of the earth; he was also acquainted with astral melothesy (the study of the correspondences between the human body and planets, signs, and decans) and Hermetic astrology.

Hermetic lay astrology was concerned with the study of universal astrology *(genika),* world periods and cycles *(apokatastaseis),* planetary lots *(klēroi),* and the horoscope of the world traced according to the position of the planets in the signs at the time the earth was formed *(thema mundi)*. It was also concerned with the interpretation of signs as manifested in the omens given by thunder *(brontologia)* and the prognoses given at the New Year *(apotelesmata)*. In addition, Hermetic astrology involved the study of correspondences between astral phenomena and the human body or material objects, as in the study of individual or medical (iatrological) astrology; astrological medicine *(iatromathēmatika)*, based on a complicated astral melothesy; and the study of the correspondences between stars, precious stones, plants, and metals. Most of the texts of Hermetic astrology are no longer extant, but they were frequently quoted by writers of late antiquity and the Renaissance.

The development of astrology was decisively influenced by the great astronomer Ptolemy (Claudius Ptolemaeus, c. 100–178 CE), the author of the *Apotelesmatika* (also known as *Tetrabiblos* or *Quadripartitum*), who made popular the pseudepigraphon *Karpos,* or *Centiloquium*. Other important astrologers of late antiquity were Vettius Valens, author of the *Anthologeuon biblia* (written between 152 and 188 CE), and Firmicus Maternus, who wrote the *Matheseos libri VIII* around 335, before he became a Christian.

After the closing of the philosophical school of Athens in 529 CE, several Greek scholars emigrated to Persia, where they were granted asylum by the emperor Khosrow I (531–579). There they translated several Greek texts, some of which were astrological treatises, into Pahlavi (Middle Persian). These treatises were later translated from Pahlavi into Arabic by Abū Ma'shar (787–886), known also as Albumasar, a scholar in the court of the caliph al-Ma'mūn of Baghdad. Many texts entered the corpus of Arabic works on astrology through Persia: the Arab Masala (c. 770–820), in his compilation of a catalog of books on astrology, listed forty-six titles of Persian provenance. By around 750 CE the Arabs had developed a considerable interest in astrology. Arabic translations of astrological texts greatly influenced the thought of the late Middle Ages and the Renaissance.

Greek astrology reached India between the first and third centuries CE, introduced possibly by a Buddhist monk. The most important Indian astrologer was the sixth-century philosopher Varāhamihira, the author of astrological treatises and of the *Pañca-siddhāntikā*, a work that contained what was then known of Indian, Egyptian, Greek, and Roman astronomy. However, Indian astrology, despite its subsequent development and later influence, was unoriginal. Chinese astrology may have derived from Indian astrology, but it is based primarily on an impressive indigenous system of correspondences between the microcosm and macrocosm.

The role of astrology in the cultural and political life of Europe from the fifteenth to eighteenth centuries is only partially known. Astrology had a prominent place in Renaissance science, but it gradually lost this position when the church disassociated itself from astrology at the end of the sixteenth century during the Reformation. Only the names of a few of the greatest astrologers of the Renaissance are still known today: Johann Müller (known as Regiomontanus), Guido Bonato of Forli, and Luca Gaurico, bishop of Civitate (Naples), who worked for Catherine de Médicis.

Some astrologers who are almost unknown today were once famous for having prophesied public events. Their predictions were associated with the theory suggesting the universal influence of Great Conjunctions of planets and signs upon religious and political matters. This theory dates to antiquity and was much discussed by the Arab thinkers al-Kindi and Abū Ma'shar. One of the best-known prophesies stated that Luther and the Reformation were the consequences of the conjunction of the superior planets Jupiter and Saturn in Scorpio during November of 1484. Interpreting this conjunction, Johann Lichtenberger predicted that a German reformer would be born who would become a monk and would have another monk as a counselor. The prediction was later rediscovered and associated with Luther (b. 1483) and Philipp Melanchthon.

During the sixteenth century, the theory of conjunctions played an important role in the works of Cyprianus von Leowitz and of the Englishman Richard Harvey. At the beginning of the seventeenth century, the theory was used by Johannes Kepler in his astrological calculations concerning a star that had appeared in 1604. On the basis of the appearance of this nova, Kepler claimed to be able to calculate the precise date of the nativity of Jesus Christ, who, because he was a great prophet, was to have been born at the time of a Great Conjunction. His birth was also to have been announced by a nova, the star of the Magi. These calculations fostered the hope that a general reformation of faith would change the deplorable conditions of contemporary humanity. This hope was also expressed by the followers of Johann Valentin Andreae (1586–1654), the author of the Rosicrucian manifestos. The dates of the last two Great Conjunctions figure importantly in the apocryphal history of the founder of the Rosicrucian order.

Astrological predictions were feared by the authorities for their possible deleterious political consequences. Astrology was often condemned or suppressed during antiquity and the Renaissance. [*See* Occultism.] For example, to counteract the effect of the prophecy concerning the church reformer born under the 1484 conjunction, Innocent VIII issued the bull *Summis desiderantes affectibus,* which had some effect on the great witch craze of the sixteenth and seventeenth centuries. Eventually astrology was officially condemned by the church at the end of the sixteenth century, as a consequence of other disastrous predictions. However, the liberal trends at the beginning of the seventeenth century were in great measure dependent upon astrological predictions. Astrology seems to continue to exert a certain influence on the political and cultural life of modern Europe, although it is much less influential than it was during the fifteenth to seventeenth centuries.

Confutations of astrology have a common pattern, which usually consists of denying the possibility that the stars could influence human affairs. Some of these confutations are famous, such as those of Girolamo Savonarola, Giovanni Pico della Mirandola, and John Calvin. Although Pico's *Disputationes astrologiam adversus divinatricem* was left unprinted because of his sudden death in 1494, it is very possible that this semiofficial treatise was meant to put forth the antiastrological policies of Innocent VIII and his successor, and to obtain for Pico a full pardon for his past errors and prepare the way for a high ecclesiastical career.

THE METHODS OF ASTROLOGY

Greek astrology was based on Greek astronomy, which was abstruse and difficult to practice. This is one of the principal reasons why many of the authors of astrological treatises in antiquity and late antiquity made inadvertent mistakes in astrological formulations that were by their very nature almost impossible to apply. Another reason for the varied and even contradictory astrological systems of late antiquity was the weight of tradition. Traditionally complex numerical systems of astrology were inevitably altered in their transmission and were rarely interpreted in the same way by any two different authors. For example, the numerical systems of specific astrological tables could be interpreted in various ways: the *horia (fines, termini)*, or portions of a sign distributed among the five planets; the tables of *hupsōmata*, or "exaltations" of the planets in different signs; the tables of *tapeinōmata (deiectiones)*, or "depressions" of the planets; the tables of the so-called *partes vacuae* or *vacantes*, the "empty spaces" of the zodiac; and so on. Ptolemy tried to eliminate discrepancies among different traditions by replacing corrupt or unintelligible traditions with numerical series linked by logical, arithmetical operations.

Astrology superimposes two different complex systems: that of the heavens and that of the collective and individual destinies of the human beings on earth. Through the observation of the heavens (and the interpretation of those observations according to a framework of theoretical, nonobservational assumptions), these systems attempt to account for the changes within the human system, which are otherwise unpredictable, unobservable, and unsystematic. It is true that from a scientific viewpoint there is no real connection between the two systems, and thus Greek astrology has been perceived as an attempt to give mathematical justification to absurd theoretical assumptions. However, instead of emphasizing the arbitrary nature and incorrect theoretical basis of astrology, one might consider its contributions from a psychological point of view. The choice of an analogous system for human fate reflects a deep insight into the transience and singularity of human lives and human events.

Astrological systems are multiple-choice systems based on several informational operators that are capable of accounting for an almost unrestricted number of operations. This astrological "computer program" was used to store information in the memory by several mnemotechnical systems.

The first operator in the zodiac, or wheel, composed of the twelve constellations (more or less arbitrary groups of stars) through which the planets circulate. In addition to these constellations, there are several others that are not in the path of the planets; as extrazodiacal signs *(paranatellonta)* that rise together with the signs of the zodiac, they can also figure in astrological computations and analyses. Beginning from the sign rising at the spring equinox, the twelve constellations are the Ram (*Krios*, Aries), the Bull (*Tauros*, Taurus), the Twins (*Didumoi*, Gemini), the Crab (*Karkinos*, Cancer), the Lion (*Leōn*, Leo), the Virgin (*Parthenos*, Virgo), the Scales (*Zugos*, Libra), the Scorpion (*Skorpios*, Scorpio), the Archer (*Toxotēs*, Sagittarius), the Goat (*Aigokerōs*, Capricorn), the Waterbearer (*Hudrochoos*, Aquarius), and the Fish (*Ichthues*, Pisces). The twelve signs of the zodiac are further grouped into triangles according to their form, sex, quality (cold, warm, wet, or dry), and the element to which they belong. Thus Aries, Leo, and Sagittarius constitute the fire triangle; Taurus, Virgo, and Capricorn, the earth triangle; Gemini, Libra, and Aquarius, the air triangle; and Cancer, Scorpio, and Pisces, the water triangle.

Each of the twelve signs occupies 30 degrees of a 360- degree circle. Each sign is further divided into three decans *(dekanoi)* of 10 degrees each; they are sometimes divided into single degrees *(monomoiriai)*. To each sign are assigned constant features according to its element, quality, sex, shape, and position. The zodiac revolves on an ideal plane divided into *topoi* ("places" or "houses"). There are two systems of *topoi*: (1) a system of eight houses *(oktōtopos)*, which is described only by Marcus Manilius and Firmicus Maternus, and (2) a more general system of twelve houses *(dōdekatopos)*. The twelve houses are life *(vita)*, wealth *(lucrum)*, brothers and sisters *(fratres)*, parents *(parentes)*, sons *(filii)*, health *(valetudo)*, marriage *(nuptiae)*, death *(mors)*, travels *(peregrinationes)*, honors *(honores)*, friends *(amici)*, and enemies *(inimici)*. According to a medieval mnemonic couplet, these are

> Vita, lucrum, fratres, genitor, nati, valetudo
> Uxor, mors, pietas, regnum benefactaque, carcer.

The revolution of the zodiac within the houses makes possible many significant combinations; however, the great variability of the system is due to the movements of the planets. According to the geocentric system, there are seven "planets," arranged according to their distance from the earth and by the length of their respective revolutions: the moon, Mercury, Venus, the sun, Mars, Jupiter, and Saturn. These were further classified according to sex and quality. Mars and Saturn were specifically designated as "malefics," a feature inherited from Babylonian astrology.

Ptolemy stated that the planets have two kinds of "aspects": (1) the aspect determined both by their positions in the zodiac and by their positions relative to one another and (2) the aspect determined only by their positions relative to one another. The most important position of the first aspect is the so-called *idioprosōpos*, the position of a planet when it is located at the same circular distance from the sun and moon that its domicile is from the domiciles of the sun and moon. The domiciles *(oikoi)* are the signs ruled by each planet. The sun and moon each rule only one sign, Leo and Cancer, respectively; the other planets each rule two signs. Mercury rules Gemini and Virgo; Venus, Taurus and Libra; Mars, Aries and Scorpio; Jupiter, Sagittarius and Pisces; and Saturn, Capricorn and Aquarius. In addition to the domiciles, each planet has an "exaltation" at a special place in one sign, and a "depression" (or "exile") in another.

Of the second kind of aspect, Ptolemy cites only two positions. the *sunaphē*, "contact," or *kollēsis*, "sticking" (Lat., *contactus, coniunctio, applicatio,* or *glutinatio*), positions that occur when two planets meet on the same meridian. The conjunction is followed by a separation or *aporroia* (Lat., *defluxio*). Several other positions were successively added to these two, but they were not based on the relative positions of planets but on their *aktinobolia (emissio radiorum)*, or power to emit rays. When these rays meet under certain conditions they form "figures" *(schēmata)*, called *adspectus* in Latin because of the way the planets are "looking" *(adspicio)* at one another. The term *aktinobolia* itself was usually employed to indicate a negative aspect in which a planet could be "blocked" or "sieged" (Gr., *perischesis* or *emperischesis;* Lat., *detentio* or *obsidio,* etc.). While conjunction with the malefic planets is usually maleficent, there are two aspects that are always benefic (120° and 60°) and two others (opposition, or 180°, and square, or 90°) that are always negative.

Signs, decans, and planets are said to rule both the zones of the earth and the human body. The correspondences between them are classified according to astrological chorography, or the distribution of the sidereal influences of the *oikoumenē,* and melothesy, or the doctrine of the correspondences between stars and the human body. There are three kinds of melothesy, which consider the influence of the signs, decans, or planets respectively. The seven planets are ascribed correspondences with metals, stones, plants, and animals. These are used in astrological medicine, or *iatromathēmatikē,* a complicated science of ascribing drugs or other remedies according to the momentary position and influence of the planets, especially the moon.

Astrological predictions are of two kinds: (1) general or catholic (*katholikos*, "universal") predictions, which are based on portentous events such as eclipses, comets, meteors, Great Conjunctions, the aurora borealis, and so on; and (2) particular, or genethliac, predictions, which are concerned with the position and influence of the stars at one's birth. The astrologer draws a "birth theme" (Lat., *thema,* or *diathema tēs geneseōs;* Lat., *constellatio*) by determining first the *hōroskopos* (Lat., *ascendens),* or "indicator," of the sign or planet rising at the eastern horizon at the precise moment of the client's birth. After the ascendant, three other points are determined on the zodiac: the zenith (Gr., *mesouranēma;* Lat., *medium coelum*), the nadir (Gr., *antimesouranēma* or *hupogeion;* Lat., *imum caelum*), and the western horizon (Gr., *dusis;* Lat., *occasus*).

The meridian line is not perpendicular to the horizon line, and thus the problem of the "ascensions" *(anaphorai)* of each sign is not a simple one; their oblique ascension, according to the real inclination of the zodiac, has to be translated on the equatorial plane, and their angular speed depends on the latitude of the geographic location where the calculations are made. During antiquity, tables were drawn for "seven climates" or latitudes. The astrologer is supposed to calculate with accuracy the ascensions of the signs and planets, and to exhaust, on a birth theme, all possible combinations of the constituents of the system.

[*See also* Divination.]

BIBLIOGRAPHY

The best work on Greek and Roman astrology is Auguste Bouché-Leclercq's *L'astrologie grecque* (Paris, 1899). It should be supplemented now with Wilhelm Gundel and Hans Georg Gundel's *Astrologumena: Die astrologische Literatur in der Antike und ihre Geschichte,* "Sudhoffs Archiv," no. 6 (Wiesbaden, 1966). The latter also contains valuable information on the history of astrology outside Greece and Rome. An excellent popular work on astrology is Wilhelm Gundel's *Sternglaube, Sternreligion und Sternorakel: Aus der Geschichte der Astrologie,* 2d ed. (Heidelberg, 1959). Another valuable popular work is Franz Johannes Boll and Carl Bezold's *Sternglaube und Sterndeutung: Die Geschichte und das Wesen der Astrologie,* edited by Wilhelm Gundel (Leipzig, 1926).

Numerous original Greek astrological works have been collected in the *Catalogus codicum astrologorum graecorum,* edited by Franz Cumont and Franz Johannes Boll (Brussels, 1898–).

There is no catalog of Renaissance works on astrology. Some general information is provided in Wayne Shumaker's *The Occult Sciences in the Renaissance* (Berkeley, 1972). Some details on Renaissance astrology are found in Will-Erich Peuckert's *Astrologie* (Stuttgart, 1960).

Information on Renaissance astrology can also be found in the writings of little-known astrologers such as Richard Argentine, Lucio Bellanti, Petrus Buccius, Joachim Camerarius, Johann Clario, A. Couillard, Claude Dariot, L. Digges, John Eschuid, Oger Ferrier of Toulouse, Thomas Finck, Oronce Fine, Giovanni Maria Fiornovelli, Jacques Fontaine, Marcus Frytschius, Alonso de Fuentes, W. Fulke, Giovanni Paolo Gallucci, Jean Ganivet, J. Garcaeus, A. P. Gasser, Francesco Giuntini, Bernardo de Granollachs of Barcelona, Joseph Grünbeck, J. Guido, A Guillermin, Richard Harvey, Jacob Koebel, Edmond Le Maistre, Cyprianus von Leowitz, Johann Lichtenberger, R. Lindenberg, G. Marstallerus, Giacomo Marzari, Antoine Mizauld, Sebastian Münster, V. Nabod, Paolo Nicoletto of Venice, Augustinus Niphus, Caspar Peucer, Alessandro Piccolomini, Annibale Raimondo, Henricus Rantzovius (governor of Holstein and owner of a 7,000-volume library), Gregorius Reisch, J. F. Ringelbergius of Anvers, Cornelius Scepperus, Johann Schöner,

Jac. Schonheintsz, Joh. Stadius, Joh. Taisnier, Georg Taunstetter-Collimitus, Johannes Virdung of Hasfurt, et al.

For works discussing theories of Great Conjunctions, see Abū Ma'shar's *De Magnis Conjunctionibus Annorum revolutionibus ac eorum perfectionibus octo continens tractatus* (Venice, 1515), Johann Lichtenberger's *Prognosticatio Latina Anno LXXXIII/1483 ad magnam coniunctionem Saturni et Jovis quae fuit anno LXXXIIII/1484 ac eclipsis solis anni sequentis sc. LXXXV/1485 confecta ac nunc de nouo emendata* (Moguntiae, 1492); Cyprianus von Leowitz's *De Conjunctionibus magnis insignibus superiorum planetarum, Solis defectionibus et Cometis* (1564); and Richard Harvey's *An Astrological Discourse upon the great and notable Conjunction of the two superior planets, Saturn and Jupiter, which shall happen the 28th day of April, 1583* (London, 1583).

18 BINDING

GIULIA PICCALUGA
Translated from Italian by Roger DeGaris

The motif of binding is widespread in the history of religions, in both the so-called primitive religions and in the religions of both ancient and modern higher civilizations. Its many, complex transpositions, often quite original, vary according to the cultural milieu and the historical moment of which they are the expressions.

Drawing on extraordinarily rich examples taken from the most diverse civilizations, phenomenologists of religion have called attention to the enormous sacred potential that is polarized around acts of physical and symbolic binding, to the concretization of this potential in the form of knots, and to the importance of the opposing act of loosening a bond. In many traditional cultures, important mythical events are believed to be the result of the fastening or loosening of bonds. Actions of binding and loosing frequently occur at the center of rituals, both cultic rituals that involve superhuman beings, and autonomous rituals that are efficacious in themselves, such as the so-called rites of passage, rites of purification, and, above all, magic.

The agents of these actions of binding and loosing vary according to circumstances. They may be superhuman beings of the most diverse kinds, whether located at the time of origins (as, for example, the creator, the first man, the *dema,* the trickster, the culture hero, the totemic ancestor, and so on), or believed to be still acting in the present (as, for example, the supreme being, the earth mother, fetishes, spirits, ancestors, polytheistic gods, or the god of monotheistic religions). Or it may be ordinary mortals who bind and loose, especially those who belong to a specialized sacred group (priests, shamans, wizards, magicians, etc.). The materials with which the bond is made are extremely diverse but generally may be distinguished as either concrete or abstract. Equally numerous are the ends that the binding or loosing action is intended to serve, whether positive or negative. This variety has been well illustrated in the works of Arnold van Gennep, Gerardus van der Leeuw, and Mircea Eliade.

Scholarly interest in binding began in the first half of the nineteenth century, when scholars such as Jacob B. Listing (1847) and Peter Guthrie Tait (1879) became interested in the question of knots. It was James G. Frazer, however, who finally brought the problem to the attention of historians of religion in the first decade of the present century. In the wake of his studies of the concept of taboo and the binding action it exercised, Frazer (1911) saw the need to broaden the scope of his research to include the special type of restraint constituted by the bond as such, its varieties and its functions. Given Frazer's predominant interest in magic, it is not surprising that he interpreted bonds as magical impediments. Despite the problems involved with such an emphasis on the magical—itself inadequately conceived as prior to or even opposed to religion—Frazer's work had the merit of interpreting sacred bonds in terms of the specific historical circumstances in which they are found, showing that the significance of a bond is relative to the positive or negative nature of what it restrains. This latter aspect of Frazer's work unfortunately left little trace in the works of his successors, such as Isidor Scheftelowitz (1912) and Walter J. Dilling (1914). Today this historical dimension to the study of bonds and binding, initially opened up by the great English scholar, remains to be developed.

The less positive side of Frazer's theory, namely the emphasis on magic, has by contrast provided the direction for more recent studies. This can be seen in the case of Georges Dumézil. Dumézil's researches, carried out in the 1930s, were based upon studies of deities of the Vedic religion of ancient India, Varuṇa most especially, but also Mitra, Vṛtra, Indra, Yama, and Nirṛti. These deities were believed to possess snares or at least to be endowed with the ability to bind their enemies and ensnare evil human beings. Accepting the thesis of the magical value of binding *in toto* and uncritically, Dumézil identified a structure of magical binding within the royal function of ancient Indo-European culture, a function that was itself associated with magic.

Dumézil's findings were based largely on Indo-European cultures. A decade later, however, Eliade, in an elegant effort to reinterpret Dumézil's conclusions, demonstrated the presence of what he called the "binding complex" in other civilizations as well, both higher civilizations (for example, in the Semitic world) and in primitive ones, and on several different planes: cosmological, magical, religious, initiatory, metaphysical, and soteriological. Although he initially followed the Frazer-Dumézil line, Eliade soon departed from it, distancing himself from the conflicts over the presumed necessity of interpreting every binding action exclusively in terms of magic or in strict accordance with French trifunctionalism. Beyond the diverse historical forms assumed by the binding motif in the most diverse cultural surroundings, Eliade attempted to identify an archetypal form of binding that would find different realizations on an infinite variety of levels. In the process, he demonstrated that it was possible to interpret the various forms of binding in nonmagical terms. At the same time, however, his work was indicative of the problematic status that the question of binding continues to have in historical comparative studies. Although there are particular studies concerning this or that type of sacred bond that are founded on a rigorously historical basis, in general the scholarly world continues to address the issue merely on the phenomenological level, thereby leaving the question of the historical foundations of the binding motif unresolved.

On the properly historical level, however, it seems possible, and indeed necessary, to establish the precise relation between the sacred value of the bond and the type of reality that lies at the origin of this value; to explain why such a phenomenon arises, and under what circumstances.

The fact that sacred bonds are known in even the most archaic cultures suggests that we should seek an answer to these questions in primitive societies before confronting them on the level of higher civilizations, with their more abstract symbolism. To take only one example, an observation made by Raffaele Pettazzoni in his comparative study of the confession of sins contributes more to our understanding of the "snares" used by the Vedic god Varuṇa than does the sophisticated trifunctional theory of Dumézil. Pettazzoni noted how often primitive peoples try to concretize their sins in the form of knots, tied in various kinds of material (ropes, lianas, vegetable fibers, etc.). He went on to interpret the Vedic motif of binding as "the primitive idea of evil-sin as a fluid wrapping the sinner like the meshes of a net" (*La confessione dei peccati,* vol. 1, Bologna, 1929, p. 230).

It is characteristic of the religions of primitive peoples that sacred bonds, of whatever type they may be and whatever their function, are viewed in a way that is not at all dissimilar to the normal, concrete bonds used in the most varied circumstances of everyday life: the means by which a shaman attempts to "capture" the soul of a sick person to bring it back to the body is an ordinary lasso, of the type ordinarily used to stop a running animal or to prevent it from straying off. Similarly, among the Aranda, an ordinary rope represents the means by which the Tjimbarkna demons tie up at night men whom they want to harm. Akaanga, the lord of the dead for the Aranda inhabitants of Harvey Island, Australia, is believed to capture the deceased by means of a real net, of the kind used by fishermen. There are many such examples.

The same parallel between sacred and ordinary bonds is found in the mythologies of primitive peoples. Here the lassos, traps, nets, and so forth, with which the sun, moon, or clouds are captured, or with which one snares the spirits, are the same as those with which on other occasions poles are tied together in the construction of a hut, wild animals are captured, and fish caught. There is nothing extraordinary in these bonds, except for the increase in power that their use normally confers on the person who employs them.

These facts should lead us to reflect on the enormous importance that fibers used for weaving and spinning, ropes, lassos, nets, and other means of binding have for peoples with a technology that is still at a rudimentary level. Such simple materials and implements are needed for the capture and domestication of animals, and for making weapons, garments, utensils, containers, pottery, and so on. These are the tools and instruments by which the labor potential of *homo faber* can be significantly increased beyond its natural limits, so as to enable the social group to establish greater control over reality, especially over those sectors that most closely concern economic interests and that would otherwise be too difficult to master. There is nothing strange, therefore, in the constant tendency of primitive cultures to transpose the techniques and the tools used to perform a binding action onto a superhuman level. The main goal of this transposition is to strengthen their supposedly extraordinary nature and to place their beneficial effects under the care of the supernatural beings who are often believed to be the source of these marvels. In this way their use can also be protected from possible risks by means of appropriate ritual practices.

Spinning and weaving provide numerous examples of such transposition. These techniques in particular involve the activity of binding and tying (one thinks of the countless loops, weaves, and knots to be found in even a tiny piece of fabric). For example, among the Bambara of Mali, the spindle and the batten, originally the possessions of Faro, the lord of the waters, were granted by him to human beings, whom he also instructed in their use. Thus the first work of a weaver cannot be used, but must be thrown into the river in honor of the superhuman being. The Dogon, on the other hand, link the invention of spinning and weaving directly with the myth of the origin of the world. Among the Ashanti various sacred precautions are taken to protect weaving. It is usually exclusively reserved for men, or else for women who have passed menopause; the work cannot be begun or finished on Friday, the day on which, according to tradition, the use of weaving had been introduced into the land; menstruating wives of weavers must not touch the loom or speak to their husband for the entire duration of the period of impurity; and in the case of adultery with another weaver, a goat must be sacrificed on the loom. In the so-called weaving schools found among the Maori of New Zealand, the technical procedures and the sacred practices are taught at the same time. The sacred practices must be scrupulously observed throughout the work in order to increase the weaver's skill. Weavers must be initiated into the profession by a priest, and are required to follow various alimentary taboos and protect their work from the harmful gaze of strangers, in order to prevent the loss of their own inventiveness and mastery. [See Webs and Nets.]

In addition to spinning and weaving, other specific binding actions, such as the working of fibers and wicker to produce ropes, baskets, nets, traps, and so forth, are projected onto the sacred plane. In the beginning they are the exclusive property of superhuman beings of various kinds, who decide at a certain point to transmit the practice to human beings. The Athapascan-speaking Wailaki of northwestern California relate that the culture hero Kettanagai taught people to weave ropes, baskets, and fishing nets after the flood. Among the Diegueño of southern California the art of working wicker through weaving was included in the comprehensive knowledge that exploded from the head of the primordial serpent and spread throughout the world. The Hopi, for their part, maintain that Spider Woman, a superhuman being connected for several reasons with spiders, and who had directly collaborated in creation, taught the Indians to spin and weave cotton. Among the eastern Pomo (north central California), Marunda first created men by weaving his own hair and, immediately thereafter, wicker; he then taught the art of working wicker to humanity.

The ever closer relationship that is being established by the comparative history of religions between the sphere of work and the sphere of the sacred in the explanation of the activity of binding may furnish us with the possibility of going back to quite precise and concrete historical roots, and to the corresponding economic substrata of all types of bonds, temporarily bypassing the complex and sophisticated symbolism with which they are often associated in higher civilizations. This more complex symbolism, once condemned to obscurity through the now outmoded label of "magical," may itself finally find a more fitting, definite, and substantial clarification.

Thus we may expect to find that behind the "snares" so skillfully manipulated by this or that god in the Indo-European, Indo-Iranian, or Semitic areas (zones with a pastoral economy in antiquity) in order to prevent deviations from the just order of things stand the actual snares (or lassos) with which the society of primitive stockbreeders, during their continual migrations in search of new pastures, maintained control over their herds, the almost unique source of their subsistence. Snares stood, therefore, as a precious guarantee of the proper course of reality.

[*See also* Knots.]

BIBLIOGRAPHY

For research on the extent to which binding is associated with religious activity, three works dating from the 1910s are still indispensable: James G. Frazer's *The Golden Bough,* 3d ed., rev. & enl., vol. 3, *Taboo and the Perils of the Soul* (London, 1911); Isidor Scheftelowitz's *Das Schlingen- und Netzmotiv im Glauben und Brauch der Völker* (Giessen, 1912); and Walter J. Dilling's "Knots," in the *Encyclopaedia of Religion and Ethics,* edited by James Hastings, vol. 7 (Edinburgh, 1914). Rich in examples of the use of sacred bonds are Arnold van Gennep's *Les rites de passage* (Paris, 1909), translated as *The Rites of Passage* (Chicago, 1960); Gerardus van der Leeuw's *Phänomenologie der Religion* (Tübingen, 1933), translated as *Religion in Essence and Manifestation,* rev. ed. (New York, 1963); and Mircea Eliade's *Patterns in Comparative Religion* (New York, 1958). More detailed studies are two now-classic works of Georges Dumézil, *Ouranós-Váruṇa* (Paris, 1934) and *Mitra-Varuṇa,* 4th ed. (Paris, 1948), and Mircea Eliade's "The 'God Who Binds' and Symbolism of Knots," in his *Images and Symbols: Studies in Religious Symbolism* (New York, 1961), chap. 3.

Reinterpretations of the concept of magic in rigorously historical terms can be found in *Il mondo magico,* by Ernesto de Martino (Turin, 1948), and in *Magia: Studi di storia delle religioni in memoria di Raffaela Garosi,* edited by Paolo Xella et al. (Rome, 1976). Enrico Cerulli discusses the sublimation at the sacred level of the arts of spinning and weaving in "Industrie e tecniche," in *Ethnologica,* vol. 2, *Le opere dell'uomo,* edited by Vinigi Grottanelli (Milan, 1965). On the theme of binding action and bonds, see both Raffaele Pettazzoni's *Miti e leggende,* 4 vols. (Turin, 1948–1963), and G. M. Mullett's *Spider Woman Stories* (Tucson, 1979).

19 CARDS

Richard W. Thurn

Cards function in the religious context both as instruments for performing divination rituals and as repositories of esoteric sacred teaching. Current historical evidence suggests that cards originated in China and that their sacred usage developed from shamanistic or Taoist divinatory rituals that predated cards themselves. The oldest extant card, found in Chinese Turkistan, dates from no later than the eleventh century. The design of Chinese cards was copied from paper money first used in the T'ang dynasty (618–908 CE). The design of an arrow on the back of the oldest Korean cards suggests that those cards developed from a divination technique for interpreting the pattern of arrows randomly cast onto a circle divided into quadrants.

Number and pattern, and their orderly transformations, are in sacred mathematics symbolic expressions, or hierophanies, of the eternal divine essences and processes that manifest themselves to us in time as the visible cosmos. The pack of divination cards is a homologue of the set of divine mathematical potentialities that can manifest itself in the time and space of the cosmos. The spontaneous play of the cards, like in any other particular act of divination, reveals a meaningful structure homologous to the divine creative process, which manifests itself within worldly events. The interpretation, or reading, of any particular play of cards is essentially a matter of intuiting from the sacred mathematical symbolism of the cards the worldly events whose structure corresponds to that symbolism.

It is not certain when and where cards first appeared in Europe. One hypothesis is that they were brought into southern Europe by the Moors as early as the eighth century. The earliest mention of numbered cards is in Covelluzo's *Istoria della città di Viterbo* (1480). Covelluzo says that they were brought to the city of Viterbo by the Saracens in 1379. In her extensive study *A History of Playing Cards* (New York, 1966), Catherine P. Hargrave says that these early numbered cards were probably European copies of Chinese cards that arrived through Venice. The oldest extant European cards are several tarot cards from a pack designed for Charles VI of France in 1392.

The two most prominent packs of cards used in Europe for divination are the ordinary pack, consisting of fifty-two cards, and the tarot pack, consisting of seventy-eight cards. The ordinary pack is divided into four suits—diamonds, clubs, hearts, and spades. Joseph Campbell (in Campbell and Roberts, 1979) has suggested that the four suits represent the four estates, or classes, of the medieval social order: clergy (hearts), knights (spades), merchants (diamonds), and peasants (clubs). The four suits of the ordinary pack possibly developed under Protestant influence from the earlier tarot suits of chalices, swords, coins, and staves. The fact that the four suits of the ordinary pack culminate in the figures of knave, queen, and king leads Campbell to suppose that the pictorial symbolism of the cards expresses a medieval esoteric initiatory tradition wherein ascent along any of the four lines represented by the suits leads to spiritual realizations of equivalent value and importance.

The tarot pack falls into two sections: the "minor arcana" of fifty-six cards, divided equally into four suits, and the "major arcana" of twenty-one numbered picture cards and one unnumbered card, the Fool. The origin of the tarot deck is not known. The first history of the tarot, *Le jeu des tarots* (Paris, 1781), was written by Court de Gebelin. Gebelin claims that the deck originated in ancient Egypt and represents the esoteric teaching of the god Thoth, recorded and expressed in a hieroglyphic alphabet, in which all the gods are symbolized by pictorial signs and numbers. While Gebelin's theory of Egyptian origins is clearly itself of a mythic nature (the Rosetta Stone, which made translation of hieroglyphics possible, was not discovered until 1790), the evidence of recent research on the history of symbols indicates that the deck is indeed, as Gebelin supposed, a repository of sacred teaching and esoteric knowledge. The pictorial symbolism of the deck is known to have much in common with the symbolism of spiritual initiation rites and instruction in Hellenistic mystery cults, ancient astrology, and medieval alchemy, wherein the processes of manifesting divine energies are represented in the progression of visual and numerical symbols.

BIBLIOGRAPHY

Tarot Revelations by Joseph Campbell and Richard Roberts (San Anselmo, Calif., 1979) is a detailed work summarizing the phenomenological evidence linking the tarot to Hellenistic religion and alchemy as well as the tarot's place in nineteenth-century esoteric societies.

20 DIVINATION

Evan M. Zuesse

Divination is the art or practice of discovering the personal, human significance of future or, more commonly, present or past events. A preoccupation with the import of events and specific methods to discover it are found in almost all cultures. The culture possibly least interested in divination is that of the traditional Australian Aborigines, yet even they hold divinatory "inquests" at funerals to discover the identity of the sorcerers responsible for the deaths.

Much of science itself has evolved from forms of divination and may be said to continue certain aspects of it. Astronomy, for example, is deeply indebted to ancient Near Eastern and Hellenistic astrological researches; mathematics and physics were advanced by Indian, Pythagorean, and Arabic divinatory cosmological speculations; and several leading Renaissance scientists were inspired by the divinatory schemes of Qabbalah and hermeticism in their search for the moral harmonies and direction of the universe. Yet it would be incorrect to label divination a mere infantile science or pseudoscientific magic, for modern science and traditional divination are concerned with essentially distinct goals. This helps to explain the continuing fascination with divination even today on the part of well-educated people, notably in regard to astrology, the *I ching*, and spiritualism or necromancy (séances with the dead). Divination involves communication with personally binding realities and seeks to discover the "ought" addressed specifically to the personal self or to a group. Science, however, if faithful to its own axioms, cannot enunciate any "oughts" because of its methodological, cognitive, and moral neutrality: it only offers hypotheses about reality and is concerned with general statistical regularities, not with unique persons or events. The existential situation and binding transcendental realities are beyond its concern. It may be argued that, precisely to the degree that such modern disciplines as psychotherapy and Marxist theory leave science behind, they take on divinatory (and therefore religious) functions, and represent modern contributions to the history of divination.

BASIC FORMS

Anything can be used to divine the meaning of events. It is very common to assign spontaneous and arbitrary meaning to signs or omens when one is deeply anxious about the outcome of a personal situation. But the cultural form of divinatory methods and signs is seldom entirely random: each one expresses a specific logic.

A full list of divinatory agents, therefore, would amount to a catalog of both nature and culture. H. J. Rose, in his article "Divination, Introductory and Primitive," in volume 4 of the *Encyclopaedia of Religion and Ethics* (Edinburgh, 1911), classifies the most common means used to obtain insight as follows: dreams (oneiromancy); hunches and presentiments; involuntary body actions (twinges, sneezes, etc.); ordeals; mediumistic possession; consulting the dead (necromancy); observing animal behavior (e.g., ornithomancy, interpreting the flight of birds); noting the form of entrails of sacrificial victims (extaspicy or haruspicy), or the victims' last movements before death; making mechanical manipulations with small objects such as dice, drawing long or short stalks from a bundle, and so on (sortilege); reading tea leaves (tasseography), or using playing cards (cartography), etc.; decoding natural phenomena (as in geomancy, palmistry, phrenology, or astrology); and—of course—"miscellaneous." Plato—in an analysis that still forms the basis of most modern treatments (as in the world survey of divination edited by Caquot and Leibovici, 1968)—distinguished "ecstatic" and "nonecstatic" types, with the latter including all inductive and empirical systems of noting portents, studying entrails, and so forth. But ecstatic states and inductive methods can be mingled confusingly; indigenous interpretations of so-called objective omens often assume spirit possession of the omens and/or ecstatic insight in the diviner, while some mediums appear quite normal when "possessed."

It would be more useful to establish what the indigenous theory of divination is, rather than to attempt to assay the states of mind actually experienced by diviners in different cultures and periods. The same conscious experience of heightened awareness can be interpreted in one culture as deep wisdom and in another as spirit possession. Under the influence of such interpretations, in fact, an individual diviner might permit himself to drift into a deeper mediumistic trance, or on the contrary strive toward a more intense lucidity. How a condition is interpreted influences the way it unfolds and realizes itself.

Stressing the indigenous theory of divination also directs us to the cosmological assumptions and the attitudes toward the self that unit various seemingly unrelated methods. For example, cultures that stress mediumistic interpretations of trance usually also explain the casting of lots or the conformations of entrails in terms of spirit possession: divination, according to this overarching viewpoint, consists of the forms of communication developed by invisible beings to instruct humanity on the meaning of events. But cultures that have developed a concept of a decodable impersonal and elemental divine order would see the entrails or the sortilege in terms of microcosmic echoes of vaster harmonies. In general, then, we may distinguish three general types of divination, based on indigenous meanings: those based on the immediate context when interpreted by the spiritual insight of the diviner (intuitive divination); those based on spirit manipulation (possession divination); and those reflecting the operation of impersonal laws within a coherent divine order (wisdom divination). See figure 1 for subcategories and examples of these three general types.

Intuitive Divination. The Shona of Zimbabwe esteem their *hombahomba* diviners above all other kinds because these remarkable men, consulted by strangers who

FIGURE 1. A Typology of Divination

I. INTUITIVE DIVINATION (in which the diviner spontaneously "sees" or "knows" reality or the future)

  A. Hunches and Presentiments

  B. Insights of Spiritual Masters, Saints, Gurus

II. POSSESSION DIVINATION (in which spiritual beings are said to communicate through intermediary agents)

  A. Possession of Nonhuman Agents (augury)

   Examples: Divination by arbitrary movements of heavenly bodies (meteorology)

   Divination by fire (pyromancy); divination by water (hydromancy); divination by stones, as in throwing dice (lithomancy)

   Divination by observation of the flight of birds (ornithomancy); divination by observation of quadrupeds, fish, insects, or reptiles

   Divination by lots (sortilege or cleromancy)

  B. Possession of Human Agents

   Examples: Divination by body twitches or pains

   Divination by judicial ordeal

   Divination by dreams (oneiromancy)

   Divination by glossolalia (speaking in tongues), spiritualistic séances, and prophecy (varying forms of possession in which the medium's general awareness of the world and of the self is preserved)

   Divination by full mediumism or oracular trance (in which self-awareness and world-awareness are said to be lost, as the spiritual being takes over the medium completely)

III. WISDOM DIVINATION (in which the diviner decodes impersonal patterns of reality)

   Examples: Divination by temporal patterns in movements of heavenly bodies (astrology)

   Divination by patterns in earth formations (geomancy)

   Divination by body forms, often said to be influenced by astrological forces (morphoscopy): in the hand (palmistry or chiromancy); in the liver (hepatoscopy) or entrails (extaspicy or haruspicy); in the head shape (phrenology)

   Divination through mathematical correspondences (numerology; *I ching; hati*) travel from far off to seek their help, can spontaneously tell their visitors' names, family connections, urgent problems, and even minor experiences encountered on the journey. People speak in awe of the piercing eyes and aura of penetrating awareness of these diviners, whose fame can spread over great distances. And yet—an example of how types of divination can run into one another—the *hombahomba* may attune himself to the consultation by casting *hakata* dice (a form of wisdom divination), after which, in one reported case, the diviner became possessed before returning to a state of mind in which he could begin the inquiry.

Intuitive divination is perhaps the elementary form out of which, through various interpretations, the other two developed. It is seldom much stressed, although its distribution as hunches and presentiments is universal. The reliability of amateur intuitions is not usually considered very great, yet in many cultures extraordinary spiritual masters are often credited with this type of divinatory insight, which then has more prestige and credence than any other. For example, disciples of a *tsaddiq* or saintly master in Hasidic Judaism frequently claim that their master can look into a person's soul at first meeting and determine not only the past lives but also the future course of that person. Precisely the same claims are made for many Hindu gurus. These insights by the guru are regarded as far more reliable and authoritative than the various forms of wisdom divination common to India, and these in turn are more esteemed than folk mediumistic and possession divination methods.

Possession Divination. There are many varieties of possession divination. The most common is augury: divining the message sent by spiritual beings through non-human creatures or things. The classic form of augury, much used in ancient Greece and Rome, consisted of attending to the flight of birds, which were thought to be seized by the gods or spirits and directed according to a code known to the diviner. But all other forms of interpreting supposedly objective spirit messages were also included in the Latin term *augurium*.

Even when human agents are seized by the spiritual beings, this does not always imply trance: a popular form of divination in ancient Near Eastern, medieval European, and even modern societies such as Mexico, is to pose a question and then attend to the first chance words one overhears from passing strangers on the street. Another almost universal method whereby spirits or divinities communicate with a person is to induce twitches or sudden pains in the body. Quite explicit meanings can be derived from this, depending on the part of the body affected and other indications, and of course varying according to the specific cultural context. The theory behind the contemporary use of the Ouija board is explicitly spiritualistic, yet all that one must do to use it is put oneself in a receptive mood: ordinary awareness remains. A very similar state is apparently involved in some cases of glossolalia, according to American Pentecostals I have interviewed, but full mediumistic trance is reported in many studies (see, for example, Felicitas Goodman, *Speaking in Tongues,* Chicago, 1979). The divinatory interpretation of dreams is another very widely used method; here manipulation by spiritual beings begins to require outright alteration of consciousness, although only when the ego has already dimmed its awareness.

Full divinatory possession of human beings may be of several theoretical forms: prophetic inspiration, shamanistic ecstasy, mystical illuminations and visions, and mediumistic or oracular trance. They differ according to the degree of ego awareness and lucidity, awareness of the ordinary world, and the theoretical recipient of the divinatory message. The prophets of the Bible seem to retain a lucid sense of themselves and the world as they exhort their audience, although they are gripped by an overmastering sense of the integral meaning of events as illuminated by God's presence. The recipient of this revelation of temporal meaning is both the prophet and the human community. In shamanistic trance the struggle between ego awareness and the spirits is often portrayed as being so intense that it forces a displacement of the shaman from this world: the shaman may fly far away to interrogate the spirits or God, and may have to struggle with bad spirits and force them to confess their role in human events. As recipient of the divinatory communications, the shaman may later report on his conversations to an assembled audience, or may permit the audience to eavesdrop on the actual interviews or even to be directly addressed by the spirits through his mouth, but in any case he remains self-possessed and afterward can recall everything that occurred. For the mystical visionary, on the other hand, the entire ordinary world is eclipsed by the ecstatic revelations, and the mystic is the sole direct recipient of the communications. The oracular medium, however, loses all awareness, it is said, and therefore often remains ignorant of the message that is communicated directly from the spiritual being to the audience.

The dependency in particular cultures or subgroups of a culture on "objective" augury methods, or on methods that progressively encroach on or even obliterate ego awareness, suggest differing views of the self, society, and the world. Satisfactory cross-cultural studies of divinatory theories from this point of view have not yet been made, but some points may be tentatively suggested. All kinds of possession divination assume a mysterious, arbitrary world governed by personal powers who are involved with a vulnerable humanity. The human self must learn how to submit to or cajole these capricious and often dangerous spirits. However, in loosely organized, relatively egalitarian societies with an emphasis on personal initiative, we can expect more confidence in the ability of the human ego to sustain its integrity when faced with the spiritual powers. This is what we find, for example, in circumpolar and related cultures in Europe, Siberia, and North America. A study by H. Barry, I. L. Child, and M. K. Bacon (cited by Erika Bourguignon, *Possession,* San Francisco, 1976) shows that hunting-fishing cultures generally depend on short-term risks and personal initiative, so that individuals are trained from childhood to be self-reliant and self-sufficient: each adult can master all the cultural skills necessary to survive, and ego alertness is highly valued. In such societies mediumistic divination is not found; instead, individuals possess an encyclopedic knowledge of portents, and of methods for obtaining auguries of the capricious spirits' intentions. The autonomous ego can negotiate its way through a mysterious cosmos, while the shaman, able to retain ego awareness and control even in the most intimate relationship with the spirits, is the group guide.

The same cross-cultural study indicates that children in agricultural societies are trained to be obedient, reliable, cooperative, and patient—qualities needed for ceaseless cultivation of crops and for interaction with fixed communities. The social group, not the individual, is the survival unit; personal success is obtained through accommodation to others. Even the powerful must submit to the more powerful and the spirits, while the weak survive only through self-effacement. Here, mediumistic trance expresses the natural state of things. A survey of African cultures by Lenora Greenbaum (in *Religion, Altered States of Consciousness, and Social Change,* edited by Erika Bourguignon, Columbus Ohio, 1973) has shown that mediumistic divinatory trance is most common in societies having slaves and two or more hereditary (i.e., fixed) classes, such as commoners and nobility, and possessing populations over one hundred thousand. I might add that in such societies a sense of relative deprivation and ego diminution must be common, since individuals meet people every day who enjoy other roles in life. Less advantaged groups (the poor, women, and so on) might well seek transcendental release from the resultant frustrations through mediumistic trance more often than more privileged sectors of society (see I. M. Lewis, *Ecstatic Religion,* Baltimore, 1971). In any case, here one obtains power only through radical self-effacement; even kings become divine only through being possessed. This is the opposite view from that underlying shamanism.

It is perhaps inevitable that, at the center of social power, attempts are made in such cultures to master all that can be known of the arbitrary will of the gods. The court diviners frequently compile mountainous records of precedents of monster births or other omens, the results of centuries of haruspicy, and so forth, as in Babylonia, where we see the fruit of intense efforts to maintain clarity as far as is possible. The Babylonian priests noted every heavenly sign over many centuries, identifying each celestial body with a god. But no system emerged from this, for the classical Babylonian worldview was polytheistic and predicated on power, passion, and personal whims of the divinities. Yet the result was a hierarchy of divination methods: present at the courts were alert, learned priests who interpreted the will of the gods in elaborate augury ceremonials, while among the lower classes mediumism and a much more random and confused use of omens indicated the insecurity of ego control.

When the entire social structure and even the cosmos is felt to be inauthentic, as in late antiquity, mediumistic ecstasy may tend to apocalyptic predictions of the end of the age: the muted protest becomes radical and explicit. Or mystical visions may teach the negation of the entire world. In such cases, divination merges with salvation cults.

Wisdom Divination. The elaboration of divination systems based on a unified field of impersonal and universal processes that can be studied, harmonized with, and above all internalized by nonecstatic sages, is an important but rare development in the history of religion. It is most often found in complex civilizations that have been defeated by equally powerful cultures and therefore must integrate their own indigenous views with other perspectives. Wisdom divination is a syncretistic movement beyond specific cults, approaching the elemental ground from which all personal spirits and cultic gods as well as cultural groups arise. But the speculative effort must usually begin in court and priestly circles, for it depends on a cumulative effort of generations and a specialized learning of which, in most early civilizations, only centralized priesthoods are capable. Only after literacy and education become general can the sagelike diviner detach himself from court circles and apply himself to individual and nonpolitical concerns.

Thus it was only after Babylonia fell to Persian conquest in the sixth century BCE that its priestly thinkers were challenged by a view that placed "Truth" (the Zoroastrian *artha*) and a cosmic order founded in a supreme being above the capricious gods. The new empire embraced many cultures, making possible as a real option personal conversion to such missionizing, universal monotheisms as those espoused by the Jews and the Persians. The old social boundaries—and their gods—now became part of a vaster order, and an attempt was begun to link individual lives directly to a single cosmic pattern rather than to any intermediate hierarchies. Inevitably, the effort was eventually to lead to a kind of pagan monotheism, but it began as an attempt to confirm the polytheistic view. With the new radical improvements in mathematics and astronomy, the first personal horoscope known to us was made of a ruler in 410 BCE. The new cities and academies of the Hellenistic world spurred the fusion of Zoroastrian, Babylonian, Jewish, Syrian, and Greek currents; as Franz Cumont (1912) has made clear, astrology came to function as nothing less than a universal and syncretistic religious perspective that underlay or influenced all the religions of late antiquity. Even synagogues, as we know from recent excavations, commonly traced the zodiac on their sanctuary floors or walls.

The growing separation of divination and wisdom from the central institutions of power was resented by many kings and emperors. One of Augustus's first acts as emperor was the burning of about two thousand collections of pseudo-Sibylline oracles circulating among the people, since some of the oracles favored rival figures or criticized Roman policies, while others, by Jewish proselytizers, predicted the impending messianic era. Several Roman emperors outlawed all nonofficial divination; Constantine the Great and his successors used Christianity as an excuse to roast to death any astrologer and client caught in private consultation (see Cramer, 1954, and D. Grodzynski's article in Vernant et al., 1974). Even in modern times astrology can have political aspects: the Nazis directed certain agents to gain reputations in the United States and England as astrologers, and then to predict the success of Nazi endeavors or otherwise demoralize Western efforts. Within Nazi Germany itself, astrology was strictly an instrument of state.

Today, however, astrology serves usually as a muted protest against everyday social identity or generally accepted scientific values and cosmology. While interest in astrology is widespread, it has been especially favored by the so-called counterculture, and by many in the lower and lower-middle classes, particularly women, since it desubstantializes oppressive personal relationships, offering instead an exotic alternative identity in which faults are erased or elevated into association with a "star family" embracing strangers. In an increasingly fluid, anonymous, and heterogeneous society, pattern and typological identities are discovered within a larger cosmic harmony, and a sense of control is restored to personal life through the aesthetic and probabilistic terms in which predictions are couched. The power of such a vision is seen in the fact that it persists, even though the zodiac houses and their stellar correlates, fixed as they were during the hellenistic period, are now literally two thousand years out of congruence, making the system obsolete even in its own terms.

A quite similar history of a wisdom divinatory system is that of the *I ching* in China. It was the practice in court circles of the Shang dynasty to consult the nature spirits and royal ancestors—and especially the celestial supreme being—concerning all significant state decisions. Scapulimancy was the favored technique—in the late Shang period tortoise shells were generally substituted, supplemented by sortilege with long and short yarrow stalks. These methods had their roots, respectively, in hunting-fishing cultures to the north and in agricultural tribes to the south. Although these methods already involved a conception of heavenly and earthly polarities, it was apparently only after the Shang were overthrown by the Chou, and after the

Chou had expanded rapidly in succeeding centuries to embrace cultures throughout northern, central, and even southern China, that an elemental metaphysics arose that transcended all gods and spirits and was encapsulated in the *I ching* as such. There is no reference to personal spirits or gods anywhere in the text of the *I ching* in its present form, which stems from the late Chou and Former Han dynasties. Instead, all of reality is regarded as woven out of a dialectic of *yin* and *yang* forces (contracting and expanding, respectively): all things and persons are composites in the process of transformation. Using the elaborate binary code of this method, one can discover what the transformations imply, but only if one has attained true nobility and tranquility of character. Confucian mandarins and philosophers through the ages ruled their lives by this text, but only in the Ming dynasty did its use become widespread among the general populace, reflecting the growth of literacy and the escalating complexity of Chinese civilization. The *I ching* had come to serve as a quiet intellectual aid to personal transcendence and mastery of immediate social pressures. This function—the same one it serves today in the West—differed from its earlier Confucian use as a guide in official life and in social activity often associated with the court. [*See* Yin-yang Wu-hsing.]

The Chinese had a number of other forms of wisdom divination, in particular a distinctive form of astrology and an elaborate geomancy. The latter offered detailed instructions on the cosmic forces affecting any specific site, and professional geomancers were consulted whenever a house was to be built, a road laid, or a grave site chosen. Astrology too governed all aspects of village life by the later medieval period, despite the general folk use of many possession divination methods, ranging from countless omens and portents to outright mediumistic séances.

Hindu astrology combined some elements of the Chinese system and more of the Middle Eastern system into its own configuration. Other significant forms of wisdom divination include the Islamic *ḥaṭi* system *(al-khaṭṭ bi-raml)* and the several derivations of it in West Africa (especially the Yoruba and Fon Ifa systems), Zimbabwe, and Madagascar.

DIVINATION IN WESTERN RELIGIONS

The Jewish and Christian traditions are markedly ambivalent about divination. For example, the rabbis criticized the use of folk methods found in surrounding cultures, just as the Torah itself forbids all appeals to local nature spirits or to the dead. While the efficacy of such appeals is not necessarily denied (*1 Sm.* 28), such acts were thought to suggest that God is not the one source of all events and of all truly reliable knowledge. (See *Dt.* 18:10–22; *Lv.* 19:26, 19:31, 20:6–7, 20:27; *Jer.* 10:2; and the tractates *Pes.* 113a and *Ned.* 32a from the Talmud. For a full discussion, see Cohen, 1949.) Thus prophetic inspiration directly from God, the use of Urim and Tumim in the Temple, certain kinds of omens, and even dream divination by Joseph in Egypt and at local shrines in ancient Israel were certainly acceptable. So most Talmudic rabbis permitted dream divination, water gazing, and the use of omens; contradictory views were expressed concerning astrology, but by the Middle Ages most rabbis accepted what was in effect the science of the day. Moses Maimonides, however, made a scathing attack upon it: freedom of will, he said, is fundamental to Torah spirituality; those who follow God cannot in any case by subject to the stars (see, e.g., *Dt.* 4:19–20), while a close analysis of astrology shows it to be based on poor reasoning and worse science. Necromancy was explicitly condemned in the

Torah (*Dt.* 18:11), and there is very little reference to any kind of spirit possession in the Talmud; the late medieval dybbuk possession chiefly involved tormented but not malicious spirits who sought expiation for sins. Yet qabbalistic meditations resulted in a wide variety of wisdom divinatory methods based on the divine image sustaining the whole of creation, and prophetic ecstatic visions were sought by mystics from the Talmudic age on.

In Christianity some of the same themes and ambiguities reappear, but now the antithesis between good and bad divination is understood as part of a war between Christ and Satan. For example spirit possession, mediumistic and otherwise, is a frequent phenomenon and is generally viewed as demonic and requiring exorcism. However, astrological signs can be good, for they marked Jesus' birth. Dream divination by Joseph or Pilate's wife, casting lots, and mediumistic glossolalia are all approved (*Mt.* 1:20, 2:2, 2:12, 27:19; *Acts* 1:26, 10:10), unless performed by non-Christians like Simon Magus or by sorcerers (*Acts* 8:9, 13:6, 16:16. Folk methods used in the Roman empire and afterward were readily incorporated into Christian and official usage, although the fourth-century Synod of Laodicia and the contemporaneous Theodosian Code outlawed divination (drawing on earlier precedents in Roman legislation). Thus divinatory invocation of pagan deities or spirits, schismatic prophetic movements within Christianity, and even oracular attempts to criticize or delegitimize the ruling regime were all stamped as "Satanism."

Similar attitudes continued into later European cultures, but a rich and highly varied regional folk practice of divination persisted. From Islamic civilization—itself the inheritor of Middle Eastern, Persian, and even Indian methods of divination—came scholarly catalogs of divinatory significances of dreams, omens, and studies of specialized systems such as palmistry, astrology, and crystal gazing. Astrology—despite the rejection of it in the late Roman empire by church leaders who often cited critical analyses by earlier pagan philosophers—came to be regarded as a universal science in the Middle Ages. The Renaissance renewed acquaintance with classical criticisms (permitting astronomy to develop as an independent science), but the increasing literacy of later generations spread knowledge of these systems and encouraged devotees to elaborate their own methods further and publish studies of them. Cartomancy (including the use of tarot cards), phrenology (divination by head conformations), graphology (handwriting analysis), and many other novel systems or elaborations of earlier systems developed at this time. Pietists of the Reformation heartily condemned these alternative systems of wisdom, but continued to use dreams, omens, and even scriptures opened at random to comprehend events.

In the modern period, devotees of such systems as astrology or water witching often feel constrained to offer "scientific" explanations for the claimed success of their methods—explanations often extrinsic to the methods themselves. Extrasensory perceptions (precognition, etc.), for example, have been cited, or the "synchronicity" invoked by Carl Jung for the power of the *I ching*: with the mind tuned in by the divinatory apparatus and method, the diviner may notice the minute evidences of interconnections and processes in the environment that are usually ignored, or the diviner may in this heightened state even comprehend vaster elemental wholes leading inevitably to certain outcomes. It is even suggested that divinatory consciousness may be able to pick up unobservable rhythms in events, in somewhat the same way that a radio picks up invisible transmission. These hypotheses may describe real processes; unfortunately, they are at present untestable.

SACRIFICIAL MOTIFS

In any case, divination is fundamentally directed by religious, not scientific, concerns. Its basic curiosity is not about how the world is constructed apart from the pulsing heart of the observer, but about the existential meaning of particular human lives. Above all, divination illuminates suffering and alleviates doubt. It restores value and significance to lives in crisis. But to achieve this, all systems of divination demand the submission of the inquirer to transcendental realities, whether these be divine persons (possession divination) or the underlying divine order (wisdom divination). The inquirer is made to achieve spiritual distance from the self and the immediate crisis.

This recentering of the self is usually directed by sacrificial motifs and rituals. Almost all African divination, for example, ends in sacrifice to the spirits named in the consultations as responsible for the crisis, and many rites also begin with sacrifice. Very often the act of divination is simply a sacrificial rite: in Nilotic and Bantu cultures, the answer is "read" from the entrails of victims. Often the actions of the sacrificed victim give the spirit's answer. In Zaire and nearby culture areas, chickens may be fed a partially toxic substance: if the bird dies, God has accepted it and signified "yes" to the question; if not, the answer is "no." A similar logic directs witch ordeals. As in Africa, so also in Europe is the observation of the last convulsive movements of a sacrificial victim a divination practice. Strabo tells us that the ancient Gauls often killed a slave or captive by a sword stroke in the back: the future was then told from the way he fell, his movements, and the way the blood flowed. Even wisdom divination is frequently given a mythical source in a primal sacrifice (as in the case of the African Dogon and Bambara rites, and also the Yoruba and Fon systems of divination, called Ifa and Fa, respectively. The oracle bone divination of Shang dynasty China had a sacrificial context, and the actual procedure by which one consults the *I ching* is basically structured by sacrificial ideas. Mediums perhaps most dramatically embody a sacrificial logic: those initiated in the spiritualistic religions of Nigeria and Dahomey, for example, and in their perpetuations in recent centuries in the Caribbean, must undergo a symbolic and psychic death and resurrection—one so experiential that occasionally the offering to the spirits, the medium-candidate, does not rise again from the ground.

All this expresses a deeper truth, that divination requires the radical submission of the diviner and indeed the client to the transcendental sources of truth, before their lives can be transformed and set straight, before they can be reincorporated harmoniously into the world. In short, divinatory rites follow the pattern of all rites of passage. The client, having learned in the course of the rite to offer up to the divine all egocentric resistance, ends the session reoriented to the world and able to take positive and confident action in it.

G. K. Park (in Lessa and Vogt, 1965) has suggested that divination assists in political and personal decision making precisely by removing the decision from contesting parties and giving it an objective legitimacy, both through its spiritual source and its convincing ritual drama. O. K. Moore (ibid.) has added that even the "randomizing" of decision outcomes in divination is actually adaptive in situations where egoistically obvious or socially customary decisions might end up limiting personal or group survival chances. By hunting in accord with the cracks that appear on heated deer shoulder blades, the Naskapi Indians of Labrador are prevented from overhunting favorite areas and are therefore more likely to find game year-round.

Wisdom divination also often works in this way: by freeing the inquirer from customary ways of thought, it frequently reveals fresh insight into problems. Thus the cryptic proverbs or aphorisms (as in the Ifa system or the *I ching*), or the nonbinding details and universalizable generalities (as in astrology), open up a cosmic perspective that in itself bestows tranquility and a renewed ability to cope effectively with crises. One learns to see behind appearances and to cultivate a continual attitude of tranquil self-offering. The momentum of wisdom divination, in short, is to internalize the basic attitude operating in all divination; it does this by rendering the structures of the transcendent into a form in which they can be grasped consciously and autonomously. The very vagueness of the answers in most forms of wisdom divination aid in this personal appropriation, making the client participate in shaping meaning out of the session.

[*For further discussion of this topic, see* Oracles; *see also* Geomancy; Necromancy; *and* Dreams.]

BIBLIOGRAPHY

Useful historical surveys of divination and related topics in world cultures include Lynn Thorndike's monumental *A History of Magic and Experimental Science*, 3 vols. (New York, 1923–1958), and Auguste Bouché-Leclerq's still very useful *Histoire de la divination dans l'antiquité*, 4 vols. in 2 (1879–1889; reprint, New York, 1975). Thorndike's history is chiefly oriented to Western culture, but the first two volumes deal with antiquity. Bouché-Leclerq focuses on classical Greco-Roman cultures. A total of seventeen learned articles on divination in particular cultures, and an additional twelve articles on astrology and other religious aspects of heavenly phenomena in world cultures, can be found in the *Encyclopaedia of Religion and Ethics*, 13 vols., edited by James Hastings (Edinburgh, 1908–1926), under "Divination" (vol. 4, 1911) and "Sun, Moon, and Stars" (vol. 12, 1921). More up to date is the excellent survey edited by André Caquot and Marcel Leibovici, *La divination: Études recueillies*, 2 vols., (Paris, 1968), which, in addition to the expected essays on the major ancient Near Eastern, classical, and Asian cultures, contains numerous essays on pre-Christian European cultures; the ancient civilizations of the Americas; native or tribal cultures in Siberia, Africa, and elsewhere; and modern folk and urban Western societies—all with helpful bibliographies. The most recent English symposium is Michael Loewe and Carmen Blacker's *Divination and Oracles* (London, 1981), with nine authoritative essays ranging from Tibetan culture to Islam.

An anthropological symposium on divination that refers to political aspects as well is *Divination et rationalité*, by Jean-Pierre Vernant and others (Paris, 1974). A useful selection of important theoretical anthropological essays on divination is included in *Reader in Comparative Religion: An Anthropological Approach*, 2d ed., edited by William A. Lessa and Evon Z. Vogt (New York, 1965); later editions include some more recent studies but omit much from the second edition. Mediumship has evoked the greatest attention from anthropologists; see, for example, *Spirit Mediumship and Society in Africa*, edited by John Beattie and John Middleton (New York, 1969), in addition to the studies mentioned in the text of the foregoing article.

For an authorative summary of what we know about ancient Mesopotamian divination, see A. Leo Oppenheim's *Ancient Mesopotamia* (Chicago, 1964), pp. 198–227, or W. H. P. Römer's "Religion of Ancient Mesopotamia," in *Historia Religionum,* edited by C. Jouco Bleeker and Geo Widengren, vol. 1 (Leiden, 1969), especially pp. 172–178. H. W. Parke has summarized his many authoritative studies on Greek mediumship in his brief *Greek Oracles* (London, 1967); he does not ignore social and political implications. Still outstanding is Franz Cumont's *Astrol-*

ogy and Religion among the Greeks and Romans (1912; reprint, New York, 1960). More recent are Hans Lewy's *Chaldaean Oracles and Theurgy: Mysticism, Magic and Platonism in the Later Roman Empire,* new edition by Michel Tardieu (Paris, 1978), and Frederick Henry Cramer's *Astrology in Roman Law and Politics* (Philadelphia, 1954).

Talmudic views of divination are well discussed by Abraham Cohen in his *Everyman's Talmud,* new ed. (New York, 1949), pp. 274–297; further information is available in the article "Divination" by Shmuel Aḥituv and others in the *Encyclopaedia Judaica,* 16 vols. (Jerusalem, 1971). A general survey of Muslim divination is available in Toufic Fahd's *La divination arabe* (Leiden, 1966), and in the various symposia mentioned above. On *hati* geomancy, see the article by Robert Jaulin in the collection by André Caquot and Marcel Leibovici, cited above, and Robert Jaulin's *La géomancie: Analyse formelle* (Paris, 1966). For a penetrating study of the Yoruba Ifa system, see Wande Abimbola's *Ifa: An Exposition of Ifa Literary Corpus* (London, 1976).

Any study of Chinese divination should begin with Joseph Needham's brilliant study *Science and Civilisation in China,* vol. 2 (Cambridge, 1956), pp. 216–395; an excellent bibliography is appended. Among the many perceptive studies of the *I ching* is Hellmut Wilhelm's *Heaven, Earth and Man in the Book of Changes: Seven Eranos Lectures* (Seattle, 1977). A useful survey of other forms of Chinese wisdom divination as well as of allied forms of the *I ching* is Wallace A. Sherrill and Wen Kuan Chu's *An Anthology of I Ching* (London, 1977). Also see Stephan D. R. Feuchtwang's *An Anthropological Analysis of Chinese Geomancy* (Vientiane, Laos, 1974).

21 EXORCISM

Geoffrey Parrinder

The Greek root of *exorcism, exorkōsis* ("out-oath"), implies the driving out of evil powers or spirits by solemn adjuration or the performance of rituals. Such practices are worldwide, present in archaic as well as modern societies.

ANCIENT AND MODERN JAPAN

Some of the most striking descriptions of exorcisms in past and present times have come from Japan. The thirty-fifth and thirty-sixth chapters of the famous *Tale of Genji*, written by the court lady Murasaki Shikibu in the eleventh century CE, give lengthy accounts of possessions and exorcisms. The work describes Murasaki being taken ill with violent chest pains and high fever, both generalized and acute. Many prayers were said for her, and Buddhist priests performed esoteric rites. Soothsayers drew up diets and lists of abstinences, but there was no improvement for months. Finally, after their spells and fire rituals had failed, the priests said that Murasaki was dead, and they packed up their altars. But Prince Genji made more vows and summoned more powerful ascetics, who made such intense efforts that clouds of black smoke seemed to hang over their heads. Then the evil spirit suddenly passed from Murasaki to a little girl who was acting as a medium, and the girl began to weep and fling her hair about. She identified herself as the spirit which had caused all the trouble and asked for prayer, that her sins be forgiven. She said that the chanted holy texts were smoke and flames in whose crackle she could not hear the holy word. She advised Murasaki to atone for her sins and concentrate upon the Good Law.

Then Prince Kashiwagi was taken ill. His head ached, though he was not drinking, and he grew worse every day. He had no wish to live but rejected suicide because of the need to care for his parents. Soothsayers agreed that a jealous woman had taken possession of him, and mountain ascetics *(yamabushi)* of repulsive and fierce aspect flocked to his bedside. One ascetic with cold and forbidding eyes intoned mystic spells in a threatening voice. Kashiwagi implored the holy man to send away the spirit, the angry lady possessing him, but to no avail. Kashiwagi died while his wife gave birth to a son.

Murasaki's diary describes another exorcism. The empress Akiko had such a difficult labor that possession was suspected. Buddhist priests and exorcists as well as mountain ascetics were called. Some recited texts, some shouted spells in loud voices. Several court ladies offered to act as mediums. Each lay on a couch attended by an exorcist, and the night passed in a frightful clamor of chanting. When the empress was delivered of a son toward morning, the screams of the spirits were acute. One spirit threw an exorcist to the ground, though the ladies were not molested, and the exorcists lamented that they had not been more effective.

The *Pillow Book* of Sei Shōnagon, written during the same period, presents another vivid picture of exorcism. In a house surrounded by tall pine trees and with a spacious courtyard a young, handsome Buddhist priest, in gray robe and fine silk stole, knelt on a round hassock fanning himself with a scented fan while he recited the *Senju Darani,* a section of the *Thousand Hand Sutra*. This was used especially by Shingon Buddhists to avert all manner of evils. In an inner room invisible to the writer lay someone afflicted by an evil spirit. A medium was brought, a heavily built girl with a fine head of hair, dressed in a long stiff robe and light trousers. The girl sat next to the priest, who gave her a thin, polished wand. With eyes shut the priest recited the sacred syllables, and after a time the medium trembled and went into a trance, while her young brother stood behind fanning her. The medium wailed and groaned in a terrible way as friends rearranged her disordered clothing. After a while the patient began to improve, and attendants brought her hot water. By afternoon the priest had brought the spirit under control, forced it to beg for mercy, and then dismissed it. When the medium came to herself she was filled with embarrassment but was encouraged by the priest with a few more incantations. He was thanked by the lady of the house and offered gifts, but he excused himself, as it was time for evening prayers. It was a very obstinate spirit, he explained, and we must not be off our guard. He left with such dignity that everyone felt that the Buddha himself had appeared on earth. Such an elegant priest at an exorcism may well have been an exception.

Linking such classical examples to modern times, Carmen Blacker (1975) has given accounts of present-day exorcisms, as revealed by her own research among Nichiren Buddhist priests in Japan. Four kinds of possession are distinguished. The first kind, when only the body is affected by mysterious pains, frequently is attributed to an angry spirit. The second kind consists of hallucinations; the third, of an altered personality which could be blamed on possession by an animal such as a fox. The fourth kind consists of more rare cases when different voices and personalities appear and indicate possession. Blacker notes that the Roman Catholic church now recognizes only cases in the fourth category as true possession.

Any of these afflictions may be treated in Nichiren Buddhist temples. There, exorcisms are based on the teachings of the *Lotus Sutra*. Methods of prayer spells with the help of a medium are used in some temples, but in others, mediums have been generally abandoned "in favour of a direct confrontation between exorcist and patient" (Blacker, 1975, p. 302).

In preparation for exorcisms, Nichiren priests undergo a very severe training in austerities, consisting of a hundred of the coldest days of winter spent on mountaintops or in temples. The training comprises brief periods of sleep, repeated cold baths, two meals a day of thin rice gruel, chants of the *Lotus Sutra,* and practice in the use of magic castanets *(bokken)*. The sharp click of the castanets is thought to have a powerful effect on the spirits.

In exorcisms witnessed by Blacker at a temple in Kanazawa in 1967, the priest's mother acted as a medium. One morning a fox, three snakes, a jealous woman, a frantic man, and a cat spoke through her mouth. During each morning's service of exorcism the priest, dressed in white, sat in front of the altar chanting verses from the *Lotus Sutra* and sharply tapping a shelf with a wooden mallet. When the medium entered and knelt at the foot of the dais on which the priest sat, he "turned to face the room with a rosary in his hand" (Blacker, 1975, p. 303). A pile of papers at his side contained problems given by patients and petitioners. As the priest read them aloud in a firm voice, the medium gave answers which were said to come from the guardian deity of the temple. The deity diagnosed the patient's trouble and declared whether it came from simple tiredness or from a possessing spirit, such as a fox, a snake, or a neglected ghost. Cases of general illness were given instructions and reassurance, but in cases of possession the spirit would be forced to name itself, leave the body of the patient, and speak through the medium. The priest read out the name and age of the patient, recited verses from the *Lotus Sutra* in nasal tones, struck sparks from a flint, and made sharp clicks on the *bokken*, all of which were intended to force the spirit into the medium so that it could be brought into submission. When a fox spoke through the medium's mouth, she crouched in a position like a fox, begged forgiveness of the priest, and joined him in singsong recitations of sacred passages. More simple cases of possession, where snakes and a cat were identified, were dealt with by scriptural recitations repeated to lay the spirits to rest.

In another temple of the Nakayama branch of the Nichiren sect, the use of mediums had been abandoned about a century ago. In 1963 Blacker there witnessed exorcisms in which there was direct confrontation between the exorcising priest and the patient. At this temple the patients could stay days or weeks until they were completely cured. The patients were obliged to cooperate fully with the priest, reciting nearly all day long, with only brief intervals for rest and food, repeating the powerful formula, "Hail to the Lotus of the Wonderful Law." This was believed to convince the evil spirit that it was in the wrong abode, cause it to change its nature, and make it wish to leave.

The priest, in a cape of white muslin and a cope of red brocade, recited verses from the *Lotus Sutra* in stern tones for ten minutes. Wheeling around to face the patients, his right hand raised the wooden *bokken* and flashed it to and fro with sharp clacks. At this, some of the patients began to shake and twist about, and one woman who jumped up and down on her heels was sternly addressed by the priest. He shook the *bokken* at her and told her fiercely to change for the better, addressing the spirit inside her. He asked how many years it had possessed the woman and where, what ward, what street, and why. When the spirit confessed that it had possessed the woman out of spite, it was told to leave her and agreed to go at once. The promise to leave was repeated three times, as the woman shrieked and then collapsed on the floor, before the priest turned to the next sufferer. People came to congratulate the exorcised woman, who sat limp and dazed on the floor, and then they continued their recitations. The priest later explained that he always began by demanding a change from the possessing entity, after detailing the symptoms and the time of suffering. After the exorcism it was always necessary to set up a small shrine to the spirit and give daily offerings to keep the spirit in peace.

The majority of patients were women, and Blacker suggests that "symptoms of malevolent spirit possession are an unconscious attempt by women to protest against neglect and oppression in a society largely dominated by men" (Blacker, 1975, p. 312). In this way these possessions may parallel spirit possessions in Africa, notably Somalia. However, Blacker notes that the Japanese possessions are not public, in the sense of seeking to draw attention to women's lot. The exorcisms take place in temples or even in private houses. The results are not material gains but spiritual rewards like peace of mind. There are mental hospitals in Japan, but many people prefer the exorcisms to be conducted in religious terms by priests initiated into the sacred life.

CHINA AND NORTH ASIA

Doctrines and practices used in Japanese Buddhist exorcisms were partly brought from China, usually by Tendai and Shingon sects, and introduced to Japan by the eminent monks Kūkai and Ennin about the ninth century CE. The Nichiren school, after the thirteenth-century reformer of that name, was a Japanese development and no doubt, like the Tendai and Shingon sects, incorporated Shintō and nature beliefs.

The use of small children as mediums for divining the future and for serving as mouthpieces for gods and spirits is said to have been brought from China and ultimately from India. In Japan such rituals were called *abisha no hō,* a term derived from the Sanskrit word *āveśa,* signifying possession by a spiritual entity or its entry into a medium. Unblemished children were selected, bathed, dressed, purified, and anointed in order to reveal hidden or future things. At times they served as organs of prophecy, and more often as mediums for exorcists or as vessels for the subjection of malignant spirits.

The activities of shamans in ancient China may be gathered from the *Nine Songs* of the fourth century BCE. These intermediaries in the cult of spirits were called *wu.* Experts in exorcism, predictions, rainmaking, and healing, they were men and women whose services seem to have been widely available. Like Siberian shamans, they went into ecstatic states, descending into the underworld and propitiating evil powers.

There were many Chinese religious officials of various ranks and grades who maintained local or state rites and ceremonies, but the *wu* of both sexes belonged to lower classes of officials, though they were probably the most ancient priests in China. Male *wu* were said to call spirits from all directions by exclaiming and waving long grasses. In winter they ejected evil from halls, and in spring they warded off disease by averting the demons. Female *wu* performed exorcisms at fixed times annually, using ablutions with aromatics, dancing during sacrifices for rain, and chanting and wailing at times of natural calamities.

The *wu* specialists who acted as exorcists, seers, and soothsayers either were possessed by spirits themselves or employed mediums who were so possessed. In times of epidemics they joined in processions, stripped to the waist, dancing frantically, pricking themselves with knives and swords, thrusting needles through their tongues, or carrying heavy lamps from hooks thrust through their arms like the ecstatics in some Hindu and Sinhalese temples. Their aim was to frighten evil spirits away by displays of power, slashing the air with double-edged swords to drive off demons or wounding themselves with swords or with balls studded with sharp iron points. J. J. M. de Groot describes the *wu* in great detail in *The Religious System of China* (6 vols., 1892–1910).

In China down to modern times exorcisms are held more frequently on behalf of the sick than for any other purpose. De Groot describes a typical healing exorcism. After reciting spells, burning papers of incantations, and offering incense, the shaman began his or her "communication with the medium" (de Groot, 1892–1910, vol. 6, p. 1274). The medium shivered and yawned, but as incantations became louder to the accompaniment of drums and as "eye-opening papers" were burnt in quick succession, he or she began to jump about. Assistants forced the medium to a seat, his limbs shaking, his head and shoulders jerking from side to side, and his eyes staring as if into the invisible world. The consultant (the sufferer or the shaman) put questions to the medium, who replied with incoherent sounds which were interpreted as a divine language and were written down on paper. When the spirit announced its intention to depart, drums were beaten, water and ashes were spurted over the medium, and gold paper money was burned for the spirit. The medium swooned, and when he revived he declared that he had no recollection of the event.

De Groot also describes a more direct exorcism of the demon of sickness. The medium was stripped of most of his clothes, and on his stomach was placed a piece of red cloth or silk with two embroidered dragons, emblems of the Emperor of Heaven. His hair was unbraided and a sword placed in his hand. In this dress the exorcist yelled and jumped through the room, brandishing his sword over the patient and even beating him with the flat of the blade, knocking the sword against the bed and the door. If the patient panted and groaned, that was a sign of the dismay of the possessing spirit. The exorcist waved a whip, strewed uncooked rice and salt about the room, and wounded his own body with the sword or with a prick-ball. After a short time, or after many dances and woundings, the medium might declare which spirit was the author of the illness, how it had been offended unwittingly by the patient, and what sacrifice would pacify it. To drive the evil spirit away dances were sometimes taken into the streets, with mock fights and the burning of incense sticks and paper money. If the patient recovered, the family god was thanked, but if he did not get better, further expensive exorcisms were required.

Exorcism was practiced both by Taoist priests and by esoteric Buddhist sects. They performed before altars, surrounded by candles, incense, long scrolls with painted figures, and the accompaniment of drums. Reciting texts from the *Shih ching* (Book of Odes) and later writings, they expelled demons by making noise, striking out at the demons with clubs, and spitting water from the mouth in the four cardinal directions. The educated, however, came to dislike such practices. These opponents of shamanism and exorcisms quoted a saying attributed to Confucius that one should "revere spirits, but keep them at a distance."

Opposition to shamanism seems to have grown along with the spread of Confucianism. When the shamans' performances were abolished at the Chinese court in 32 BCE, the minister who sponsored the reform quoted Confucius as justification. Other commentators of the time noted that when rulers encouraged shamanism cases of haunting became more frequent. With the establishment of Confucianism as state religion in the first century BCE, the ruling classes more and more looked down on the *wu*, putting them on the same low level as professional entertainers and musicians. From the point of view of the elite, even if the *wu* were not impostors, they certainly were not gentlemen either.

In the Han dynasty Wang Ch'ung wrote a short dissertation refuting the necessity of exorcism. His work provides a good picture of contemporary beliefs about the spirit world, revealing that exorcism was widely practiced. He acknowledges that his contemporaries trust the power of sacrifices and exorcisms to remove evil. They first hospitably set out sacrifices for the entertainment of the spirits, then chase them away with swords and sticks after they have enjoyed the sacrifice. According to Wang Ch'ung's account, if these spirits have any sense, they will refuse to go but stand and fight, causing more misfortune. On the other hand, if the spirits have no knowledge they cannot cause any evil. Therefore exorcism represents meaningless labor and no harm is caused by its omission.

Further, if spirits have no material shape, they are like vapor or clouds and cannot be chased away. If we do not know their shape, we cannot guess their feelings, and if they are disposed to murder, they will hide and come back again after exorcism. The most elaborate system of exorcism can no more ensure the banishment of misfortune than the killing of tigers and wolves can undo the effects of misgovernment. Exorcism has no use, therefore, since the spirits either do not leave the house or will return to it. "The conclusion is, that man has his own happiness in his own hands, and that it is not in the hands of specters, being determined by his virtues, not by his sacrifices" (de Groot, 1892–1910, vol. 6, pp. 938f.).

Despite this criticism, exorcisms continued, and Confucians found approval for some of the rituals in Confucian texts. In the *Analects* of Confucius (10.10), it is said that when the men of the village hold their expulsion rite, the gentleman puts on his court dress and stands on the eastern steps. The expulsion rite, called No, was performed by an exorcist and four wild assistants, "inspectors or rescuers of the country to the four quarters" (de Groot, 1892–1910, vol. 6, p. 974). Over their heads they wore bears' skins decorated with four eyes of yellow metal. Dressed in black coats and red skirts and grasping halberds and shields, they led the house servants on a search through the buildings in order to drive out evil influences. It is said in the *Lun-yü* that Confucius stood at the east of the ancestral shrine in order to reassure the ancestral spirits so that they would not take flight along with other spirits and noxious influences. This No ritual was later stylized as a court dance, and the Son of Heaven performed the No to give succor against disease, ordering his officers to offer sacrifices at the same time.

Popular No ceremonies were performed in China in many places down to this century not only at the end of the year but also at times when there was high mortality from the demons of cholera. Through a medium, the god of the temple gave orders for a procession in which his image and a board bearing his name and titles were to be carried through the town so that the environs might be purified by the god's presence. Male and female *wu* were possessed by the divinity, dancing about with drums and cymbals. Other participants in specter masks, or in brilliantly colored dresses, armed with spears and banners, represented good powers suitably attired to terrify demons.

Siberian techniques of exorcism, at least in their modern forms, appear to have been strongly influenced by Chinese and Tibetan techniques and ideas. The Tunguz reindeer herders believe that sickness and misfortune come from the malice of the protective spirits of other clans or from the neglect of their own clan spirits. Shamans, as described by Soviet ethnographers, exorcise the foreign demons by driving them into the lower world. In retaliation, they then seek to send out their own guardian spirits in monstrous forms to fight the invading spirits.

Séances are undertaken in order to know and master the spirits by means of sacrifices. Disease may be attributed to the soul staying away from the body, or to its being stolen, or to its possession by evil spirits. The expulsion of the demons can only be undertaken by the shaman, for he alone can perceive the spirits and know how to exorcise them. Only he recognizes that the soul has disappeared, and only he, in his ecstatic state, can overtake the soul and return it to its body.

Séances described among the Yakut usually include four stages: the evocation of the helping spirits, the discovery of the cause of illness (generally thought to come from an evil spirit), the expulsion of this evil spirit, and finally the shaman's ascent to the sky. The shaman summons the clan spirits to help fight the invading evil; he goes into a trance and chants solemn verses to the rhythm of a drum, calling on the highest powers to prepare his way. He invokes the help of his tutelary spirit as well as other familiar spirits, who can arrive so violently as to throw him over backward. Finally, drumming and dancing, jumping in the air, chanting and shrieking, he goes to the patient and commands the cause of the illness to depart, "or he lays hold of the trouble, carries it to the middle of the room and, never stopping his imprecations, chases it away, spits it from his mouth, kicks it, drives it with his hands and breath" (account recorded by W. Sieroszewski and quoted in Eliade, 1964, pp. 231f.).

The shamanistic tradition of the ancient Bon religion of Tibet was preserved almost in its entirety in Buddhist Lamaism. The most famous Tibetan Buddhist monks were said to have performed miracles and exorcisms like other shamans. In one Tibetan legend a notable lama expelled the spirit of sickness in the form of a black pin from a queen, and his fellow worker flew through the air and danced on the roof of a house. However, not a great deal has been done to investigate the shamanistic elements in Bon and Lamaism.

In Tibet and Sikkim, demons who had caused death were exorcised within two days of the removal of the corpse. This ritual was called "turning away the face of the destroying devil" (Waddell, 1895, p. 494). The head lama, invoking his tutelary deity, blew upon human and animal images while assistants beat drums and cried "Begone." The chief lama then ordered the death demon to leave the house and sent it away to oppress his enemies. The images were deposited at crossroads while the lama uttered spells and made passes with a bell and a model thunderbolt *(rdo rje)* to ensure that no evil lurked behind.

In an example recorded in Tibet in 1940, an exorcist of demons was called from Lhasa to summon back the soul of a woman. After using magical devices and burning twigs, he went into a trance, first staring fixedly and then dancing wildly. By so doing, he called up the spirit, who demanded through a medium, "Who called me?" The spirit, through the medium, was then required to identify the sickness and indicate the means by which life could be restored to the woman. Once a sacrificial ceremomy was arranged and gifts offered, the woman recovered (Hoffmann, 1961, p. 26).

INDIA AND SOUTH ASIA

Parallels to shamanistic techniques and exorcisms are found in Indian classical texts. The *Atharvaveda* (5.15–16) gives spells for exorcising, "speaking away " *(apa-vaktri),* warding off or averting pests and their leaders, as well as rites against demons. "O Agni, burn against the demons. . . . Let Rudra crush the ribs of sorcerers . . . Mitra-Varuṇa drive back the devourers" (6.32). Charms were recommended for the expulsion of adversaries, rivals, wizards, and assorted demons (2.18). In particular, the fire god, Agni, was offered sacrifice so that he would slay the demons and touch sorcerers with his flame. Agni would pierce the demons with arrows and thunderbolts or shut them up in his mouth, grind them with his teeth, split their skin, and crush their joints (8.3).

Āyurveda ("science of life, health") was closely associated with the *Artharvaveda*. One of its eight departments was *bhūta-vidyā* ("knowledge of evil beings"), which was demonology, or the treatment of diseases produced by evil influences. After describing how spirits are sent by sorcerers to plague individuals, Āyurveda recommends employing an exorcist who by means of spells and propitiatory formulas can send the malady back to its author or transfer it to a tree, animal, or human being. More philosophically, the *Chāndogya Upaniṣad* (7.7) affirms that understanding *(vijñāna)* gives knowledge of the Vedas and sciences, including *bhūta-vidyā*, and that therefore *vijñāna* should be revered as *brahman*.

In Indian village religion the activities of professional exorcisers ranged from warding off hailstorms to expelling evil spirits from those possessed by them. L. S. S. O'Malley (1935) describes an exorcism during an epidemic in the sub-Himalayan districts of Uttar Pradesh. The exorcist was simply carried outside the village tied upside down on a bedstead. Driving a wooden peg into the ground, he assured the villagers that the evil spirit had been tied up. Spirits that possessed men or women might be induced by the exorcist to leave by offerings of sweetmeats or sacrifices of goats. If this persuasion failed, harsher methods were used: beating the sufferer, applying red pepper to his nose, or undertaking the fire-walking ceremony. "Only those possessed by an evil spirit are affected by the fire, and, if their skin is burnt, it is a sign of deliverance from demonical possession" (O'Malley, 1935, p. 160).

In South India and in Sri Lanka professional exorcisers paint their faces, put on hideous masks, dress in gaudy costumes, arm themselves with symbolic weapons, and take to dancing in order to impersonate particular demons. In this way they induce evil spirits to leave the persons they have possessed. Sinhala exorcism has been described in detail by Paul Wirz (1954).

The Sinhala exorcist (*edura* or *kattadiya*, "devil-charmer") is distinct from the general medical practitioner or natural healer. He usually comes from a lower caste, though he is just as prominent in his social activities. Exorcists preserve the ancient folk religion's belief in demons, spirits, and the occult powers needed in dealing with them. But the exorcists also link their practices to Hinduism and Buddhism. Like Āyurveda, medical science in Sri Lanka includes a section on *bhūta-viya*, those illnesses *(viya)* believed to be caused by demons or ghosts. They include epidemics sent by the gods in response to human offenses, illnesses caused by the unfavorable conjunctions of the planets and constellations, and sicknesses caused by the human "evil eye" or "evil talk." The demons may be appeased by the presentation of offerings or driven away by exorcists.

In addition to the Sinhala *edura*, devil-charmer or exorcist, there is a *bandhanaya*, whose task it is to "bind" *(bandhana)* or confine evil beings and render them harmless. There are also astrologers, though the three professions are difficult to separate. The *edura* is one of the best-known figures in Sinhala villages, making offerings to spirits and demons, persuading them to release the persons they have made sick and make them healthy again. Most *edura* belong to the low castes of fishermen, land workers, drummers, or chair carriers. They are trained through a long apprenticeship to a teacher *(guru)*, often in their own family, learning *mantras* that eventually enable them to perform ceremonies independently.

When a person is ill in Sri Lanka, he sends first for the general medical practitioner, but if the practitioner's remedies do not help the invalid, a soothsayer is called in to determine the cause of the sickness. The soothsayer may suggest an astrologer, who is cheaper, or an exorcist. The exorcist makes his diagnosis by asking where the patient has stayed, whether he has come into contact with harmful spirits, eaten food that attracted them, or lived in a haunted house. He ties a charm on the patient to prevent the sickness from getting worse and to show the demons that a fuller ritual offering will be made.

Wirz gives several detailed descriptions of exorcism ceremonies, including the following account (Wirz, 1954, pp. 41ff.). For every great ceremony an auspicious day must be selected by consulting the patient's horoscope and noting, above all, the quarter of the compass where Mārea is to be found. Mārea or Māraya (Skt., Māra, "death, the evil one") is the mischievous and evil being, the leader of the demons, the personification of death, and the great adversary of the Buddha in mythology. Mārea changes his place in the sky each day. The exorcist and his assistants must never face in his direction lest their spells be rendered useless. Their spells would also be ineffective on the four days of the moon's phases that are Buddhist holidays. Saturdays and Wednesdays are the most auspicious days, other things being equal, because demons are hungry then and most likely to obey a summons.

The patient's relatives are told by the exorcist to procure certain herbs and roots, especially a large number of small lemons or limes, palm leaves, and banana stems. Other herbs and leaves are brought by the exorcist himself. Although the fee for the ceremony is fixed according to how elaborate it is to be, the exorcist must have at least one drummer and one or two assistants who help with arrangements and participate in dances. The ritual must always take place at night and continue until dawn, because that is the only time the spirit *(yakku;* Skt., *yakṣa)* may be called up. Ceremonies and dances are performed in front of the house where the patient is seated. From a small leaf hut to one side the dancers emerge. On the other sides of the house are another hut, stands for offerings and branches, and chairs for water, flowers, and roots.

The ceremony begins with a dance "by three or four persons who are supposed to represent the *yakku* at their evening-dance or their assembly" (Wirz, 1954, p. 52). A dialogue between a *yakku* and a drummer reveals that somebody has fallen ill and has been prescribed certain medicines. The *yakku* says that the medicines are no good, but that if he is given twelve presents, he will cure the patient. After two or three hours of dancing, herbs are placed at the patient's feet. Then the chief exorcist dances, utters spells, passes a mat through smoke, and lies on it in front of the patient. At the same time incense is carried around the exorcist.

After further dances and offerings, the *yakku* severally promise to restore the patient to health. The climax of the ceremony is a dance by a *yakku* with double torches in his mouth, which builds to a peak of intensity until he collapses in exhaustion. The patient is paraded round the hut and the stands of offerings and then gives gifts to the chief *yakku,* who promises recovery and health in words such as these: "Om, honour to Buddha, honour to Shiva, the eighteen mental disorders, the eighteen convulsion diseases, the eighteen fevers . . . may they be put to an end by the help of the deities and of glorious Buddha" (Wirz, 1954, p. 61).

At last the exorcist sings a magic word or exclamation *(dehena)* which assures the patient of his recovery. He passes a ritual brush over the patient's head and body, and all the *yakku* and bystanders join in the exclamation to confirm that the exorcism has been successful.

Such famous "devil dances," elaborate exorcisms of the demons of disease, take place in southern and western provinces of Sri Lanka, but these performances are not practiced everywhere in the rural highlands. However, Richard F. Gombrich (1971) has described more simple forms of exorcism in the highlands. Gombrich recounts how a sick patient believed that he had been plagued by an evil spirit sent by malicious neighbors and called in an exorcist to nullify the spell by performing a lime-cutting ceremony. The exorcist prepared offerings of five kinds of grain and meat. The offerings were placed at a crossroads so that when the spirit *(yakku)* had left the patient it would be unable to find its way back. Incense sticks were burned before pictures of the Buddha and the gods which were hanging on the wall of the patient's house. Twenty-one limes were placed at crucial points on the patient's body, then they were cut and thrown into sizzling oil. Finally, an egg was passed down the sufferer's body from head to feet, then broken and thrown into the pot along with the limes and the cutters that had sliced them. This indicated that all the evil influence *(dosa)* had been drained out of the patient and burned (Gombrich, 1971, p. 199).

Other sufferers from evil spirits go to popular shrines, such as the famous center of Kataragama in southeastern Sri Lanka, named after a god who is the second son of the Hindu god Śiva. Although primarily a Hindu center for the Tamils, this shrine attracts members of other religions. Enthusiastic devotees have become notorious for walking on fire or hanging in the air by means of skewers through their back muscles. At Kataragama are claimed cures of physical, mental, and spiritual possession. More simply, Buddhists may claim that evil spirits can be exorcised by recitation of the Three Refuges, which causes spirits and ghosts to flee.

In Burma and other countries of Southeast Asia, Buddhist sects practice exorcism for diseases believed to be caused by witchcraft or demonic possession. Combining ancient indigenous beliefs in spirits with faith in the Buddha and his attendants, some monks exorcise evil spirits by enlisting both traditional esoteric skills and the powers of benign Buddhist gods.

In Thailand the concept of *phii* includes a wide range of spirits. The *phii paub* is a particularly malevolent type of spirit whose removal requires the services of an exorcist. Women, married and single, are the most common victims of this kind of possession. Children also are affected, but very rarely adult men. Symptoms of hysteria—crying out, laughing loudly, hiding the face, and general depression—are diagnosed as possession.

Stanley J. Tambiah argues that the Thai exorcist is "an inversion of the orthodox Buddhist monk" (Tambiah, 1970, p. 322). The Thai exorcist uses Buddhist texts, but in diametrically opposed ways to those of the monk who uses these texts to teach morality and transfer blessings. The exorcist uses "the sacred words to frighten the spirits and drive them away," and he treats diseases of women, whereas the monk keeps his distance from women.

The Thai exorcist *(mau tham)* is an expert in reciting the Buddhist sacred texts (Dhamma), for they are considered to have great power. At the beginning of a séance the exorcist sits facing the propitious east and first worships the Buddha, the Sangha, the Dhamma—the Three Refuges. Then he invokes the powers of his teacher and other benevolent spirits to come wage war against the evil. He goes into a trance, trembling, waving his arms, shaking his body, gabbling magical spells, rushing to confront the patient. To make the spirit reveal itself, the exorcist may attack the patient, beating her with a whip or a fern, even scratching her with a tiger's tooth.

Once the spirit is identified, the exorcist and patient quiet down and proceed to the phase of purification. By reciting charms, washing with and drinking charmed water, and chanting outside and inside the house, the patient is purified. Her neck, wrists, and ankles are bound with cord to prevent the spirit from entering her body again. The exorcist teaches her the five Buddhist precepts of morality, usually recited only by monks. Lastly, she is given five pairs of flowers and candles to place by her bed until she is fully cured. To help toward this end the patient may visit the exorcist several times more to receive further washings with sacred water.

AFRICA AND ISLAMIC LANDS

In Africa, belief in possession by good or evil spirits flourished in ancient indigenous religions and has survived in modern Islamic and Christian contexts. Such beliefs have been noted in northern desert regions—Egypt, Arabia, and Ethiopia—as well as in tropical regions where both Islam and Christianity have flourished in modern times.

In Somalia a victim is said to have been entered or seized by spirits. When this happens, both the spirits and the resulting illness are called *sar* (*zār* in Ethiopia). Somalians believe that these evil spirits are consumed with greed and lust after luxurious food, clothing, jewelry, and perfume. Women, especially married women, are particularly vulnerable to such possession. I. M. Lewis (1971) suggests that this results from women's depressed social status, for divorce and absent husbands are common. Speaking through the lips of the possessed woman, the spirits demand fine clothes, perfumes, and dainties with an authority that the women rarely achieve in ordinary life. When a *sar* specialist recognizes this possession, the woman's husband pays large sums of money for dances for "beating the *sar*" to bring relief and recovery. Some men are skeptical of this possession, regarding it as female trickery, noting that it occurs more often among the wives of the wealthy than among the poor. The women retort that some *sar* spirits attack the wealthy and others molest the poor, but that in any case the *sar* spirits hate men.

In Tanzania a similar "devil's disease" reveals its presence by hysterical symptoms of craving for food and presents. The exorcism includes not only cathartic dances but also the continuing presence of the exorcist in the house of the possessed woman. The exorcist's presence makes the woman feel like the center of attention and persuades her husband to show kindness. Similarly possessed women of the Luo in Kenya are treated by female exorcisers, who summon up the possessing spirits, find out their requirements, and expel them with dancing and feasting. The victim may be taken to the exorciser's home in order to find relief from the drudgery of her own household. Some possessed women dress in male clothing, and by so doing perhaps show their envy of the higher status of men. When they have undergone exorcism they return to a more respected position in their own home.

The Hausa cult of spirit possession is widely distributed in West Africa. The cult includes some two hundred spirits (*bori*), many of which are named and characterized by a specific behavior. These spirits are also called by words related to Arabic, for example *iblisi* ("devil") or *aljannu* (related to the Arabic word for Gehenna). Such spirits are believed to control different illnesses. Each spirit requires an appropriate type of sacrifice to propitiate it, such as a white sheep or a red cock. The "children of the *bori*" is the Hausa term for members of the cult of spirit possession. Dancers are referred to as "mares," and possession is described as "the spirit mounted her" or "she mounted the spirit." The spirit indicates its name and nature by distinctive behavior and gestures. At its departure the medium sneezes and recovers from trance. Interpreters believe that women accept the afflictions caused by the spirits as release from situations of domestic conflict. After their cure they are treated with deference.

In West Africa evil may also be expelled or transferred in a manner reminiscent of the ancient Hebrew practice of transferring a social evil to a scapegoat who carries it away into the wilderness. In ancient Dahomey the mother of twins that had died knelt in front of a priest. The priest proceeded to dust her chest, brow, knees, and feet with a fowl that she had brought. She was then instructed to take a goat by the horns and place her forehead three times against it in order to transfer her evil. The fowl and goat were then set loose to wander away from the village, while the woman was dusted with powdered clay in order to prevent a return of the evil.

The Islamic world tolerates the belief in witchcraft and possession. Although such beliefs at times are condemned, their prevalence is not questioned. *Siḥr* ("glamour, magic") is based upon belief in a world of spirits. Magicians claim that they can control the spirits by obeying Allāh and using his name in exorcisms. Illicit magicians are believed to enslave spirits for evil purposes and do so by performing deeds displeasing to God.

A crucial verse in the Qur'ān states that unbelievers "follow what the devils used to recite in the reign of Solomon. Solomon did not disbelieve, but the devils disbelieved, teaching the people magic . . . and they learn what injures them and does not profit" (2:96–102). Later Islam traced all good magic back to Solomon, and the devils listened at the walls of heaven and added lies to what they heard. In the traditions it is said that Muḥammad permitted the use of spells to counteract the effects of the evil eye or to remove the yellowness which came from a malignant eye.

Exorcism was *da'wah*, a call or invocation, interpreted by the orthodox as permissible only through the invocation of God himself. A further tradition said, "There is nothing wrong in using spells as long as you do not associate anything with God." Exorcists and licit magicians claim that they control the spirits by supplicating God and bringing adjurations to bear on the spirits. Illicit magicians are said to enslave spirits by making evil offerings and by performing deeds displeasing to God. Incantations used by exorcists consist of the recital of the names and attributes of God, either "amiable attributes" or "terrible attributes." The name and initials of the person to be influenced are also considered by many popular exorcists to be connected with the twelve signs of the zodiac, the seven planets, and the four elements. Books on exorcism correlate these signs with types of incense and with the names of presiding spirits which make other souls obedient to the will of the exorcist.

The *jinn*, or genies, of Islamic belief are fiery spirits, some of whom are believers and will enter paradise, while others will go to the fire of hell. They appear in many popular stories, as in the *Thousand and One Nights*. Solomon had great power over the *jinn* by means of his seal or ring, on which was engraved "the most great name" of God. He built the Temple at Jerusalem with the help of thousands of *jinn*. But the relation of the *jinn* to the evil spirits or *shaytān*s is obscure, for Iblīs, the devil *(diabolos)*, is said to be both a *jinnī* and an angel. The presence of the *jinn* in many strange events leads people to invoke the name of God against possession by them. Mental and physical illnesses are often ascribed to *jinn*, and prayers for protection against them are uttered on entering a house or taking a bath. *Jinn* are frightened away by strong smells or sounds, by salt or water or smoke, but only with the help of the invocation of God.

In Morocco the *jinn* were exorcised from sick people by persons who had plenty of *jinn* themselves and never ate salted food. The exorcist required that the sick person bring clothes of a certain color and a cock or hen of the same color. The exorcist then dressed in the clothes brought by the patient and killed the fowl over a vessel held above the patient's head. The fowl was boiled and eaten by the exorcist and the patient, while a company of dancers played music, sang, and invoked various saints. If the patient was seriously ill, he might remain with the exorcist for seven days and nights. During this time they both ate only unsalted food. Other exorcists also sacrificed fowls and performed dances so that the *jinn* afflicting the patients would be identified. The dances continued up to seven days, during which time the house was fumigated.

Some other Semitic exorcisms are illustrated in the Old Testament Apocrypha, the writings of Josephus, and the New Testament. Generally these exorcisms use no magic rituals or mediums to contact or contain the possessing spirits but rely on powerful words in the name of God.

[*See also* Healing; Diseases and Cures; Shamanism; *and* Spirit Possession. *For discussion of exorcism in specific contexts, see* Drums; Folk Religion, *article on* Folk Judaism; *and* Affliction.]

BIBLIOGRAPHY

For general studies of exorcism and its practitioners, see Traugott K. Oesterreich's *Possession, Demoniacal and Other* (New York, 1930) and Mircea Eliade's *Shamanism: Archaic Techniques of Ecstasy*, rev. & enl. ed. (New York, 1964). Arthur Waley's translation of *The Tale of Genji* (London, 1925) was long the standard version, but Edward G. Seidensticker's translation under the same title (New York, 1978) is complete and beautifully done. Carmen Blacker's *The Catalpa Bow* (London, 1975)—the title taken from an instrument used by a Japanese exorcist— is an invaluable study of popular religion past and present based on firsthand experience. *The Pillow Book of Sei Shōnagon* has been translated and annotated by Ivan I. Morris (Baltimore, 1970). *The Religious System of China,* 6 vols., by J. J. M. de Groot (1892–1910; Taipei, 1967), is full of detail on traditional beliefs and practices, as is L. Austine Waddell's *The Buddhism of Tibet* (1895; Cambridge, 1971). Helmut Hoffmann outlines more modern practices in *The Religions of Tibet* (New York, 1961). *Popular Hinduism* by L. S. S. O'Malley (New York, 1935) provides brief studies. *Exorcism and the Art of Healing in Ceylon* by Paul Wirz (Leiden, 1954) is more detailed and analytical. Stanley J. Tambiah's *Buddhism and the Spirit Cults in North-East Thailand* (Cambridge, 1970) is a more anthropological study. Richard F. Gombrich examines the relationship between "cognitive" and practiced religion in Sri Lanka in *Precept and Practice* (Oxford, 1971). An anthropological study of possession and exorcism with special reference to Africa is found in I. M. Lewis's *Ecstatic Religion* (Harmondsworth, 1971). For a comparative study of beliefs see my *West African Psychology* (London, 1951). On exorcism in popular Islam, see Edward A. Westermarck's *Ritual and Belief in Morocco,* 2 vols. (1926; New Hyde Park, N.Y., 1968).

22 GEOMANCY

Erika Bourguignon

Geomancy is a form of divination based on the interpretation of figures or patterns drawn on the ground or other flat surface by means of sand or similar granular materials. The term is also used for the interpretation of geographic features. Among the Chinese, in particular, this practice of geomancy is rooted in traditional philosophic conceptions of the relationship that exists between human beings and the vital forces of their environment and the need to achieve a harmonious balance between the two to ensure well-being.

The Western form of geomancy, widespread in the Arab world, was also of importance in medieval Europe, where it was closely linked with alchemy and astrology. Geomancy of this kind is likely to have originated in the ancient Near East and may also have been developed further by Greek mathematical speculations. In the eighth and ninth centuries, during the period of Arab cultural florescence and expansion, it became systematized and was then widely distributed from its center to Byzantium and across North Africa and into Spain. From Spain it was also probably spread along a second route into Christian Europe. From Egypt and North Africa, geomancy was carried south with Islam and then even beyond, so that it is now found both in West Africa (for example, among the Yoruba of Nigeria) and in East Africa, including Madagascar.

The Arab system called *ram'l* ("sand") is based on complex mathematical calculations and involves conceptions of an orderly universe. Its numerical order provides the underlying framework for all other Western systems of geomancy. The fundamental common feature of geomancy is a pattern of binary oppositions of markings grouped into sixteen combinations of four positions. In both the Arab system and that of medieval Europe *(ars punctatoria),* points or lines were drawn on sand in a pattern based on chance. In the Yoruba system (Ifa), which has been particularly well described, markings are based on the casting of palm kernels or cowrie shells according to prescribed procedures. For each of the resulting figures, from among a total of 256 possible combinations and permutations there is a set of verses that the diviner *(babalawo)* will have memorized to interpret the pattern and to apply to the case at hand. In general, the aim of this practice is not to divine future events but to discover the supernatural causes of present situations and their remedies.

In the European system the sixteen figures are related to astronomical signs of the planets and the zodiac; the scheme also includes four elements and four qualities. Although various authors have offered divergent interpretations of this system, its basic structure is remarkably constant and has been integrated into different philosophical conceptions with striking flexibility.

The system of medieval European geomancy appears to have had a brief revival in the occultism of the nineteenth century. The African systems are still viable, and forms of the Yoruba practice, in particular, have even been discovered in the Americas, notably in Cuba and Brazil.

Less complex systems of geomancy, apparently unrelated to those of the West, are to be found in Tibet in the form of "stone divination" and "pebble divination." These systems each have their own sets of rules, recorded in manuals. They are quite distinct from those discussed above.

The term *geomancy* is also used to refer to *feng-shui* ("winds and waters"), the traditional Chinese technique for determining propitious locations for towns, dwellings, and tombs. This system, which is still in very widespread use, concerns the distribution over the earth, by winds and water currents, of various terrestrial and atmospheric emanations that are believed to exert important influences on people. In addition to being a system of calculations for establishing favorable sites, geomancy is also a method for discerning the causes of human illness and suffering. Geomancers may claim that these causes lie in the negative influences on people of badly placed residences or of the unfortunate positioning of the tombs of ancestors, who consequently send illness and misfortune to their descendants as expressions of anger. Moreover, a given dwelling or tomb, which was originally well placed, may, in time, have its geomantic position shifted as a result of changes in the area, such as new constructions that produce an alteration in the balance of positive and negative currents. A geomancer will not only divine such causes but will also seek to remedy the situation by recommending reburial at a better spot, changing the position of a tomb, or urging the building of a wall or other structure to modify the direction of the currents. Because of the belief that illness may be due to such influences, geomancers must be included in any list of traditional Chinese diagnosticians and medical practitioners.

[*See also* Divination.]

BIBLIOGRAPHY

Bascom, William R. *Ifa Divination*. Bloomington, Ind., 1969.

Bascom, William R. *Sixteen Cowries: Yoruba Divination from Africa to the New World*. Bloomington, Ind., 1980.

Caslant, Eugène. *Traité élémentaire de géomancie*. Paris. 1935.

Ekvall, Robert B. *Religious Observances in Tibet*. Chicago, 1964.

Granet, Marcel. *The Religion of the Chinese People*. Translated by Maurice Freedman. New York, 1975.

Jaulin, Robert. *La géomancie: Analyse formelle*. Paris, 1966.

23 INCANTATION

THEODORE M. LUDWIG

The practice of incantation (Lat., *incantatio,* from *incantare,* "to chant a religious formula") differs considerably from culture to culture. For the purposes of this cross-cultural overview, however, incantation can be understood as the authorized use of rhythmically organized words of power that are chanted, spoken, or written to accomplish a desired goal by binding spiritual powers to act in a favorable way.

Since incantation uses words to move spiritual powers and accomplish a desired result, this practice is related to other uses of sacred language such as prayer, invocation, blessing, and cursing. Verbal formulas associated with prayer beseech the spiritual powers for certain actions or maintain communication by praise and submission. However, verbal formulas associated with incantation are designed to perform the desired result by "obliging" (Lat., *ob-ligare,* "to bind") spiritual powers. Invocation, blessing, and cursing are used with both prayer and incantation.

THE POWER OF INCANTATION

Even though practices of incantation differ widely from culture to culture, its validity or efficacy appears to depend on cultural consensus about a number of primary factors, namely, the power of the chanted verbal formula, the authority of the incantor, the receptivity of spiritual forces both good and evil, the connection with the religious or mythological tradition, and the power of the accompanying ritual.

The Power of the Formula. Societies that use incantations understand them to be performative, that is, they accomplish what they say. The act of chanting the verbal formula itself has power. Scholars have put forth a variety of explanations concerning the effect incantations have for people. Older theories considered incantation to be a form of magic, an attempt to control and manipulate the forces of nature. More recent theories have suggested that incantations are expressive of needs and wishes or symbolize a desired result, or that they have the psychological effect of restructuring reality in the minds of people. Although these explanations may provide certain insights into the meaning of incantation, it must be remembered that, to the people involved, the proper chanting of the formula itself has performative power. To them it does not express or symbolize some other action—it *does* it. When, for example, the incantation experts of the Trobriand Islanders chant over the newly planted yam vines, "Raise thy stalk, O taytu. Make it flare up, make it lie across!" (Malinowski, 1935, vol. 1, p. 146), the people know that the "hearing" of these commands by the tubers is what makes them sprout and grow.

It is not, however, just any words that have such power. Incantations are special verbal formulas that in a variety of ways, depending upon the particular cultural tradition, tap into sacred power. They may, for example, contain powerful scriptural expressions, *mantra*s, or sacred names. [*See, for example,* Mantra *and* Names and Naming.] They are usually rhythmically organized and chanted repeatedly. They may use special devices such as foreign or unintelligible words, "abracadabra" nonsense phrases. The Anglo-Saxon medical-incantation treatise *Lacnunga* provides an example, using powerful names and impressive nonsense words:

> *Sing this prayer over the black blains nine times: first, Paternoster. "Tigath tigath tigath calicet aclu cluel sedes adclocles acre earcre arnem nonabiuth aer aernem nidren arcum cunath arcum arctua fligara uflen binchi cutern nicuparam raf afth egal uflen arta arta arta trauncula trauncula. [In Latin:] Seek and you shall find. I adjure you by the Father, Son, and Holy Spirit that you grow no larger but that you dry up.* . . . *Cross Matthew, cross Mark, cross Luke, cross John."*
> (Grattan and Singer, 1952, p. 107; my trans.)

It should be noted that, although the primary power of an incantation resides in its oral presentation, once these formulas could be written down, the chirographic (handwritten) text itself contributed to the potency of the incantation. From before 600 CE come Jewish-related Aramaic incantation texts written by experts on bowls and designed to ward off various sorts of evil. Such power could now be extended even into the realm of the dead, as in the case of Middle Kingdom Egyptian incantations inscribed on the inside wall of coffins, by which the various gods and demons encountered by the soul would be bound to act beneficially.

The Chanter's Authority. Closely connected to the power of the verbal formula is the authority of the incantors. These may be experts in terms of learning or ecclesiastical authority, like Taoist priests or Christian monks; they may be people who have been specially initiated into the use of such power, like various kinds of shamans; they may be charismatic holy ones who keep certain special observances or practices that sanction their authority. In the incantation itself, the chanter often clothes himself in the aura of divine authority and power. A Malay shaman, drawing authority from both Hinduism and Islam, outroars a thunderstorm:

> Om! Virgin goddess, Mahadewi! Om!
> Cub am I of mighty tiger!
> 'Ali's line through me descends!
> My voice is the rumble of thunder, . . .
> By virtue of my charm got from 'Ali
> And of Islam's confession of faith.
> (Winstedt, 1925, p. 59)

Receptivity of the Spiritual Forces. The power of the incantation further derives from the people's shared understanding of the nature and receptivity of the spiritual powers to be moved and bound by the powerful words. That spiritual entity may be simply an object or person that is to perform in a certain way. At other times, the incantation invokes, with careful mention of names, spirits, or gods who control aspects of nature and life, empowering or binding them to act beneficially. Ritual specialists of Java, when burying the umbilical cord of a newborn baby, intone the following words: "In the name of God, the Merciful, the Compassionate! Father Earth, Mother Earth, I am about to leave in your care the birthcord of the baby. . . . Don't bother the baby. This is necessary because of Allah. If you do bother him, you will by punished by God" (Geertz, 1960, p. 46).

A great many incantations are addressed to evil spirits or demons, conjuring them to leave or stay away. It is extremely important that the incantor name and identify the origin and characteristics of the evil power in order to bind it. Pre-Spanish Maya incantations, for example, list detailed knowledge about the evil spirit of the disease, recounting its parentage, its lustful impulses that inspired its shameful birth, and all its characteristics; they then proceed to consign the spirit to the foul-smelling underworld or to cast it into the wind to fall behind the sky. An Aramaic incantation becomes very specific in naming one of the many demons: "I adjure you, Lilith Hablas, granddaughter of Lilith Zarnai, . . . the one who fills deep places, strikes, smites, casts down, strangles, kills, and casts down boys and girls, male and female foetuses," while another text conjures by name nearly eighty demons and spirits of evils or sicknesses (Isbell, 1975, pp. 61, 121–122), showing that, occasionally, an incantation will name a whole series of evil spirits and demons—just to be sure that the right one is included.

Connection of the Chant with Tradition. The successful operation of the incantation depends on its connection with the religious or mythological tradition of the people. In one way or another, the incantation fits the specific human circumstance into the larger pattern of sacred existence and power as known in the religion of the people. Incantations in which such patterns are made explicit can be called narrative incantations. For example, Scottish incantations are regularly grounded in stories or legends about Christ and his disciples, as in this example: "Christ went on an ass, / She sprained her foot, / He came down / And healed her foot; / As He healed that / May He heal this, / And greater than this, / If it be His will to do" (Carmichael, 1928, vol. 2, p. 17). An ancient Egyptian narrative incantation, relating at great length how Isis rescued her son Horus from a scorpion's bite, concludes with the main point: "It means that Horus lives for his mother—and that the sufferer lives for his mother likewise; the poison is powerless!" (Bourghouts, 1978, pp. 62–69).

The Accompanying Ritual Actions. While incantations can be used alone without any accompanying actions, in most cultures the chanting of incantations is usually associated with the power of other ritual actions. The incantation may be related to a ritual object that it empowers with sacred force. For treating a child with worms, the Javanese doctor chants over a special herb: "In the name of God, the Merciful, the Compassionate! Grandmother spirit, Grandfather spirit. . . . The harmful worms—may they all die. The good worms—may they stay for the whole length of the child's life" (Geertz, 1960, p. 93). Cherokee specialists almost always chant their incantations over tobacco, "remaking" or empowering the tobacco to perform the desired benefit. A Taoist priest chants this incantation over a small puppet as he rubs it over a patient: "Substitute, be thou in place of the fore part of the body, . . . be thou in place of the back parts, . . . be thou in place of the left side, that health may be ensured to him for year upon year" (de Groot, 1967, vol. 6, p. 1260). Incantation texts are often accompanied by directions for ritual actions. For example, an ancient Mesopotamian incantation for potency commands: "Let the ass swell up! Let him mount the jenny! Let the buck get an erection! Let him again and again mount the young she-goat!"; then the ritual directions follow: "Pulverized magnetic iron ore you put [into] puru oil; you recite the incantation over it seven times; the man rubs his penis, the woman her vagina with the oil, then he can have intercourse" (Biggs, 1967, p. 33). Incantation and ritual together accomplish the desired result.

FORMS OF ADDRESS

Within the great diversity of forms taken by the incantation formulas in different cultures and even within the same culture, a number of standard types can be discerned in the way spiritual powers are addressed. Many operate with the command form, using imperatives or statements of obligation to bind the spiritual powers to the desired action. Other incantations use the declaratory mode to establish the hoped-for result. And there are other incantations that approach the prayer mode, beseeching or charming the spiritual powers to take the beneficial action. Many times, of course, incantations use a combination of these three forms.

The command form, at its simplest, consists in naming the spiritual power and binding it to the desired action with an imperative. The High German "Pro Nessia" incantation from the ninth century AD, driving out the worm spirit that causes disease, is pure command:

> Go out, nesso,
> with the nine little ones,
> out from the marrow into the veins,
> from the veins into the flesh,
> from the flesh into the hide,
> from the hide into this arrow.
> Three paternosters.
>   (Hampp, 1967, p. 118; my trans.)

In Burma, an exorcist addresses many powers of the supernatural world in a general incantation in order to focus his powerful command on the *ouktazaun* (minor spirit) that is possessing his client: "To all the *samma* and *brahma devas* of the sky heavens; to all the ghosts, monsters, and other evil creatures; to the ogres of the earth; to the master witches and the wizards; to the evil nats and the *ouktazauns:* I command you to leave. I command you by the glory of the Triple Gems [Buddha, Dhamma, and Sangha]" (Spiro, 1967, p. 177).

Very often incantations use a declaratory mode to perform the intended result of binding evil forces or compelling the good, declaring the desired state to be a reality in the present or the future. A Cherokee incantation designed to break up a happily married couple, for the benefit of a forgotten lover, simply declares the result to be so:

> Now! Very quickly pillow your head upon the Soul of
>   the Dog, outside, where there is loneliness!
> Your name is _____.

> In the very middle of your two bodies loneliness has
> just come to think.
> You are to be broken in the Pathway.
> Now! Where the joining is has just come to be divided.
> Your two souls have just come to be divided somewhere
> in the Valley.
> Without breaking your soul, I have just come to stupefy
> you with the Smoke of the Blue Tobacco.
> (Kilpatrick and Kilpatrick, 1965, pp. 139–140)

When the Trobriand sorcerer tours the gardens with their budding leaves, he intones, "The yam rises and swells like a bush-hen's nest. The yam rises and swells like a baking-mound. . . . For these are my yams, and my kinsmen will eat them up. My mother will die of surfeit, I myself will die of repletion" (Malinowski, 1935, vol. 1, p. 146). It is in this declaratory mode that blessings and curses are often formulated, focusing on the person or thing to be involved and declaring the favorable or unfavorable state to be a reality.

A third mode of expression in many incantations is that of beseeching or charming the sacred powers to act benevolently. This form approaches that of prayer and, at times, is indistinguishable from it. Yet the typical expressions, "May you," "Let God," "I ask you," and the like, can also be understood as compelling or binding the spiritual powers, not just beseeching them. A Burmese doctor chants a prayer-spell over a sick girl, repeating it three times as he empowers many spiritual beings for action: "May the five Buddhas, the nats, and the Brahmas rest on the forehead [of the patient]; may Sakka rest on the eyes and ears, Thurasandi Devi on the mouth, and Matali on the hands, feet, and body, . . . and may they guard and protect me" (Spiro, 1967, p. 152). And the Malay incantor turns even to Iblīs (Satan) and the other spirits and devils and firmly requests direct action on behalf of his lovesick client:

> In the name of God, the Merciful, the Compassionate!
> Friend of mine, Iblis!
> And all ye spirits and devils that love to trouble man!
> I ask you to go and enter the body of this girl,
> Burning her heart as this sand burns,
> Fired with love for me.   (Winstedt, 1925, p. 165)

PURPOSES OF INCANTATION

Purposes for the use of incantation differ widely and cover the whole gamut of life needs of individuals and societies. It is possible, however, to classify incantations, according to their purpose, into three broad categories: defensive, productive, and malevolent.

Defensive Incantations. Among defensive incantations, a major purpose is prophylactic or apotropaic, that is, warding off evil spirits and their troubles, especially in the critical passages of life. Classic among apotropaic incantations are those widespread in the ancient Near East, directed against demonic powers called liliths—

ghostly paramours of men, who attack women during their periods and at childbirth and who devour children. An incantation bowl binds these demons:

> *I adjure you, every species of lilith, in the name of your offspring which demons and liliths bore. . . . Woe, tramplers, scourgers, mutilaters, breakers, disturbers, squeezers, muzzlers, and dissolvers like water. . . . You are fearful, terrified, and bound to my exorcism, you who appear to the sons of men—to men in the likeness of women and to women in the likeness of men—you who lie with people during the night and during the day.* (Isbell, 1975, pp. 17–18)

Vedic incantation from ancient India is directed against the fiends who cause pregnant women to abort: "The blood-sucking demon, and him that tries to rob health, Kanva, the devourer of our offspring, destroy, O Prisniparni [medicinal plant], and overcome!" (*Atharvaveda* 2.25.4, as cited in Bloomfield, 1964, p. 22). The Egyptian Coffin Texts testify to the need for incantations to ward off the evil powers who feast on the soul in the passage of death.

The other major use of defensive incantations is for the expulsion of evil powers that have taken up abode. A Malay Muslim shaman exorcises the demon of disease, reciting first the creation story and then chanting,

> Where is this genie lodging and taking shelter?. . .
> Genie! if thou art in the feet of this patient,
> Know that these feet are moved by Allah and His prophet;
> If thou are in the belly of this patient,
> His belly is God's sea, the sea, too, of Muhammad. . . .
> (Winstedt, 1925, pp. 62–63)

Sickness can also be seen as the result of attack by rival humans, and then the appropriate measure is a counterincantation. The Atharva priest of ancient India chants over a special ritual plant: "The spell which they skillfully prepare . . . we drive it away! . . . With this herb have I destroyed all spells. . . . Evil be to him that prepares evil, the curse shall recoil upon him that utters curses: back do we hurl it against him, that it may slay him that fashions the spell" (*Atharvaveda* 10.1.1, 4–5, as cited in Bloomfield, 1964, p. 72).

Productive Incantations. A second purpose of incantation is beneficial, that is, it promotes growth, health, and happiness either by urging on the responsible inherent powers or by causing beneficial interference by divine powers. A curer in Java uses a massage and a spitting ritual with this incantation:

> In the name of God, the Merciful, the Compassionate!
> May the Prophet Adam repair [the person],
> May Eve order [the person].
> Untangle the tangled veins,
> Right the dislocated bones,
> Make the fluids of the body feel pleasant, . . .
> Health falls with my white spittle,
> Well, well, well, by the will of God.
> (Geertz, 1960, p. 94)

A great many incantations of the productive type have to do with love and sexual attraction, marriage, home and family, potency, successful birth, and the like. The Cherokee, for example, have a large variety of love incantations, for creating loneliness in the desired person, for retaining affection of a wandering mate, for acclimatizing a newlywed wife, or compelling a runaway spouse to return. Cherokee men and women can use incantations to "rebeautify" themselves and thus become attractive to a potential mate:

> Now! I am as beautiful as the very blossoms themselves!
> I am a man, you lovely ones, you women of the Seven
>   Clans! . . .
> All of you have just come to gaze upon me alone, the
>   most beautiful.
> Now! You lovely women, already I just took your souls!
> I am a man!
> You women will live in the very middle of my soul.
> Forever I will be as beautiful as the bright red blossoms!
>   (Kilpatrick and Kilpatrick, 1965, pp. 86–87)

At times, productive incantations are needed to bring about pregnancy, as this one from ancient India: "Into thy womb shall enter a male germ, as an arrow into a quiver! May a man be born there, a son ten months old!" (*Atharvaveda* 3.23.2, as cited in Bloomfield, 1964, p. 97).

Malevolent Incantations. A third purpose of incantation is related to the need to harm, punish, or take revenge on enemies or rivals. A jilted woman can target her erstwhile lover with this fierce imprecation:

As the best of the plants thou art reputed, O herb; turn this man for me today into a eunuch that wears his hair dressed! . . . Then Indra with a pair of stones shall break his testicles both! O eunuch, into a eunuch thee I have turned; O castrate, into a castrate thee I have turned!
            (*Atharvaveda* 6.138.1–3, as cited in Bloomfield, 1964, p. 108)

The Cherokee bent on revenge learns from the shaman to recite the name of his adversary, repeating the following incantation four times and blowing his breath toward him after each rendition: "Your Pathways are Black: it was wood, not a human being! Dog excrement will cling nastily to you. You will be living intermittently. . . . Your Black Viscera will be lying all about. . . . Your Pathway lies toward the Nightland!" (Kilpatrick and Kilpatrick, 1967, p. 127).

CONCLUSION
Incantations, as rhythmic or formulaic words of power used to accomplish a desired goal by binding spiritual powers, have sometimes been considered as magic rather than religion, or as a form of religious practice lower than prayer. It is true that incantations oblige the powers to perform the action rather than prayerfully request them for it. And it is also true that incantations have to do with self-interest, sometimes at the expense of others. Yet they do represent a religious mode of being in

the world, albeit a mode of aggression rather than simple submission to spiritual powers. The power of chanted words fits the events of human life into the pattern of the sacred realities that underlie and support human existence. Far from being trivial, incantations provide help for whatever deeply troubles or concerns humans: health, birth, love, marriage, family, prosperity, death. Human existence is understood as a drama involving the interaction of many spiritual powers, and, through the power of the chanted formula, a restructuring of these powers is performed so that life can become more healthy, secure, prosperous, and happy.

[*See also* Magic *and* Spells.]

BIBLIOGRAPHY

Among the many works that include incantations from all over the world, the following provide a representative survey from ancient, medieval, and modern cultures.

Biggs, Robert D. *Šà.zi.ga: Ancient Mesopotamian Potency Incantations.* Locust Valley, N.Y., 1967. Translations and textual studies of incantations used in Mesopotamian society for this universal sexual problem.

Bloomfield, Maurice, trans. and ed. *Hymns of the Atharva-Veda.* Delhi, 1964. Reprint of "Sacred Books of the East," vol. 42 (Oxford, 1897). Translations and interpretations of the most important incantations and hymns of the fourth Veda from ancient India by one of the outstanding American Sanskritists of the nineteenth century.

Borghouts, J. F., trans. *Ancient Egyptian Magical Texts.* Leiden, 1978. Translations of a representative range of incantations from ancient Egypt, dealing with concerns of everyday life, mostly from the Middle Kingdom and later.

Carmichael, Alexander. *Carmina Gadelica: Hymns and Incantations,* vol. 2. Edinburgh, 1928. Various incantations collected orally in the highlands and islands of Scotland and translated into English.

Geertz, Clifford. *The Religion of Java.* Glencoe, Ill., 1960. Extensive information about incantations in this important study of the Javanese religious system, which combines Islam and native spirit beliefs.

Grattan, J. H. G., and Charles Singer. *Anglo-Saxon Magic and Medicine.* Oxford, 1952. Some incantations and healing rituals especially from the semipagan text *Lacnunga,* translated into modern English.

Groot, J. J. M. de. *The Religious System of China* (1892–1910). 6 vols. Reprint, Taipei, 1967. Especially volume 6 of this multivolumed work contains traditional Chinese rituals and incantations against specters.

Hampp, Irmgard. *Beschwörung, Segen, Gebet: Untersuchung zum Zauberspruch aus dem Bereich der Volksheilkunde.* Stuttgart, 1961. A rich sourcebook for incantations from German cultures, providing also a study of types and purposes.

Isbell, Charles D. *Corpus of the Aramaic Incantation Bowls.* Missoula, Mont., 1975. Texts and translations of all the published Aramaic texts inscribed on incantation bowls, from Jewish-related societies in Babylon.

Kilpatrick, Jack Frederick, and Anna Gritts Kilpatrick. *Walk in Your Soul: Love Incantations of the Oklahoma Cherokees.* Dallas, 1965. Incantations used in situations of love and marriage among the Cherokee.

Kilpatrick, Jack Frederick, and Anna Gritts Kilpatrick. *Run toward the Nightland: Magic of the Oklahoma Cherokees.* Dallas, 1967. Incantations of the Cherokee for use in various situations.

Malinowski, Bronislaw. *Coral Gardens and Their Magic.* 2 vols. London, 1935. Texts of many incantations interspersed with descriptions of the Trobriand Islanders to the east of New Guinea, with important interpretations by this famous anthropologist.

Roys, Ralph L., trans. and ed. *Ritual of the Bacabs.* Norman, Okla., 1965. Translations of healing incantations from the pre-Spanish Maya culture.

Spiro, Melford E. *Burmese Supernaturalism: A Study in the Explanation and Reduction of Suffering.* Englewood Cliffs, N.J., 1967. A careful study of the Burmese spiritual world, including translations of incantations used in this Buddhist culture.

Winstedt, R. O. *Shaman, Saiva and Sufi: A Study of the Evolution of Malay Magic.* London, 1925. Includes translations of many incantations in a study of religious practices in Malay culture, which mixes Islamic, Hindu, and indigenous religious influences.

24 NECROMANCY

Erika Bourguignon

Necromancy, the art or practice of magically conjuring up the souls of the dead, is primarily a form of divination. The principal purpose of seeking such communication with the dead is to obtain information from them, generally regarding the revelation of unknown causes or the future course of events. The cause of the death of the deceased who is questioned may be among the facts sought.

More generally, necromancy is often considered synonymous with magic, sorcery, or witchcraft, perhaps because the calling up of the dead may occur for purposes other than information seeking, or because the separation of divination from its consequences is not always clear. There is also a linguistic basis for the expanded use of the word: the term *black art* for magic appears to be based on a corruption of *necromancy* (from Greek *necros*, "dead") to *negromancy* (from Latin *niger*, "black").

Limited to the practice of magical conjuration of the dead, necromancy does not include communication employing mediums, as in spiritualism or spiritism. Nor does it include encounters with the souls of the departed during the spirit journeys of shamans, apparitions of ghosts, or communications in dreams, with the possible exception of those in dreams resulting from incubation.

Divination is undoubtedly a universal phenomenon, to be found in all cultures. In the form of necromancy, however, it is relatively infrequent, though widespread. We possess only limited descriptions and documentation of the phenomenon and only for certain periods and regions. Necromancy presupposes belief in a form of life after death and the continued interest of the dead in the affairs of the living. As such, it may well be associated with complex funerary and postfunerary customs and with ancestor worship.

TECHNIQUES OF NECROMANCY

Necromancy is a theme often found in myths, legends, and literary works. Such texts may describe communications with the dead or state their messages, but they seldom provide information on techniques employed in a given community. Where actual descriptions exist, rather than fabulous accounts or rumors and accusations, we find inquiries connected with burial and burial preparation. Here the questioning of the corpse may concern the cause of death and the identification of a murderer. Other necromantic practices involve rites at the grave site with the use of some part of the deceased, often his or her skull, or name. The response may be in the form of an utterance produced by the diviner, either in a trance state or through ventriloquism. It may also be revealed in the form of a sign; this may involve the interpretation of an omen or the drawing of lots.

The concept of necromancy is of limited utility for at least two reasons. (1) It is linked to its history in the Western tradition and therefore difficult to employ in analyzing beliefs and practices of other cultures, with different traditions. (2) Necromancy is also only one of several types of divinatory practices, and these tend to shade into each other. For both of these reasons the term is of limited value in cross-cultural research, and it is not generally utilized in modern ethnographic studies.

NECROMANCY IN ANTIQUITY

The ancient Greeks believed that the dead had great prophetic powers and that it was possible to consult them by performing sacrifices or pouring libations at their tombs. Such offerings were also part of the funerary and postfunerary ceremonies. The visit of Odysseus to Hades to consult Tiresias, as described in book 11 of the *Odyssey,* has also been classified as an instance of necromancy. There are references in various other classical texts to formal oracles of the dead; however, these are generally to practices in remote locations or among barbarians.

Most of our information on necromancy among Nordic and Germanic peoples comes from the sagas. A number of references appear, for example, in the Eddas. Óðinn (Odin) is, among other things, god of the dead, and in one account he awakens a dead prophetess in order to consult her. In addition to conjurations, interpretation of the movement of rune-inscribed sticks appears to have been practiced. Necromancy was only one of numerous techniques of divination, and one considered to be particularly dangerous, especially when the dead were not family members. It appears to have been prohibited even prior to the conversion of these peoples to Christianity.

Necromancy appears to have been unknown, or at least unreported, among the Etruscans and in the earlier periods of Roman history. It may have been introduced with other Hellenistic and Oriental divinatory and magic practices, all of which were prohibited by Augustus. Like other forms of divination and magic, which might include the use of poisons, necromancy was perceived as a potential political tool, dangerous in a world of personal power and ambition. The emperors, however, surrounded themselves with diviners of all sorts. The concerns of medieval Christianity with necromancy and magic have their roots in this period, as well as in biblical prohibitions.

Numerous divinatory techniques are mentioned in the Bible. The account of the so-called Witch of Endor (*1 Sm.* 28) is frequently cited as an example of necromancy and of the prohibitions attached to it (cf. *Deuteronomy, Leviticus,* and *Isaiah*). Necromancy is mentioned in the Talmud among other divinatory practices. Although it is severely condemned, several examples are cited. The practice appears to have been rare, but it left its trace in rabbinic sources and medieval Jewish magical beliefs, perhaps reinforced by the beliefs of the Christians among whom the Jews lived.

Magical beliefs, many of pre-Christian origins, continued throughout the Middle Ages. It was, however, between the late Middle Ages and the beginning of the Renaissance that a great fear and persecution of witches took hold. One of the crimes of which witches were accused was necromancy, conjuring up the dead as well as (or with the help of) the Devil. Indeed, the term *necromancy* is primarily associated with this period.

NECROMANCY IN ARCHAIC CULTURES

Spanish chronicles composed shortly after the conquest of Peru record that the Inca had two special classes of diviners who consulted the dead, one group specializing in dealing with mummies of the dead and another consulting various spirit beings and their representations, which the Spaniards referred to as idols. The reports are written from the perspective of sixteenth-century Spaniards, at a time when, in their own country, the Inquisition searched out necromancers and others considered sorcerers and heretics.

In the Huon Gulf region of New Guinea, throughout the nineteenth century and prior to the arrival of missionaries, all deaths were attributed to magic. The identification of the sorcerer who had caused the death was carried out by a diviner, who conjured the spirit of the deceased into one of several types of objects. It was then questioned, and "yes" or "no" responses were obtained from the motion of the object. The most common object used was a stunned eel, whose convulsions were interpreted as "yes" responses. Other objects might be an upturned shell or a piece of bamboo held in the hand. The movements of these objects were subject to some manipulations, and the answers were often used to confirm suspicions held by popular opinion.

In Haiti, a tradition exists that is derived from both European influences of the colonial period and West African traditions. As part of postfunerary rites of Voodoo initiates, one of the two souls with which every person is endowed is removed from a temporary sojourn underwater and settled in a family shrine. During this ceremony, the soul is questioned on various matters of interest. At a later time, it may be called into a jar for purposes of consultation. Like conversations with the dead in parts of Africa, as, for instance, among the Zulu, this process appears to involve ventriloquism by the performing ritual specialist. It is also believed that sorcerers can send the spirit of one or more dead persons into the body of a victim, to cause illness and eventual death if appropriate counterrites are not performed. These involve the identification of the dead and of the sender. The diagnostic process may involve the direct questioning of the dead using the patient as a medium, or by scrying (water gazing) or other divinatory techniques. The Haitian example suggests the difficulty in drawing clear lines between divination, sorcery, diagnosis, and healing, or even among the various divinatory techniques.

[*See also* Divination.]

BIBLIOGRAPHY

Callaway, Henry. *The Religious System of the Amazulu* (1870). Africana Collectanea, vol. 35. Reprint, Cape Town, 1970.

Caquot, André, and Marcel Leibovici, eds. *La divination*. 2 vols. Paris, 1968.

Caro Baroja, Julio. *The World of Witches*. Chicago, 1964.

Godwin, William. *Lives of the Necromancers*. London, 1834.
Hogbin, Herbert Ian. *The Island of Menstruating Men: Religion in Wogeo, New Guinea*. Scranton, Pa., 1970.
Hughes, Pennethorne. *Witchcraft* (1952). Reprint, Baltimore, 1965.
Junod, Henri A. *The Life of a South African Tribe*. 2d ed., rev. & enl. 2 vols. London, 1927. The 1912 first edition has been reprinted (New Hyde Park, N.Y., 1962).
Kramer, Heinrich, and James Sprenger. *The Malleus Maleficarum* (1928). Reprint, New York, 1971.
Métraux, Alfred. *Voodoo in Haiti*. New York, 1959.
Trachtenberg, Joshua. *Jewish Magic and Superstition: A Study in Folk Religion* (1939). Reprint, New York, 1982.
Williams, Charles. *Witchcraft* (1941). Reprint, New York, 1959.

25 ORACLES

DAVID E. AUNE

The word *oracle* is derived from the Latin word *oraculum,* which referred both to a divine pronouncement or response concerning the future or the unknown as well as to the place where such pronouncements were given. (The Latin verb *orare* means "to speak" or "to request.") In English, *oracle* is also used to designate the human medium through whom such prophetic declarations or oracular sayings are given.

ORACLES AND PROPHECY
In Western civilization the connotations of the word *oracle* (variously rendered in European languages) have been largely determined by traditional perceptions of ancient Greek oracles, particularly the oracle of Apollo at Delphi. The term *prophecy,* on the other hand (from the Greek word *prophēteia,* meaning "prophecy" or "oracular response"), has been more closely associated with traditions of divine revelation through human mediums in ancient Israel and early Christianity. One major cause of this state of affairs is that in the Septuagint (the Greek translation of the Hebrew scriptures made during the third and second centuries BCE) Greek words from the *prophēt-* family were used to translate words derived from the biblical Hebrew root *nv'* ("prophet, to prophesy"). Since most oracles in the Greek world were given in response to inquiries, oracles are often regarded as verbal responses by a supernatural being, in contrast to prophecy, which is thought of as unsolicited verbal revelations given through human mediums and often directed toward instigating social change. In actuality, question-and-answer revelatory "séances" were common in ancient Israel, and it was only with the appearance in the eighth century BCE of free prophets such as Amos, Isaiah, and Hosea that unsolicited prophecy became common. Further, the preservation of the prophetic speeches of the classical Israelite prophets in the Hebrew scriptures has served to ensure the dominance of this particular image of Israelite prophets and prophecy. Therefore, modern distinctions between "oracles" and "prophecy" are largely based on the discrete conventions of classical and biblical tradition rather than upon a cross-cultural study of the subject, though the terms themselves are often used and interchanged indiscriminately in modern anthropological studies. [*See* Prophecy.]

ORACLES AND DIVINATION

Oracles are but one of several types of divination, which is the art or science of interpreting symbols understood as messages from the gods. Such symbols often require the interpretive expertise of a trained specialist and are frequently based on phenomena of an unpredictable or even trivial nature. The more common types of divination in the Greco-Roman world included the casting of lots (sortilege), the flight and behavior of birds (ornithomancy), the behavior of sacrificial animals and the condition of their vital organs (e.g., hepatoscopy, or liver divination), various omens or sounds (cledonomancy), and dreams (oneiromancy). Chinese civilization made elaborate use of divination, partly as an expression of the Confucian belief in fate. Some of the more popular methods included the use of divining sticks and blocks (the latter called *yin-yang kua*), used together or separately; body divination to predict the character and future behavior of select individuals (palmistry, physiognomy); astrology; the determination of the proper location of buildings and graves in accordance with *yin* and *yang* factors and the five elements (geomancy); coin divination; planchette divination or spirit writing; and the use of the *I ching* (Book of Changes) for divination based on the symbol *pa-kua,* that is, the eight trigrams constituting the sixty-four hexagrams that provide the basis for the book. [*See* Divination.]

Oracles (or prophecies) themselves are messages from the gods in human language concerning the future or the unknown and are usually received in response to specific inquiries, often through the agency of inspired mediums. Oracles have, in other words, a basic linguistic character not found in other forms of divination. This linguistic character is evident in the sometimes elaborately articulated inquiries made of the deities in either spoken or written form. In addition, oracles themselves exhibit a linguistic character ranging from the symbolized "yes" or "no" response, or "auspicious" or "inauspicious" response, of many lot oracles, to the elaborately crafted replies spoken and/or written by mediums while experiencing possession trance or vision trance, or shortly thereafter. This linguistic character of oracles presupposes an anthropomorphic conception of the supernatural beings concerned.

In actuality, oracles are usually so closely associated with other forms of divination that it is difficult to insist on rigid distinctions. Some commentators have vainly attempted to distinguish between oracles and divination by claiming that *oracle* is used only in connection with a specific deity, one often connected with a particular place. Other forms of divination were in fact used in all the ancient Greek oracle sanctuaries, often as an alternate form of consultation. At the oracle of Delphi, for example, where Apollo was believed to be present only nine months each year, oracular consultations were held in ancient times on only one day each year, the seventh day of the seventh month (seven was Apollo's sacred number), though they became more frequent with the passing centuries. On other auspicious days it has been supposed that the god could be consulted by means of a lot oracle, the exact nature of which is disputed. Questions were formulated to receive a yes or no answer, and oracular personnel may have used some type of lot oracle to answer such inquiries. In China divination was employed in all except Confucian temples; even in temples specializing in spirit mediumship, divinatory techniques such as divining sticks and divining blocks were regularly used.

A distinction between oracles and divination was made by the Roman orator Cicero (106–43 BCE), following Plato (c. 429–347 BCE) and the philosopher Posidonius

(c. 135–50 BCE). This distinction was between (1) "technical" or "inductive" divination (Lat., *artificiosa divinatio;* Gr., *technikē mantikē*), based on special training in the interpretation of signs, sacrifices, dreams, prodigies, and the like, and (2) "natural" or "intuitive" divination (Lat., *naturalis divinatio;* Gr., *atechnos* or *adidaktos mantikē*), based on the direct inspiration of the practitioner through trance or vision (Cicero, *De divinatio* 1.6.12; cf. Plato, *Ion* 534c). The Greek term for all forms of divination is *mantikē*, which, on account of its etymological relation to the term *mania* ("madness, inspired frenzy"), might appear a more appropriate designation for intuitive divination, yet even in the most archaic Greek texts it was not so used. A third category can be added, "interpretive" divination, in which a combination of inspired insight and technical skill is required.

TYPES OF ORACLES

Oracles are usually associated either with a sacred place where they are available in the setting of a public religious institution or with a specially endowed person who acts as a paid functionary or a free-lance practitioner.

Oracular Places. In the ancient Mediterranean world certain places were thought to enjoy a special sanctity, particularly caves, springs, elevations, and places struck by lightning (especially oak trees). The emphasis on the oracular powers inherent in particular sites is due to the ancient Greek belief that the primal goddess Gaia ("earth") was the source of oracular inspiration. While oracle shrines were rare among the Romans (the lot oracle of Fortuna Primigenia, goddess of fertility, at Praeneste was the most popular), they were very common in the Greek world. Apollo, the primary oracular divinity among the Greeks, had oracles at Delphi, Claros, and Didyma. Zeus had oracles at Dodona, Olympia, and the Oasis of Siwa in Libya (as the Egyptian god Amun); the healing god Asklepios had them at Epidaurus and Rome; and the heroes Amphiaraos and Trophonios had oracular grottoes in Lebadea and Oropus respectively. Each of these oracle shrines required supplicants to fulfill a distinctive set of traditional procedures, and each site had a natural feature connected with its oracular potencies. Springs or pools were closely associated with the oracles of Apollo at Delphi, Claros, and Didyma and in Lycia, with the healing oracle of Demeter at Patrae, with the oracle of Glykon-Asklepios at Abonuteichos, and with the oracle of Amphilochos in Cilicia. Further, the Pythia prepared for oracular consultations by drinking water from the Kassotis spring, and the priest-prophets of Apollo at Colophon and Claros did the same (Iamblichus, *De mysteriis* 3.11; Tacitus, *Annals* 2.54). Caverns or grottoes were associated with the lot oracle of Herakles Buraikos in Achaea, with the oracles of Apollo at Delphi (where the presence of a cave—a widespread ancient opinion—has been disproved by modern archaeology) and at Claros, and with the oracle of Trophonios in Lebadea. An oak tree was a central feature of the cult of Zeus and Dione at Dodona.

In the ancient Mediterranean world three distinctive techniques were used at oracular shrines to secure three kinds of oracles: the lot oracle, the incubation (or dream) oracle, and the inspired oracle.

Lot Oracles. The process of random selection that is the basis of all lot oracles is based on the supposition that the result either expresses the will of the gods or occasions insight into the course of events by providing a clue to an aspect of that interrelated chain of events that constitutes the cosmic harmony. Lot oracles used a variety of random techniques to indicate either a positive or a negative response to prepared queries, or to select one of a more elaborate set of prepared responses. Both types of response had a basic linguistic character and for that reason must be regarded as oracular. Questions to the ancient Greek oracles were typically put in such forms as "Shall I, or shall I not, do such and such?" and "Is it better and more beneficial that we do such and such?" The oracle of Zeus at Dodona was primarily a lot oracle in which questions framed by supplicants were inscribed on lead strips and rolled up. Though the exact procedure is not known, cultic personnel probably deposited the inscribed questions in a container and simultaneously drew out a question and an object from another container signifying a positive or negative answer from Zeus. The lot oracle of Herakles Buraikos used a form of divination called astragalomancy, or knucklebone divination. Knucklebones with numbers on their four flat sides were cast; the resultant numbers indicated a prepared oracle engraved on the walls of the sanctuary. One such oracular inscription, with the number of each of five knucklebones on the left and their total in the center, is the following (from G. Kaibel, *Epigrammata Graeca,* Berlin, 1878, p. 455, no. 1038; my trans.):

> 66633   24   From Pythian Apollo
> Wait and do nothing, but obey the oracles of Phoebus.
> Watch for another opportunity; for the present, leave quietly.
> Shortly all your concerns will find fulfillment.

For centuries the Chinese have used divining sticks and divining blocks as a lot oracle similar in basic structure to the system of astragalomancy just described. Temples commonly have bamboo tubes containing a number of sticks, each marked with a number corresponding to a slip of paper containing written advice (i.e., an oracle) in verse. The kneeling worshiper shakes a stick out of the container, and the priest then reads and explains the response in relation to the inquirer's specific problem. Divining blocks may be thrown to determine whether the correct stick has been shaken out. Like the astragalomancy inscriptions, the advice is suitably vague, but usually it suffices. A typical example is the following:

> *Food and clothing are present wherever there is life, and I advise you not to worry excessively; if you will only practice filial piety, brotherliness, loyalty and fidelity, then, when wealth and happiness come to you, no more evil will harm you.*
>
> (Yang, 1961, p. 262)

Such oracular responses frequently express Confucian values that are received as expressions of the will of the spirit *(shen)* whose advice is being sought.

Incubation Oracles. Incubation oracles in the ancient Mediterranean world were revelatory dreams sought in temples after completion of preliminary ritual requirements. Most incubation oracles were sought in connection with healing. The most popular healing god in antiquity was Asklepios, who had more than two hundred sanctuaries by the beginning of the Christian era. Typically, preparation for a revelatory dream or vision from Asklepios included a ritual bath and a sacrificial offering; fees were paid only if the healing was successful. After the lights in the temple or, in some cases, the incubation building *(abaton)* were extinguished, Asklepios was expected to appear in either a dream or a vision and to perform a medical procedure or surgical operation, to prescribe a particular regimen, or to make some kind of oracular pronouncement, usually of a predictive nature. Another type of incubation oracle in the ancient Greco-Roman world was the oracle of the dead *(psuchomanteion)*, a shrine that facilitated consultations with the dead through dream or vision oracles. [*See* Asklepios.]

One famous ancient oracle, that of Trophonios at Lebadea in Boeotia (central Greece), was described in some detail in the early second century CE by the traveler Pausanias (9.39.5–14). While this was not technically an incubation oracle, worshipers sought and received there a visionary experience of an oracular character. Both the protocol and the mythological features of the consultations strongly suggest that the worshiper was to visit the dead in the underworld so as to receive a revelatory experience. Isolated for several days, consultants abstained from hot baths, bathed only in the river Hercyna, made numerous sacrifices, and on the night before the consultation sacrificed a ram over a pit, following the sacrificial protocol appropriate for earth or chthonic divinities. Next, two young boys called Hermais (after Hermes Psuchopompos, conductor of souls to the afterlife) led each supplicant to the river, washed him, and anointed him with oil, as in the preparation of a corpse. Priests then had the worshiper drink from the waters of forgetfulness and memory (in accordance with Greek underworld mythology), and finally they led him to the opening of a chasm, where he had to descend to meet Trophonios. Consultants emerged badly shaken and unable to laugh—a state associated by the Greeks with death. [*See* Descent into the Underworld.]

Inspired Oracles. In the Greco-Roman world many of the local oracles of Apollo employed a cult functionary who acted as an intermediary of the god and responded to questions with oracular responses pronounced in the god's name. Such mediums experience the cross-cultural phenomenon of an altered state of consciousness. Bourguignon (1973) has suggested that the two primary patterns of altered conscious states be designated "possession trance" (possession by spirits) and "vision trance" (visions, hallucinations, and out-of-body experiences). Of the more than six hundred Delphic oracles collected by Parke and Wormell (1956), only sixteen are not presented as the direct pronouncements of Apollo himself. Similarly, the *tang-chi* ("divining youth") of the Chinese spirit medium cults of Singapore and mainland China south of Fukien (the mainland origin of immigrants to Singapore) speaks in the first person of the *shen* who possesses him. Though the evidence is ambiguous, it appears that forms of divination other than oracular pronouncements through mediums were preferred at oracles of gods other than Apollo.

The oracle of Apollo at Delphi was in many ways a unique religious institution that exerted a strong influence on other ancient Greek oracles. [*See* Delphi.] At Delphi, Apollo's intermediary was always a woman called the Pythia, a priestess but also a *promantis* ("diviner") and *prophētis* ("spokeswoman"), who occupied a permanent position. There is no evidence to suggest that she was selected for her clairvoyant powers. The attendants at Delphi also included five male *hosioi* ("holy ones") and two male priests called *prophētai* ("spokesmen"). Prior to the sixth century BCE, Apollo could be consulted at Delphi only on the seventh day of the seventh month; thereafter consultations were held more frequently, on the seventh day of each of the nine months when Apollo was believed to be present at Delphi. (According to

Delphic legend, he spent the three winter months far to the north among the Hyperboreans.)

On a day of consultation, a goat received a ritual bath in a spring; it was then sacrificed if, by trembling appropriately, it signaled the god's presence. Next, the Pythia took her seat within the *aduton* (inmost sanctuary) of the temple upon a tripod that represented the throne of Apollo. Though ancients believed that the tripod was situated over a fissure or chasm that emitted vapors causing divine inspiration, modern archaeology has disproved this notion. But the Pythia did drink water from the Kassotis spring, and later evidence reports that she chewed laurel leaves. Inquirers were assembled in an outer room and apparently spoke directly to the Pythia, who answered them. (No evidence suggests that their questions were submitted in written form.) The priest-prophets *(prophētai)* probably wrote out responses for inquirers who were represented by envoys.

The traditional view, now discredited, held that the Pythia spoke incomprehensibly and that her utterances were interpreted and reduced to written form (often in verse) by one of the priest-prophets. Ancient and modern beliefs that the Pythia was in a state of hysterical ecstasy manifested in bizarre behavior are belied both by ancient literary evidence and by her calm demeanor in ancient vase paintings. The possession trance experienced by the Pythia appears to have been, in the categories of I. M. Lewis (1971), a state of "controlled possession," in distinction to the uncontrolled possession experienced by those not yet fully adept in managing the onset of possession. [*See* Inspiration.]

A similar phenomenon is found in Chinese spirit possession cults. The intermediaries *(tang-chi* or *chi-t'ung)* are not hereditary professionals; as a rule, they are young men or women, usually under twenty, who have an aptitude for experiencing altered states of consciousness, either involuntarily or through conscious cultivation. They are almost exclusively associated with temple worship where the *shen* who possesses the *tang-chi* is one that is customarily worshiped, and where the *tang-chi* are subordinate to the owners of the temple (the promoters of its religious ceremonies), and usually to the *sai-kung* (Taoist priests). A consultation is usually planned at a temple for a particular time when the *shen* is called down by invocation. The *tang-chi* must fast beforehand and avoid sexual intercourse, and no pregnant or menstruating woman can be present at the oracular séance. The worshipers usually number about one dozen, though larger groups are possible. Outside the temple, a flag with the eight-trigram *(pa-kua)* design indicates the presence of a *tang-chi*. The *tang-chi* both begins and ends the possession trance on a ceremonial dragon throne, which probably represents the imperial dragon throne where generations of Chinese emperors sat, representing divine ancestors.

The session begins with drums, gongs, and chants. Gradually, the *tang-chi* starts to exhibit the characteristics of possession (swaying, rolling of the head, staggering, uttering strange sounds) and often at the same time commits acts of self-injury without experiencing pain (cutting the tongue, extinguishing incense sticks with the tongue, piercing the cheeks with sticks). Consultations follow in which the *tang-chi* gives advice to worshipers, cures their illnesses, and either speaks incomprehensibly with divine wisdom (requiring the interpretation of colleagues) or addresses his colleagues in a shrill, unnatural voice representing ancient Chinese. Clothing and household items are brought to be stamped with the *tang-chi*'s blood for good luck.

When no more business remains, the *tang-chi* signals that the *shen* is about to return; he then leaps into the air and is caught by assistants who lower him onto the dragon chair. Afterward, he does not remember what took place during the consultation.

Oracular Persons. Professional diviners and intermediaries often have no permanent relationship to temples or shrines. They may practice their divinatory and oracular arts in their homes, in the marketplace, or in various places of employment such as army posts or governmental offices. These specialists often practice either possession trance or vision trance, but there are other possibilities as well.

Oracle Diviners. During the late Shang dynasty in China (under the eight or nine kings from Wu Ting to Ti Hsin, c. 1200–1050 BCE), the *wu* (shamans) in the service of kings and nobles employed a type of oracle divination called pyroscapulimancy. More than 107,000 "oracle bones" have been excavated (47,000 inscriptions have now been published); about 80,000 were found during excavations from 1899 to 1928, and the remainder from 1928 to 1937 during excavations by the Academia Sinica. Besides being of great value for understanding Shang religion, they are of incalculable importance for Chinese linguistics. The bones themselves consist of bovid scapulae and turtle plastrons. At the moment of consultation heat was applied to a drilled hollow on the inside or back of the shell or bone, causing a crack shaped like the Chinese character *pu* (meaning "to divine, to foretell") to appear on the other side. Both question and answer were recorded on the bone or shell itself, which then became part of the royal archives. The inscriptions usually consist of several parts: (1) preface (cyclical day, name of diviner, and sometimes the place of divination), (2) injunction (usually put into a positive or negative mode), (3) crack number, (4) crack notation, (5) prognostication (e.g., "The king, reading the cracks, said: 'Auspicious'"), and rarely (6) verification. Though most of the oracle inscriptions focus on the nature and timing of sacrifices (a preoccupation of most oracle questions and responses at ancient Greek oracles), others include announcements made to spirits or concern arrivals and departures, hunting and fishing, wars and expeditions, crops, weather, and sickness and health. The oracle questions used in pyroscapulimancy were directed to the great ancestral spirit and the spirits of the deceased kings, who were expected to send down their advice and commands.

Oracular Possession-Trance. Two legendary figures of ancient Greece and Rome, the *sibulla* (sibyl) and the less popular *bakchis,* were paradigms of possession-trance. The number of sibyls multiplied in antiquity, and lists of them distinguished by epithets formed of place names are not uncommon (see Varro as quoted in Lactantius, *Divine Institutes* 1.6); by the end of antiquity more than forty sibyls had been distinguished. The sibyls (always female) and the *bakchides* (always male) were believed to belong to the remote past; though connected with specific regions, they were often thought of as having traveled extensively. Their oracles, which were preserved in widely circulated collections, were believed to have been uttered in hexameter without solicitation while in a state of divine inspiration or possession. The inspiring deity was invariably Apollo, with whose oracle shrines the various sibyls tended to be associated. However, the oracular utterances of the sibyls and *bakchides* were never formulated as the first-person speech of Apollo but always referred to him in the third person. The popularity of the sibyl among Jews resulted in the composition and circulation of oracles in Greek hexameter uttered in the person of Yahveh, the God of Israel.

The oracles that circulated in collections under the names of various sibyls and *bakchides* were regarded as enigmatic and in need of interpretation. One collection of sibylline oracles was kept in Rome under the supervision of the *quindecimviri sacris faciundis,* a college of fifteen priests, and was consulted only in time of national emergency, so as to obtain instructions for avoiding the peril. When this collection was accidentally destroyed by fire in 83 BCE, a new collection was made. The last consultation occurred in the fourth century CE. The fourteen books of sibylline oracles now preserved are a mixture of pagan and Jewish materials. The content of the sibylline oracles was originally dominated by matters relating to portents, prodigies, and ritual procedures, but they also came to express political and religious protest, particularly against Hellenistic Greek and then Roman hegemony in the eastern Mediterranean area. [*See also* Sibylline Oracles.]

In the Chinese tradition, female *wu* specifically called *wang-i* ("women who raise the spirits of the dead") dominate the practice of necromancy. They are frequently widows and over thirty years of age. In contrast to the *t'ung-chi,* the *wang-i* operate almost exclusively in private company and may charge fees for consultations. When consulted, a *wang-i* requires the name of the deceased and the date of death. Using incense sticks and "good luck papers," the medium invokes a particular *shen* to lead her to the kingdom of the dead. The *shen* takes possession of the medium and describes a tour of the underworld. When the correct soul is located (and it has confirmed the identification by describing, for instance, the circumstances of death), its needs are determined for later offerings and sacrifices. Often the soul (who assumes its former kinship status for the duration) speaks to family members present through the medium, in order of seniority. Rarely are more than two or three souls consulted during a séance. When the consultations are concluded, the *shen* emerges chanting from the gates of the underworld; the medium then stands up and falls back on the chair. [*See* Necromancy.]

Another type of possession trance found in Chinese tradition is *fu chi,* or spirit writing, in which the medium receives the pronouncements or responses of the possessing *shen* in writing. Consultations may be held in temples, but they occur more often in private homes. The writing stick, or planchette *(chi),* is in the shape of a Y, with the lower writing end often carved in the shape of a dragon's head. The top two handles of the stick are grasped by two bearers, one with mediumisticpowers and the other a passive participant. A tray of sand is placed before the altar of the invoked *shen,* and the writing stick begins to move, often with initially violent motions, as if of its own accord. According to de Groot (1892–1910), the *shen* often identifies himself by saying "I am Kwan so-and-so of the Great Han dynasty; I have something to announce to you, people that are now seeking for medicines" (de Groot, vol. 6, 1910, p. 1303). An interpreter with pencil and paper stands ready to interpret the incomprehensible marks in the sand. Requests may be addressed to the inspiring *shen* silently, written on paper that is then burned, or read aloud. The answers or pronouncements are discussed by those present. When the session is to be concluded, the *shen* announces his decision to return. Often automatic writing is used, not to answer specific queries but to compile sacred writings consisting of poems, myths, and histories.

Oracular Vision-Trance. This altered state of consciousness presupposes Ernst Arbman's widely accepted dualistic distinction between the "free soul," which is passive during consciousness but active during unconsciousness (i.e., during a trance), and the "body soul," which endows the body with life and consciousness. This shamanistic experience, however, is only very rarely connected with oracles or prophecy. The ancient Greeks had legends about those whose souls wandered away during trances, as for example Aristeas of Proconnesus, a devotee of Apollo (Herodotus 4.13–15), and Hermotimos of Clazomenae in western Asia Minor (Apollonius, *Mirabilia* 3; Pliny, *Natural History* 7.174). Two other Greek shamanistic figures shrouded in legend were Empedocles (c. 493–433 BCE) and his teacher Parmenides of Elea (late sixth to mid-fifth centuries BCE). A great deal of the revelatory literature from the Greco-Roman world and the ancient Near East uses the literary motif of the vision-trance to secure divine revelation in a literary genre known as the apocalypse.

The magical diviner, a common figure in the ancient Greco-Roman world, used vision-trance to secure oracular revelation for himself and his clients. Though the oracles themselves have not survived, many magical recipe books have been preserved on Egyptian papyri dating from the third through the fifth century CE. Along with love magic, revelatory magic constitutes one of the dominant concerns of the magical papyri. In addition to the many methods of divination attested in the papyri (e.g., lamp divination, saucer divination, dream divination), several types of oracular magic are also in evidence. These include procedures for obtaining such things as visions *(autopsia)*, foreknowledge *(prognōsis)*, a supernatural assistant *(paredros daimōn)*, and oracular responses through a boy medium; there are also forms of bowl divination in which the summoned being would appear in a liquid. Several of these procedures seek to invoke the presence of a supernatural being (usually one of minor status) who will answer questions posed by the diviner regarding the future or the unknown, often on behalf of paying clients. In one example of a personal vision recipe, the diviner says "I am a prophet" and then continues with "Open my ears that you may grant oracles to me concerning the things about which I expect a response. Now, now! Quick, quick! Hurry, hurry! Tell me about those matters about which I asked you" (Karl Preisendanz and Albert Henrichs, *Papyri Graecae Magicae,* Stuttgart, 1974, vol. 2, papyrus 6, lines 323–331; my trans.).

CHARACTERISTICS OF ORACLES

The linguistic character of oracles does not necessarily render their meaning unambiguous. While lot oracles in a positive or negative mode and oracles dealing with sacrifice and expiation are usually clearly expressed, those dealing with other matters often require the skill of an interpreter. Outside the temple of Apollo at Delphi, free-lance *exēgētai* ("expounders") would interpret the meaning of oracles for a fee. Similarly, interpreters are essential in the consultations of the *tang-chi* and in sessions involving automatic writing. In ancient Greek and Roman literature, the ambiguity of oracles that often find unexpected fulfillment became a common motif. Ambiguity also characterizes the prepared oracular responses in certain lot oracles, which must be phrased so as to apply to many situations. A similar ambiguity is found in the verses and commentaries accompanying each of the sixty-four hexagrams in the *I ching* (Book of Changes).

The inherent ambiguity of oracles was an important factor leading to the formation of oracle collections. Since their original fulfillment remained in doubt, they could be subject to new interpretations. In the Greco-Roman world, professional oracle collectors and interpreters *(chrēsmologoi)* sold their skills in the marketplace. They possessed oracle collections attributed to various sibyls and *bakchides* as well as to other legendary figures such as Orpheus and Musaeus. The archives of oracle temples often contained such collections, and in the Hellenistic period certain individuals traveled to the more famous oracles and made their own collections, which they published with commentary. Though the origin of the Confucian classic *I ching* is shrouded in legend, it too functions as an oracle book.

FUNCTION OF ORACLES

Oracles, like other forms of divination, are means of acquiring critical information regarding the future or the unknown that is unavailable through more conventional or rational channels. The very act of consultation requires that what may have been a vague and amorphous concern or anxiety be articulated in a specific, defined, and delimiting manner. Oracles function in a variety of ways, some of which concern the audience (i.e., the inquirer or recipient of an oracle), while others concern the mediums or specialists who obtain oracles, as well as the institutions with which these persons may be associated. In some instances divinatory techniques are consciously monopolized by the state as a means of both maintaining and legitimating political power, as for instance by the Shang dynasty of China. In other instances respected oracles beyond the control of the state are consulted in an attempt to provide religious legitimation for particular decisions or plans inherently fraught with peril or uncertainty (e.g., the utilization of Delphi by the Greek city-states). Rulers and nobles of states are necessarily concerned above all with matters of corporate interest such as war and peace, colonization, expiation and sacrifice, plagues and drought, crops and weather, coronations and succession, and ratification of laws and constitutions. Private individuals, on the other hand, tend to focus on such matters as sickness and health, travel, business ventures, marriage and childbirth, happiness and wealth, good fortune, and recovery of lost or stolen property. Seeking oracular advice on these and other vital matters helps reduce the risks inherent in human experience.

[*See also* Portents and Prodigies.]

BIBLIOGRAPHY

The only comparative study of oracles and prophecy in the ancient Mediterranean world (including Greco-Roman, Israelite, early Jewish, and early Christian oracular and prophetic traditions) is my *Prophecy in Early Christianity and the Ancient Mediterranean World* (Grand Rapids, Mich., 1983), which has a lengthy, up-to-date bibliography. Two important general cross-cultural studies of possession are Erika Bourguignon's *Religion, Altered States of Consciousness, and Social Change* (Columbus, Ohio, 1973) and I. M. Lewis's *Ecstatic Religion: An Anthropological Study of Spirit Possession and Shamanism* (Harmondsworth, 1971). Still valuable is the older study by Traugott K. Oesterreich, *Possession, Demoniacal and Other* (New York, 1930).

The best book on the oracle of Delphi is Joseph Fontenrose's *The Delphic Oracle: Its Responses and Operations* (Berkeley, 1978), with a catalog of all known Delphic oracles in English translation classified according to grades of authenticity; it includes an extensive bibliography. The earlier standard work on Delphi, with a complete catalog of oracles in Greek, is H. W. Parke and D. E. W. Wormell's *The Delphic Oracle*, 2 vols. (Oxford, 1956); the more recent book by Fontenrose, however, is far superior.

An important introduction to some non-Apollonian oracles, including a collection in English translation of written oracle questions excavated at Dodona, is H. W. Parke's *The Oracles of Zeus: Dodona, Olympia, Ammon* (Oxford, 1967). Two very readable introductions to Greek oracles are H. W. Parke's *Greek Oracles* (London, 1967) and Robert Flacelière's *Greek Oracles* (London, 1965). An important discussion of the function of orcles in ancient Greek city-states is Martin P. Nilsson's *Cults, Myths, Oracles, and Politics in Ancient Greece* (1951; New York, 1972). An older but still useful comparative study of ancient Mediterranean views of revelation is Edwyn Robert Bevan's *Sibyls and Seers: A Survey of Some Ancient Theories of Revelation and Inspiration* (London, 1928). Though now out of date, the most detailed study of Greek divination, useful for putting oracular divination in proper context, is W. R. Halliday's *Greek Divination: A Study of Its Methods and Principles* (1913; reprint, Chicago, 1967). An English translation of the Greek Magical Papyri, including many procedures for securing oracles, is now available in *The Greek Magical Papyri in Translation,* edited by Hans Dieter Betz (Chicago, 1985).

The most important recent study of the sibylline oracles is John J. Collins's *The Sibylline Oracles of Egyptian Judaism* (Missoula, Mont., 1974). A recent translation of the extant fourteen books of sibylline oracles is available in *The Old Testament Pseudepigrapha,* vol. 1, *Apocalyptic Literature and Testaments,* edited by James H. Charlesworth (Garden City, N.Y., 1983), pp. 317–472.

An older work that is still valuable for its consideration of Israelite and Arab traditions with a wide spectrum of prophetic phenomena including "divinatory prophecy," dreams and visions, ecstasy, and magic is Alfred Guillaume's *Prophecy and Divination among the Hebrews and Other Semites* (London, 1938). A book that includes many texts in English translation but that lacks critical discussion is Violet MacDermot's *The Cult of the Seer in the Ancient Middle East* (London, 1971). More recent is a book that considers Old Testament prophecy in the context of comparative studies of possession phenomena: Robert R. Wilson's *Prophecy and Society in Ancient Israel* (Philadelphia, 1980), which includes an extensive bibliography.

The most important work in English on Chinese religion continues to be the magisterial work by J. J. M. de Groot, *The Religious System of China,* 6 vols. (1892–1910; Taipei, 1967); particularly relevant is part 5 in volume 6, "The Priesthood of Animism," pp. 1187ff. A more up-to-date study is Ch'ing-k'un Yang's *Religion in Chinese Society: A Study of Contemporary Social Functions of Religion and Some of Their Historical Factors* (Berkeley, 1961), where aspects of both ancient and modern divination and oracles are considered. Also useful is David Crockett Graham's *Folk Religion in Southwest China* (Washington, D.C., 1961). An excellent anthropological study of modern trance-possession cults among the Chinese of Singapore is Alan J. A. Elliot's *Chinese Spirit-Medium Cults in Singapore* (London, 1955). The most important study of the oracle bones and shells of the Shang period, with an extensive bibliography, is David N. Keightley's *Sources of Shang History: The Oracle-Bone Inscriptions of Bronze Age China* (Berkeley, 1978). Also useful is a book written by one of the excavators, Tung Tso-pin's *Hsü chia ku nien piao* (Tokyo, 1967).

26 SPELLS

Beatriz Barba de Piña Chán
Translated from Spanish by Erica Meltzer

Spells belong to the general context of magical thought. They consist of words or sets of words that issue a command that is efficacious merely because it has been pronounced. Spells represent one of the many techniques used to control nature and the evils arising in a given society. They are found universally and are probably as old as language itself, having been in existence since the Lower Paleolithic.

The basis of the power of spells is the primitive idea that nothing exists without a name and that to know the names of things is to possess them. [*See* Names and Naming.] Thus, to give orders with the appropriate words is to ensure success, made even more certain when the speaker is a witch, shaman, holy man, or anyone else whose profession it is to deal with mystery.

Stated in other terms, spells are all-powerful spoken formulas, words, or phrases of power. They are definitive: once uttered, the desired chain of events is set irrevocably in motion. Each word, once enunciated, has a magical value and weight that none can control.

The order given in the spell, addressed to deities, spirits, or the forces of nature, can be creative, destructive, protective, or medicinal; it can demand triumph over an enemy, or the attainment of impossible powers or things. It can be used to break spells, cast spells, or obtain love.

CONDITIONS OF SPELLS

According to magical thought, only prayers can be spoken by anyone at any time and remain effective. [*See* Prayer.] Spells, by contrast, and other such magical activities, have many prerequisites. Spells in particular must be pronounced by a person who is initiated into the mysteries or endowed with supernatural powers, and who is sexually, dietetically, and socially pure. The person casting the spell must know with precision the words he will pronounce, the time when they must be uttered, the cardinal point toward which he will face, what he will stand or sit on, how his person must be arranged, the clothing, colors, ornaments, and objects he will use, the number of times he must repeat the words, and the psychological attitude and manners he must assume. Everything must be precise. As a part of religious and magical activities, spells sometimes require musical backgrounds, specially prepared settings, appropriate instruments, prudent timing, and attention to taboos that might be violated, such as sex, the lack of initiation, or impurity.

Spells can serve either collective ends, such as victory in battle, the banishing of plagues and epidemics, or the bringing of rain, or they can serve personal ends, such as the attainment of love, health, power, wealth, virility, fertility, finding out who has stolen something, or causing harm to an enemy. The former collective spells require a complex ceremony and initiates. The latter, usually carried out on a popular level, generally need only to be repeated continually or for a magical number of times.

As a general rule, spells accompany the preparation of potions, amulets, weapons, magical paraphernalia, scepters, and objects of sorcery. They are recited over sick people, addressed to the natural elements one wants to control, or murmured softly and continuously. Rarely are they repeated by large groups of people, although this does happen occasionally.

POWERFUL SOUNDS AND WORDS

Many scholars have concentrated on the study of the word as a symbol. [*See* Language.] These scholars include linguists, sociologists, anthropologists, philosophers, educators, psychiatrists, and occultists. Many of these researchers are inclined to give an onomatopoeic value to sounds: for example, /m/ and /n/ are related to the mother because of the sound made during breastfeeding; /g/ is related to water, because that is how it sounds when swallowed; and /a/ is an imperative for calling attention. Since ancient times, philosophers such as Plato (in his dialogue *Cratylus*) have remarked on how words somehow take on the form of the things they name.

Nevertheless, a serious analysis gives us very few sounds or words that have the same value in all cultures. Greater universality can be found, perhaps, in the language of gestures: assenting by moving the head up and down, negating by moving it from right to left, beckoning with the arm and hand, pointing things out with the index finger or the eyes and brows, or threatening by raising a fist. [*See* Postures and Gestures.]

In Qabbalah, the interest in a knowledge of sounds, written letters, and words was intensified. Each sign was given a magical value that had a religious meaning and a numerical relationship. For example, the Hebrew letter *alef* became the symbol of mankind and the abstract principle of material objects; it is the trinity in unity and its numerical value is 1 (Scholem, 1974). Freemasonry also produced speculations in this field, but it assigned many meanings to the same letter. The letter *A* became an emblem of the first of the three faculties of divinity—creative power— in addition to being the abbreviation for the word *architect* (Powells, 1982). This association of the word with creation is found among many peoples of the world.

The history of religions has given us several words or short phrases that have been believed to be particularly powerful. The gnostics of North Africa, for instance, made an abundant use of talismans and incantations. Two words in particular have survived to our day: *abraxas* and *abracadabra*. The word *abraxas* represents the supreme deity and his supreme power. Numerically ($a = 1, b = 2, r = 100, a = 1, x = 60, a = 1, s = 200$) it adds up to 365, or the number of days in the solar year, the cycle of divine action. The word was carved into stone as a talisman and pronounced as a protective device. The word *abracadabra*, derived from the Aramaic phrase "Avreiq 'ad havra' " ("Hurl thunderbolts to [unto? at?] darkness"), was used to invoke the aid of the supreme spirits. Inscribed as an inverted triangle, with one less letter on each successive line, it was considered a powerful talisman.

The Jews, a people rich in esoteric and magical lore, were the inventors of Qabbalah, which includes one of the most important techniques for the numerological analysis of words and letters, intended to reveal their esoteric meaning. Four words in particular deserve mention. *Adonai,* which means "supreme lord," was spoken as an infallible invocation of aid. *Haleluyah,* translated as "hymn to the lord," also served as an invocation. *Amen* was a term that gave a full and definitive meaning to whatever was expressed. It was understood as "So be it," but with the magical sense that things could not be otherwise. Some think it was derived from invocations to Amun. *Golem* referred to the basic substance from which God created man. When deprived of a soul, it could be used to create evil beings, who could be controlled only by pronouncing the true and secret name of God.

Within Islam, three phrases are believed by some to have a magical power. The phrase "Lā ilāha illā Allāh" ("There is no god but God") has been used to perform miracles (Idries Shah, 1968). The phrase "Allāh akbar" ("God is great") serves as a basis for white magic, and the words "Ism al-a'zam" are used to subjugate or subdue evil spirits.

Among Christians, the names *Christ* and *Jesus* serve to stave off evil. Roman Catholics may seek triple insurance by naming all three members of the holy family: "Jesus, Mary, and Joseph."

For Tibetan Buddhists, the phrase "Oṃ maṇi padme hūṃ" contains many occult meanings. It is believed that the first word, *oṃ,* emanates from the cosmic vibration essential to creation. [*See* Oṃ.] Some scholars maintain that it is equivalent to the *Amin* of the Muslims and the *Amen* of the Jews. It is the basic name of the creator god. The complete phrase expresses a desire to be pure and to be part of the universal spirit.

SPELLS IN THE HISTORY OF RELIGIONS
Since ancient times people have uttered and written words, phrases, and formulas that they have believed to have some magic power or irresistible influence. Spells to ward off what is evil or undesirable and to bring about what is good or desirable are known in many cultures.

Egypt. The basic esoteric activity of the ancient Egyptians was preparation for life after death. For this purpose they developed high levels of art, magic, and religion. The preparation of a scarab, carved from semiprecious stone to replace the heart of the deceased, required that the artisan recite the following spell: "I am Thoth, the inventor and founder of medicine and letters; come to me, thou who art under the earth, rise up to me, great spirit." This spell was to be uttered without fail on a set number of days after the new moon (Idries Shah, 1968). Many similar spells are known to have been used, usually with apotropaic intent. In addition, the Egyptian *Book of Going Forth by Day* records spells that were to be used for each moment after a person's death.

Mesopotamia. The earliest Mesopotamian cultures have left very few records of their magico-religious thought. Later Assyro-Babylonian translations make it seem that one of the most crucial concerns of these peoples was the evil eye, the evil that surrounds men on all sides and affects them especially in the form of the envy of enemies. One spell against the evil eye went as follows:

> Let the finger point to the evil desires,
> the word of ill omen.
> Evil is the eye, the enemy eye,
> eye of woman, eye of man,
> eye of a rival, anyone's eye.
> Eye, you have nailed yourself to the door
> and have made the doorsill tremble.
> You have penetrated the house. . . .
> Destroy that eye! Drive out that eye!
> Cast it off! Block its path!
> Break the eye like an earthen bowl!
> (Garcia Font, 1963)

The old spells used in Assyrian medicine had something of a mythical nature. Take, for instance, this spell for toothache:

After Anu made the heavens, the heavens made the earth, the earth made the rivers, the rivers made the canals, the canals made the swamps, and the swamps, in turn, made the Worm. The Worm, crying, approached Shamash, and he approached Ea, spilling tears: "What will you give me to eat and what will you give me to destroy?" "I will give you dried figs and apricots." "Of what use are they to me? Put me between your teeth and let me live in your gums, so that I can destroy the blood of the teeth and gnaw at the marrow of the gums. . . ." "Since you have spoken thus, O Worm, let Ea crush you with his powerful fist."

(Hocart, 1975)

This was repeated until the pain disappeared.

Greece. The Greeks imagined their gods as having human form and character, and they occasionally ordered them to help the needy by means of magical formulas, as in the following spell addressed to Hekate:

Come, infernal, earthly and heavenly one . . . goddess of the crossroads, bearer of light, queen of the night, enemy of the sun, friend and companion of the darkness; you who are happy with the barking of dogs and bloodshed, and who wander in the darkness, near the tombs, thirsty for blood, the terror of mortals, Gorgon, Mormon, moon of a thousand forms, accept my sacrifice. (Caro Baroja, 1964)

Medieval Europe. In Europe, the practitioners of witchcraft developed multiple spells for defense against enemies, always preceded by the name of God and the archangels. We also find terrible spells that try to control enemies. In the anonymous medieval work *Clavicula Salomonis* (Small Key of Salomo), one reads: "Man or woman! Young man or old! Whoever might be the evil person trying to harm me, either directly or indirectly, bodily or spiritually . . . MALEDICTUS ETERNAM EST, by the holy names of Adonai, Elohim, and Semaforas. Amen." After reciting this spell, a candle was extinguished as a sign of the finality of the curse.

Sudan. The Sudan covers a territory between Egypt and Ethiopia, where the magic of Egyptian antiquity and the later Muslims is mixed with primitive animistic magic. Popular sorcerers and magicians abound, openly offering their services. Frequently they exalt their own powers, which they obtain through their spells. For example, when a hunter hires one to obtain luck at hunting, the magician says: "I am a magician, all powerful in spells. What I say comes true. I say, 'Give victory to so and so.' He will have victory in all things." Afterward, the magician goes about filled with the desire that events might occur that will instill the hunter and the warrior with luck. This is accompanied by whistlelike sounds and by facing toward different cardinal points, whistling three times in each direction while holding a receptacle of water. The Sudanese believe that spells are more powerful when pronounced over running water.

The Sudanese also have spells to give power to certain leaves that are used in the preparation of medicines. The spells are recited over the leaves a specific number of times in order to bring about the desired effect.

To obtain the love of the opposite sex, the magician draws a magic circle within which he prepares a potion of herbs and feathers. In order to give the potion the necessary potency, he repeats the following spell: "I am a magician, O Pot, you contain the medicines of love, the spell of love, of passion. My heart throbs like the drum, my blood boils like water." This is repeated three times, and afterward another spell is intoned: "Bring my desire to me, my name is so-and-so, and my desire is the one whom I love." This spell requires solemnity and precision. To make it more effective, one has to open and close one's eyes four times, slowly, while saying it

Such spells are not taught to laymen, only to initiates. To be able to pronounce them one has to undertake a series of purifications, such as abstaining from food and sex for forty to sixty days (Idries Shah, 1968).

India. The sheer number of spells used in the sacred books of India is noteworthy in itself. The *Atharvaveda* in particular is full of them. Here I shall mention only one, dedicated to obtaining a man's love: "By the power and laws of Varuna, I invoke the burning force of love, in thee, for thee. The desire, the potent love-spirit which all the gods have created in the waters, this I invoke, this I employ, to secure thee for me" (Idries Shah, 1968).

China. One result of China's use of ideograms is that its magic produces mostly written talismans, although spells abound, greatly influenced by their historical past. A spell written on the blade of a sword could make it invincible: "I wield the large sword of Heaven to cut down specters in their five shapes; one stroke of this divine blade disperses a myriad of these beings" (Idries Shah, 1968).

Mesoamerica. As in most cultures, magic in pre-Conquest Mexico was highly specialized, permitted only to initiates. The spells themselves prove this, since their language was comprehensible only to occultists of the time; for example, a spell for alleviating intestinal pain—very common in tropical countries—was recorded in the seventeenth century by Jacinto de la Serna:

Ea, white serpent, yellow serpent, observe that you are damaging the coffer . . . the tendons of meat. . . . But the white eagle already goes ahead, but it is not my intention to harm or destroy you, I want only to stop the harm you cause by withdrawing . . . by stopping your powerful hands and feet. But should you rebel and disobey, I will call to my aid the pledged spirit Huactzin and also call the black chichimeco, who is also hungry and thirsty, and who rips out his intentines, to follow you. I will also call my sister, the one with the skirt of jade, who soils and disorders stones and trees, and in whose company will go the pledged leopard, who will go and make noise in the place of the precious stones and treasures: the skeletal green leopard will also accompany her.

(de la Serna, [1656] 1953)

The serpents mentioned at the beginning are the intestinal maladies (intestinal worms, pinworms, tapeworms, etc.) that harm the stomach and intestines. They are threatened with the eagle, which represents the needle used to pierce the stomach for bloodletting. They are also threatened with the spirit of medicinal plants and liquids.

Modern-Day Spells. With the development of experimental science, one would expect magic and religion to decline. In fact all three remain active, although magic has certainly yielded ground. (Magic tends to gain ground in times of crisis.) We find both ancient and modern spells disguised in the folk tales recorded by the brothers Grimm, such as the traditional "Magic wand, by the powers you possess, I command you to make me [rich, invisible, etc.]."

Mexico provides an interesting example of the survival of ancient spells. In pre-Conquest Mexico, death was believed to be a change of life, and it was thought that the god of the underworld, Mictlantecuhtli, was a disembodied, skeletal being with whom those who died natural deaths were united in burial. After the Spanish conquest, the figure was assimilated, ending up as a being who lends aid when the request is made in the appropriate fashion. Thus today, at the entrance to thousands of churches throughout Mexico, one can buy prayers and spells "To Most Holy Death." The most common of these tries to obtain the love of some indifferent person and says: "Death, beloved of my heart, do not separate me from your protection; do not leave him a quiet moment, bother him every instant, frighten him, worry him so that he will always think of me." This is repeated as often as possible, with the interjection of Catholic prayers.

The new mythology is even felt in the kitchen. For example, when there is some fear the the cooking will not turn out well, the following spell is recited: "Saint Theresa, you who found God in the stew, help my stew not to be [salty, burned, overcooked, etc.]." It must be admitted, however, that this and many other spells are usually said out of habit, not from a certainty that the words, through their intrinsic power, will bring the desired results. Nevertheless, a belief in the power of spells can still be found among marginal groups even today, as it has been found in the past.

[*See also* Incantations *and* Magic.]

BIBLIOGRAPHY

Caro Baroja, Julio. *The World of Witches.* Translated by O. N. V. Glendinning. Chicago, 1984.
Cassirer, Ernst. *Language and Myth.* Translated by Susanne K. Langer. New York, 1948.
Cirlot, J. E. *Simbolismo fonetico.* Barcelona, 1973.
Garcia Font, Juan. *El mundo de la magia.* Madrid, 1963.
Hitschler, K. *Pouvoirs secrets des mots et des symboles.* Paris, 1968.
Hocart, A. M. *Mito, ritual y costumbre.* Barcelona, 1975.
Idries Shah, Sayed. *Oriental Magic.* New ed. London, 1968.
Jung, C. G. *Symbols of Transformation,* vol. 5 of *Collected Works of Carl G. Jung.* 2d ed. Edited by Gerhard Adler and translated by R. F. Hull. Princeton, 1967.
Powells, L. *La sociedad secreta y la iluminación interior.* Buenos Aires, 1982.
Scholem, Gershom. *Kabbalah.* New York, 1974.
Serna, Jacinto de la. *Manual de Ministros de Indios para el conocimiento de sus idolatrías y extirpación de ellas* (1656). Reprint, Mexico City, 1953.
Suares, Carlo. *The Sepher Yetsira: Including the Original Astrology according to the Qabala and Its Zodiac.* Translated by Vincent Stuart. Boulder, 1976.

27 MAGICO-RELIGIOUS POWERS

Robert A. F. Thurman

The term *power* here refers to the energy or ability that enables an individual to cause a desired effect. The essence of magic is that it utilizes techniques that are mysterious to its beholders and commonplace to its masters. [*See* Magic.] Religious powers are magical in the above sense but are equally mysterious to master and beholder. Those who wield religious powers may operate as mediums for some higher divine being, who is presumed to be the master of the power and who knows how the effects are caused.

Belief in the existence of magical powers has existed in many cultures. One of the most elaborate formulations of various kinds of magico-religious powers is found in the Buddhist Abhidharma Piṭaka, the multivolumed philosophical commentary on the teachings of the Buddha. In the "inner sciences" *(adhyātmavidyā)* section of the Abhidharma Piṭaka, magical powers are classified according to a basic scheme of six "superknowledges" *(abhijña),* as follows: (1) magical power, or *ṛddhi,* which derives from the concentration of the will—it makes possible teleportation, thought transference, and the ability to see things from a great distance, (2) clairaudience, (3) telepathy, (4) memory of former lives, (5) knowledge of future lives, and (6) liberation, or cessation of mental defilements. The first five powers can be attained by both ordinary people and saints, but the sixth can be attained only by saints. All six are wisdoms *(prajñā)* derived from ectatic releases attained in the four contemplative realms of the heavens of form.

In this Abhidharma scheme are also magical creations, or *nirmāṇa,* which belong either to the desire realm (the realm of bodies that consist of matter, odor, taste, and texture) or the form heavens (the heavens where bodies consist only of matter and texture). These two categories are further subdivided into those creations formed when a magician either transforms only himself or creates another being entirely. Only a Buddha can emanate limitless creations. Magical powers can be innate among nonhuman beings; for humans, they can be generated by meditation, spells, *mantras,* medicines, or past karmic actions.

Such typologies of superknowledges and powers are connected with Buddhist categories of beings, of which there are six types: gods, titans, humans, animals, hungry ghosts, and hell-beings. In addition, there are selfless beings, saints, *bodhi-*

*sattva*s, and Buddhas. Some of the superknowledges are possessed naturally by gods. Even hell-beings are naturally telepathic and can remember previous lives. Humans can achieve superknowledges by entering into the contemplative states of the realm-form abodes of the gods, which can be done by systematic trance, the use of drugs, incantations, or by a powerful evolutionary imprint derived from an act in a former life.

A Hindu classification of magical powers is found in the *Yoga Sūtras* of Patañjali, an Indian scholar of the second century BCE. The *Yoga Sūtras* discuss those powers attainable through the withdrawal of subtle energies from their habitual investment in the gross physical body of the yogin. A modern scholar of yoga, H. Chaudhuri, has divided these powers as follows: (1) extrasensory perceptions and mental powers, (2) physical powers, (3) wisdom powers and transcendent powers, and (4) ecstatic powers. Under the first category are included the first five superknowledges of the Buddhist classification, with the addition of heightened senses, knowledge of the cosmos, knowledge of the interior aspects of the body, knowledge of all words, and comprehension of the sounds of animals. Under the second category of physical powers are included the eight great powers of the body: the ability to (1) shrink into the microworld, (2) expand into the macroworld, (3) levitate, (4) increase in weight, (5) travel through the cosmos, (6) manifest instant wish-fulfillment, (7) create objects, minds, souls, and societies and transform oneself and others, and (8) control one's own physiology and emotions and the thoughts and actions of others. In addition, the powers of the body include the powers to transmit psychic energy, heal, feed on air, generate inner bliss, raise the dead, create mass illusions, shine radiantly, and so on. Under the category of wisdom powers and transcendent powers are included knowledge of reality, the absolute, the subtle and causal realms, the essence of forms, oneness, law, bliss, and so on. Finally, the category of ecstatic powers consists of ecstasies that arise from union with the divine, which is seen as the creative energy at the root of all life in its playful restoration of the world.

Mircea Eliade (1969), seeking to develop a typology that would incorporate religious phenomena from all cultures, discerned three main types of powers: (1) shamanic or "ecstatic" powers; (2) yogic or "enstatic" powers; and (3) the powers of a *jīvanmukta,* one who has attained liberation while still living. Ecstatic practices are externally directed experiences in which the practitioner attempts to leave his physical body; enstatic practices are internally directed experiences in which the practitioner attempts to withdraw himself from the physical world. Among shamanic phenomena, he has discerned as essential four types: (1) an initiatory experience involving dismemberment and descent and ascent within a multilevel cosmos, (2) the ability to the soul to travel, (3) the mastery of fire; and (4) the ability to change shape and assume animal forms.

The Hindu and Buddhist Tantras provide the most complete explanation of magical powers and the psychophysical causality underlying their manifestations. Key to Tantric analyses of powers are notions of the subtle body and mind. Tantric theories are concerned with both the physical and the mental in their metaphysical assumptions. They tend to repudiate the relevance of body-mind dualism, yet they consider analyses of the relationship of the body and mind to be philosophically useful.

Buddhist Tantric theoreticians refer to the final nature of reality as "emptiness" *(śūnyatā);* Hindu Tantric theoreticians refer to it as the Absolute *(brahman).* They consider that the cosmos follows a coherent patterning that is beyond final characterization as matter or mind. It is pure energy that can be reached and controlled most effectively by the human nervous system while focused on precise and subtle imagery. According to the Tantras, no machine can be as sensitive and finely tuned as the mind. Every being has unconscious contact with this subtlest energy of life. In dreams, it is this energy that constructs the experiential facsimile of self and environment. In death, it is this energy that gradually withdraws from the senses and body and then constructs a "between state" *(bar do)* form that seeks a new rebirth.

The shaman or yogin who seeks to transcend the ordinary gross world of birth and death employs ecstatic and contemplative techniques to withdraw this energy from its habitual investment in the activities of the senses and the gross body. Once the identification with the gross body/mind complex is abandoned, a subtle form emerges that can identify directly with the subtle energy on the subatomic level. This level is beyond the three normal states of waking, dreaming, and sleeping/ unconsciousness. Using a building code of "seed mantras," the yogin then builds a new gross reality where the sleep/unconsciousness is fused with absolute reality and the dream consciousness is fused with a beatific, heavenly reality. In this reality, the yogin is no longer subject to the rigid "laws" of a material objective world but is in a dreamlike world that can be shaped at will. If the yogin is still egotistical, then his ability to influence the world is very limited, but if, in the process of disidentification with the gross material self, he has transcended habitual ego drives, then his will is directed only by compassion for others, and his ability to reshape the world is enormous.

In the case of the shaman, the same processes are involved, but there is no technical description of the coarse and subtle body/mind complex. The wisdom the shaman desires to attain is available in culturally developed archetypes: in the nature spirits and deities that emerge from the subtle reality to shape the world. Thus, the initiatory experiences of the shaman involve images of dissolution and dismemberment and correspond to the yogic process of withdrawal from the gross physical body. For the shaman, the subtle energy is dismembered from the gross senses and body. The shaman's ecstatic journeys to heavens and hells correspond to the yogin's experimentation with the simulated "between state" or "dream state"; it is in this state that the subtle energy, in the form of a subtle body/mind, explores the inner universe and learns to wield the seed patterns of world-construction. The shaman's mastery of fire (and of the other gross elements, especially wind, the subtlest) corresponds to the yogin's mastery of the process of reconstruction of gross reality. And the feats of soul catching, shape changing, and so on are all part of the repertoire of healing and world-mending techniques through which the fully adept shaman serves his or her community.

This general Tantric explanatory framework makes it possible to understand the ecstatic and enstatic tendencies observed by Eliade, not as exclusive techniques of contradictory disciplines, but as phases or aspects of a universal process, the development of magico-religious powers. Thus the enstatic preoccupations of the Hindu yogin or Buddhist monk *(bhikṣu)*, while clearly concerned with liberation from the world, correspond to the initiatory dissolution stage for the shaman or adept. Here the term *world* refers to the entrapment of the subtle body/mind energies in the gross body and senses. The individual must first enstatically withdraw from the world; once freedom from it has been attained, true ecstatic experiences can ensue, as the subtle body/mind journeys in the dream state or between state beyond the realm of the gross body/mind. The next stage, that of the "liberated person" *(jīvan-mukta)* or "great adept" *(mahāsiddha)*, is a stage where the subtle form is voluntarily (according to Buddhist Tantra) or playfully (according to Hindu Tantra) engaged with the world of social reality, and where the enstatic/ecstatic dichotomy has been reconciled in balance. In this stage, the yogin as *bodhisattva-siddha* or *jīvanmukta* creates manifestations, self-transformations, transmutations of others, and so on, in order to help others overcome their delusions and passions, just as the shaman works to heal his community.

The above framework for understanding magico-religious powers in general helps to organize the variety of such religious phenomena that occur in all cultures. In most cultures, such powers are routinely attributed to superhuman or subhuman species, such as gods, angels, fairies, dragons, underworld serpent-spirits, demons, and sometimes malevolent ancestors or ghosts who have somehow been stuck in a between state from which they discontentedly molest the world. Some cultures, such as the Tibetan or the Amerindian, have hundreds of species of such nonhuman beings.

According to the Tantras, magical powers can be inborn or can be obtained through drugs, spells, ascetic energy, or contemplation *(samādhi)*. Any of these methods can be combined with the propitiation of a deity or spirit who possesses such powers and who can be cajoled or coerced into sharing them. In shamanic cultures, a person might have an innate calling to be a shaman or might be inducted into shamanic practices by means of ceremonies using drugs. He also might receive shamanic powers as the gift of a deity or spirit or might develop them by generating ascetic energy through an ordeal or vision quest. Spells and contemplations are widely used, but they are not systematically employed in shamanic cultures as they are in the magical traditions of the East.

In general, it seems that humans who come to possess magical powers may do so in three main ways: as mediums, by way of possession by a deity or spirit; as instruments, by way of election or commission by a spirit or deity; and as free agents, by way of their own attainment of mastery of the subtle body/mind.

In the Buddhist Tantras, powers are first divided into extraordinary and ordinary. The extraordinary power is that of Buddhahood. The general power of Buddhahood is considered to be total freedom from all faults as well as possession of all excellences, including a virtual omniscience. With Buddhahood comes an enormous number of specific powers. A Buddha's powers are thought to be greater than those of a god (neither a Buddha nor a god possesses the power to create a universe, which is an evolutionary or karmic development in one respect and is beginningless in another). A Buddha is defined as one who is able to transform himself into anything, including inanimate objects (as many at a time as he wishes), out of his interest in helping beings. A Buddha can travel anywhere (even many places at once) at the speed of thought and can temporarily transform any other person into another form. The supreme miracle he works is the education of others, thereby providing them with the means of achieving their own freedom. A Buddha's powers are believed to be inconceivable in scope.

The Buddhist Tantras divide the ordinary powers into categories of inferior, mediocre, and superior. The inferior ones are attained through ritual and contemplative magic and are said to consist of pacifying (diseases, evil forces, or obstacles), increasing (life, harvests, wealth, or happiness), controlling (enemies, demons, or oppressors), and destroying (evil). The mediocre powers include the ability to levitate, become invisible, control zombies, and so on. They are organized into the "eight great powers," whose vehicles are (1) eye ointment, (2) foot ointment, (3) mouth-sword (enabling one to fly), (4) magic pill of invisibility and transformation, (5) alchemy of life and body, and (6) alchemy of fortune. They also include (7) the power to find underworld treasure and (8) mastery of women and female spirits. The superior powers include sky walking (the ability to visit different universes), *mantra* holding (similar to the control of the subtle patterning force discussed earlier), and universal sovereignty (enabling one to pacify the world).

The world of magical powers bears a striking resemblance to the world of scientific technology in that it is an expression of the age-old human desire to understand, control, and even to transform nature. This goal is clearly expressed in the desire to attain magical powers, in the systems of knowledge and means of practice designed to attain them, and in the mythic vistas of how they should be employed to better human life. The difference in the nonmodern systems is that the emphasis is on *inner* understanding, control, and transformation. The "outer sciences" of material technologies *(śilpa)*, medicine *(vicikitsā)*, reason and communication *(pramāṇa)*, and linguistics *(śabda)* all deal with the natural and social environments. But the supreme science for the ancients of India was the "inner science" *(adhyātmavidyā)*, the philosophies, psychologies, and interior technologies of understanding, controlling and transforming the subjective self. This was considered the most practical method of mastery of the world.

[*See also* Shamanism; Yoga; *and* Tantrism.]

BIBLIOGRAPHY

Bengali Baba, ed. and trans. *Yogasūtra of Patañjali, with the Commentary of Vyāsa.* Delhi, 1976.
Beyer, Stephan. *The Cult of Tārā: Magic and Ritual in Tibet.* Berkeley, 1973.
Bhattacharyya, Benoytosh. *Introduction to Buddhist Esotericism.* London, 1932.
Eliade, Mircea. *Yoga: Immortality and Freedom.* 2d ed. Princeton, 1969.
La Vallée Poussin, Louis de, trans. *L'Abhidharmakośa de Vasubandhu* (1923–1931). 6 vols. Brussels, 1971.

28 PORTENTS AND PRODIGIES

RAYMOND BLOCH
Translated from French by Marilyn Gaddis Rose

Portents and prodigies are signs that, if understood or interpreted correctly, can reveal personal destinies and the will of the gods. They may be observed and interpreted either by the person who witnessed them or, more usually, by a priest specializing in the science required.

Portents and prodigies are one of the sources of the art of divination (*divinatio* in Latin, *mantikē technē* in Greek). The diviner, who is capable of predicting the future, could have recourse either to the exegesis of observed signs or to prophetic inspiration, a kind of delirium *(mania)* deriving from his possession by some divinity who comes into contact with diviners, sibyls, or Pythian priestesses.

Some of the words designating portent or prodigy in the languages of classical antiquity (Greek, Latin, and also Etruscan, which remains largely obscure to us) have a clear origin and significance; others have an original meaning that eludes us.

Sēmeion in Greek and *signum* in Latin correspond closely to the word *sign*. The ancients lived in a world where signs were ever present and were to be found in the most diverse parts of the universe: heaven, earth, and underworld. Portents and prodigies often appeared in everyday observation. Even today, popular belief often attributes favorable or unfavorable meanings to apparitions, no matter how natural: to animals of certain breeds, aspects, or colors, or to certain ecclesial phenomena like a flash of lightning or a thunderclap in a peaceful sky.

OMENS

The most universal portent is the word or phrase heard by chance. Although it is not intended for the listener, it is perceived to have some bearing on one's daily life. In antiquity, as today, people imagined that utterances spoken or heard fortuitously could foretell a dark future or a bright and happy one. The listener, of course, might fail to recognize the omen for what it was, and remain deaf to its warning.

The Roman had the right to accept a portent—an *omen*—by declaring it in a loud and clear voice. This was the meaning of the expression *omen accipere* ("to accept the omen"). But the Roman could just as easily strip the omen of its value and efficacy by declaring in a loud and clear voice that he or she refused to take it into account: *omen exsecrari, abominari* ("omen execrated, abominated"). The ancients also knew how to transform the omen's value and meaning by adroit wording that modified or transformed its scope. Celebrated narratives from Latin writers illustrate the efficacy of human speech in this regard, as in Ovid's *Fasti* (3.330ff.), in which he legendary king of Rome, the pious Numa Pompilius, avoided by clever replies Jupiter's cruel demand for human lives to expiate the stain left on the soil by a bolt of lightning.

AUSPICES

As with all peoples of Indo-European origin, the most important and frequent portents for the Greeks and Romans were furnished by the flights, cries, and behavior of birds. The importance of birds as portents is clear in Aristophanes' comedy *The Birds*, which was performed at the festival of the Great Dionysia in Athens in 414 BCE. In this play, in which distant memories are muted by the satiric medium, the birds proudly bestow upon themselves leading roles as true guides, not mere advisers of human beings. Although this might simply be poetic fancy, it must reflect the memory of a very ancient reality whose origins are lost in the mists of protohistory.

In the vast domain of portents conveyed by birds, ancient Italy deserves attention. From its origins, Rome had a very important priestly college, the augurs, whose responsibility was to preserve scrupulously and apply methodically the religious regulations pertaining to signs given by birds, that is, auspices. By their presence, advice, and collaboration, the augurs could ensure the propriety of the actions of the magistrates. They possessed the compilations of sacred precepts, the *Libri augurales*, which preserved in full detail the rules of auspication and the precise record of controversies over procedure.

Numerous Greek and Latin texts describe minutely the ritual capture of the auspices, a ceremony dating from the beginnings of Rome. The fratricidal rivalry of the twins Romulus and Remus was adjudicated and the founder of the city selected through precise augural interrogation of the divine will. Romulus's *lituus*, a curved stick, which he used to take the portents, became the characteristic emblem of the augural *sacerdotia*.

The object of augury was to obtain signs testifying to the agreement of the gods with the city in any political, religious, or military actions it wanted to undertake. The juridical and pragmatic Roman mind knew how to organize the ritual needed to obtain this assent in the most efficacious way possible. A sacred formula, which served as a veritable pact between humans and gods, was read in a loud and clear voice by the priest who was to perform the augury. The formula specified both the time and place in which the signs were to be observed. The augurs thus received certified, enabling signs that had legal force and value in themselves. But the ceremony could be marked also by accidental, unforeseen phenomena that had to be taken into account.

The Romans were not, to be sure, the only people in Italy who possessed such an augural law. The longest religious inscription that classical antiquity has left us, the Eugubine tablets, attest to the existence of augural law among other Italic peoples, especially the Umbrians. According to this well-known text, a sacerdotal college called the Attiedii Brotherhood practiced a system of explication very similar to that used by the Roman augurs. In both cases, the observation and interpretation of portents was carried out with the same formalism and attention to minute detail in the ritual procedures. The question put to the gods was the same among both peoples: were they in agreement with the proposed enterprise or not?

HARUSPICES

Among the series of portents that lent themselves to observation, those furnished by a sacrificial victim consecrated on the altar of a divinity held a major importance in classical antiquity and in other civilizations. The reason is clear. By virtue of its consecration, the sacrificial animal passes from the domain of the human to that of the god. The gods express their disposition by means of the victim itself in the moments preceding, accompanying, and following the sacrifice. It was important, then, to observe everything in the victim's behavior with the greatest attention: when it was led to the altar and when it received the mortal blow, the crackling of flesh on the brazier, the colors of the flame, and the speed of the smoke's ascent into the sky.

But the clearest and most decisive indications were provided by the examination of the entrails of the sacrificial animal by experienced specialists: in Greece, the Iamides, diviners at Olympia; in Etruria and Rome, the haruspices. The haruspices, according to the ancients, enjoyed an immense reputation and seemed to practice a science that was infallible. They can be compared only with the *baru*, Babylonian priests who in the second millennium BCE had a veritable library of clay tablets at their disposal. These tablets detailed a complex doctrine based on minute observation of the organs of victims that was transmitted from one generation to the next.

For the haruspex, as for the *baru*, each fact noted at the sacrifice—i.e., form, color, presence or absence of specific parts of the viscera—unfailingly foretold the approach of specific events, favorable or foreboding, in human society. Rome received its haruspicinal science primarily from Etruria, which, long before it was conquered, had entrusted its best diviners to Rome. But did Etruria develop this discipline independently, or did it borrow elements from the Greek world or even from regions of the Near East? The latter is more likely, although the paths such influences followed are difficult to determine.

In various lands of the Near East, numerous terra-cotta models have been discovered. These models represent organs of sacrificed sheep and bear inscriptions clearly indicating the portents foretold by anomalies in the organs. Etruria is the source of the famous bronze liver found in the Po plain in 1877 near the city of Piacenza. The convex surface of the Piacenza Liver is divided into two lobes bearing the names of the sun (Usil) and the moon (Tiur). The concave surface, admirably sculptured and engraved, is divided into a large number of compartments, on which can be read forty-two inscriptions and twenty-seven names of divinities. This is a graphic illustration of the haruspex's fundamental belief: that the gods actually occupy different parts of the sacrificed animal, and their places there correspond to those they occupy in the sky.

OTHER PORTENTS

The sky, in antiquity, was the home of reigning gods and the place from which they launched comets, falling stars, lightning, and thunder (sources of joy or, more often, terror), considered in some places portents, in other places prodigies. [*See* Sky.] Lightning and thunder were major phenomena, intended to warn humans, who noted with the keenest attention the path of meteorites and deep claps of thunder, foretelling, according to Cicero, the most serious perils for the city and state.

The Etruscans developed most fully the so-called science of interpretation of major celestial portents. [*See* Etruscan Religion.] Indeed, the master of thunder and lightning, the Etruscan Tinia, was the homologue of the Hellenic Zeus, undisputed master of meteorological phenomena, and of the Roman Jupiter, who hurled thunderbolts during the day (Summanus was master during the night). The Etruscans developed a complete methodology for the interpretation of thunderbolts, including directions for expiation if the portents were unfavorable.

The Greek historian Diodorus was not exaggerating when he wrote, "Etruscan keraunoscopia [*keraunos* was the Greek word for thunder and lightning] was renowned throughout nearly the whole earth" (5.40.2). Seneca, in *Natural Questions* (2.32ff.), discourses knowingly on the differences between Roman and Etruscan approaches to portents, and on the importance the Etruscans placed on thunder portents. He wrote, "Since the Etruscans relate everything to divinity, they are persuaded not that thunderclaps foretell the future because they have been formed, but that they take form because they must foretell the future."

If portents are taken to include inanimate objects and the earth itself, they are even more numerous in the Greek, Roman, and Etruscan traditions. The importance of portents furnished by waters, especially the waters of springs, is attested by texts and archaeological data. These portents depended on the way the water spurted out from the depths of the earth, and also on the way that objects thrown into them were carried along or sank. They were attributed to nymphs reigning over these streams and to various female divinities who were objects of popular devotions in different parts of the ancient world.

Like the surface of water, the mirror was thought to present future events in its reflected images. Drawing lots by choosing among similar objects also appeared to translate either the will of the gods or the will of destiny. Thus, as a response to a question, the white bean drawn by the Greek diviner represented a positive answer, the black bean a negative answer. At Delphi, the center of divination in the ancient world, Apollo spoke through the mouth of his priestess, the Pythia, but she, too, in certain cases, had recourse to drawing lots.

In inspired divination, the priest or prophetess, after attaining the necessary precondition, entered into direct contact with the deity. The god then spoke through their voices and permitted them to prophesy the future, albeit in obscure terms that required professional exegesis.

The premonitory dream is the object of one of the most widespread human beliefs, and in antiquity it was connected with rituals of incubation. The believer, after carrying out certain rituals before induced sleep, sees in a dream what the priests interpret upon awakening.

THE WORLD OF PRODIGIES

To move from portents to the world of prodigies is not really to change domains, because the prodigy, like the portent, is a sign, a warning the gods transmit to humans. Nevertheless, there is a serious difference between the two, which lies in the importance and gravity of the sign. The prodigy, wherever it appears, is a truly exceptional phenomenon that disrupts the normal course of things for a time.

The Greeks could call the prodigy *sēmeion*, but the proper term is *teras*, whose semantic field is the same as that of the archaic term *pelōr*. Both words lack an Indo-European etymology and undoubtedly represent loan words derived perhaps from one of the Near Eastern civilizations. Despite their importance in Etruscan divination, we do not know the Etruscan word or words designating prodigies. Although the word *teras* is found in one of two Etruscan inscriptions, the exact meaning of the word in this context cannot be confirmed.

In Latin, the numerous names for the prodigy reveal the importance the notion possessed in the Roman mind. It is called *prodigium, monstrum, miraculum, ostentum,* and *portentum*. It is not easy to distinguish among the usages of these different words. *Prodigium* is the most often used; its etymology is unclear. *Monstrum* and *miraculum* are applied to something unexplainable in a living creature, human or animal. *Ostentum* and *portentum,* properly speaking, designate what the gods present to humans. None of these terms implied, however, the idea of portent, in the sense of warning about the future. We should note finally that the Roman term *miraculum* became specialized in modern languages to designate all events that ignored natural laws, particularly those associated with Christ. In the shift from paganism to Christianity, the word remained very much alive.

In Etruria, as well as in Rome and the rest of the Italic world, prodigies appeared in various forms. In Greece, as in many other countries, the prodigy could occur in any aspect of nature: earth, sea, sky, underground, in the realms of humans, animals, vegetables, and inanimate objects. The prodigy was attributed to one or another of the gods. The most diverse chthonian phenomena—subterranean rumbles, volcanic displays, earthquakes, and tidal waves—terribly feared in themselves, were also considered forewarnings of the most dire events. Sources of terror for the ancients, these phenomena required expiatory ceremonies intended to pacify the gods.

PRODIGIES IN ETRUSCAN LIFE

Etruria devoted a part of its sacred books to *ostentaria,* collections of rules for observing, explicating, and expiating prodigies. For this function, Rome called on the knowledge of the haruspices. For these priests, as for the Greeks, a prodigy could have a favorable or an evil and disastrous meaning. Presumably it was different in Rome, at least at the beginning of its history. We know the world of Etruscan prodigies rather well because Roman writings accord them considerable importance and familiarize us with the haruspices' behavior vis-à-vis the most extraordinary phenomena. The exegeses were often subtle, but usually based on a rather clear symbolism. A comet, a meteor, or a ringing that seemed to burst out of a serene sky could mark the end of a *saeculum,* one of those centuries that formed the history of Etruria. As in Greece, seismic activity on Tuscan soil foretold the most serious events. Conversely, however, certain prodigies could foretell the high destiny of humans, often divining in certain individuals the charisma necessary for kingship. Before the first two Etruscan kings of Rome, Tarquinius Priscus and Servius Tullius, acceded to the throne, they had been marked by prodigies announcing their elevated destiny. The former, upon arriving in Rome had his hat removed by an eagle, which then replaced it, uttering loud cries. Divine favor distinguished Servius Tullius during his childhood, for flames would surround his head for long periods, frightening those around him, and then flicker out.

It is clear that haruspices did not need uncommon wisdom to interpret correctly miraculous phenomena by means of transparent symbolism. But the priests were also masters of ritual as well as of the propitiatory expiations rendered necessary by any prodigy that they thought defiled the land or the city. The priests purified places that had been struck by lightning by interring all objects that it had touched. Compelled by a deep sense of cosmic order, they pitilessly eliminated abnormal creatures as products of the cruelty of nature. The appearance of monsters in the animal or human realm was a tangible sign of divine wrath, representing a disturbance of the rhythm and laws of the universe. Thus, the haruspices made monsters disappear from the face of the earth by fire or drowning, but without laying hands on them, lest they suffer contagion from the contamination.

PRODIGIES IN ROMAN LIFE

In Rome, the prodigy went through a perceptible evolution; its characteristics were modified during the course of history. In the beginning, according to Greek and Roman historians, the prodigy was not a divinatory sign, not a simple presaging of an important event. An unforeseen event that appeared in some form of nature broke the course of natural laws and indicated the wrath of the gods, a rupture of the peace the gods maintained with Rome. A sudden disruption of the *pax deum* represented a terrible threat. Such a situation most often came about through the failure of either citizens or the state to fulfill religious duties. To obtain the reestablishment of the crucial *pax deum,* high authorities had at their disposal an arsenal of expiatory measures. They addressed the keepers of whatever religious traditions were indicated—the pontiffs, the guardians of the Sibylline Books, or even the haruspices—to act without delay in restoring calm to a world momentarily threatened. This was known as *procuratio prodigiorum* ("prodigy management"), and it influenced greatly the evolution of Roman religion. [*See* Prodigia.]

In the crises that characterized Roman religious history from the time of the Second Punic War, an anxious public felt new divinatory needs. Portents and prodigies became nearly indistinguishable, except for the force of the meaning they signified. To be sure, the expiation of contamination continued, but the search for divinatory meaning now intervened. At the end of the republic and the beginning of the empire, Hellenic mystery religions and religions of the Near East increased in popularity, and Christian monotheism made gradual inroads. The person of the emperor, now the center of religious life, was surrounded by an entire series of charismatic signs, portents, or prodigies. The belief in traditional prodigies, however, gave way gradually to other more complex and increasingly widespread beliefs that came from Greece and the East. Astrology and magic became more important, and it was only in great crises that the haruspices, the most ancient priests in Italy, dared to show their strength by calling attention to the prodigies whose secrets they had jealously guarded.

[*See also* Oracles *and* Divination.]

BIBLIOGRAPHY

Works on Portents

Bouché-Leclercq, Auguste. *L'astrologie grecque.* Paris, 1899.
Catalano, Pierangelo. *Contributi allo studio del diritto augurale,* vol. 1. Turin, 1960.

Nougayrol, Jean. "Les rapports des haruspicines étrusque et assyro-babylonienne, et le foie d'argile de *Falerii veteres.*" In *Comptes rendus, Académie des Inscriptions et Belles Lettres,* pp. 509–519. Paris, 1955.

Thulin, Carl O. *Die etruskische Disciplin* (1906–1909). 3 vols. Reprint, Darmstadt, 1968.

Works on Prodigies

Aumüller, Ernst. "Das Prodigium bei Tacitus." Ph.D. diss., University of Frankfurt, 1948.

Bloch, Raymond. *Les prodiges dans l'Antiquité classique: Grèce, Etrurie et Rome.* Paris, 1963.

Brassmann-Fischer, Brigitte. *Die Prodigien in Vergils Aeneis.* Munich, 1966.

Macbain, Bruce. *Prodigy and Expiation: A Study in Religion and Politics in Republican Rome.* Brussels, 1982.

Weinstock, Stefan. "Libri Fulgurales." *Papers of the British School at Rome* 19 (1951): 122–153.

29 FETISHISM

MESQUITELA LIMA
Translated from Portuguese by Monica Varese Andrade

The term *fetishism* derives from the Portuguese *feitiço*, which literally means "that which is made in order to make." The word *feitiço* appears to have been in use already in the fourteenth century. As applied to an object such as a basket, for instance, it could mean either that the basket was "made" (manufactured) or that it was bewitched *(encantado, feiticeiro)*. When, during the fifteenth, sixteenth, and seventeenth centuries, Portuguese navigators and merchants sailing along the coasts of Africa (particularly the west coast) noticed the carved figurines made by Africans and used by them in their magico-religious cults, they accordingly described these figurines as *feitiços*, or as "having *feitiço*." The French, who were soon competing with the Portuguese along the Guinea seaboard, translated the Portuguese word as *fétiche*, and in this form the word became current in those parts of Europe where French culture was most influential. Any carved or sculpted figure made in sub-Saharan Africa came to be known as a fetish. It is interesting to note that until very recently, Portuguese ethnographers used the term *fétiche* instead of *feitiço*.

In 1760, Charles de Brosses (1709–1777) published in Paris his *Du culte des dieux fétiches: Parallèle de l'ancienne religion de l'Égypte avec la religion actuelle de Nigritie*, in which he propounded the view that all religions had derived from fetishist cults. Later, this view was taken up by Auguste Comte (1798–1857) in his *Cours de philosophie positive*, when formulating the well-known and much-debated "law of the three stages" in the development of human intelligence: the theological (temporary and preparatory); the metaphysical (transitory); and the positive (normal). According to Comte, the first stage consists of three phases. One of these is fetishism, which endows all external objects with human forms of life and culminates in the worship of the celestial bodies. Comte further taught that primitive peoples believe in an intimate and exact correspondence between man and the world; hence their belief in fetishes, which are regarded as living creatures. For Comte, such a belief is a step forward in the evolution of the human mind from its animal-like torpor. The fetishist is a step closer to positivist science than is the theologian.

Comte's theories influenced the philosophical and socioethnological thought of his time. Opinion gradually changed, however, due to more extensive information and renewed attempts to explain peoples of non-European stock. In the end, African cults were seen to involve the worship of fetishes not as material objects but as objects housing forces akin to spiritual forces. The notion of fetishism was therefore replaced by those of animism, manism, animatism, totemism, and so forth, which began to be applied to the magico-religious practices of Africans and other so-called primitive peoples.

E. B. Tylor introduced the theory of animism, which describes the magico-religious belief that everything is endowed with soul *(anima)* or power *(mana,* from the Melanesian languages). [*See* Animism and Animatism.] Tylor's interpretation of *mana* as energy, power, and so forth, was reinforced by Maurice Leenhardt in his study on the religion of the Melanesians *(Do Kamo,* Chicago 1979). Placide Tempels, writing about the Bantu-speaking peoples of Africa, preferred to speak of "life force" *(Bantu Philosophy,* Paris, 1952). It is interesting to note that these definitions are very close to that of the word *energy* used by Western scientists with differing meanings in physics, chemistry, biology, and so on. This is perhaps why Freud took animism to be the most complete religious system *(Totem and Taboo).* In his well-known essay "The Worship of Animals and Plants," John McLennan, taking theories about fetishism as his starting point, introduced his notion of totemism, asserting that it could be understood by means of a single formula: totemism = fetishism + exogamy + matrilinear descent. This was a mistaken view, however, due no doubt to McLennan's lack of data. Frazer, Spencer, Rivers, Reinah, Lang, and Durkheim have in turn all presented totemic hypotheses of their own. The death blow has been dealt to totemism by Claude Lévi-Strauss *(Totemism,* Boston, 1963). [*See* Totemism.]

Today it is possible to say that, as far as the language of anthropology is concerned, the word *fetishism* has been abolished for the description of religious practices. In ethnographic studies, however, it is not unusual to encounter the term *fetish* applied to figurines used in magico-religious cults. As Jean Pouillon has written, these are fetishes without fetishism.

Both Karl Marx and Sigmund Freud employed the notion of fetishism, giving it specific meanings of their own. For Marx, fetishism consists of attributing objective reality to nonexistent things. It is a process that grows out of alienation, one where man, when dominated by the products of his own labor, expresses his alienation by projecting ontological status onto idols (or ideas). Submitting himself in turn to these idols, he is in the end crushed by them. As an example, Marx refers to the "fetishism of goods." Freudian psychoanalysts use the terms *fetish* and *fetishism* in a similar fashion in their writings.

Marcel Mauss rejected the word *fetishism,* claiming that it was the result of a misunderstanding and was useless as a scientific concept. He argued that the notions of fetish and fetishism should be eliminated from sociological theories of African religions (particularly that of the Bantu-speaking peoples) and that they should be replaced by the concept of *nkiosi* (or *nkisi*), which is close to that of *mana.*

We have seen that the notion of fetishism derives from the term *feitiço,* which is to be found in historical sources dating back to the fifteenth century, when the Portuguese first came into contact with the west coast of Africa and spoke of the magico-religious practices of Bantu-speaking peoples, especially those of the Zaire or Kongo Basin. In fact, our present knowledge of these peoples confirms that their magico-religious practices contain much of what came to be known under the terms *fetishism, totemism* or *totemic reminiscences, animism, animatism, life force,* and even *euhemerism.* Most of these ethnic groups use a large number of natural and manufactured objects that could fall into the category of fetishes: diviners' implements (i.e., the figurines contained in the diviner's basket, most of which are carved from any one of a variety of materials); figurines sculpted in clay or in termite secretion; small dried trees or even parts of a tree, such as roots, twigs, leaves, branches, and fruit; coarsely sculpted tree trunks; small dolls clothed in net; miniature musical instruments or miniature agricultural or hunting implements; a large number of figurines carved in wood, bone, or ivory in the shape of human beings, animals or even abstract forms; horns, nails, or claws, or bits of human or animal skin; small tortoise shells; sacred rocks or minerals; crucifixes, medals, or images used in Christian cults; philters or magic substances and medicines. All these objects are believed to contain force and power and are capable of achieving that which is beyond the grasp of ordinary individuals. They are imbued with an underlying power that must be manipulated by human beings if it is to be put to use. This power is always connected with a spirit or genie embodying special qualities and can even be connected with an ancestor, located in either historical or mythic time. In certain cases, this power is the mythic ancestor himself, who for a time resides in the object.

Some of these objects possess propitiatory, repulsive, regressive, or otherwise "positive" functions, whereas others carry out the opposite "negative" functions. The latter category includes objects intended to cause harm or to protect against the evil spells of the *nganga* ("witch doctor"), who in such societies plays an important but ambiguous role. The *nganga* is a legendary figure, half man, half beast. He is often spoken of, but only rarely is anybody ever said to be a true *nganga*. Whenever a charge of witchcraft is leveled at a member of the group, such a charge is made timidly, and there is always difficulty in finding the culprit: so-and-so and so-and-so are said to have fetish or to possess a specific fetish (among certain Kasai ethnic groups, they are said to have *wanga*). Thus one may say that the *nganga* is a quasi-metaphysical, extraterrestrial, "supernatural" personage, who wields and captures the mysterious forces of the universe, possessing the power to unleash them at will, whenever he is asked to do so and most often with evil intent. In the mental makeup of the groups under consideration, the *nganga* is an ever-present being and force that acts even when not actually invoked; the figurine in which he resides need not even be handled and the user need not make his intention or desire clear. [*See* Witchcraft, *article on* African Witchcraft.]

Among the Chokwe (a Kasai people), for instance, the notion of *nganga* is paradoxical. Where evil spells are concerned, they say that the real culprit is not the *nganga* himself but the individual or group who invoked him, whether through threats, through either a nonverbalized or a conscious intention, through prayers or by any other means. This individual or group is made to bear full responsibility for invoking the *nganga* and to suffer the full weight of social sanctions.

The name *nganga* is connected with certain acoustic phenomena that are deemed inexplicable by these peoples: the sounds of the forest, the cries of certain night birds, the croaking of frogs, the hissing of snakes, and so forth, particularly if these unusual sounds occur in isolated or eerie spots. Everybody knows that the *nganga* has the power to turn himself into certain beasts and that he can, by direct or indirect means, either destabilize the social fabric or bring harmony to it. However, not everybody can gain access to the powers of the *nganga*. Only certain members of the group can do so: the medicine men, doctors, diviners, magicians, for example, who in most cases also prescribe and make the so-called fetishes. These persons are to a certain extent immune to the evil spells of the *nganga,* since in addition to undergoing specific initiation rites, they can also make use of processes that protect them against the occult powers; their immunity is not complete, however, for if they fail to follow the rules of the game, they can be harmed by their own fetishes.

In the foregoing examples, we detect two principles or attitudes in the magico-religious practices of the Bantu-speaking peoples, represented above all by those living in the Zaire-Kasai area: one belonging to the public domain and the other to the private domain of the witch doctors. Similarly, we should note two opposed functions connected with the power of the fetish: the positive and the negative, the public and the private—in a word, the good and the evil. In their attempts to define and signify the forces of this ambiguous power, these societies possess paired words such as *hamba* and *wanga* (among the Lunda Chokwe of the Kasai Basin, for instance) and *nkisi* and *ndoki* (among the Kongo and other peoples of the Zaire Basin). With regard to concrete representations of these forces, one of these principles can be and very often is turned into its opposite: this is achieved simply by placing a series of ingredients in the object, such as magic substances or philters. Thus, the Chokwe are able to transform a *hamba* figurine into *wanga* by making a small hole in the figurine and placing magical substances in it. Finally, we may say that the above two principles represent, at one and the same time, force, action, quality, and a concrete object, although one aspect may be less personalized and less ubiquitous than another.

In short, fetishism is not found in an absolute and exclusive form within the known magico-religious systems. Nevertheless, it is an extremely important component in our understanding of the behavior of the individuals and groups under consideration. Fetishism is signified by the fetish, a symbol of a "supernatural-divine" energy which can be harnessed and used. It would appear, therefore, that the sixteenth-century Portuguese were not altogether mistaken in applying the word *fetish* to the figurines used in the cults they encountered on the west coast of Africa.

[*See also* Images; Idolatry; *and the biographies of the principal scholars mentioned herein.*]

BIBLIOGRAPHY

Almada, André Alvares de. *Tratado breve dos rios de Guiné do Cabo-Verde désde o Rio Sanagá até aos baixos de Sant' Anna de todas as nações de negros que há na dita costa e dos seus costumes, armas, trajes, juramentos, e guerras, anno de 1594.* Porto (Oporto), 1841. Basic work for ethnographic knowledge of the Guinea coast (in the widest sense) at the end of the sixteenth century, written by a Coloured inhabitant of Cape Verde.

Brosses, Charles de. *Du culte des dieux fétiches: Parallèle de l'ancienne religion de l'Egypte avec la religion actuelle de Nigritie.* Paris, 1760. One of the first European works to try to widen the definition of *fetish* used by the Portuguese sailors of the African coast. Affirms that fetishism is a direct cult of the "object" or "thing," of an animal or element of the sky, of its power, of its force, and of its experience; that there is nothing symbolic in the relationship between the object and the believer; that the "fetish" is not the transformation of a spiritual or superior power. Brosses believes that fetishism is the cult of the beginnings of humanity, and so constitutes, in some way, an "infantile" or "childish" cult.

Comte, Auguste. *The Positive Philosophy of Auguste Comte* (1855). 2 vols. New York, 1970. Comte believes that positivism represents the final stage of humanity, following a theological stage and a metaphysical stage. The theological stage is characterized by fetishism.

Freud, Sigmund. "Unsuitable Substitutes for the Sexual Object: Fetishism" (1905) and "Fetishism" (1927). In *The Standard Edition of the Complete Psychological Works of Sigmund Freud,* translated by James Strachey, vol. 7, pp. 153–155, and vol. 21, pp. 149–157. London, 1953, 1961. For Freud, fetishism involves an individual attitude and is pathological in origin. For the psychopath, the fetish is a "substitute" for the penis or the clitoris.

Himmelheber, Hans. "Le système de la religion des Dan." In *Les religions africaines traditionnelles,* pp. 75–96. Paris, 1965. Attempts to define *fetish* and presents an important classification.

Lima, Mesquitela. *Fonctions sociologiques des figurines de culte hamba dans la société et dans la culture tshokwé (Angola).* Luanda, 1971. Includes a systematic study of a large number of sculpted figures of the Chokwe ethnic group of northeast Angola (Kasai Basin), related to magico-religious cults and rites. The great majority of these figurines can be categorized as fetishes.

Lopes, Fernão. *Crónica del Rei Dom Joãom I de Boa Memória e dos reis de Portugal o decimo* (1443?). Lisbon, 1973. An account, written in a masterly style, of the accession to power of John I, first king of the second Portuguese dynasty, and of his reign (1385–1433).

Marx, Karl. *Capital: A Critique of Political Economy,* vol. 1, *The Process of Capitalist Production* (1867). New York, 1977. Marx tries to demonstrate that merchandise as value-object in a capitalist society possesses not only worldly value but also religious values, which lead to illusion and alienation. He denounces the "fetishism of values," since he believes that it is in the religious form of fetishism that the sacred is most thoroughly made objective. Such values have their own life, he says, not merely in practical terms but in religious terms. He thus affirms that fetishism is inseparable from the production of goods.

Mauss, Marcel. "Notes à l'essai sur 'L'art et le mythe.'" In *Oeuvres,* vol. 2, pp. 244–246. Paris, 1974. In making a critique of Wilhelm Wundt's *Völkerpsychologie* (Leipzig, 1900– 1909), Mauss focuses on Wundt's conceptions of art and myth, giving at the same time a series of notes in which he raises the problem of fetishism, especially the religious concept of fetishism, an expression that he says should be banished from sociological terminology applied to African religions.

Philippart, L. *Le Bas-Congo.* 2d ed. Louvain, 1947. Albeit an ethnocentric work, chapter 3 deals in a reasonable way with the problem of *fétichisme* and *féticheurs* or *sorciers.*

Pouillon, Jean. "Fétiches sans fétichisme." *Nouvelle revue de psychanalyse* 2 (Autumn 1970): 135–147. Discusses fetishism in the thought of Marx, Freud, Hegel, and Mauss, agreeing with Mauss's theory that there can be *fétiches* without *fétichisme.*

Redinha, José. *Etnossociologia do nordeste de Angola.* Lisbon, 1958. Chapter 2, section 4, deals with the question of *feiticeiro, feitiço,* and *feiticismo* in northeast Angola, especially among the Chokwe ethnic group. Does not supply a precise definition of the *feiticeiro nganga.*

Zurara, Gomes Eanes de. *Crónica da tomada de Ceuta por el rei D. João I* (1450?). Lisbon, 1942. Vigorous narrative of the taking of the city of Ceuta by the Portuguese in 1415. Full of rich detail about the strategic, economic, and commercial importance of Ceuta in the context of Moorish power in the Maghreb and on the Iberian Peninsula. Recounts some customs of the city's residents.

FOUR
ALCHEMY

30

WHAT IS ALCHEMY?

Mircea Eliade

The vocable *alchemia* (or some alternate form such as *ars chemica*) appears in the West from the twelfth century onward in reference to the medieval quest for a means of transmuting base metals into gold, for a universal cure, and for the "elixir of immortality." The origin of the root *chem* is not yet satisfactorily explained. In Chinese, Indian, and Greek texts alchemy is referred to as "the Art," or by terms indicating radical and beneficial change, for example, *transmutation*. Until quite recently, historians of science have studied alchemy as a protochemistry, that is, an embryonic science. Indeed, like the early chemist, the practitioner of "the Art" made use of a laboratory and of certain specific instruments; more important, alchemists were the authors of a number of discoveries that later played roles in the development of the science of chemistry. To quote only a few examples: the isolation of mercury around 300 BCE; the discovery of *aqua vitae* (alcohol) and of the mineral acids, both before the thirteenth century; the preparation of vitriol and the alums.

But the methods, the ideology, and the goals of the early chemists did not prolong the alchemical heritage. The alchemists were not interested—or only subsidiarily—in the scientific study of nature. Where the early Greek mind applies itself to science it evinces an extraordinary sense of observation and argument. Yet the Greek alchemists show an inexplicable lack of interest in the physico-chemical phenomena of their work. To cite a single example, no one who has ever used sulfur could fail to observe "the curious phenomena which attend its fusion and the subsequent heating of the liquid. Now, while sulphur is mentioned hundreds of times [in Greek alchemical texts], there is no allusion to any of its characteristic properties except its action on metals" (Sherwood Taylor, quoted in Eliade, 1978, p. 147). As we shall see presently, the alchemist's quest was not scientific but spiritual.

ESOTERIC TRADITIONS AND THE IMPORTANCE OF SECRECY

In every culture where alchemy has flourished, it has always been intimately related to an esoteric or "mystical" tradition: in China to Taoism, in India to Yoga and Tantrism, in Hellenistic Egypt to *gnōsis,* in Islamic countries to Hermetic and esoteric mystical schools, in the Western Middle Ages and Renaissance to Hermeticism, Christian and sectarian mysticism, and Qabbalah. In brief, all alchemists have proclaimed their art to be an esoteric technique pursuing a goal similar or comparable to that of the major esoteric and "mystical" traditions.

For this reason, great emphasis is placed by the alchemist on secrecy, that is, the esoteric transmission of alchemical doctrines and techniques. The oldest Hellenistic text, *Physikē kai mystikē* (probably written around 200 BCE), relates how this book was discovered hidden in a column of an Egyptian temple. In the prologue to one of the classical Indian alchemical treatises, *Rasārnava,* the Goddess asks Śiva for the secret of becoming a *jīvanmuleta,* that is, one "liberated in life." Śiva tells her that this secret is seldom known, even among the gods. Again, the importance of secrecy is emphasized by the most famous Chinese alchemist, Ko Hung (260–340 CE), who stated that "secrecy is thrown over the efficacious recipes. . . . The substances referred to are commonplaces which nevertheless cannot be identified without knowledge of the code concerned" (*Pao-p'ru–tzu,* chap. 16). The deliberate incomprehensibility of alchemical texts for the noninitiate becomes almost a cliché in Western post-Renaissance alchemical literature. An author quoted by the fifteenth-century *Rosarium philosophorum* declares that "only he who knows how to make the Philosophers' Stone understands the words which relate to it." And the *Rosarium* warns the reader that these questions must be transmitted "mystically," just as poetry uses fables and parables. In short, we are confronted with a secret language. According to some authorities, there was even an oath not to divulge the secret in books (texts quoted in Eliade, 1978, p. 164).

The stages of the alchemical opus constitute an initiation, a series of specific experiences aimed at the radical transformation of the human condition. But the successful initiate cannot adequately express his new mode of being in a profane language. He is compelled to use a "secret language." Of course, secrecy was a general rule with almost all techniques and sciences in their early stages—from pottery, mining, and metallurgy to medicine and mathematics. The secret transmission of methods, tools, and recipes is abundantly documented in China and in India, as well as in the ancient Near East and Greece. Even so late an author as Galen warns one of his disciples that the medical knowledge that he communicates must be received as an aspirant receives the *teletē* (initiation) in the Eleusinian mysteries. As a matter of fact, being introduced into the secrets of a craft, of a technique, or of a science was tantamount to undergoing an initiation.

It is significant that the injunction to secrecy and occultation is *not* abolished by the successful accomplishment of the alchemical work. According to Ko Hung, the adepts who obtain the elixir and become "immortals" *(hsien)* continue to wander on earth, but they conceal their condition, that is, their immortality, and are recognized as such only by a few fellow alchemists. Likewise, in India there is a vast literature, both in Sanskrit and in the vernaculars, in relation to certain famous *siddhi*s, yogin-alchemists who live for centuries but who seldom disclose their identity. One encounters the same belief in central and western Europe: certain Hermetists and alchemists (such as Nicolas Flamel and his wife, Pernelle) were reputed to have lived indefinitely without being recognized by their contemporaries. In the seventeenth century a similar legend circulated about the Rosicrucians and, in the following century, on a more popular level, in relation to the mysterious Comte de Saint-Germain.

ORIGINS OF ALCHEMY

The objects of the alchemical quest—namely, health and longevity, transmutation of base metals into gold, production of the elixir of immortality—have a long prehistory in the East as well as in the West. [*See* Elixir.] Significantly, this prehistory reveals a specific mythico-religious structure. Innumerable myths, for instance, tell of a spring, a tree, a plant, or some other substance capable of bestowing longevity, rejuvenation, or even immortality. Now, in all alchemical traditions, but particularly in Chinese alchemy, specific plants and fruits play an important role in the art of prolonging life and recovering perennial youth.

But the central aim of the alchemist was the transformation of ordinary metals into gold. This "noble" metal was imbued with sacrality. According to the Egyptians, the flesh of gods and of pharaohs was made of gold. In ancient India, a text from the eighth century BCE (*Śatapatha Brāhmana* 3.8.2.27) proclaims that "gold is immortality." Interpreting alchemy as a mere technique for "turning base metals into precious ones," that is, for *imitating* gold, H. H. Dubs has suggested that the technique originated during the fourth century BCE in China, where the test for gold (which had been practiced in Mesopotamia since the fourteenth century BCE) was unknown. This hypothesis has been rejected, however, by most scholars. According to Nathan Sivin, the belief in physical immortality is documented in China by the eighth century BCE, but not until the fourth century was immortality considered attainable through the use of drugs and other techniques, and "the transformation of cinnabar into gold is not spoken of as possible, according to extant sources, before 133 B.C." (Sivin, 1968, p. 25).

MINING, METALLURGY, AND ALCHEMY

Even if the historical beginnings of alchemy are as yet obscure, parallels between certain alchemical beliefs and rituals and those of early miners and metallurgists are clear. [*See* Metals and Metallurgy.] Indeed, all these techniques reflect the idea that man can influence the temporal flux. Mineral substances, hidden in the womb of Mother Earth, shared in the sacredness attached to the goddess. Very early we are confronted with the idea that ores "grow" in the belly of the earth after the manner of embryos. Metallurgy thus takes on the character of obstetrics. The miner and metalworker intervene in the unfolding of subterranean embryology: they accelerate the rhythm of the growth of ores; they collaborate in the work of nature and assist it in giving birth more rapidly. In a word, man, with his various techniques, gradually takes the place of time: his labors replace the work of time.

With the help of fire, metalworkers transform the ores (the "embryos") into metals (the "adults"). The underlying belief is that, given enough time, the ores would have become "pure" metals in the womb of Mother Earth. Further, the "pure" metals would have become gold if they had been allowed to "grow" undisturbed for a few more thousand years. Such beliefs are well known in many traditional societies. As early as the second century BCE, Chinese alchemists declared that the "baser" minerals develop after many years into "nobler" minerals, and finally become silver or gold. Similar beliefs are shared by a number of Southeast Asian populations. For instance, the Annamites were convinced that the gold found in mines is formed slowly *in situ* over the course of centuries, and that if one had probed the earth long ago, one would have discovered bronze in the place where gold is found today.

These beliefs survived in western Europe until the industrial revolution. In the seventeenth century one Western alchemist wrote:

> *If there were no exterior obstacles to the execution of her designs, Nature would always complete what she wishes to produce. . . . That is why we have to look*

upon the birth of imperfect metals as we would on abortions and freaks which come about only because Nature has been, as it were, misdirected or because she has encountered some fettering resistance or certain obstacles which prevent her from behaving in her accustomed way. . . . Hence although she wishes to produce only one metal, she finds herself constrained to create several. Gold and only gold is the child of her desires. Gold is her legitimate son because only gold is a genuine production of her efforts. (quoted in Eliade, 1978, p. 50)

THE ALCHEMIST COMPLETES THE WORK OF NATURE

The transmutation of base metals into gold is tantamount to a miraculously rapid maturation. As Simone da Colonia put it: "This Art teaches us to make a remedy called the Elixir, which, being poured on imperfect metals, perfects them completely, and it is for this reason that it was invented" (quoted in Eliade, 1978, p. 166). The same idea is clearly expounded by Ben Jonson in his play *The Alchemist* (1610). One character says that "lead and other metals . . . would be gold if they had time," and another adds, "And that our Art doth further."

Moreover, the elixir is said to be capable of accelerating the temporal rhythm of all organisms and thus of quickening their growth. In a text erroneously attributed to Ramón Lull, one can read that "in Spring, by its great and marvelous heat, the Stone brings life to the plants: if thou dissolve the equivalent of a grain of salt in water, taking from this water enough to fill a nutshell, and then if thou water with it a vinestock, thy vinestock will bring forth ripe grapes in May" (quoted in Ganzenmüller, 1940, p. 159). Furthermore, Chinese as well as Islamic and Western alchemists exalted the elixir for its universal therapeutic virtues: it was said to cure all maladies, to restore youth to the old, and to prolong life by several centuries.

ALCHEMY AND MASTERY OF TIME

Thus it seems that the central secret of "the Art" is related to the alchemist's mastery of cosmic and human time. The early miners and metallurgists thought that, with the help of fire, they could speed up the growth of ores. The alchemists were more ambitious: they thought they could "heal" base metals and accelerate their "maturation," thereby transmuting them into nobler metals and finally into gold. But the alchemists went even further: their elixir was reputed to heal and to rejuvenate men as well, indefinitely prolonging their lives. In the alchemist's eyes, man is *creative:* he redeems nature, masters time; in sum, he perfects God's creation. The myth of alchemy is an optimistic myth; it constitutes, as it were, a "natural eschatology."

It is certainly this conception of man, as an imaginative and inexhaustibly creative being, that explains the survival of the alchemist's ideals in nineteenth-century ideology. Of course, these ideals were radically secularized in that period. Moreover, the fact that they had survived was not immediately evident at the moment when alchemy itself disappeared. Yet the triumph of experimental science did not abolish the dreams and ideals of the alchemist; on the contrary, the new ideology of the nineteenth century crystallized around the myth of infinite progress. Boosted by the development of the experimental sciences and the progress of industrialization, this ideology took up and carried forward—radical secularization notwithstanding—the millenarian dream of the alchemist. The myth of the perfection and redemption of nature has survived in camouflaged form in the Promethean program of industrialized societies, whose aim is the transformation of nature, and especially the transmutation of matter into energy. It was also in the nineteenth century that man succeeded in supplanting time. His desire to accelerate the natural tempo of organic and inorganic beings now began to be realized, as organic chemists demonstrated the possibility of accelerating and even eliminating time by preparing in laboratories and factories substances that would have taken nature thousands of years to produce. With what he recognizes as most essential in himself—his applied intelligence and his capacity for work—modern man takes upon himself the function of temporal duration; in other words, he takes on the role of time.

[*See also* Gold and Silver; Immortality; *and* Nature, *article on* Religious and Philosophical Speculations.]

BIBLIOGRAPHY

For the earliest relations between the rituals and mythologies of mining, metallurgy, and alchemy, see my book *The Forge and the Crucible: The Origins and Structures of Alchemy*, 2d ed. (Chicago, 1978); critical bibliographies are given therein. For a cultural history of mining, see T. A. Rickard's *Man and Metals: A History of Mining in Relation to the Development of Civilizations*, 2 vols. (New York, 1932). For the history of metallurgy, see R. J. Forbes's *Metallurgy in Antiquity: A Notebook for Archaeologists and Technologists* (Leiden, 1950) and Leslie Aitchison's *A History of Metals*, 2 vols. (London, 1960).

The origin and development of alchemy are presented from different perspectives by several authors: by Edmund von Lippmann in a three-volume work, *Entstehung und Ausbreitung der Alchemie* (Berlin, 1919–1954), of which volume 3 is indispensable; by John Reed in *Through Alchemy to Chemistry* (London, 1957); by Eric John Holmyard in *Alchemy* (Baltimore, 1957); and by Robert P. Multhauf in *The Origins of Chemistry* (London, 1966). On origins and development, see also three articles by Allan G. Debus: "The Significance of the History of Early Chemistry," *Cahiers d'histoire mondiale* 9 (1965): 39–58; "Alchemy and the Historian of Science," *History of Science* 6 (1967): 128–138; and "The Chemical Philosophers: Chemical Medicine from Paracelsus to van Helmont," *History of Science* 12 (1974): 235–259.

The works cited in this article on specific alchemical traditions are Wilhelm Ganzenmüller's *Die Alchemie im Mittelalter* (Paderborn, West Germany, 1938), translated into French as *L'alchimie au Moyen-Âge* (Paris, 1940), and Nathan Sivin's *Chinese Alchemy: Preliminary Studies* (Cambridge, Mass., 1968).

31 ELIXIRS

ALLISON COUDERT

Elixir, a latinized form of the Arabic word *al-iksīr*, is related to the Greek word *xērion* denoting a dry powder used for medicine and alchemical transmutation. Elixirs are potions believed to have restorative and curative powers. The term was first used by alchemists to describe the substance (also known as the philosophers' stone) that was believed to transmute base metal into gold, cure disease, and promise immortality. Although alchemists coined the word, belief in the existence of such a substance predates alchemy and appears throughout the history of mythology and religion.

CHARACTERISTICS AND SIGNIFICANCE

In religions, myths, and fairy tales, the fantasy has prevailed that there exists, somewhere, a plant, fountain, stone, intoxicating beverage, or noxious potion brewed in a witch's caldron, that rejuvenates the old, cures the sick, and confers wealth and eternal life on those wise, lucky, or cunning enough to snatch a bite, a sip, or a sniff. In the *Epic of Gilgamesh*, the mighty king of Uruk, Gilgamesh, sets out to discover the secret of eternal life and is fortunate to find the miraculous plant of immortality growing at the bottom of the sea. He plucks it, but carelessly leaves it unguarded, and it is stolen by a water snake.

Countless others have tried to find what Gilgamesh lost. The belief that magical substances exist that can confer health, wealth, and eternal life represents a powerful example of wishful thinking that goes back to the time when men first attempted to circumvent their mortality. Far from accepting death as the natural end of life, men everywhere have considered it the unnatural consequence of ignorance and malice. The belief that man was once immortal, and should be still, is enshrined in the many myths that tell the disastrous tale of how death entered the world. Stories such as the *Epic of Gilgamesh*, in which the plant of immortality is stolen by a serpent, appear throughout the world; all are variations on the myth in which a serpent or sea monster guards a sacred spring of immortality, a tree of life, a fountain of youth, golden apples, and the like. Behind these stories lies the fear that the gods themselves are jealous and wish to keep the elixir of immortality beyond the reach of mortal hands (see *Genesis* 3:22). Men have gone to incredible lengths, both physical and spiritual, to charm or circumvent the gods and reclaim their rightful immortality. Taking their cue from the periodic regeneration in heaven and on earth, they have tried to locate the source of this eternal renewal and apply it to themselves. They have found the most potent symbols of regeneration in the sun and moon, and the "waters" associated with them.

THE WATER OF LIFE

In Egyptian, Hindu, Greek, Babylonian, and Hebrew creation myths, life emerges from the waters, the primal substance containing the seeds of all things. [*See* Water.] In deluge myths, life returns to the waters (undifferentiated form), from which it can reemerge in new forms. The rite of baptism originated in the belief that water is the source of life and consequently the source of rebirth and immortality. [*See* Baptism.] As such, water becomes the supreme magical and medicinal substance. It purifies, restores youth, and ensures eternal life in this world or the next. This magical "water of life" has been given many different names—soma, haoma, ambrosia, wine—each one a sacred beverage with the power to confer knowledge, strength, and immortality on gods and men alike. [*See* Beverages.]

The moon is the ultimate symbol of regeneration, both because of its own monthly renewal and because of the control it exerts over the ebb and flow of water, the source of all life. The symbolism linking the moon with seawater, rain, plant life, female fertility, birth, death, initiation, and regeneration goes back to the Neolithic period, if not earlier. The sun is also a potent symbol of regeneration and immortality. The mythological and religious associations linking the sun and moon with life and rebirth explain why men have sought to concoct elixirs from the liquids, plants, animals, minerals, and metals associated with both heavenly bodies.

ANCIENT AND TRIBAL RELIGIONS

In ancient and tribal religions characterized by shamanism, elixirs are available to the community at large in the form of drugs. The use of hallucinogens, intoxicants, and narcotics is extremely important for inducing the ecstatic visions that are regarded as being able to bring shamans and their followers into contact with a spiritual world more perfect and real than that in which they live. [*See* Psychedelic Drugs.] These visions reinforce (and perhaps even produce) the belief that a supernatural world exists in which poverty, disease, and death have no part. It is a short step from the vision of immortality to the quest for immortality. The substances that occasioned the vision were used in healing rituals or taken as medicines. Sometimes they were deified and worshiped in their own right, as was Soma in Vedic ritual and "Father Peyote," the hallucinogen used by the Plains Indians of North America. Men believed they had the gods within their grasp and could literally eat them and thereby absorb their power and immortality. Behind this notion lies the belief that man is what he eats and can absorb animal, human, and divine power through his digestive tract. This belief, taken literally or figuratively, provided the rationale for sacrificial meals in different religions (Dionysian, Attic, Eleusinian, Christian).

The Soma ritual described in the *Ṛgveda* is the oldest recorded religious ritual involving the preparation and use of an elixir. [*See* Soma.] Opinion varies as to what *soma* actually was. From the research of R. Gordon Wasson (1969), however, it now seems likely that *soma* was originally extracted from the mushroom *Amanita mus-*

caria, the juices of which are lethal at full strength but hallucinogenic when diluted. In the case of *soma*, the vision of immortality inspired by the drink became identified with the drink itself. *Soma* was deified and the men who drank it became immortal gods:

> We have drunk the Soma and become immortal;
> We have attained the light the gods discovered.
> What can hostility now do against us?
> And what, immortal God, the spite of mortals?
> (*Ṛgveda* 8.48.3)

The use of soma disappeared by the end of the Vedic period. Some scholars attribute this development to the migration of the Indo-Aryans away from sites where the mushrooms grew. A more compelling reason, perhaps, is the emergence of priestly religion, with its emphasis on institutionalized, nonorgiastic forms of worship.

WORLD RELIGIONS

As shamanism gave way to more organized religious worship, the ritual use of elixirs in the form of mind-altering drugs was gradually restricted to the priestly caste. Eventually it was discontinued altogether or replaced by symbolic rituals (involving powerless substances) that were carefully controlled by the priestly hierarchy. Such was the case both in Indian worship during the post-Vedic period, when rhubarb juice and other liquids were substituted for soma, and in early Zoroastrianism, where the practice of drinking haoma was discouraged by no less a figure than Zarathushtra (Zoroaster). [*See* Haoma.] The individual ecstasy that characterizes shamanistic trance is incompatible with religious organizations based on hierarchy and the maintenance of orthodoxy. The ritual consumption of the sacred drink *kukeōn* in the Eleusinian mysteries provides an example of the way organized religion transformed individual ecstatic experience into a communal event mediated by an ordained priest.

Another example is the Christian sacrament of the Eucharist. The promise of immortality implicit in the concept of an elixir is at the very heart of this ritual. According to the *Gospel of John* (6:51ff.), the bread and wine are literally the body and blood of Christ, and the communicant receiving them is ensured eternal life. Ignatius of Antioch (d. around 113) described the bread as the medicine of immortality and the antidote against death. But Christian theologians were fully aware of the dangers of antinomianism and self-deification inherent in the eucharistic doctrine of the real presence (of Christ), and constantly warned against both. Paul's condemnation of the Agape, or Love Feast, celebrated by early Christians (see *1 Cor.* 10–11), reflects the fear that intoxication might lead to heterodoxy. As the church became more powerful, individuals who continued the older shamanistic practices were labeled heretics, and persecuted. Such was the fate of witches, magicians, and alchemists.

ALCHEMY

Eastern and Western alchemists alike claimed to have produced elixirs that rendered men immortal. [*See* Alchemy.] But Chinese alchemists were more single-minded in their quest for physical immortality than Indian, Greek, or Western alchemists. The Chinese never made the invidious distinction between this world and the next so characteristic of Western thought, nor did they seek eventual liberation from the cosmos like Greek and Indian alchemists. For the Chinese, matter and spirit were part of an organic continuum, and the function of elixirs was to act as a kind of permanent glue, keeping body and soul eternally united, and thus preserving "spirit" *(shen)*.

The Chinese were always interested in prolonging life, but the idea of an elixir of immortality appears to have first emerged in the fourth century BCE as a result of a literal interpretation of early Taoist philosophy. The term *tao* originally stood for the life force that makes material bodies develop and function. Over time, Taoist alchemists transformed this abstract principle into an edible elixir. The only difficulty lay in determining the material constituents of the Tao and putting them in a digestible form. The consensus was that gold and cinnabar were the two most promising ingredients because of their immutability and color, respectively. Throughout the world, men have tried to capture the perfection and indestructibility of gold and to instill it in less perfect things, including themselves. To achieve this, they ate powdered gold and drank golden brews. [*See* Gold and Silver.] (Western alchemists dubbed Moses an alchemist on the basis of *Exodus* 32:20, where it is said he forced the Israelites to drink the golden calf, ground up and mixed with water.)

The claim that cinnabar was the ideal substance for the elixir rested on its color and chemical composition. Cinnabar is red, the color of blood, and, since cinnabar is mercuric sulfide, it can be transformed into mercury (quicksilver), the most "alive" of all the metals. The problem, of course, was that cinnabar is poisonous; but immortality was a powerful vision, and alchemists, like many others, accepted suffering as the necessary price. Between 820 and 859 CE, no fewer than six emperors were poisoned by the elixirs they took in the confident expectation that they would live forever. Joseph Needham (1957) suggests that elixir poisoning was an important factor in the decline of Chinese alchemy after the ninth century.

The idea of an alchemical elixir came to the West, via Islam, in the early Middle Ages. But the Christian distinction between matter and spirit, and emphasis on the afterlife, made it more difficult for Western alchemists to accept immortality in this world. Although some alchemists did try to concoct elixirs of immortality, and in so doing contributed to medical theory and practice, the majority espoused the more limited and mercenary goal of discovering elixirs with the power to transmute base metal into gold. A select group of spiritual alchemists scorned both aims, however. They sought spiritual elixirs that would elevate the soul and enable it to reach its divine origins.

Of all those who tried to discover an elixir of immortality, no one, so far as we know, succeeded. However, the exhilarating idea that a substance exists that can free men forever from poverty, sickness, and death has provided a powerful spur to religious, philosophical, and scientific thought.

BIBLIOGRAPHY

For an excellent discussion of rebirth and regeneration and the part played in both by sun, moon, and water symbolism, see Mircea Eliade's *Patterns in Comparative Religion* (New York, 1958). On shamanism, see Eliade's *Shamanism: Archaic Techniques of Ecstasy*, rev. & enl. ed.

(New York, 1964), Weston La Barre's *The Peyote Cult*, enl. ed. (New York, 1969), and *Hallucinogens and Shamanism*, edited by Michael J. Harner (Oxford, 1973). R. Gordon Wasson identifies soma and describes its effects in *Soma: Divine Mushroom of Immortality* (New York, 1968), and Joseph Needham gives a full account of Taoist elixir addicts in *Science and Civilisation in China*, vol. 5 (Cambridge, 1983). I have discussed elixirs in Eastern and Western alchemy in *Alchemy: The Philosopher's Stone* (Boulder, 1980).

32 CHINESE ALCHEMY

Nathan Sivin

Definitions of alchemy have generally been based on the experience of a single civilization—usually but not always Europe—and tend to imply that traditions that do not follow the chosen pattern are not the real thing. The sole exception is the definition of H. J. Sheppard: "Alchemy is the art of liberating parts of the Cosmos from temporal existence and achieving perfection which for metals is gold, and, for man, longevity, then immortality, and finally, redemption." This definition might be slightly qualified. Longevity and material immortality may or may not accompany salvation in a given time and place. The evolution of other substances from base materials may be more important than that of gold. In China, for instance, cinnabar was the prototype of elixir substances. Adding the specification that the alchemical art uses chemical change to symbolize the processes by which perfection is attained, we can recognize a pattern common to Hellenistic Alexandria, China, Islam, India, and early modern Europe.

The alchemy of each of the great civilizations was distinct in the knowledge on which it drew, in the symbols it created, and in the purposes for which it was used. These peculiarities depended on public structures of meaning as well as on the private discourse of the groups that took up alchemy.

Alchemy began in close alignment with popular religion, especially among educated groups in the Yangtze region. It was considered one of several disciplines that could lead to individual spiritual perfection and immortality. Some Taoist movements took up its practice after about 500 CE; it influenced both Buddhist and Taoist symbolism and liturgy. The aims and means of alchemy, some important issues in its history, and its far from clear-cut relations with Taoism and with science are discussed below.

AIMS AND MEANS

Chinese ideals of individual perfection combined three ideas that would have been incompatible in Egypt or Persia. The desire for immortality, which long preceded formal philosophy or religion, was the first of these ideas. [*See* Imoortality.] In popular culture ideals of long life evolved into the notion that life need not end. This was not immortality of the soul in isolation, but immortality of the personality—of all that selfhood implied—within an imperishable physical body. In the most highly elaborated doctrines of immortality, this new physical self was nurtured within by a variety of disciplines including alchemy until, at the moment the "naked child" was fully formed, it would burst forth like a butterfly leaving behind an empty chrysalis, an almost weightless corpse.

The portent personal force that may linger on after someone dies was undifferentiated in the thought of the uneducated, but in the conceptions of specialists it was separated into ten "souls" (three *yang hun* and seven *yin p'o*). [*See* Soul, *article on* Chinese Concepts.] Their normal postmortem dissipation could be prevented only if the body, their common site, could be made to survive with them. That, as Lu Gwei-djen and Jsoeph Needham have suggested, is why Chinese immortality was bound to be material.

A second implication of immortality was perfection of the spirit. Because there was no dichotomy between the spiritual and the somatic, the refining of the body was not distinct from the activity of spiritual self-cultivation. Immortality was salvation from decrepitude and death. Piety, ritual, morality, and hygiene were equally essential to the prolongation of life. Regardless of whether we consider popular views or those of Taoist, Buddhist, or Confucian initiates, all these kinds of striving were also requisite for the proper orientation of the individual toward the transcendent Way, the Tao, as each tradition defined it. [*See* Tao and Te.]

A third implication of immortality, alongside spiritual and physical perfection, was assumption into a divine hierarchy. In popular thought this hierarchy was bureaucratic, a mirror of the temporal order. In fact, the bureaucratic ideal—of a symmetrical organization in which power and responsibility belonged to the post, and only temporarily to the individual who filled it—evolved more or less simultaneously in politics and religion.

There were many paths to simultaneous longevity, salvation, and celestial appointment. Meditational, devotional, and ascetic exercises carried out communally by organized religious movements or privately by individual initiates could be supplemented by physiological disciplines, sexual techniques for augmenting the vital forces, dietary regimens, or alchemy.

Why should alchemy have a part to play in this spiritual quest? To rephrase the question, what could the symbology of chemical interaction contribute? Despite the worldly implications of appointment in the divine order, this aim was reached by a mystic path, a process in which the individual attained union with the Way. This process, itself called the Way, perfectly integrated the cosmos, society, and the person.

To embody the Way one had to experience it, whether through direct illumination or through insight. This experience might begin with knowing, but deepened far beyond the limits of rational cognition. As an early alchemical poem from the *Arcane Memorandum of the Red Pine Master* (*Ch'ih-sung-tzu hsüan chi,* probably seventh century or earlier) put it,

> The Perfect Tao is a perfect emptying of heart and mind.
> Within the darkness, unknowable wonders.
> When the wise man has attained the August Source
> In time he will truly reach the clouds.
> (*Yün-chi ch'i-ch'ien* 66.14a)

The nurturant aspect of the Way—seen as activity that brings about perfection in the macrocosm or microcosm—could be observed in the life cycles of living things in nature. One could speak of life cycles not only in plants and animals but in minerals, which, as in Aristotle, matured from earth. Mineral evolution could transcend decay and death, for its end point was the immutable perfection of cinnabar or gold. The evolution of these two substances from base starting points was an obvious metaphor for the process that made mortals immortal. The elixir *(tan)*, originally cinnabar perfected by the Way of nature, came to embody in alchemical thought the potential of humans for perfection. Thus the elixir and the art of making it came to be named for cinnabar *(tan)*, even in instances when the latter was not an ingredient.

The "great work" of the alchemist reproduced the perfecting activity of nature. As a text of circa 900 puts it, "natural cyclically transformed elixir is formed when flowing mercury, embracing [lead], becomes pregnant. . . . In 4,320 years the elixir is finished. . . . It embraces the *ch'i* of sun and moon, *yin* and *yang,* for 4,320 years; thus, upon repletion of its own *ch'i,* it becomes a cyclically transformed elixir for immortals of the highest grade and for celestial beings. When in the world below lead and mercury are subjected to the alchemical process for purposes of immortality, [the artificial elixir] is finished in one year. . . . What the alchemist prepares succeeds because of its correspondence on a scale of thousandths" (*Tan lun chüeh chih hsin chien,* p. 126). In other words, the alchemist accomplishes in one year of 4,320 hours (12 Chinese hours per day for a round year of 360 days) what takes nature 4,320 years.

The alchemical process, in other words, is a kind of pilot model of cosmic evolution. The seeker not only shrinks time but reproduces the dimensions of the universe within the confines of his laboratory. He reduces the operation of the Way to spatial and temporal dimensions that he can encompass in contemplation, in the hope of becoming one with it.

The alchemist used a great variety of means—mainly quantitative and qualitative correspondences—to manipulate space and time in this way. His laboratory might be oriented to the cardinal directions, his furnace at the very center, both replete with uranic diagrams. The dimensions of the furnace, the emplacement of steps in its platform, the number and placement of doors for firing, all aligned it with respect to sky and earth.

Since the heat of the fire stood for the nurturant cosmic forces, to recreate these forces required that fire be bound by time. The intensity of fire was thus gradually increased and decreased in carefully timed cycles, using weighed amounts of fuel. The cycle of warmth and cold in the four seasons was reproduced, in the absence of thermometers, by the one precision measuring instrument readily available, the balance. Several carefully designed schedules for increasing and decreasing the weight of charcoal, and charging it into the furnace through a succession of doors, survive. They are not simple cycles, in which the end point is the same as the beginning. Successive end points slowly increase, representing the notion of a change in the alchemical ingredients at once cyclic and progressive.

This cyclic approach to modeling was also apparent in the ingredients. The most influential early processes used two ingredients or two main ingredients that were *yin* and *yang* with respect to each other. They were conjugated and separated through one cycle after another, yielding (in the eyes of the alchemist) a series of progressively more perfect products. The mercury and lead mentioned earlier are examples; another frequently encountered pair is mercury and sulfur, which combine to form vermillion (artificial cinnabar), from which, by heating at a higher temperature, mercury can be recovered. As an alchemist about a thousand years ago phrased it, "That cinnbar should emerge from mercury and again be killed by mercury; this is the mystery within the mystery" (*Pi yü chu sha han lin yü shu kuei* of Ch'en Ta-shih, in *Cheng-t'ung tao tsang,* vol. 587). Sometimes the progressive cycle-by-cycle changes were achieved by adding additional ingredients, but in the alchemist's eyes the process remained in principle dyadic.

This does not exhaust the metaphors available to the alchemist for his use in reproducing the cyclical energetics of the Way. The figure of the cosmic egg, nurturing from the yolk the gradual differentiation of the fully formed chick, is familiar in all the great alchemical traditions. The alchemical vessel is often referred to as an egg. Persistently in China the alchemical ingredients were actually sealed inside an eggshell; the earliest detailed instructions come from the ninth century CE or somewhat later, the latest from the mid-seventeenth century. A Ming imperial prince of the early fifteenth century carried this approach to its logical conclusion by incubating his cinnabar-filled eggshell under a hen.

Cosmic process could be reenacted not only in a single room but entirely within the adept's body. Meditative techniques of self-cultivation that involve visualizing the circulation of vital energies or cosmic effluvia within the body are ambiguously documented in the fourth century BCE. By the first century CE adepts were establishing relations with a hierarchy of gods within their bodies.

There is nothing intrinsically alchemical (or Taoist) about these exercises, but they provided a basis for internalizing the alchemical process. Metaphors were borrowed from the work of the furnace to express the union of opposites in full realization of the Way. As Farzeen Baldrian-Hussein puts it, "it is from his own body that the adept of internal alchemy *(nei-tan)* constructs his laboratory. In fact he finds within himself all the ingredients and apparatus of traditional alchemy: furnace, reaction vessel, mercury, cinnabar, lead, and other minerals. By a mental and physiological process he furnishes the laboratory, lights the fire of the furnace, keeps watch over the heat, brings about the marriage of the ingredients in the reaction vessel and, once the desired result has been obtained, begins the process anew on a different level" (Hussein, 1984, p. 14).

In an important scripture revealed around 300 CE, the adept controls the movement of the solar pneuma connected with cardiac functions and the lunar pneuma connected with renal functions. The first of these pneumas is called "divine elixir" and the second "liquefied gold." This interiorization of alchemy grew naturally out of the prevalent belief that the body is a microcosm, its vital processes corresponding to those of the physical world, its spirituality embodied in inner gods organized as a mirror image of the celestial and terrestrial bureaucracies.

In the pursuit of these disciplines it is not the product that matters but the process. Even in some texts of external alchemy, either nothing is said about ingesting the elixir, or immortality is said to result from witnessing the "great work." Some descriptions of the forms and colors of the elixir when the reaction vessel is opened suggest that it was contemplated in a heightened state of consciousness.

If a protracted personal experience is the means to immunity from death, the benefits of alchemy are not transferable. But alchemy had other dimensions that made the transfer of elixirs highly desirable. This art could be a source of patronage, whether to underwrite its substantial expenses or to yield profit. A pre-alchemical tradition in medicine made natural drugs of the highest grade effective means to immortality (the two lower grades of drugs replenish depleted vitalities and cure illness). By a natural extension of this line of thought, many physicians studied alchemy as a source of new medicines, and alchemists adapted established drugs to their work.

Many surviving alchemical writings aim at the straightforward preparation of economically or therapeutically desirable substances. Such sources tend naturally to discuss the preparation of alchemical gold as well as elixirs related to cinnabar. Gold is a matter of relatively minor concern in the central tradition of alchemy, with its emphasis on individual self-cultivation.

HISTORY

This section will explore three issues pertinent to the relations of religion and alchemy: the beginnings of alchemy in China, the character of change in alchemy, and the historical relations of external and internal alchemy.

Whether alchemy originated earlier in Hellenistic Egypt or China remains uncertain. The earliest testimony from either society has not yet been rigorously dated to within a century. Differing views about Chinese origins vary largely with willingness to accept legends as historical statements.

Cinnabar and similar blood-colored compounds have been connected with ideas of death and immortality since the Neolithic period; that is how most scholars interpret the archaic custom of sprinkling red powders on corpses to be buried. The splendidly preserved corpse of the Lady of Tai (or Dai; died shortly after 168 BCE, excavated 1972) contained high concentrations of mercury and lead. These elements were distributed in a way consistent with ingestion before death. Traces in the intestines include native cinnabar, frequently prescribed by physicians as an immortality drug, rather than an artificial elixir. An edict dated 144 BCE against falsifying gold is sometimes said to show the prevalence of alchemy, but it presents no evidence that anything more was involved than artisans' use of alloys. In 133 BCE the Martial Emperor was told by an occultist that eating from plates of artificial gold would lengthen his life so that he could seek out certain immortals and, with their help, become an immortal himself by performing certain rituals. This request for patronage links gold indirectly with immortality and suggests that the direct alchemical linkage had not yet been made. As patronage increasingly became available in the decades that followed, the lore of immortals with whom patrons could be put in touch proliferated. "Medicines of immortality" were frequently mentioned, but these were not said to be artificial. Critical scholars find clear proof of the emergence of alchemy only in the earliest treatises on the subject: *Chou i ts'an t'ung ch'i* (Concordance of the Three; partly c. 140 CE, partly ninth century), and the first chapter of the *Huang ti chiu ting shen tan ching* (Canon of the Nine-Vessel Divine Elixir of the Yellow Lord), almost certainly written in the second half of the second century CE.

The chronological priority of East or West is not in fact a pressing issue unless the undertaking in question is substantially the same in both parts of the world. That is not the case. Joseph Needham pinpoints one significant difference when he defines Chinese alchemy as a combination of macrobiotics (the quest for material immortality through drugs) and aurifaction (the attempt to make true gold by artificial means, as distinguished from "aurifiction," in which gold is consciously faked). The centrality of cinnabar is ignored in these definitions. Needham notes that macrobiotics was conspicuously missing from the early occidental art, which he therefore does not consider "true" alchemy.

Other scholars evaluate not only the techniques of the alchemists but also their beliefs. The types of spiritual experience outlined above and the relation of alchemical success to appointment in a divine hierarchy are unique to China. They suggest that the alchemical quest in East Asia, as in Alexandria, cannot be adequately defined by technical goals. Both civilizations used chemical methods and metaphors for redemptive ends. The goals differed because Chinese and Hellenistic Egyptian structures of meaning and values differed. It is fitting to speak of the corresponding arts of both as "true" alchemy and to conclude that—on present knowledge—they emerged at roughly the same time.

The alchemists, unlike modern historians, did not believe that their art evolved or changed. As in any other Chinese religious or technical tradition, its practitioners assumed that its every possibility had been laid out in the archaic, divine revelations that founded it. In alchemy there were several of these seminal works, including the two already mentioned. These scriptures were to be passed down intact to those worthy to receive them, supplemented by oral explanations. Much explanation was needed, for these founding works (especially the *Concordance of the Three*) were packed with metaphor and symbol, their density multilayered. The inexhaustible meanings of the Sages, in a lesser age, could only be grasped approximately. The issue was not progress in knowledge but regaining ancient wisdom.

Nevertheless alchemical writings over the centuries exhibit an increasingly comprehensive knowledge of chemical processes. They were also increasingly able to accommodate new impulses from popular religion. Some adepts were aware of this new content in alchemy. They attributed it to additional (but in principle timeless) revelations. These are often said to be given by immortals in disguise, "remarkable men" met in strange circumstances or seen in dreams or visions. The static ideal did not rule out change.

Current understanding suggests that external and internal alchemy began together. There is no reason to believe that the practice of both at the same time was a late or gradual development. The *Concordance of the Three* brings an elaborate symbolism to bear on processes that can be understood equally well as external or internal to the body. The book refers not only to the internal alchemy of imaginative visualization but also to sexual disciplines that give the marriage of opposites its ultimately literal expression. Later alchemists disagree about whether sexual practices further or hinder immortality, but a number of important adepts follow the *Concordance of the Three* in seeing external, internal, and sexual alchemy as aspects of a single process. Historians of chemistry thus find it difficult to achieve consensus on whether certain texts are concerned with operations on mineral ingredients.

External alchemy did not retain the vitality of its internal analogue. Writings that reflect new knowledge of chemical processes rarely appear after about 1000. Later writers often said that only outsiders believe that alchemy is to be done—or was ever done—in the laboratory. It thus appears that practice, or at least innovation, in external alchemy had largely ceased. This has been explained by a revival of Confucian ideals that discouraged educated people from doing artisanal work. Another reason may be the ascendancy of meditation and visualization over practical operations in the schools of Taoism that attracted elite enthusiasts in the eleventh and twelfth centuries. Occult and manual practices, as noted above, were not mutually exclusive earlier. Another likely cause is general awareness that a number of emperors and high officials had died as a result of taking alchemical elixirs. To the adept the appearance of death was a sign that the perfected self had hatched out of the old body and taken office among the immortals. To secular humanists intolerant of popular beliefs, this seemed a foolish rationale for suicide.

ALCHEMY, SCIENCE, AND RELIGION

Alchemy has been studied mainly by historians of chemistry, who have shown that the Chinese art exploited the properties of many chemical substances and even incorporated considerable knowledge of quantitative relations. Scholars of medical history have demonstrated close connections between alchemy and medicine, in the substances and processes on which both drew and in the use of artificial, mainly inorganic "elixirs" by physicians to treat disease and lengthen life. Historians have tended to see alchemy as a fledgling science, a precursor of modern inorganic chemistry and iatrochemistry. Lu and Needham speak of internal alchemy as "proto-biochemistry."

This view overlooks the fact that the goals of alchemy were not cognitive. They were consistently focused on immortality and largely concerned with reenacting cosmic process for purposes of contemplation. It is impossible to say with certainty that alchemists discovered any new chemical interaction or process. Since alchemists were literate and craftsmen were not, it is only to be expected that innovations by the latter would be first recorded by the former (who were almost the only members of the elite greatly interested in the chemical arts). Claims that alchemists played major roles in developing gunpowder and distillation apparatus are not supported by independent evidence about the state of contemporary industrial processes, which remained poorly explored for the first millennium CE. Similarly, too little of the medical literature has been studied to permit the generalization that alchemists gave more to medicine than they took from it.

The idea that alchemy is Taoist by nature, or was invented by Taoists, has not survived advances since about 1970 in historical studies of Taoism. In the Celestial Master sect and other early Taoist movements drugs (including artificial preparations) were forbidden; only religious exercises could procure health and divine status. Upper-class initiates gradually began to use fashionable immortality drugs in the north. As refugees after the fall of Lo-yang in 311 they encountered elixirs in the Yangtze region, where alchemy had long been established among popular immortality practices. The aristocratic southerners they displaced in positions of temporal power invented new religious structures to assert, by way of compensation, their spiritual superiority. Michel Strickmann (1979) has demonstrated that in doing so they adapted northern Taoist usages to local popular practices, in which immortality and alchemy were central, and in which the religious use of inorganic drugs was usual. T'ao Hung-ching, a man of noble southern antecedents, drew on revelations inherited from fourth-century predecessors when he founded the Supreme Purity (or Mao-shan) Taoist movement under imperial patronage in about 500. T'ao adapted not only old southern techniques but elaborate structures of alchemical and astral imagery. T'ao thus formed a movement that captured upper-class allegiance, supported state power, and was supported in return for more than five centuries. He united alchemy with Taoism—the particular Taoism that he created—for the first time. Alchemy did not originate in the Taoist milieu and was never confined to it. Similarly, the role of alchemy in movements other than T'ao's varied too greatly to constitute a fixed relationship.

BIBLIOGRAPHY

The most detailed modern study of Chinese alchemy is in Joseph Needham's *Science and Civilisation in China* (Cambridge, 1954), vol. 5, pts. 2–5. For a brief summary, see Needham's *The Refiner's Fire: The Enigma of Alchemy in East and West* (London, 1971), the second J. D. Bernal Lecture, or, for cross-cultural comparisons, "Comparative Macrobiotics," in his *Science in Traditional China* (Cambridge, Mass., 1981), pp. 57–84. I discuss the symbolic structures used in alchemy at length in volume 5 of *Science and Civilisation in China*, pt. 4, pp. 210–305, summarized in more final form in "Chinese Alchemy and the Manipulation of Time," *Isis* 67 (1976): 513–526, and reprinted in *Science and Technology in East Asia,* edited by me (New York, 1977). On the religious significance of internal alchemy, see Farzeen Baldrian-Hussein's *Procédés secrets au Joyau magique: Traité d'alchimie taoïste du onzième siècle* (Paris, 1984). Pre-Taoist southern occult traditions, including alchemy, are discussed in Isabelle Robinet's "La revelation du Shangqing dans l'histoire du taoïsme" (Ph.D. diss., University of Paris, 1981). The relation between alchemy and Taoist movements has been trenchantly analyzed in Michel Strickmann's "On the Alchemy of T'ao Hung-ching," in *Facets of Taoism: Essays in Chinese Religion,* edited by Holmes Welch and Anna Seidel (New Haven, 1979), pp. 123–192; see also his *Le taoïsme du Mao-Chan: Chronique d'une révélation,* 2 vols., "Mémoires de l'Institut des Hautes Études Chinoises," no. 17 (Paris, 1981). Guides to methods of research in Chinese alchemy are my *Chinese Alchemy: Preliminary Studies,* "Harvard Monographs in the History of Science," vol. 1 (Cambridge, Mass., 1968), and Ch'en Kuo-fu's *Tao tsang yüan liu hsü k'ao* (Taipei, 1983).

33 INDIAN ALCHEMY

DAVID WHITE

"Gold is immortality." This correspondence from the Brāhmaṇas grounds the worldview of the Indian alchemist. Just as gold neither corrodes nor loses its brilliance with time, so too the human body may realize a perfect and immutable state. In Indian alchemy, this is accomplished through *rasāyana*, "the way of *rasa*" (i.e., of essences), which is the Sanskrit term for the alchemist's craft.

There are early references to chemical and metallurgical alchemical processes in the *Arthaśāstra*, the *Suśruta Saṃhitā*, and the so-called Bower manuscript. But the Indian alchemical tradition proper did not begin until these processes were correlated with techniques and goals of perfecting the body. The history of the word *rasāyana* illustrates this primary concern with bodily perfection. In the ancient Ayurvedic tradition of the *Caraka Saṃhitā*, the term *rasāyana* refers to techniques and processes leading to bodily invigoration and rejuvenation. [*See also* Āyurveda.]

The Indian alchemist's cosmology and metaphysics have their roots in the "emanationism" and microcosm-macrocosm analogues of Sāṃkhya philosophy, of the yogic Upaniṣads, and of Vedānta. According to these philosophies, everything that exists is an emanation or emission (*vyāpana* or *sṛṣṭi*) from an original source or essence. It is destined for reabsorption (*laya* or *pralaya*) into the same. The emanated universe is hierarchical in structure. At the top of the hierarchy is the Absolute, which is variously conceived as Puruṣa, Prakṛti, *brahman,* or a union of Śiva and Śakti. Emanation proceeds down from the Absolute into the manifested world of the five sentient qualities, the senses, and the elements. These also are hierarchically organized, following the system of the *tanmātra*s. Ether, along with its corresponding sense and sentient quality, diffuses downward into air, fire, water, and earth. One can return these gross *(sthūla)* elements of the manifested world to their original, subtle *(sūkṣma),* and perfect state through *saṃskāra*s ("transforming processes"). Here the elements are conceived as stages rather than substances. The process of reintegration conceptually entails the stripping away of sheaths of ultimately illusory form in order to reveal a true and perfect essence.

The semilegendary Nāgārjuna is considered the father of Indian alchemy. There were possibly no less than five alchemists named Nāgārjuna in India between the second and twelfth centuries CE, but their histories are so entangled that scholars have all but been reduced to accepting the general Indian consensus—that "Nāgārjuna" lived for at least eight hundred years! Nāgārjuna is the reputed author or editor of such diverse alchemical texts as the "magic" *Kakṣapuṭa Tantra*, the "mercurial" *Rasendramaṅgalam*, and the "Ayurvedic" *Suśruta Saṃhitā*. [*See also the biography of Nāgārjuna.*]

Buddhist alchemy differs from Hindu alchemy inasmuch as it places greater emphasis on internal yogic processes than on external chemical or mercurial processes. Buddhist alchemy *(rasāyana)* uses chemical substances to prolong the life of the body, but only as a means to the higher end of realizing total liberation through sexual, yogic, and meditative techniques.

Because it emphasizes the use of mercury and drugs in transmutation and in the realization of a perfect *(siddha)* and immortal body, Hindu alchemy is also known as mercurial *(dhātuvāda)* alchemy, in contrast to Buddhist *rasāyana*. The Buddhist yogic and Hindu chemical approaches often overlap, however, and one finds elements of both in the Nāth, Siddha, Sahajiyā, and Vajrayāna Tantric traditions. The flowering of alchemical thought and practice was contemporaneous with that of Tantra, spanning roughly the sixth to the fifteenth centuries CE. Indian alchemists were often characterized as *siddha*s whose metaphysics and techniques at once embraced alchemy, yoga, and Tantra. These traditions also overlap in their "historical" lineages of gurus. Thus the alchemists Gorakh, Carpaṭe, Vyāḍi, and Nāgārjuna figure in the lineages of numerous Tantric traditions, from the Sittar (Siddha) alchemists of South India to the Vajrayāna Buddhists of Tibet. [*See also the biography of Gorakhnāth.*]

The Hindu mercurial alchemist's laboratory is portrayed as a microcosm of the universe. Just as the gross elements of the manifested world ultimately return to the Absolute according to Vedantic philosophy, here the alchemist attempts to effect an analogous reintegration by using physical substances. He makes use of plant, animal, and mineral substances to remount the hierarchy of metals: lead, tin, copper, silver, and gold. The most essential elements that he employs are mercury *(rasa* or *pārada)* and sulphur *(gandhaka)*. In Hindu alchemy these elements are conceived as the seed *(bīja* or *bindu)* of the male Śiva and the sexual essence or blood *(śonita* or *rajas)* of the female Śakti, respectively.

According to Indian alchemy, yoga, and Tantra, every substance and combination of elements in the universe has its sexual valence. In the Hindu Tantric worldview, the manifest world is the emanation of the eternal union of Śiva and Śakti. Their sexual essences, of which mercury and sulphur are hierophanies, are the means for reintegrating and perfecting the world. The alchemical *saṃskāra*s are described in highly evocative language: mercury pierces or penetrates *(vedhana)* sulphur in order that it may be killed *(mṛta)* and be "reborn" into a purer, more stable state *(bandha)* where it has a greater capacity for transmuting other elements. In the transmutation process mercury penetrates base metals. They are "killed" and "reborn" into increasingly higher states in the hierarchy of metals until finally perfect alchemical gold emerges from the sloughed-off sheaths of its grosser stages. The language of these *saṃskāra*s is simultaneously one of initiation (as *dīkṣa*), sexuality, and rebirth. The alchemist's craft is conceived of as a spiritual exercise, a ritual, a sacrifice, an act of devotion, and a participation in the divine play of an expanding or contracting universe. It is in such a context that we may best understand immortality as the ultimate goal of mercurial alchemy. In the alchemical universe, mercury (i.e., Śiva's seed or *bīja*) is capable of purifying and perfecting the human body in the same way that it perfects metallic "bodies."

It is through the correspondence of *amṛta-bīja-rasa* that the alchemical hierarchies and processes become fused to the psychochemical system of *kuṇḍalinī* and other forms of yoga. In *kuṇḍalinī* yoga, the yogin, through his austerities, causes his own seed *(bīja)* to mount the six *cakras* through the agency of the internal (female) *kuṇḍalinī* serpent. As the *kuṇḍalinī* pierces each of the *cakras*, the heat thus generated transmutes that seed until it becomes pure ambrosia *(amṛta)* in the highest *cakra*, the *sahasrāra*, located in the skull. (In Buddhist alchemy, the analogous sexual yogic practice of "fixing the *bodhicitta*" is the primary means of transmuting the seed into *amṛta*.) The *kuṇḍalinī* then unites with the (male) "full moon" of the *sahasrāra*, such that the *amṛta* built up there rushes down through the body, rejuvenating it and rendering it immortal. [*See also* Kuṇḍalinī.] By taking in compounds of mercury in conjunction with using *mantras*, *mudrā*s, breathing techniques, and other yogic practices, the alchemist catalyzes psychochemical processes so as to facilitate the perfecting of his body.

The end of these complementary practices is a perfect *(siddha)* body of stable *(sthīra)* processes. This body shines like gold, is as hard and impenetrable as a diamond *(vajra)*, and is possessed of supernatural powers *(siddhis)*. The *siddha*'s body is as if reborn from a body that was previously subject to aging, sickness, and death; now he is *jīvanmukta* (liberated in the body), immortal, and as powerful as the gods themselves. [*See also* Jīvanmukti.] Should he choose to do so, he may enter into *samādhi*, ultimate reintegration with the Absolute. In doing so, he sheds his physical form for total liberation, known as *mokṣa* or *mahāsukha* in Tantric Hinduism and Buddhism, respectively.

BIBLIOGRAPHY

The broadest-ranging scientific approach to Indian alchemy remains Prafulla Chandra Ray's *A History of Hindu Chemistry*, 2 vols. (Calcutta, 1904–1909); a revised edition, edited by Priyadaranjan Ray under the title *History of Chemistry in Ancient and Medieval India* (Calcutta, 1956), contains excerpts and partial translations of some alchemical texts. Also highly useful for their compelling syntheses are Mircea Eliade's *The Forge and the Crucible: The Origins and Structures of Alchemy*, 2d ed. (Chicago, 1978), and Sashibhusan Dasgupta's *Obscure Religious Cults*, 3d ed. (Calcutta, 1969). Two excellent recent studies of Indo-Tibetan Buddhist alchemy are Michael Walter's "The Role of Alchemy and Medicine in Indo-Tibetan Tantra" (Ph.D. diss., University of Indiana, Bloomington, 1982) and Edward Todd Fenner's *Rasāyana Siddhi: Medicine and Alchemy in the Buddhist Tantras* (Madison, Wis., 1983); the latter contains a translation of the alchemical section of the *Vimala-prabhā*, a commentary on the *Kālacakra Tantra*.

Madhava's fourteenth-century work *Sarva-darśana-saṃgraha*, translated by Edward B. Cowell, 7th ed. (Varanasi, 1978), includes a section on the "Mercurial school" of Indian philosophy, which passes in review the teachings of the major texts of the Hindu alchemical tradition. Most important among these is the Sanskrit *Rasārṇavam* (c. tenth century), edited by Indradeo Tripathi, 2d ed. (Varanasi, 1978), which contains references to devotional aspects of alchemy (see 1.37–38, 1.43–52, and 1.109–116) and to the origin myth of sulphur (7.57–66). The *Rasaratnasamucchaya* of Vāgbhaṭa (c. fourteenth century), edited by Shridharmananda Sharma, 2d ed. (Delhi, 1962), contains an origin myth of mercury (1.60–66). For discussion of the "historical Nāgārjuna" and other alchemists, see K. Satchidananda Murty's *Nagarjuna* (New Delhi, 1971) and Giuseppe Tucci's "Animadversiones Indicae," *Journal of the Asiatic Society of Bengal* 26 (1930): 125–160.

34 ISLAMIC ALCHEMY

Habibeh Rahim

The Arabic term for alchemy is *al-kīmiyā'*. The word *kīmiyā'* is alternately derived from the Greek *chumeia* (or *chēmeia*), denoting the "art of transmutation," or from *kim-iya,* a South Chinese term meaning "gold-making juice." Greek and later Hellenistic writings are generally regarded as the initial impetus behind Muslim learning, thus the wide acceptance of the Greek origin of the word.

In the Islamic context, *al-kīmiyā'* refers to the "art" of transmuting substances, both material and spiritual, to their highest form of perfection. The word *kīmiyā'* also refers to the agent or catalyst that effects the transmutation and hence is used as a synonym for *al-iksīr* ("elixir") and *ḥajar al-falāsifah* ("philosopher's stone"). The search for the ideal elixir has been an ancient quest in many cultures of the world; it was supposed to transform metals to their most perfect form (gold) and minerals to their best potency and, if the correct elixir were to be found, to achieve immortality. [*See* Elixir.] All matter of a particular type, metals for example, were supposed to consist of the same elements. The correct *kīmiyā'* or *iksīr* would enable the transposition of the elements into ideal proportions and cause the metal concerned to be changed from a base form to a perfected form, for instance, copper to gold.

On another level, the philosophical theory of alchemy was used to conceptualize the purification of the soul. The terminology and procedures of alchemy were allegorized and applied to the transformation of the soul from its base, earthly, impure state to pure perfection. Elementary psychological postulations were allegorized as chemical properties. For the mystics, the *iksīr* served as a symbol of the divine truth that changed an unbeliever into a believer. In Ṣūfī literature, the spiritual master purifies the soul of the adept via various processes of spiritual alchemy. This usage of alchemical principles in the spiritual realm reflects the worldview of the ancients, including those of medieval Islam, whereby the human soul was regarded as a microcosm of the forces and principles contained in the macrocosm of the universe.

HISTORICAL BACKGROUND

In Muslim tradition, alchemy enjoys ancient roots. The cultivation of alchemy is traced back to Adam, followed by most of the major prophets and sages. This chain of transmission is then connected to the "masters" from the ancient world, including Aristotle, Galen, Socrates, Plato, and others. Muslims are considered to have received the art from these masters. In Islamic times, the prophet Muḥammad (d. 632 CE), is said to have endorsed the art, lending it grace and power; his cousin and son-in-law, ʿAlī ibn Abī Ṭālib (d. 661), is regarded as its patron. ʿAlī's descendant Jaʿfar al-Ṣādiq (d. 765) is portrayed as the next major transmitter. The Umayyad prince Khālid ibn Yazīd (660–704) is depicted as both a practitioner and a patron of alchemy who encouraged the translation of relevant Greek and Syriac texts into Arabic. Legendary tales indicate that he learned the art from a Syrian monk named Marianos, whom he sought out on long journeys to strange lands. Jābir ibn Ḥayyān (d. c. 815), who is held to be the disciple of Jaʿfar al-Ṣādiq, is credited with over three hundred treatises on alchemy; consequently, the name of this quasi-historical figure came to imply the authority and teacher *par excellence*.

The Jabirian Corpus. By contrast with these legendary accounts, modern scholarship places the development of Islamic alchemy in the ninth century. Jābir ibn Ḥayyān is indeed recorded as the first major alchemist, but the writings attributed to him are mainly pseudepigraphical, and many appeared as late as the tenth century. The *Book of Mercy,* the *Book of the Balances,* the *Book of One Hundred and Twelve,* the *Seventy Books,* and the *Five Hundred Books* are some of the important works in the collection. Movements such as the Ikhwān al-Ṣafāʾ (Brethren of Purity) probably influenced or even contributed to some of the treatises in the Jabirian corpus, which forms an important source of information on alchemic techniques, equipment, materials, and attitudes.

According to the sulfur-mercury theory of metals introduced in the corpus, all metals were considered to possess these two elements, or the two principles they represent, in varying proportions, the combination of which lends each metal its peculiarities. Sulfur was responsible for the hot/dry features and mercury, the cold/moist ones. (Aristotle considered these four features to be represented by fire, earth, air, and water respectively.) Sulfur and mercury embody the positive and negative aspects of matter, also referred to as male and female properties.

The *Book of Balances* theorizes that the metals are generated from contrary elements. Each body expresses an equilibrium of the natures composing it, and this harmony can be expressed numerically by the musical harmony that governs the heavens. The qualitative differences and degrees of intensity of the natures are analogous to the differences of tone in the musical scale. Further, each body represents a balance between internal and two external qualities, with each metal characterized by two internal and two external qualities. The transmutation of one metal into another is thus an adjustment of the ratio of the latent and manifest constituents of the first to the second, an adjustment to be brought about by an elixir. Each metal is regarded as an inversion of one of the others, and transmutation is a simple changing of qualities, which could be accomplished the same way that a physician cures by counterbalancing an excessive humor with one of contrary quality. The elixirs, in other words, were the alchemists' medicines.

According to the Jabirian corpus, there are various elixirs suitable for specific transmutations, but transmutations of every kind could be brought about by a grand or master elixir, the prime focus of the alchemists' endeavors. An important and original link between theory and practice is provided by the Jabirian author of the

Seventy Books, who explains that material phenomena can be separated not only into their elements but into the contrary qualities by distillation. The inflammable and nonflammable vapors that are usually evolved when organic matter is subject to heat for distillation are considered to represent "fire" and "air." The condensable liquid that follows from the process is called "water," and the residue "earth." The author then attempts the division of these elements into the pair of qualities of which each was made. He claims not only that this process is applicable to organic matter but that even the hardest stones are distillable. The use of elixirs from the distillation of organic materials, which has been called a Jabirian innovation, indicates the medical orientation of alchemy. It is in their extensive pursuit of the elixir that the Jabirian treatises resemble those of al-Rāzī.

Al-Rāzī. The physician and philosopher Muḥammad ibn Zakariyā' al-Rāzī (d. 925) is the next Muslim alchemist who made a major impact on the art. To the sulfur-mercury theory of the constitution of metals he added the attribute of salinity. The popular conception of alchemy with three elements—sulfur, mercury, and salt—reappeared in Europe and played an important role in Western alchemy. According to al-Rāzī, bodies were composed of invisible elements (atoms) and of empty space that lay between them. These atoms were eternal and possessed a certain size. This conception seems close to the explanation of the structure of matter in modern physics. Al-Rāzī's books, *Sirr al asrār* (The Secret of Secrets) and *Madkhal al-ta'līmī* (Instructive [or Practical] Introduction), are important sources for understanding the principles and techniques of alchemy as practiced in the tenth-century Muslim world, specifically Iran. In them, he provides a systematic classification of carefully observed and verified facts regarding chemical substances, reactions, and apparatus, described in language that is free of mysticism and ambiguity. Of the voluminous Jabirian writings only the *Book of Mercy* is mentioned by al-Rāzī, perhaps because the other works were composed after his lifetime.

Other Masters. Muḥammad ibn 'Umayil (tenth century) was famous for his *Kitāb al-ma' al-waraqī* (The Book of the Silvery Water and the Starry Earth) and *Kitāb al'ilm al-muktasab,* two of his main works on alchemy. The writings attributed to 'Ali ibn Waḥshīyā' (a legendary figure of the tenth century) provided encyclopedic information on the tradition of alchemy in Islam. He is an important source of information on the alchemists and their art. He also provides the views of prominent nonalchemists on the subject. Another important work compiled at this time is the *Muṣḥaf al-jamā'ah,* known as the *Turba philosophorum* in its famous Latin translation; here the author, who has yet to be definitely identified, describes an ancient congress of alchemists chaired by Pythagoras, with Archelaus recording the doctrines expounded by nine pre-Socratic philosophers. Maslamah al-Majrīṭī (d. 1007?) was the author of the famous alchemical guide *Rutbat al-ḥakīm* (The Step of the Sages); his book on practical magic, *Gha'yat al-ḥakīm* (The Limit of the Sages), was also very popular and was translated in the West. A notable figure in the following century is Ḥusayn 'Ali al-Tughrā'i (d. 1121?), author of the important defense of alchemy *Kitāb ḥaqā'iq al-isthishād fī-al-kīmiyā'* (Truths of the Evidence Submitted with Regard to Alchemy). Written in 1112, the work is a strong refutation of the negative polemics of Ibn Sīnā. Later documentation of the practice of alchemy is provided by the Egyptian Aydamir ibn 'Ali al-Jildakī (d. 1360), whose encyclopedic works provide us with summaries of and commentaries upon everything that had been written on alchemy and magic before him.

OPPOSITION TO THE ART

Although widespread, alchemy did not have the approval of all Muslim scholars. Thus Ibn Sīnā (d. 1035) censured it as a futile activity and contested the assertion that man is able to imitate nature. He asserted that the alchemists were only able to make something that externally resembles the precious metals, since the actual substance of base metals remained unchanged. The great North African historian Ibn Khaldūn (d. 1406) also made a critical assessment of Arab-Islamic alchemical activities. He characterized alchemy as the study of the properties, virtues, and temperatures of the elements used for the preparation of and search for an elixir that could transform lesser metals into gold. Elements used for the elixir included animal refuse, urine, manure, bones, feathers, blood, hair, eggs, and nails, as well as minerals. Distillation, sublimation, calcination, and other techniques were used to separate elements in the extracts used in the preparation of the elixir. Alchemists believed that if the correct elixir could be obtained by these methods, it could then be added to concocted lead, copper, or tin over fire to yield pure gold. For his part, Ibn Khaldūn rejected the alchemists' claims that their transmutations were intended to perfect the work of nature by mechanical and technical procedures. He also criticized the authenticity of works ascribed to Khālid ibn Yazīd and argued that the elaborate sciences and arts of Islam had not been developed in that early time.

INFLUENCE ON THE WEST

Islamic alchemy was brought to the West in the twelfth century, mostly through translations. The earliest extant Latin translation of an Arabic treatise on alchemy is generally considered to be Robert of Chester's work *De compositione alchemiae*, dating from 1144. Some scholars consider it as a possible later Latin forgery, but this issue is very complicated and requires further study. About the same time, Gerard of Cremona (1114–1187) translated the Jabirian *Seventy Books* into Latin; *De aluminibus et salibus* and *Liber luminis luminum* are considered his translations. Other works that seem to be translations from Arabic prior to the appearance of the first indigenous European alchemical writing (the *Ars alchemia*, c. 1225, attributed to Michael Scot, d. 1232) were the *De anima* of Ibn Sīnā, the *Turba philosophorum*, the *Emerald Tablet*, the *Secret of Creation*, and al-Rāzī's *Secret of Secrets*. Thus it seems that the majority of celebrated Islamic alchemical works were known in Europe by the middle of the thirteenth century.

BIBLIOGRAPHY

For general surveys of Islamic alchemy, the following essays are useful: Salimuzzaman Siddiqi and S. Mahdihassan's "Chemistry," in *A History of Muslim Philosophy*, edited by M. M. Sharif (Wiesbaden, 1966), vol. 2, pp. 1296–1316; Seyyed Hossein Nasr's "Alchemy and Other Occult Sciences," in his *Islamic Science: An Illustrated Study* (Westerham, England, 1976), pp. 193–208; Eric J. Holmyard's "Alchemy in Medieval Islam," *Endeavour* 14 (July 1955): 117–125; Julius Ruska's *Turba Philosophorum: Ein Beitrag zur Geschichte der Alchemie* (Berlin, 1931); and Manfred Ullmann's "al-Kīmiyā," in *The Encyclopaedia of Islam*, new ed. (Leiden, 1960–).

As yet no comprehensive critical study of the origin, development, and practices of traditional Islamic alchemy is available.

Overviews of Islamic alchemy within the context of global surveys of alchemy or chemistry can be found in Eric J. Holmyard's *Alchemy* (Baltimore, 1957), chap. 5; George Sarton's *Introduction to the History of Science*, 3 vols. in 5 (Washington, D.C, 1927–1948); Robert P. Multhauf's *The Origins of Chemistry* (London, 1966); *Studien zur Geschichte der Chemie,* edited by Julius Ruska (Berlin, 1927); and Homer H. Dub's "The Beginnings of Alchemy," *Isis* 38 (November 1947): 62–86. Dubs argues that alchemy in Islam originated in China.

Julius Ruska and Karl Garbers discuss the mutual relation of the corpus Jabirian and the writings of al-Rāzī, large alchemical works written at the end of the ninth and tenth centuries, in "Vorschriften zur Herstellung von scharfen Wässern bei Ğābir und Rāzī," *Islam* 25 (1938): 1–35. Some of the problems surrounding these writings are studied in Ruska's *Chālid ibn Jazīd ibn Mu'āwija* and *Gā'far al-Sādiq der sechste Imām,* volumes 1 and 2 of *Arabische Alchemisten* (Heidelberg, 1924); in Paul Kraus's "Studien zu Jâbir Ibn Hayyân," *Isis* (February 1931): 7–30; and in Gerard Heym's "Al-Rāzī and Alchemy," *Ambix* 1 (March 1938): 184–191.

A valuable study of the secret names used by Arab alchemists is Julius Ruska and E. Wiedemann's "Alchemistische Decknamen," in *Sitzungsberichte der physikalisch-medicinische Sozietät* (Erlangen, 1924). Their study partially utilizes al-Tugra'ī's *Kitāb al-Jawhar al-nādir* (Book of the Brilliant Stone).

35 HELLENISTIC AND MEDIEVAL ALCHEMY

Henry and Renée Kahane

By the beginning of the Christian era, a change in secular and religious attitudes can be discerned. The rationalism that had guided the thinking of the elite in previous times waned, and the rise of skepticism and loss of direction led to a philosophical vacuum that stimulated a recourse to mystic intuition and divine mysteries. The area of the Roman empire in which this process became primarily manifest was Egypt, where, after the conquest by Alexander the Great (in 332 BCE), the culture of Hellenism with its fusion of Greek and Eastern features was centered. The fashionable mystery beliefs subsumed under the names of gnosticism and Hermetism exerted a strong attraction for practitioners of the occult sciences (astrology, magic, and medicine) as well as alchemy, the art of making gold. previously, men of science had by thought process and investigations obtained what they now expected to receive through divine revelation or supernatural inspiration. In short, science—as revealed knowledge and, for the alchemist, as a means of creating gold—turned into religion.

Such a link between alchemy and gnosticism and Hermetism is most tangibly documented in the occult literature of Hellenistic Egypt from about the second to the fourth century. This emphasizes, first, the fact that alchemy, beyond being a craft devoted to changing matter, has a place also within the history of religions and, second, that in the alchemist's religious beliefs the general gnostic tenets blended with his specific alchemical approach to the world. The impact of the craft can be discerned in four aspects of the cult: its doctrine, its ritual, its language, and its roots.

DOCTRINE

The soul is enchained in matter and is to be freed. Science as traditionally expounded in the schools was unable to liberate it. Only gnosis, the knowledge of God, could accomplish the task, and to convey gnosis, alchemy transformed itself into an esoteric religion. The beliefs were fantastic: visions, the chemical apparatus as a temple, the alchemical operation as a sacrificial act, mental baptism in the Hermetic vessel called the *kratēr*, and the ascension to God by means of a mystic ladder that transports the soul from the discord and suffering below to the divine order above. The doctrines of alchemy as a religion echoed the principles of alchemy as a science. These were essentially three: primal matter, sympathy, and transmutation.

Primal Matter. The *opus alchimicum*, ("the alchemist's labor") centered on matter. Nobody knew, of course, what matter was, and it remained a secret of alchemy, although many chemical, mythological, and philosophical definitions were ventured in the course of time (Jung, 1953, p. 317). Thus, the *Tabula Smaragdina* (the revelation of secret alchemical teaching, of the ninth century but based on Hermetic sources) identified matter with God, because all created objects come from a single primal matter; and Comarius, an alchemist-philosopher (first century CE?) identified it with Hades, to whom the imperfect souls were chained (Jung, pp. 299, 319). Such perceptions of matter echo the alchemist's craft: his operation was, in mythical terms, a replica of divine creativity, aiming at the liberation of imprisoned matter. The inherent anthropomorphic view of matter, the "vitalist hypothesis," was going to play a fundamental role in the "sacred art," alchemy: metals, that is, matter, were considered living organisms, which are born, grow, and multiply. With the alchemist's preoccupation with matter and his belief that the divine soul is enchained in matter, he "takes upon himself the duty of carrying out the redeeming *opus*" (Jung, p. 306). Thus seen, the alchemist evolves into a priest.

Sympathy. The anthropomorphic perception of matter that assigned to the metal a human soul correlated with an occult system according to which the supposed affinity between substances expressed itself in a mutual attraction or rejection, that is, either "sympathy" or "antipathy." Such a bond linked, in particular, our world "below" to the world "above," the microcosm of man to the macrocosm of planetary divinities. The system of correspondences elaborated, for example, by the second-century astrologer Antiochus of Athens (Sheppard, *Ambix* 7, p. 46) embraced, in addition to "above" and "below," also elements, metals, and colors:

COLOR	ELEMENT	METAL	MACROCOSM	MICROCOSM
black	earth	lead	Saturn	body
white	water	silver	Moon	spirit
yellow	fire	gold	Sun	soul

Already Maria Prophetissa (fl. early third century), also known as the "founding mother of alchemy," heralded the principle of parallelism: "Just as man results [from the association] of liquids, of solids, and of spirit, so does copper." Zosimos of Panopolis in Egypt (fl. c. 300), recognizing the identity between the behavior of matter and the events in his own (unconscious) psyche, condensed this complex insight into the formula "What is within is also without."

Transmutation. The third facet of alchemical religiosity was also linked to the alchemist's practice. A basic alchemical tenet stated that all substances could be derived through transmutation from primal matter. The technique of change consisted essentially in "coloring": the Egyptian alchemists did not intend to "make" gold but to color *(baptein)* metals and textiles through tinctures and elixirs so that they would "appear" like gold (or silver or some other metal). A "changed" metal, then, was a "new" metal. The technique of coloring evolved, in the end, into a powerful symbol of alchemical doctrine; for just as the alchemist transformed lead into silver, and silver into gold, so too he posited for matter, in his anthropomorphic view of it, a similar change, from body to spirit to soul. And in the frame of his doctrine, he identified this escalation with the renewal of man, to which he assigned the same chain of transmutations to reach the goal of redemption.

THE RITUAL

Although the alchemist, who represented the religious bent of his profession, has been viewed as a priest, the identity of his congregation remains unknown. The sources, reading somewhat like tracts of edification, transmit no detail. Some have sensed in the texts evidence of the existence of a loosely structured brotherhood. Others, above all Festugière (1950, pp. 427–428), took the alchemical devotion (like the Hermetic) to be a cult adhered to by individuals or groups who practiced the "sacred art" and came under the spell of the mystic beliefs inherent in their work. Those nonpractitioners of alchemy who felt attracted were possibly members of the intelligentsia drawn to that particular version of modish gnosticism.

The code that the devotee observed had various specific features. They concern the transmission of the creed, first to him and then from him, and the way of life expected of a spiritual father.

The Mystagogues. The myth of transmission added the religious component to alchemical mysticism. The spokesmen invoked the authority of the supreme being, or its prophets, or the sages of old: "Behold [says Isis to her son as alchemist], the mystery has been revealed to you!" (Festugière, 1950, p. 260). Maria Prophetissa claimed that alchemical secrets were revealed to her by God. The Byzantine monk Marianus quoted alchemists saying to Maria: "The divine, hidden, and always splendid, secret is revealed to you."

With Egypt providing the setting of the cult, Egyptian mythical figures and divinities were the prime wellspring of inspiration: chiefly Thoth (hellenized as Hermes Trismegistos), the legendary author of the Hermetica, and Isis, turned into the creators and teachers of alchemy to whom alchemical sayings and doctrines were attributed. Various Greek writings on alchemy that contained traces of Jewish monotheism were ascribed to Moses, probably in a homonymic transfer from the alchemist Moses of Alexandria. Later on, Jewish alchemical tradition evoked Enoch, the Jewish counterpart to Hermes. The Greek alchemist Pseudo-Democritus, looking in Memphis for enlightenment, conjured the ghost of the Persian Ostanes, the "hellenized magus" of alchemy, who advised him: "The books are in the temple." Zosimos, our major source, owed his knowledge to the wisdom of Hermes.

Traditio Mystica. The "sacred craft" was a secret craft. The goddess Isis instructs her son Horus: "Keep it a great secret [*megalomustērion*]." The initiated were forbidden to divulge their knowledge; they could pass it on only to their "legitimate sons" and to those who were "worthy." Alchemy, known through revelation, remained a privilege of the few, and the taboo of disclosure, well guarded through the ages, in an impressive example of *traditio mystica,* a very Hermetic feature.

Portrait of the Alchemist. Just as revelation strikes the priest, so the divine mystery overwhelms the alchemist and shapes his way of life. His *opus* is not so much determined by technical knowledge and manual skill but, rather, by its true goal, redemption. His soul is to be saved. He has to strive for detachment from matter, for liberation from his passions, and for suppression of his body. He is spiritual man, alone, in search of himself, on a silent quest for God.

THE LANGUAGE OF ALCHEMY

Alchemy, like every other movement in the history of civilization, found its own forms of expression. Their pseudoscientific orientation imparted to the alchemical writings the stamp of mystery, and by displaying the "jargon of mysteries" (Festugière, 1950, p. 82) these texts produced the effect of liturgy and secured a screen against the profane. Three stylistic markers stand out:

Symbols. The alchemist, in the formulation of Wayne Shuhmaker, "did not analyze but analogized," and his own universe, metallurgy, provided the mythical imagery and stimulated new meanings. The alchemical *opus* centered on the change of matter, and transmutation of matter turned into the recurrent theme of the alchemist's cult. To him, the soul imprisoned in matter symbolized the spirit striving to purify itself from the roughage of the flesh. Matter was represented above all by metal and symbolized life and man, its growth comparable to the growth of the fetus. "The achievement of metallic transmutation became symbolic of the religious regeneration of the human soul" (Sheppard, *Ambix* 17, p. 77). With technical alchemy providing the similes that expressed gnostic religiosity, the two-tiered semantic construct evolved that was characteristic of Hellenistic and medieval mystic language: the worldly, exoteric lexicon furnished the "surface," the *sensus litteralis,* but when applied to esoteric experience it yielded the hidden meaning, the *sensus allegoricus.*

Many lexical items were drawn into the process: thus, in the Valentinian system of gnosticism (deriving from the second-century Egyptian Valentinus), metallurgical terms such as the following symbolized spiritual concepts. *Pneuma* signified, first, the product of natural sublimation, then, "divine spirit"; *ebullient* ("boiling up"), referring to the alchemical process of "separating the pure from the impure," was applied to wisdom; *sperma* (the "embryonic germ") yielded the "seed" of gnosis; in a similar way, such terms as *refine, filter,* and *purify* acquired spiritualized meanings. The transfer, through alchemy, from the literal to the symbolic realm contributed richly to the language of religion and, generally, abstraction. It indicates a conscious effort of the alchemist to frame his views in the terms of his craft.

Antonyms. Hellenistic alchemy tended to emphasize the varied contraries inherent in the craft: hot/cold, moist/dry, earth/air, fire/water. Antonymic structure was symbolically superimposed on matter: Maria Prophetissa distinguished metals as male and female as if they were human, and Zosimos distinguished between the metals' souls and bodies. The same antonymy, but with the focus on man himself, characterizes gnostic dualism with its model of spiritual versus carnal man.

Aphorisms. Technical prescriptions, and in particular those that aimed at the transformation of matter, tended to be sharpened and honed so as to sound, in their lapidary style, like keys to mysteries. Such aphorisms, often bordering on the abstruse, were a favored feature of alchemical doctrine. For example, the first commandment requires secrecy and elitism: "One man to one man." Pseudo-Democritus, on the subject of liberating the imprisoned soul, declared "Transform the nature and make the spirit that is hidden inside the body come out." Maria Prophetissa said likewise, "Invert nature and you will find that which you seek."

Transmutation was tied to the law of sympathy and antipathy: "One nature rejoices in another nature; one nature triumphs over another nature; one nature masters another nature." One of Maria's axioms that subsumed a complex alchemical procedure was read by Jung (1953, p. 23) in psychological terms, according to which the even numbers signified the female principle and the odd numbers the male, the latter overwhelming the former: "One becomes two, two becomes three, and by means of the third the fourth achieves unity; thus two are but one." Maria focuses also on an analogy made between metals and mankind: "Join the male and the female, and you will find what you seek." A well-known aphorism expresses the analogy between macrocosm and microcosm: "That which is above is like to that which is below, and that which is below is like to that which is above." Several maxims rest on the principle of antonymy. The symbol of the serpent biting its tail is used to circumscribe diversity in unity: "The All is one and the All is through itself and the All goes to itself, and if it had not the All there would be no All." The philosophers' stone is simply defined as "a stone that is not a stone."

ROOTS

The essence of the strange and complex phenomenon of alchemy is elusive, and its various interpreters were inclined to stress the feature that each considered, in genetic terms, to be its foundation. In particular, four possible sources have been isolated: classical philosophy, mystery creeds, the lore of the craft, and the workings of the unconscious.

Classical Philosophy. The great cognitions of the classical tradition, from the pre-Socratics to Plato, Aristotle, and the Stoics, resurfaced in eclectic Hellenistic philosophy. Numerous doctrines prefigured crucial phases of the alchemical worldview: the concept of a primal matter; the unity of matter (seen in, say, water or fire); cosmic correspondences; the affinity of the similar; the microcosm reflecting the macrocosm; the notion of sympathy; transformation through *pneuma,* the all pervading spirit; genesis, that is, the origin of one element from another, proceeding by way of opposites.

Mystery Creeds. Hermetism and the alchemical cult overlap in various features. The tie between them is substantiated in the writings of Zosimos, the "divine," the "highly learned," and the outstanding representative of both creeds. The common ground consisted of "mystic reveries" (Festugière): observation and inquiry were rejected, and intuition replaced science; the "sacred craft" was revealed through divine grace; the chosen were few, bound to secrecy; and the goal was the liberation of the soul from the body.

The Lore of the Craft. Alchemy, hopelessly aiming at the transformation of metals into gold, has often been viewed as something like a misguided application of chemistry. Yet its significance lies, indeed lay even for its practitioners, not so much in the experimental method and the outcome of metallic transmutation as in other spheres, notably anthropology, religion, and folklore. The story has been reconstructed by Mircea Eliade: it goes back to archaic times and surfaced in Hellenistic Egypt. Its protagonist was the smith, the adept who dominated matter by transforming it. The insights deriving from his work gave rise to new meanings and symbols: matter was suffering; transmutation perfected matter; redemption was freedom from matter. In short, the primary function of alchemy, physical transmutation, escalated into metaphysical transmutation: the *opus alchimicum* became a symbol of the *opus divinum.* The title of one of the prominent alchemical works of the early post-

Christian era by Pseudo-Democritus (and ascribed to Bolos from Mendes, in Egypt) stressed the dichotomy: *Phusika kai mustika* (Natural and Mystical Matters).

Depth Psychology. The attribution of life to matter was the foundation of alchemical belief. Enticed by the resemblances between the dreams of his patients and alchemical symbols, C. G. Jung read this belief from his psychoanalytic standpoint as the projection of inner experience onto matter, and thus as the identification of matter with the Self. "Matter" evolved as a name for the "self." It represented an unconscious archetype, primordial images, and the alchemical *opus,* aiming at freeing, saving, and perfecting matter, and was a symbolic replica of the universal quest for the Self. Jung called it the "individuation" process.

Convergence. These four components of spiritual alchemy can be traced in Hellenistic Egypt. The craft of the goldsmith was flourishing, and metallurgy yielded the imagery while boosting, by its very nature, the identification, ever present in the human mind, of self and matter; Greek philosophy, in a stage of revival then and there, provided the basic concepts of the doctrine; and Hermetism supplied the vital climate of mystery.

Alchemy is described here as a facet of the ancient mystery religions, and this description centers on its style and manifestations in the Hellenistic period. But other cultures, tending in a similar direction, produced other varieties of spiritual alchemy. In China, it aimed at physical immortality and thus came into the orbit of medicine, with some link to the religious movement of Taoism. In India, as Eliade has shown, alchemy evolved as an analogue to the mystic discipline of yoga: that purification sought by the yogin for the body, the alchemist seeks through the purification of metals. The relationship (involving the question of polygenesis or monogenesis) between the Chinese, Indian, and Hellenic forms of spiritual alchemy is not very clear. Islamic culture, on the other hand, played a vital role in the transmission of alchemical knowledge; many of the Greek texts were translated into Arabic and through this link, reached the West during the late Middle Ages. Thus, the transmutation of matter continued, with its occult framework, into the Renaissance and beyond. But then modern science rejected ideology, and with the loss of its "exoteric" component to chemistry, alchemy was reduced to its "esoteric" questions about man's relation to the cosmos. In our day the mystic movement of the Rosicrucians, which appeared during the seventeenth century, is a typical relic—and faint echo—of the vanished Hellenistic cult.

[*See also* Hermetism; Gnosticism; *and* Rosicrucians.]

BIBLIOGRAPHY

The literature is large and rapidly growing. A comprehensive bibliography is Alan Pritchard's *Alchemy: A Bibliography of English-Language Writings* (London and Boston, 1980). The previous standard, *Collection des anciens alchimistes grecs,* edited and translated by Marcellin P. E. Berthelot and Charles-Émile Ruelle, 3 vols. (1887–1888; reprint, Osnabrück, 1967), will be superseded by *Les alchimistes grecs,* 12 vols. (1981–), a comprehensive edition of the texts, with French translations.

Good surveys, from varying standpoints and usually with bibliographical information, may be consulted in the standard cyclopedias: Wilhelm Gundel's "Alchemie," in *Reallexikon für Antike und Christentum* (Stuttgart, 1950); Franz Strunz's "Alchemie," in *Die Religion in Ges-*

chichte und Gegenwart, 3d ed., vol. 1 (Tübingen, 1957); René Alleau's "Alchimie," in *Encyclopaedia Universalis,* vol. 1 (Paris, 1968); Bernard Suler's "Alchemy," in *Encyclopaedia Judaica,* vol. 2 (Jerusalem, 1971); Manfred Ullmann's "Al-Kīmiyā," in *The Encyclopaedia of Islam,* new ed., vol. 5 (Leiden, 1979); and Robert P. Multhauf's "Alchemy," in *Encyclopaedia Britannica,* 15th ed., vol. 1 (Chicago, 1983).

The present overview draws, in particular, on the studies by A.-J. Festugière, *La révélation d'Hermès Trismégiste,* vol. 1 (Paris, 1950), and "Alchymica" (1939), reprinted in *Hermétisme et mystique païenne* (Paris, 1967); Mircea Eliade's *The Forge and the Crucible,* 2d ed. (Chicago, 1978); C. G. Jung's *Psychology and Alchemy,* translated by R. F. C. Hull (Princeton, 1953); and the various articles and reviews by H. J. Sheppard in the journal *Ambix,* listed in the index for volumes 1–17.

36 RENAISSANCE ALCHEMY

Allison Coudert

The Renaissance and post-Renaissance period marked both the high point and the turning point of alchemy in the West. During the same years in which Kepler, Galileo, Descartes, Boyle, and Newton wrote their revolutionary scientific works, more alchemical texts were published than ever before. But under the impact first of the Reformation and later of the seventeenth-century scientific revolution, alchemy was profoundly changed and ultimately discredited. The organic, qualitative theories of the alchemists were replaced by an atomistic, mechanical model of change, which eventually undermined the alchemical theory of transmutation. The balance between the spiritual and the physical, which had characterized alchemical thought throughout its long history, was shattered, and alchemy was split into two halves, theosophy and the practical laboratory science of chemistry. [*See* Theosophy.]

THE PRACTICE OF ALCHEMY

For the most part Renaissance alchemists accepted the theories and practices of their ancient and medieval predecessors. By the time the study of alchemy came to Europe, it was already an established discipline with a respected past. The theories upon which it was based were an integral part of ancient philosophy. Western scientists accepted these theories precisely because they provided plausible explanations for the way events were observed to occur in nature and the laboratory. Transmutation was seen to be an aspect of all forms of change. Caterpillars turn into butterflies; ice melts; food becomes flesh. Long before there were practicing alchemists, the mechanism behind these transformations was investigated. The ancients had supplied explanations that satisfied most alchemists up to the seventeenth century. By combining Aristotelian physics, Stoicism, and Hermetism, Western alchemists evolved a vitalistic philosophy that viewed all phenomena as alive and striving for perfection. Whatever is imperfect (the base metal lead, for example) will eventually become perfect (gold) in the course of time or with the help of the mysterious substance known to alchemists as the philosopher's stone.

Although transmutation appeared straightforward on a theoretical level, it proved more difficult to accomplish in practice. Thomas Norton, a famous fifteenth-century English alchemist whose *Ordinall of Alkimy* was one of the most popular alchemical works of the period, describes how frustrating the work of an alchemist could be. Just finding the appropriate raw materials was difficult enough. Norton gives a poignant portrait of an alchemist who has fallen into despair because after years of fruitless experimenting he cannot decide what to try next. Even if an alchemist was lucky enough to choose the right ingredients, he had the additional problem of determining what to do with them.

The steps of transmutation were laid out clearly in respect to color. The work had to proceed from the black stage, during which time the alchemists believed they killed the substances in their vessels, through the white stage, during which period the ingredients were purified, to the final red stage, which marked the successful fabrication of the philosopher's stone. As Norton explains, "Red is the last work in Alkimy."

Although the color sequence was well established, Renaissance alchemists could not agree on the chemical processes necessary to produce the change from black to white to red. The most optimistic practitioners said the stone was made from one substance in one vessel in one operation, but judging from pictures depicting the cluttered array of apparatus littering laboratory floors, most alchemists took a less sanguine and simplistic view of their task. Daniel Stolcius illustrates eleven chemical processes in his book on alchemical emblems (*Viridarium chymicum* . . . , 1624). Salomon Trismosin reduced the number to seven in his *Splendor Solis*. George Ripley, another respected English adept, describes twelve steps in his *Twelve Gates of Alchemy*. Dom Pernety, a French alchemist living in the eighteenth century, associates each process with one sign of the zodiac:

1. calcination (Aries)
2. congelation (Taurus)
3. fixation (Gemini)
4. dissolution (Cancer)
5. digestion (Leo)
6. distillation (Virgo)
7. sublimation (Libra)
8. separation (Scorpio)
9. ceration (Sagittarius)
10. fermentation (Capricorn)
11. multiplication (Aquarius)
12. projection (Pisces)

Alchemy had always been profoundly influenced by astrology. Since the alchemical signs of the seven metals were those of the seven planets, it seemed reasonable to assume that in their reactions they would respond to the movements of their namesakes in the heavens above.

It is not easy to describe and distinguish all the different alchemical processes. Calcination is simple enough: it involved heating a substance in an open or closed vessel and usually included oxidation and the blackening of the substance. (This process may have given alchemy one of its many names, "the black art".) Calcination was described by alchemists as "mortification," "death," or "putrefaction," and the alchemical vessel in which it occurred was the "tomb," the "coffin," even "Hades" or "Hell." Congelation and fixation consisted of making the substances solid and nonvolatile. This essential step brought the alchemist closer to gold, the most stable and "fixed" of all the metals. Dissolution and digestion were connected with the white stage and purification. Distillation and sublimation were confused by alchemists until the eighteenth century, but both processes awed them. When they saw vapors rise, condense, and revaporize, they thought they were witnessing a miraculous transformation in which the "soul" of matter separated from its "body" and reunited with it in a purer state.

Separation was an elastic term describing the filtration, decantation, or distillation of a liquid from its residue. With fermentation, multiplication, and projection, we arrive at the heart of the alchemical work of making the philosopher's stone. Through fermentation, the stone became akin to yeast and acquired the power to transmute substances. Multiplication augmented the power of the stone to such a degree that it could transmute many times its weight of base metal without losing its strength. In the final process, projection, the stone was made into a powder and thrown on whatever was to be transmuted.

Estimates about the length of time it took to make the philosopher's stone varied from one day to twelve years. The common analogy between the stone and a child (the stone was often referred to as the "royal child" or "son") explains why nine months was frequently cited. The conflicting estimates lead one to agree with Thomas Norton that for the alchemist patience was a preeminent virtue.

Another difficulty facing the alchemist was the regulation of his fire. Since a practical thermometer was not invented until the eighteenth century, this was an almost impossible task. Many alchemists inadvertently blew up their experiments by applying too much heat or ruined months of work by allowing the fire to die out. The problem of heat was so crucial that Norton devoted a chapter of his *Ordinall* to the subject and describes the alchemist who properly controls his fire as "a parfet Master."

The obscurity of alchemical texts provided a final and often insurmountable obstacle facing Renaissance alchemists. Alchemists were masters of metaphor. They dressed up their instructions in parables and allegories, veiled them in symbols, delighted in enigmas, and preferred to call a substance by any name other than its common one. Even the great genius Sir Isaac Newton found himself baffled by the obscurity of alchemical literature and symbolism.

The opacity of alchemical writings was partly a response to opposition from the church, which was suspicious of the religious implications of alchemical symbolism. Alchemists were also justifiably afraid of running afoul of national laws against counterfeiting; they were afraid of being kidnapped as well. Alchemical literature is filled with stories of adepts captured by impoverished adventurers intent on wresting the secret of transmutation from them. It was therefore only prudent for alchemists to disguise their secret wisdom as well as their own identities.

Aside from the real dangers of imprisonment, excommunication, or capture, there were other reasons for the obscurity of alchemical writings. Over the centuries, the meaning of many alchemical terms changed, and the continual translation of alchemical texts (from Greek to Arabic to Latin and then into the vernaculars) compounded the confusion. The most important reason for their obscurity, however, is rooted in the nature of alchemy itself. Alchemy shared the same mystical associations that surrounded mining and metallurgy among ancient and primitive peoples. [*See* Metals and Metallurgy.] Alchemy was as much a spiritual process as a physical one, and the obscurity of alchemical language reflects its religious orientation.

ALCHEMY AS A SPIRITUAL DISCIPLINE

Mystery and religion, which were a part of alchemy from its beginnings, gained in importance from the Renaissance onward. In many cases alchemy moved out of the laboratory altogether and into the monk's cell or philosopher's study. "Our gold is not common gold," wrote the sixteenth-century author of the *Rosary of Philosophers*. The popularity of alchemy as a spiritual discipline coincided with the breakdown of religious orthodoxy and social organization during the Renaissance and the Reformation. Petrus Bonus was one of the many alchemists to emphasize the spiritual nature of alchemy. It was, he says in his work *The New Pearl of Great Price*, revealed by God, not for man's material comfort, but for his spiritual well-being. For these spiritual alchemists, alchemy had nothing to do with the making of gold. (They dismissed those alchemists benighted enough to think it did as "sooty empiricks" or "puffers.") All the ingredients mentioned in alchemical recipes—the minerals, metals, acids, compounds, and mixtures—were in truth only one, the alchemist himself. He was the base matter in need of purification by the fire; and the acid needed to accomplish this transformation came from his own spiritual malaise and longing for wholeness and peace. The various alchemical processes had nothing to do with chemical change; they were steps in the mysterious process of spiritual regeneration. Spiritual alchemists constantly stress the moral requirements of their art. The author of *Aurora Consurgens*, for example, insists that alchemists must be humble, holy, chaste, virtuous, faithful, charitable, temperate, and obedient. These are not qualities expected of a practical chemist. That they were emphasized by spiritual alchemists demonstrates how dominant the religious aspects of alchemy had become.

The interpretation of alchemy as a spiritual discipline offended many churchmen, who viewed the combination of alchemical concepts and Christian dogma in the writings of spiritual alchemists as dangerous heresy. One of the most daring appropriations of Christian symbolism was made by Nicholas Melchior of Hermanstadt, who expounded the alchemical work in the form of a mass. Melchior had been anticipated to some extent by Thomas Norton, who had called his book an "Ordinall." Heinrich Khunrath (1560–1601) provides another example of alchemy's spiritual extremists. In his *The Amphitheatre of Eternal Wisdom*, Khunrath interprets transmutation as a mystical process occurring within the adept's soul. He calls the alchemist's laboratory a *Lab Oratorium*. Spiritual alchemists like Khunrath often identified the philosopher's stone with Christ on the grounds that both redeemed base matter. Hermann Kopp, the nineteenth-century historian of alchemy, was scandalized by the parallel drawn between Christ and the philosopher's stone, which subject took up more than fifty pages in the alchemical tract *Der Wasserstein der Weysen* (*Die Alchemie in älterer und neuer Zeit*, 1886, vol. I, p. 254). Not only did spiritual alchemists identify the philosopher's stone with Christ, but they identified themselves with both. The heresy involved is obvious. Luther was one of the few highly placed churchmen to praise alchemy both for its practical uses and for its verification of Christian doctrine.

Alchemists of the sixteenth and seventeenth centuries drew many of their ideas from Renaissance Neoplatonism and Hermetism. In all three systems, the world was seen as a single organism penetrated by spiritual forces that worked at all levels, the vegetable, animal, human, and spiritual. Frances Yates has brillantly described the "magus" mentality that evolved from these ideas and encouraged men to believe they could understand and control their environment. This state of mind is illustrated in the writings of Paracelsus (1493–1541). For Paracelsus, God was the divine alchemist, who created the world by calcinating, congealing, distilling, and sublimating the elements of chaos. Chemistry was the key to the universe, which would disclose the secrets of theology, physics, and medicine. The alchemist had only to read the reactions in his laboratory on a grand scale to fathom the mysteries of creation.

RENAISSANCE ALCHEMY AND MODERN SCIENCE

By instilling some of the grandiose ideas of spiritual alchemy into the practical study of chemical reactions, Paracelsus and his followers transformed alchemy into a universal science of matter concerned with every aspect of material change. "Chemistry is nothing else but the Art and Knowledge of Nature itself," wrote Nicolas le Fèvre in his popular book, *A Compleat Body of Chemistry* (1670). This greatly expanded vision of alchemy's role struck a responsive cord in the millenarian movements prevalent in Europe during the sixteenth and seventeenth centuries. The Rosicrucian manifestos were typical of the utopian visions in the air. Using the language and imagery of spiritual alchemy, they called for the regeneration of society and outlined in broad strokes the social, economic, political, and religious reforms necessary.

No one knows who wrote the Rosicrucian manifestos. They have been attributed to Johann Valentin Andrea (1586–1654), whose acknowledged writings contain a similar blend of utopianism and spiritual alchemy. In his most famous work, *Christianopolis,* Andrea describes an ideal society organized to promote the health, education, and welfare of its citizens. One of the institutions in this society is a "laboratory" dedicated to the investigation of nature and to the application of useful discoveries for the public good.

Francis Bacon (1561–1626) was one of the many philosophers influenced by the Rosicrucian manifestos. Bacon looked forward to what he called a "Great Instauration" of learning that would herald the return of the Golden Age. He described this in his own utopia, *The New Atlantis.*

Neither Andrea nor Bacon said much that was new or significant in terms of science. What was novel in their visions was the idea of a scientific institution whose members worked by a common method toward a common goal. The secrecy and mystery that had been such a basic part of alchemy played no role in the scientific societies each describes, although their visions had been sparked by the utopian schemes of spiritual alchemists. This was one of the most important innovations to emerge in all the utopian literature of the seventeenth century and the one that had the greatest impact on the decline of alchemy. Once alchemists openly communicated their discoveries, the stage was set for the tremendous advances we have come to expect from the natural sciences.

In 1655 a small book was published entitled *Chymical, Medicinal, and Churgical Addresses: Made to Samuel Hartlib, Esquire.* Between the covers of this slim volume, the old and the new alchemy lie side by side. The arcane and bombastic variety of spiritual alchemy is represented by Eirenaeus Philalethes's *Ripley's Epistle to King Edward Unfolded*; but the new alchemy, dedicated to the cooperative investigation of nature for the public good, is advocated in a treatise by Robert Boyle significantly entitled *An Invitation to a free and generous Communication of Secrets and Receits of Physick.* Boyle urged alchemists to share their secrets for the sake of common charity and scientific advancement.

The Reformation was both a cause and a consequence of a growing attitude of philosophical skepticism, which brought all the wisdom of past ages into doubt. Although skepticism was bitterly opposed by philosophers and theologians on the grounds that it undermined the very possibility of rational knowledge, it paradoxically contributed in the long run to the development of a constructive scientific method that benefited all the sciences. Observation and experiment became the shibboleths of the new science and, eventually, the cause of alchemy's undoing. As more and more negative evidence was gradually accumulated through careful laboratory experiments, the alchemical dream of transmutation faded into the recesses of history.

BIBLIOGRAPHY

General accounts of the history of Renaissance alchemy and the emergence of chemistry may be found in my *Alchemy: The Philosopher's Stone* (Boulder, 1980); Allen G. Debus's *The Chemical Philosophy: Paracelsian Science and Medicine in the Sixteenth and Seventeenth Centuries*, 2 vols. (New York, 1977); Eric J. Holmyard's *Alchemy* (Baltimore, 1957); John Read's *Through Alchemy to Chemistry* (London, 1957); and J. R. Partington's *A History of Chemistry*, 4 vols. (London, 1961–1970). *Ambix: The Journal for the Society for the Study of Alchemy and Early Chemistry* (Cambridge, 1937–1979) contains important specialized articles. Maurice P. Crosland's *Historical Studies in the Language of Chemistry* (London, 1962) provides an invaluable guide to the intricacies of alchemical terminology. Betty J. Dobbs's *The Foundations of Newton's Alchemy* (Cambridge, 1975) sheds light on the period of transition from alchemy to chemistry. The best introduction to Paracelsus is Walter Pagel's *Paracelsus* (New York, 1958). Renaissance Neoplatonism, Hermetism, and the Qabbalah are brilliantly described and analyzed in Frances Yates's *Giordano Bruno and the Hermetic Tradition* (London, 1964). She discusses the Rosicrucian manifestos in *The Rosicrucian Enlightenment* (London, 1972). H. J. Sheppard has published important articles on alchemical symbolism in *Ambix*. Jacques van Lennep's *L'art et l'alchimie* (Paris, 1966) is also useful. J. W. Montgomery discusses Luther's views on alchemy in "Cross, Constellation and Crucible: Lutheran Astrology and Alchemy in the Age of Reformation," *Ambix* 11 (1963): 65–86.

There are several collections of Renaissance alchemical texts. Thomas Norton's *Ordinall* and George Ripley's *Twelve Gates* can be found in Elias Ashmole's *Theatrum Chemicum Britannicum* (1652; reprint, New York, 1967). *Theatrum Chemicum* (1659–1661) provides six volumes of alchemical writings. Another collection, the *Musaeum Hermeticum Reformatum* (Frankfurt, 1678) has been translated by Arthur E. Waite as *The Hermetic Museum*, 2 vols. (London, 1893).

CONTRIBUTORS

IOANA ANDREESCO-MIEREANU, Centre National de la Recherche Scientifique, Paris
DAVID E. AUNE, Saint Xavier College, Chicago
BEATRIZ BARBA DE PIÑA CHÁN, Instituto Nacional de Antropología e Historia, Mexico City
HANS DIETER BETZ, University of Chicago
RAYMOND BLOCH, Académie des Inscriptions et Belles-Lettres, Paris
ERIKA BOURGUIGNON, Ohio State University
ALLISON COUDERT, State University of New York, College of Oneonta
IOAN PETRU CULIANU, Rijksuniversiteit te Groningen
MIRCEA ELIADE, University of Chicago (deceased)
TOUFIC FAHD, Université de Strasbourg II
ANTOINE FAIVRE, École Pratique des Hautes Études, Collège de France
THEODOR H. GASTER, Barnard College, Columbia University
TEUN GOUDRIAAN, Rijksuniversiteit te Utrecht
DONALD HARPER, Stanford University
DONALD R. HILL, State University of New York, College at Oneonta
HENRY KAHANE, University of Illinois at Urbana-Champaign
RENÉE KAHANE, University of Illinois at Urbana-Champaign
MESQUITELA LIMA, Universidade Nova de Lisboa
THEODORE M. LUDWIG, Valparaiso University
JOHN MIDDLETON, Yale University
GEOFFREY PARRINDER, University of London
GIULIA PICCALUGA, Università degli Studi, Rome
HABIBEH RAHIM, New York, New York
KURT RUDOLPH, Philipps-Universität Marburg
JEFFREY BURTON RUSSELL, University of California at Santa Barbara
NATHAN SIVIN, University of Pennsylvania
ROBERT A. F. THURMAN, Amherst College
RICHARD W. THURN, New York, New York
DAVID WHITE, Chicago, Illinois
EVAN M. ZUESSE, South Australian College of Advanced Education

LAWRENCE E. SULLIVAN is professor of the History of Religions and acting director of the Institute for the Advanced Study of Religion at the University of Chicago

FINDING LIST OF ARTICLE TITLES

The following table lists the article titles (in parentheses) as they originally appeared in *The Encyclopedia of Religion*. Titles not listed below are unchanged.

What is Occultism? (Occultism)
Speculations about Nature (Nature: Religious and Philosophical Speculations)
Gnosticism from the Middle Ages to the Present (Gnosticism: Gnosticism from the Middle Ages to the Present)
Witchcraft (Witchcraft: Concepts of Witchcraft)
Theories of Magic (Magic: Theories of Magic)
Magic in East Asia (Magic: Magic in East Asia)
Magic in Greco-Roman Antiquity (Magic: Magic in Greco-Roman Antiquity)
Magic in Medieval and Renaissance Europe (Magic: Magic in Medieval and Renaissance Europe)
Magic in Eastern Europe (Magic: Magic in Eastern Europe)
Magic in Islam (Magic: Magic in Islam)
Magic in South Asia (Magic: Magic in South Asia)
Magic in Tribal Societies (Magic: Magic in Primitive Societies)
What is Alchemy? (Alchemy: An Overview)
Elixirs (Elixir)
Chinese Alchemy (Alchemy: Chinese Alchemy)
Indian Alchemy (Alchemy: Indian Alchemy)
Islamic Alchemy (Alchemy: Islamic Alchemy)
Hellenistic and Medieval Alchemy (Alchemy: Hellenistic and Medieval Alchemy)
Renaissance Alchemy (Alchemy: Renaissance Alchemy)